Understanding the Neolithic

Understanding the Neolithic is a groundbreaking investigation of the Neolithic period (4000–2200 BC) in southern Britain. Whilst thoroughly examining the archaeological data of this region, Julian Thomas exposes the assumptions and prejudices which have shaped archaeologists' accounts of the distant past, and presents fresh interpretations informed by social theory, anthropology and critical hermeneutics. This volume is the fully reworked and updated edition of *Rethinking the Neolithic* (1991), which provoked much heated debate on publication, especially in providing stimulating and radical alternative ways of interpreting archaeological evidence.

Understanding the Neolithic questions the impression that there was a universal shift from hunting and gathering to farming, and argues that monuments and other material innovations were not simply the products of economic and technological developments. Rather, new forms of material culture were used in inventive ways by local communities to transform social relationships and create new worlds of meaning.

Understanding the Neolithic will be of great interest to students of prehistory and archaeological theory.

Julian Thomas is Reader in Archaeology at the University of Southampton. He has published widely on European prehistory and archaeological theory, and his publications include *Time, Culture and Identity* (1996). He is a member of the Council of the Royal Anthropological Institute.

Understanding the Neolithic

A revised second edition of *Rethinking the Neolithic*

Julian Thomas

London and New York

First edition published 1991
by Cambridge University Press as *Rethinking the Neolithic*

Second edition published
by Routledge
11 New Fetter Lane, London EC4P 4EE

Simultaneously published in the USA and Canada
by Routledge
29 West 35th Street, New York, NY 10001

Reprinted 2001

Routledge is an imprint of the Taylor & Francis Group

Typeset in Garamond by Keystroke, Jacaranda Lodge, Wolverhampton
Printed and bound in Great Britain by TJ International Ltd, Padstow, Cornwall

British Library Cataloguing in Publication Data
A catalogue record for this book is available from the British Library

Library of Congress Cataloging in Publication Data
A catalog record for this book has been requested

ISBN 0–415–20766–5 (hbk)
ISBN 0–415–20767–3 (pbk)

The age of the wholesale creation of social, economic, technical, political, and other structures, upon which we still subsist – the neolithic age . . .

(Jacques Derrida, *Of Grammatology*, p. 128)

We Neolithic folk had entirely different customs, and not just in regard to eating . . .

(Günther Grass, *The Flounder*, p. 237)

Contents

List of figures ix
Preface to the second edition xi

Chapter One
AN ARCHAEOLOGY OF DIFFERENCE 1

Chapter Two
BEYOND THE ECONOMIC SYSTEM 7

Chapter Three
READING MONUMENTS 34

Chapter Four
PITS, POTS AND DIRT: A GENEALOGY OF
DEPOSITIONAL PRACTICES 62

Chapter Five
PORTABLE ARTEFACTS: THE CASE OF POTTERY 89

Chapter Six
MORTUARY PRACTICE 126

Chapter Seven
REGIONAL SEQUENCES: THE STONEHENGE AREA 163

Chapter Eight
REGIONAL SEQUENCES: THE UPPER THAMES VALLEY 184

Chapter Nine
REGIONAL SEQUENCES: THE AVEBURY DISTRICT 199

Chapter Ten
CONCLUSION 221

Bibliography 230
Index 258

Figures

2.1   The Mesolithic/Neolithic transition   16
2.2   Earlier Neolithic settlement in the study area   19
2.3   Later Neolithic settlement in the study area   20
2.4   Landscape use in the earlier and later Neolithic: raw count of sites (above)
      and percentages (below)   22
2.5   Faunal assemblages: ratio of pigs:cattle:sheep   27
3.1   Comparative plans of causewayed enclosures   39
3.2   The enclosure complex on Hambledon Hill, Dorset   44
3.3   The Dorchester on Thames complex, Oxfordshire   49
3.4   Bryn Celli Ddu: plan   51
3.5   Maiden Castle, Dorset: causewayed enclosure and long mound   53
3.6   Comparative plans of henges   55
3.7   Plan of Durrington Walls, Wiltshire   56
3.8   Durrington Walls: plan of the Southern Circle   57
3.9   Plan of Woodhenge, Wiltshire   58
3.10 Crickley Hill, Gloucestershire: the long mound   59
4.1   Pits: length and depth   65
4.2   Pits: layers in fill   66
4.3   The Chalk Plaque Pit, Wiltshire, and pits at Fir Tree Field, Dorset   67
4.4   Numbers of pits containing particular styles of pottery from southern Britain   69
4.5   The Coneybury 'Anomaly', Wiltshire   71
4.6   Ceramic decoration from two later Neolithic pits at Heathrow   73
4.7   Deposits in the ditch of the causewayed enclosure at Staines, Middlesex   76
4.8   Thickthorn Down long barrow, Dorset: deposits in the ditch   79
4.9   Woodhenge: ratio of bones of cattle to bones of pig in successive concentric
      circles of post-holes   82
4.10 Deposits in the pit-defined henge at Wyke Down, Dorset   84
5.1   British Neolithic pottery chronology   91
5.2   Earlier Neolithic pottery   100
5.3   Distribution of earlier Neolithic pottery in southern Britain   101
5.4   Earlier Neolithic vessel forms represented in various context types   103
5.5   Vessel forms represented at causewayed enclosures   104
5.6   Earlier Neolithic (above) and Peterborough Ware (below) vessel volumes   105
5.7   Earlier Neolithic ceramic style zones in southern Britain   106
5.8   Peterborough Ware   107

5.9	Distribution of Peterborough Wares in southern Britain	108
5.10	Radiocarbon dates for Peterborough Wares, Grooved Ware and Beakers (uncalibrated dates b.p.)	110
5.11	Peterborough Wares (above) and Grooved Ware (below): contexts of deposition	112
5.12	Grooved Ware	113
5.13	Grooved Ware (above) and Beakers (below): vessel volumes	115
5.14	Distribution of Grooved Ware in southern Britain	116
5.15	Neolithic ceramic traditions: patterns of association	124
6.1	Distribution of megalithic chambered tombs and non-megalithic long barrows in southern Britain	130
6.2	Timber mortuary structure	132
6.3	The mortuary structure at Haddenham long barrow, Cambridgeshire	133
6.4	Earthen long mounds: comparative plans	135
6.5	Fussell's Lodge, Wiltshire: distribution of anatomical parts	138
6.6	Burial with flint blade at Barrow Hills, Radley	140
6.7	Barrow Hills, Radley, Oxfordshire: long barrow	141
6.8	The mortuary structures at Nutbane long barrow, Hampshire	143
6.9	Comparative plans of Cotswold–Severn long cairns	145
6.10	Burials in the North Chamber, Hazleton long cairn, Gloucestershire	146
6.11	Articulated skeleton in the north entrance at Hazleton long cairn	147
6.12	Later Neolithic single grave at Linch Hill Corner, Oxfordshire	152
6.13	Distribution of cremations within later Neolithic cemeteries at Stonehenge and Dorchester on Thames Sites VI and II	154
6.14	Hemp Knoll, Wiltshire: Beaker burial	158
6.15	Beaker barrow at Barnack, Cambridgeshire	160
7.1	Stonehenge area: earlier Neolithic	168
7.2	Stonehenge: main phases of construction	173
7.3	Stonehenge area: middle/later Neolithic	175
7.4	Stonehenge area: later Neolithic/Beaker	180
8.1	Upper Thames Valley: earlier Neolithic	186
8.2	Upper Thames Valley: middle/later Neolithic	189
8.3	Comparative plans of Neolithic ring ditches and hengiforms	191
8.4	The Dorchester on Thames complex: sequence	193
8.5	Upper Thames Valley: later Neolithic/Beaker	197
9.1	Avebury: earlier Neolithic	201
9.2	West Kennet long barrow: composition of ceramic assemblages in the secondary chamber deposits	205
9.3	West Kennet long barrow: vessels found in more than one context in the secondary chamber deposits	206
9.4	Avebury: middle/later Neolithic	211
9.5	West Kennet long barrow: entrance and forecourt area	215
9.6	West Kennet palisade enclosures	217
9.7	Avebury: later Neolithic/Beaker	219

Preface to the
second edition

A few years ago, at a conference of the Theoretical Archaeology Group, I was disturbed to hear *Rethinking the Neolithic* described by one of the speakers as a 'textbook'. I had originally intended the book as an extended version of the kind of papers that are presented at the TAG conference: speculative, critical, trying out new ideas, but hardly definitive. However, texts have a way of escaping their authors and developing a life of their own. This second edition began its existence in an attempt to recapture a wayward volume and instil it with some discipline.

Preparing the second edition has taken rather longer than I hoped, since what was originally intended as an exercise in clarification has become a complete rewriting of the book. There are several reasons for this: a great deal of new evidence has come to light over the past decade, and several major excavation reports have been published; my own theoretical orientation has developed somewhat over the same period, and I find that I have changed my mind concerning much of what was written in the first edition. This means that what follows differs considerably from the original, so that a new title is perhaps justified. I cannot satisfactorily express how weary I am of colleagues suggesting that I should name the new edition *Re-rethinking the Neolithic*. I would prefer to think of it as *Rethinking the Neolithic: The Twelve-Inch Remix*.

I should like to thank again all of those who have contributed with discussion, information, comments and criticisms to either of the two editions of the volume. They include Mary Baker, Gordon Barclay, John Barrett, Barbara Bender, Richard Bradley, Aubrey Burl, Ros Cleal, Mark Edmonds, Roy Entwistle, Andrew Fleming, Chris Fowler, Frances Healey, Ian Hodder, Ian Kinnes, Matt Leivers, Gavin Lucas, Rick Peterson, Joshua Pollard, Frances Raymond, Colin Richards, Maggie Ronayne, Nick Thorpe, Chris Tilley, Robin Torrence, Alasdair Whittle and Norman Yoffee. I should also like to thank my colleagues in Southampton and Lampeter for their support.

The illustrations for the first edition of the book were executed by Chris Jones. Those which have been added to the second edition were undertaken by Matt Leivers. They were financed by the Pantyfedwen Fund of the University of Wales, Lampeter, and the Faculty of Arts of the University of Southampton respectively. The index was compiled by Matt Leivers, Rick Peterson and Julia Roberts.

The book is dedicated to my wife, Sue Pitt, and to our daughter Morag.

Chapter One

An archaeology of difference

INTRODUCTION

It seems particularly ironic that prehistoric archaeology systematically erases those qualities of the past which attract us to it in the first place. When we come across a megalithic tomb, its presence is one which can be at once intriguing and disturbing. It is an object which is foreign to our own culture, yet it exists in the same space as we do. Although it may have been incorporated into folklore, or depicted on a road map, or included in a heritage trail, its material existence is one which can seem at odds with its surroundings. Such a monument is an indication that the world that we inhabit was once quite different. As such, it offers us the opportunity to encounter the 'otherness' of the past. It is doubtless this experience of something mysterious and alien which first inspires many of us to take up archaeology as a study. Being engaged by the past, we want to know more about it. Yet it is precisely through attempting to find out more about the past that we erode its unfamiliarity. We introduce techniques of classification and rationalisation which homogenise and tame the past.

The difference of the past is inexhaustible. But despite this, I wish to argue that our present image of the Neolithic period in Britain is one which is unnecessarily tied to a series of contemporary assumptions. It may be ultimately impossible to mentally escape our own cultural context, and to grasp a dead and alien culture in its own terms. Nevertheless, it is a reasonable goal to account for the reasons why our present understanding has been put together in the way that it has, and in the process to present a more satisfactory interpretation. It is for this reason that many of the chapters of this book will dwell at some length on the history of investigation into particular aspects of the British Neolithic. My suggestion is that successive generations of archaeologists have not simply progressed gradually toward a more perfect understanding of prehistory. On the contrary, in the course of their labours they have constructed a series of prejudices, stereotypes and assumptions which need to be exposed and evaluated before we are able to move forward. Of course, this is not to say that critique will ever be able to purge our accounts of the past of 'bias', to such an extent that we can claim neutrality. Apart from being a practical impossibility, a neutral understanding of the Neolithic would probably be quite dull. This book doubtless has its own prejudices, and consequently it is presented as a critical writing of the British Neolithic rather than a definitive account.

While the social sciences have long stressed the way in which our personal experience forms the frame through which we apprehend reality (Bourdieu 1977, 2), the problems faced by archaeologists in overcoming their preconceptions are singular. Inevitably, we judge the object of our investigation in relation to ourselves and the way that we live. But as archaeologists who inhabit the same space as the past society which we study, we are also tempted to see that society as part of an unbroken developmental continuum which leads upward to ourselves. All of prehistory and history do no more than document the process of emergence of our present order. The consequence of this for the Neolithic has been that in addition to the imposition of a modernist economism which seeks to find a 'rational' explanation for all aspects of prehistoric society, the period has been seen as a simplified and more barbaric form of the epochs which succeed it. This can take the relatively crude form of interpreting the 'Beaker folk' as a community of *foederati* brought into Britain to quell the rebellious natives (Ashbee 1978). But equally, Neolithic pits have been interpreted as storage devices, despite their manifest unsuitability for the purpose, by analogy with Iron Age pits (Field *et al.* 1964). Causewayed enclosures have been seen as the equivalent of hillforts (Renfrew 1973a; Barker and Webley 1978), and Neolithic pottery was originally categorised according to an ABC sequence which mimicked schemes devised for the Iron Age (Hawkes 1931; Piggott 1931; Warren *et al.* 1936). Arguably, all of these interpretations are grounded in a meta-narrative of continuous, seamless and progressive development toward the present. The notion that the Neolithic might in certain respects be qualitatively and categorically different from what followed it, and that major horizons of cultural discontinuity might exist in prehistory at a more fundamental level than that of migration, invasion and diffusion is one which has been difficult to entertain under these conditions. This volume is addressed to the problem that, while any prehistory we write is a modern production, written within a contingent set of historical and cultural circumstances, the past achieves its greatest political potency when it retains its sense of difference and 'otherness'. Consequently, it is not concerned with theory to the exclusion of practice, or vice versa. It has been suggested that textual production in archaeology is dominated by descriptive, 'common-sense' works, and that works of theory are few and far between (Shanks and Tilley 1987a, 14–15). However, while we might agree with this argument in principle, another point needs to be added. Texts concerning abstract theory have been a constant, if minor, element of the archaeological canon over the past thirty years (e.g. Clarke 1968; Watson *et al.* 1971; Gardin 1980; Hodder 1986; etc.). However, what have been rather less common have been works that take a body of integrated theory as the basis for a sustained evaluation of a particular period or problem. Within the 'processualist' tradition there have been useful attempts to use theory as a means to throw new light on to certain problems (e.g. Renfrew 1972; Randsborg 1980; Hodges 1982). Nevertheless, in some of these instances the method which has been followed is to recruit 'bits' of theory from various sources to explain particular phenomena, rather than to start from an integrated theoretical position.

WRITING PREHISTORY

Recently, archaeologists have become increasingly aware of the textual dimension of their enterprise. Part of this awareness has involved the adoption of a textual model for the archaeological record (Patrik 1985), but in this chapter I will concern myself more with the status of archaeological discourse as writing, and some of the implications which follow from this. History, Frederic Jameson tells us, is only available to us textually (1981, 35). This point is forcefully supported by Shanks and Tilley (1987a, 19; 1987b), when they suggest that archaeological evidence is only made comprehensible when it is placed in the context of a narrative – that is, when we tell a story. This admission clearly contradicts the positivist dictum that we should allow the facts to 'speak for themselves', and the notion that we could conceivably accumulate a complete set of evidence which would reduce the past to a transparent and self-evident state. Despite what archaeologists may claim to the contrary, our problem may not be one of a paucity of evidence, but one of defining which elements of the evidence are significant. In this connection, Michael Roth (1988, 10) considered the positivist historian's dream of a 'perfect chronicle' containing every event in history written down as it happened. Such a chronicle would still provide an inadequate vision of the past, since the significance of events is only ever understood in context, and often only in hindsight. The relevance of an historical event is judged in terms of its contribution to the development of an historical plot, a sequence of significant and related happenings. Whenever we write about prehistory we undertake a conscious or unconscious sifting and sorting of the available evidence, creating new meanings in the process. What we define as significant evidence, what we choose to look on as facts, varies depending on the preoccupations and preconceptions under which we write the past.

My investigation of the British Neolithic begins with the recognition that the archaeological past is inherently written, and is written in a present which is itself 'in history'. What makes this different from writing a novel is that what I write adheres to something which already exists, a raw material which is transformed in the act of writing: the 'trace' of the past in the present. But writing about the past involves taming it; placing the evidence in a comprehensible narrative requires us to rationalise it from a perspective which is located in the present. There are a number of different ways in which archaeologists can and do write the past, and here I should like to suggest a means of coming to terms with this problem, before addressing the difficult question of how we can evaluate rival accounts of the past. The central motif of the first part of this discussion is drawn from Paul Ricoeur's essay *The Reality of the Historical Past* (1984). Here, Ricoeur distinguishes between three tropes of historical writing: History-as-Same, History-as-Other and History-as-Analogue. Each of these 'great signs' is distinguished by a particular relationship between the past and the present. Or rather, each form of writing attributes a different status to the written past. It is arguable that the great bulk of archaeological writing is conducted under the sign of the Same. In order to make sense of the evidence available to them, archaeologists often employ some form of universalism, whether it is called analogy, uniformitarianism or middle-range theory. In this way, the palaeoeconomic school sought to explain the evidence which was available to them concerning prehistoric settlement and subsistence by recourse to presumed universal laws of behaviour based upon animal ethology (Higgs and Jarman 1975). Other forms of Past-as-Same which prevail in archaeological discourse involve attempts to isolate anthropologically defined forms of social organisation in the past. Thus, for instance, we can identify Renfrew's search for 'chiefdoms' in European prehistory (1973a), or the forms of structural Marxist archaeology which seek evidence for particular kinship systems or modes of production in the past (Thomas 1987).

Ricoeur cites the work of Collingwood as his central example of History-as-Same, and it is significant that Ian Hodder drew upon Collingwood's writings in developing one of the most sophisticated archaeologies written under the sign of the Same (Hodder 1986, 90). According to Ricoeur, Collingwood's aim in historical 're-enactment' is not the re-living of events, but the re-thinking of the thoughts of the actors concerned. To get inside the event in this way suggests that knowing what happened is already to know why it happened: understanding consists in fusing with the mental life of another. Hodder takes this line of reasoning to imply that certain universal structuring principles allow unique events to be appreciated by all people at all times.

However, even with such an advanced form of Past-as-Same there are inevitably certain problems. These stem, I think, from the medium through which the archaeologist must attempt to enter past worlds: that is, material culture. Taking the argument that we can look on material culture as being in some ways analogous to language, something which conveys or produces meanings, it is questionable whether any communicative medium can give a total and immediate access to the thoughts of another person. To suggest this would be to accept Edmund Husserl's model of the meaning-giving subject expressing primordial, internally generated meanings through communicative acts (Norris 1982, 46). This effectively implies that a pure and perfect experience is first created within a person, and then as a secondary matter expressed through the imperfect, distorted artifice of discourse, whether it be verbal or material. This would require that meaning can exist in the first instance in a form which is external to language or any other form of signification. In this way of thinking, language and material culture are relegated to the status of vessels for conveying pure ideas and impressions from place to place and mind to mind. But as Michel Foucault objects, 'there is nothing absolutely primary because, when all is said and done, underneath it all everything is already interpretation' (1967, 189).

There is something to be said for rejecting the image of deep meaning underlying more superficial communication. As in the case of Husserl's attempt to identify certain archetypal human experiences, the use of 'depth metaphors' can often be associated with the attempt to isolate some phenomenon which is timeless, ahistorical, 'hard-wired' or transcendental (Derrida 1978a). The modern West often appears to be fixated with hidden meanings and deep Freudian horrors. Yet this is a metaphysical way of thinking, in which whatever we experience is always secondary to a more fundamental order of things which can only be inferred. From an archaeological point of view, this is a counsel of despair, since it implies that the material things which we study are no more than a tattered reflection of cognitive worlds which are forever lost to us (Thomas 1996a; 1998a). Rather than search for 'deep meanings' locked away in the structure of artefacts, it is possible to argue that thought and communication are one and the same thing. Ideas cannot precede signification, since we require objects and concepts in order to structure our thought. Thinking is not an abstracted reasoning which takes place in a realm of pure consciousness: it is a practical aspect of our being in the world (Heidegger 1962). All of this makes the suggestion that material culture is language-like (Hodder 1982a; Tilley 1989) all the more significant. Material culture is a form of signification, and as such it exists not to express essences (as some forms of historical idealism might suggest) but to produce meaning (Olsen 1990). People use things to think with; things are integral to thought, and to the production of meaningful worlds.

The study of material culture is a means of engaging with those past worlds, even if this is always achieved from the context of our own world (Johnson and Olsen 1992). This need not involve any attempt to empathise with past people, or to enter into their thoughts. Meaning is not locked away in the individual mind: it is produced in public, in interaction, in the relationships between people and things. It is struggled or negotiated over, or the result of an uneasy accommodation between differently positioned people, with different understandings of the world. People live in a world of pre-understanding and interpretation, which they continually actively test and reinterpret (Thrift 1991), but which always involves imperfect and partial understandings. Their material culture is fashioned as a part of this imperfectly grasped world (as is our own). Consequently, when we interpret past material culture, we are not approaching the 'empirical reality' of the past 'as it really was' (as if such a thing were possible). We are creating an interpretation of an interpretation (or many interpretations), a cultural production fashioned from other cultural productions. This recalls Derrida's seemingly playful digression on Nietzsche's umbrella (Derrida 1978b; Norris 1982, 71; Lawson 1985, 116). Apparently, one of Nietzsche's manuscripts contains a marginal note, which says: 'I have forgotten my umbrella.' Derrida finds almost endless possible meanings for this one sentence, speculating as to whether it should be taken at face value, or whether it represents some coded comment on or key to the rest of the manuscript. Indeed, he finds it possible to argue that it is no more or less significant than any other sentence in the manuscript. This is because its meaning is ultimately unknowable; what we take it to mean depends upon our own reading. This is also the case with archaeological evidence. The paradox is that while the evidence may determine that some things cannot be written about it, there are potentially limitless things which can be written about it.

If there are problems with perspectives which link past and present, the immediate alternative is a past written under Ricoeur's sign of the Other. It is here that some more of the disturbing consequences of post-structuralist thought for archaeology start to emerge. In their different ways, Derrida and Foucault have done away with the 'points of presence', the Archimedean places of reference outside history which might act as the thread to guide us through the labyrinth (Lentricchia 1980, 166). Now, there is only the labyrinth. 'Nothing in man,' says Foucault, 'not even his body – is sufficiently stable to serve as a basis for self-recognition or for understanding other men' (1984a, 87). What, then, if there is no stable entity which we can call human nature? What if, as Nietzsche suggested, even the most seemingly stable elements of our existence, like ethics and values, can be seen as historical and transient? What if there are no structural universals which extend into the past? What if there were no chiefdoms in the Neolithic? How can we ever reach into the distant past if we have only concepts developed in the present with which to apprehend it?

It is with the attempt to get beyond 'the consoling play of recognitions' (Foucault 1984a, 88) that the idea of History-as-Other begins. Such a history is based not on searching for similarities between past and present, but in the recovery of temporal distance. By revealing the difference of the past, such a history seeks to delegitimise the present. In this way, the difference of the past becomes one of its most political characteristics. The prototype of such a history was Nietzsche's *On the Genealogy of Morals* (1969), which served as a model for Foucault's work on penal systems and sexuality. In each case the aim was to historicise the apparent universals of the human condition by contrasting past and present. All of the common-sense values dissolve before genealogical analysis – words do not keep their meanings, desires do not keep their objectives, ideas do not keep their logic.

Genealogy, a contrastive history, can be argued to provide a paradigm for effective archaeological research. It is possible to use a similar methodology to investigate particular areas of human practice through a search for points in time in which they were subject to structural changes. Our efforts can be directed at those supposedly static and ahistorical spheres like the appropriation of landscapes, the preparation and consumption of food, the disposal of household waste, the organisation of domestic space and the use of the human body in mortuary practice. Each of these has been conventionally looked on by archaeologists in universal terms: hence food remains are looked on as evidence for calorific input, while mortuary practices are seen as the raw material for mathematical indices of the degree to which a society is ranked.

This kind of an archaeology would be opposed to the forcing of the past into modernist categories and classifications. At each stage, it would attempt to recover the strangeness of the past, its alien quality. However, it must be admitted that in the final analysis such a process will always be incomplete and unfinished. One can deconstruct the forms of one's analysis of the past indefinitely. Clearly, no set of concepts or ideas developed in the present will ever grasp the whole essence of the past (see Dews 1987, 177). So just as Derrida can demonstrate the absence of any fixity of meaning by moving constantly from one signifier to the next, we might search endlessly for a written past which finally breaks its ties with the present. At some point we must come to terms with this, and simply write a story. It is at this stage that we move to Ricoeur's final great sign, that of the Analogue. Here, the narrative which we write is recognised as something which is not the real past, but which 'stands for' the past. A history written as Analogue is an account written in the present, which weaves together the traces of the past in a web of rationalisation. If we accept the point that to write at all is to tame and homogenise the past, such a writing effects some kind of reconciliation between Same and Other.

If we begin from the position that what we are striving to do is to free the past from ethnocentric and presentist deformations, our writing can begin with a radical separation of past and present through the use of genealogy and deconstruction, yet it must end with some level of domestication. Writing the past is an endless task, but one in which each act of putting pen to paper is recognised as a failure to fully articulate difference.

GENEALOGIES OF THE NEOLITHIC

These considerations stand behind the approach which will be followed in this book. The intention is to use each chapter to trace the development of a different aspect of Neolithic society in Britain: subsistence economics, monument-building, depositional practice, the making and use of ceramics, and mortuary practice. While these accounts of the period may intersect in places, their relative autonomy from each other is presented as a virtue. Each chapter will involve some degree of historiography, attempting to explain the emergence of current ideas, and this historical dimension serves as the basis for a critique, which can inform a fresh look at the evidence. These chapters (2–6) could be said to have been written as genealogies, emphasising the cultural difference between the Neolithic and the present. In the later part of the book, a series of regional studies and a conclusion attempt a reintegration of the separate strands which have been followed. Geographically, the study is principally focused on the central southern part of England (the counties of Avon, Berkshire, Dorset, Gloucestershire, Oxfordshire, Somerset and Wiltshire). However, it is recognised that some aspects of the evidence cannot readily be addressed within such a limited frame. To some extent, each class of evidence is investigated within its own appropriate scale of analysis.

Chapter Two

Beyond the economic system

Agriculture is not merely a necessary pendant to civilisation; it is its life force, the fundamental qualification of its appearance, and if the men of Avebury, whose high and laborious civilization is manifest in their works, were not agriculturalists, we are faced with a contradiction in terms.

(H.J. Massingham, *Downland Man*, p. 207)

THE IMAGE OF A 'NEOLITHIC ECONOMY'

The still dominant understanding of the Neolithic in Britain rests upon its identification as a primarily economic phenomenon. Because the essence of the Neolithic is believed to lie in agricultural practice, a relatively homogeneous economic base is presumed to underlie the evident cultural variability of the period. In this chapter I will contest this assumption, and will suggest that a quite different set of economic practices prevailed in the Neolithic of southern Britain. Some aspects of this argument may apply to other parts of Britain and Ireland, but it is not my intention to replace one set of global generalisations with another. At the larger spatial scale I will hope to stress variability: the Neolithic in Britain was not characterised by a single economic system.

When first employed by archaeologists, the term 'Neolithic' implied a technological rather than an economic phenomenon (Lubbock 1865). However, at some point in the history of the discipline the use of ground and polished stone tools, pottery and agriculture came to be seen as inextricably linked (e.g. Cole 1965). While contemporary archaeology has eroded the division between hunting and gathering and agriculture (Higgs and Jarman 1975), and has come to recognise the existence of foragers with ceramics (Rowley-Conwy 1983), the opening of the Neolithic is still seen as necessarily the occasion of the universal adoption of a reliance upon food production (Williams 1989). The term 'Neolithic', I would argue, is still often used as being synonymous with 'mixed farming economy'. In Britain, this assumption has been maintained by an orthodoxy which represents a fusion of two quite different schools of archaeological thought, one based on a traditional, culture-historical approach, and one geared to the 'palaeoeconomic' perspective which developed in Cambridge in the 1960s and 1970s. These two paradigms have found common ground in two basic suppositions: first, that a separate sphere of human action designated 'subsistence economy' can be discerned in prehistoric societies in general, and second, that this practice is in some way more fundamental than all others, forming the precondition for all aspects of human life. Thus Atkinson suggests that 'it was the practice of agriculture and stock-raising, that is, the deliberate *production* as opposed to the mere gathering of food, that allowed the population of Britain for the first time to gain mastery of its environment, and so to rise from brute savagery to the higher levels of barbarism' (1956, 148; emphasis in original). Similarly, Higgs and Jarman indicate that:

> The primary human adaptation to the environment is the economy, man's management of his household. . . . Palaeoeconomic studies lay their main stress on a basic aspect of human behaviour which can be shown to conform to predictable laws over a long period of time.
>
> (1975, 4)

What these two points of view share, then, is a form of the base/superstructure duality in which the institutions of the latter are ultimately always reducible to the former. Thus Legge (1989, 224) is able to suggest that:

> the modest achievements of Mesolithic peoples in Britain are a reflection of an economy based upon hunting and gathering. The major achievements of the Neolithic peoples of Britain were not. . . . Only agriculture could provide the essential fuel for that degree of social elaboration.

As we will see below, there are plentiful known examples of communities who built massive monumental structures without practising mixed agriculture, or in some cases any form of food production. Yet these analogies have been neglected in most discussions of Neolithic Britain. It has been this degree of agreement between traditional and economic archaeologies which has allowed the two approaches to be welded together over the years to produce a picture of a mixed farming economy driven through successive episodes of intensification and collapse by the fragile relationship which obtained between population and resources. This is not to say, however, that all commentators within this hybrid tradition draw entirely the same conclusions from this body of accepted wisdom. Given the comparative paucity of evidence for settlement patterns, permanent dwellings and horticulture in the Neolithic of lowland England, the contradictory ways in which the existing scraps have been read is quite illuminating.

The conventional narrative of economic change through the period can be outlined briefly. To begin with, the British Neolithic farming system:

> involved the cultivation of emmer wheat, supplemented by *einkorn* and barley; and the grazing of cattle, supported by pig and goat and possibly sheep.
>
> (Case 1969a, 177)

This regime was seen as being 'mature and non-experimental . . . highly likely to have been introduced' (1969a: 177), whether by colonisation as Case would have it, or by acculturation as more recent formulations suggest (Zvelebil and Rowley-Conwy 1986). Its impact on the British landscape is described as 'impressive . . . in all but a few upland areas inroads into the woodland and forest were made' (Darvill 1987, 53). The ultimate consequence of this 'most significant social transition . . . ever to have taken place' (1987, 48) was the foundation of 'networks of subsistence territories' within which was practised a 'complex agricultural system' which 'can of course be integrated with Renfrew's model of emergent chiefdoms' (Barker 1985, 200). Nevertheless:

> One must *assume* an initial period after the settlement of the British Isles in which all efforts were concentrated on the production of food and the increase in numbers both of herds and crops, where there would be little time available to devote to sites or even, perhaps, substantial settlements. One may therefore *reasonably assume* that the earliest Neolithic monuments for which there are radiocarbon dates do not in fact reflect the structures erected by the first, second, or even the third generation of agriculturalists to settle in this country.
>
> (Megaw and Simpson 1979, 79; emphasis mine)

This series of acknowledged assumptions allows the rather interesting proposition of a totally archaeologically invisible first Neolithic in Britain to be posited, a line of argument which Zvelebil and Rowley-Conwy (1986, 74) seem equally happy to accept. Both schools of thought have implicitly conceived of the Neolithic as being in the first instance primarily composed of a set of agricultural innovations, any 'cultural' elements being secondary. The eventual emergence of Renfrew's monumental landscapes is thus entirely conditional upon this agricultural achievement.

A similar set of arguments has been constructed to explain away the comparative absence of permanent domestic architecture in Neolithic southern Britain. On the one hand we have Megaw and Simpson, arguing that:

> Archaeologists have been searching in the wrong places – on the tops of the downs where in general both the barrows and causewayed enclosures lie, rather than in the valley bottoms where now more and more evidence suggests, and *common sense would indicate*, that settlements would occur adjacent to water.
>
> (1979, 86; emphasis mine)

This is surely what Bradley (1985) calls 'the archaeology of Mr. Micawber', the faith that in time 'something will turn up'. This emphasis on taphonomic factors neglects the point that the large timber-framed longhouses of the central European *Linearbandkeramik*, Rössen and Lengyel, which perhaps condition our expectations of what Neolithic settlement should look like on the ground, ceased to be built at around the same time as the inception of the British Neolithic (e.g. Kruk 1980; Whittle 1988a, Chapter 3). An elaborated focus on the domestic context was a feature of an earlier phase of Neolithic activity in Europe, and a shift to smaller, more temporary structures is widespread (Last 1996, 39). Similarly, the abrupt appearance of settlements of roundhouses set amongst field systems in the lowland British Middle Bronze Age (Barrett 1994, 150) is difficult to explain in preservational terms alone. It suggests a change in the character of domestic life.

By contrast, attempts have been made to interpret the rather scarce structures which do give the impression of timber-framed 'houses' as farmstead settlements typical of the overall Neolithic settlement pattern (Darvill 1987, 56–7). This tends to overlook the distinctly un-domestic character of the deposits encountered in most of these structures (Kinnes 1985, 26; Herne 1988, 25), their very atypical locations, and their association with monumental constructions like enclosures and cursus monuments. While these may be 'houses', in the sense of making reference to an idealised domestic context, they may not have provided the year-round dwellings of domestic communities (Thomas 1996b).

A third strategy is followed by Burl (1987, 83), who chooses to interpret the large pits with attendant stake-holes at Winterbourne Dauntsey as 'three claustrophobic round huts'.

> Their filth discouraged any idea of a prehistoric golden age. Although they were situated on a low hill, the ground appeared to have been continually sodden, bare of anything but patches of grass and scatters of decaying food thrown out from the cramped, squalid shacks.
>
> (1987, 83)

There are a very large number of ambiguous Neolithic structures which have been excavated in southern Britain, ranging from post-hole constructions beneath barrows to timber circles inside henge monuments, sunken hollows, isolated hearths and wind-breaks (Darvill 1996). It is undeniable that some of these were lived in by people, at least on a temporary basis. But what is striking is how few can unequivocally be identified as permanent dwellings, of the sort associated with agricultural settlement in subsequent periods. Moreover, this evidence presents something of a contrast with that from Orkney and Shetland, where a sedentary, agricultural Neolithic is much more plausible (Barclay 1996; Clarke and Sharples 1985; Whittle *et al.* 1986). It seems unlikely that this contrast can be put down to differences in building materials and taphonomic factors alone.

It is worth questioning the reasons why so many archaeologists have laboured so hard to convince themselves that Neolithic people in southern Britain lived permanently in substantial houses. There is no question, on the basis of the monumental architecture which survives, that these communities were sophisticated, and able to construct impressive dwellings had that been appropriate. It is possible that some of them lived in such structures, some of the time. But the evidence indicates considerable variability in patterns of both residence and mobility. As with other material traces, there seems to be an imperative to use isolated pieces of information as the basis for a generalised model of how people lived in the Neolithic. This in turn can be related to a unilinear evolutionism which demands that all Neolithic people, having advanced beyond the limitations of the Mesolithic, should practise mixed agriculture, should be sedentary and should live in houses. We might choose to connect this with the forms of technological determinism which have already been mentioned: if agriculture and houses had been introduced, all right-thinking people might be expected to have adopted them. This turn of mind seems to lie behind Fowler's remarkable suggestion that:

> It will not be too surprising when we turn up our Middle Neolithic and earlier field systems. They will turn up, perhaps not on the present land surface and probably not in the 'classic' field areas, but buried beneath the erosion deposits in a lowland English valley, or just out of sight below the rim of a bog or marsh.
>
> (1981, 39)

At present, Neolithic field systems in Britain are extremely rare. At Fengate, a series of late Neolithic boundaries may indicate paddocks for the control of cattle (Pryor 1978), and the same may be the case for Céide Fields in Ireland (Caulfield 1978) which is routinely recruited as a model for England and Scotland. More such examples may eventually come to light, but this would not alter the point that the exceptional is frequently taken as representative of a supposedly general pattern, neglecting both regional variability and the possibility that a range of different economic strategies may have been pursued simultaneously within a given area. It is because a single subsistence practice is perceived as fundamental to the Neolithic way of life that this degree of homogeneity is expected. In practice, when extensive spreads of alluvium and colluvium *have* been removed from low-lying areas of the British landscape they have not revealed Neolithic houses and field systems, but yet more monuments. For instance, in the case of the Raunds project in Northamptonshire, new complexes of long mounds, enclosures and barrows have come to light at West Cotton and Stanwick (Windell 1989).

It seems that in all its aspects, the agricultural way of life of the Neolithic is assumed to have been much the same as that which obtained in lowland England until the arrival of the Romans and beyond. People lived in houses, kept sheep, pigs and cattle, and grew cereals. This amounts to 'mixed agriculture' (e.g. Burgess 1980, 29). On this basis, Mercer suggests that 'farming practice in British prehistory had the *potential* to support massive populations' (1981a, 236; my emphasis). Here we can identify another assumption, the Malthusian dictum that population will always rise to the highest level which can be supported by resources and technology, implicit in palaeoeconomy. Population pressure has come to be seen as a driving motor in many accounts of the British Neolithic.

> With more people to feed, more crops and more cattle were needed, areas of good soil were overexploited, poorer regions were brought under cultivation, more forest was cut back and

competition for land increased. In such a period of tension there came the emergence of territories, leaders and conflict.

(Burl 1987, 32)

If the middle of the Neolithic is perceived as a period of change in the relationship between population and resources (Whittle 1978, 34), then the later third millennium is a 'period of recovery' (Whittle 1980a, 33). In this epoch is often imagined the rise of 'a largely pastoral economy' and 'a nomadic society' (Megaw and Simpson 1979, 168). The users of Grooved Ware, in particular, are seen as practising 'pastoralism and strandlooping, with no certain evidence for the cultivation of cereals' (Wainwright and Longworth 1971, 266). This is an interesting prospect, since it seems to be suggested that the major meat animal was the pig (1971, 264), whose appropriateness to a nomadic lifestyle might be questioned. Pigs are notoriously difficult to herd, and provide no secondary products beside hide (Grigson 1982a).

The prevailing image of the Neolithic in lowland Britain, then, is one of a society firmly grounded in a lifestyle of sedentary mixed farming, in many ways comparable with those which succeeded it until the Industrial Revolution, yet one dogged by its explosive population expansion and the fragility of the ecosystem it inhabited. The contemporary circumstances which lie behind the writing of this account are easy enough to identify. First, there is a hankering after the idyll of an 'eternal' British countryside, in which vestiges of a particular way of life have remained unaltered for millennia (Massingham 1926, 206; 1936, 5; Veldman 1994, Chapter 1). This is all the more potent in that so much of the image of 'Britishness' is bound up with this timeless landscape rather than any particular national characteristic (Lowenthal 1994, 20). In these terms, the inception of the Neolithic is of crucial importance, as it marks the creation of an agricultural landscape. It becomes important to distinguish this horizon from the preceding Mesolithic, in which the wildwood was peopled by hunter-gatherers behaving in a most *un-British* fashion. Second, there has been an emerging 'green' concern over the present-day environment. Within this pairing, of course, lies a contradiction between change and changelessness. Many prehistorians seem happy to assert that agriculture was the sphere of human practice in which reasons for the development of prehistoric societies must be located, yet are unwilling to acknowledge that agriculture itself changed in any fundamental way. At most, agriculture is said to 'intensify' – to increase in scale, rather than to undergo fundamental transformation. Where change is posited, it is generally in the form of that stock explanation of culture-historical archaeology, 'a shift to pastoralism'. A way of life which is outside our own immediate experience seems to be difficult to conceptualise within such a framework.

THE ARCHAEOLOGY OF PRODUCTION

One of the principal reasons why this set of commonsensical and modernist ideas has come to dominate our thinking on the economic practices of the Neolithic period has been the existence of a general resistance to theory in economic and environmental archaeology. We will never understand the significance of the acquisition of food in prehistory if our accounts begin and end with how many cattle would have been kept, how many tonnes of grain harvested per hectare. The provision of food, and equally of other goods, is always a process which takes place in the context of a set of social relationships. While it can be argued that people always have to eat, this is very much a minimum consideration with respect to the form and character of their economic life. To attempt to explain an agricultural system, or a set of exchange transactions, in abstraction from the particular social rationale which defined the objectives of production and circulation is consequently likely to be a fruitless task. Economic production is a form of engagement with the material world, which involves the investment of effort, but which also invokes the classification and categorisation of materials, living things and people. Hence what is made and what is consumed by whom is socially defined, and cannot be measured purely in terms of matter and energy (Ingold 1981, 120).

The form of words 'social relations of production' derives from Marx, and can imply an economistic and deterministic view of history. In some forms of Marxism, for instance, the relations of production are seen as depending directly upon the development of the productive forces, and in particular technology (Cohen 1978). This can promote a picture of history in which societies are driven through a series of transformations by successive technical innovations. Within archaeology, something like this can be discerned in Gordon Childe's emphasis on the agricultural and metallurgical 'revolutions' in Old World prehistory (Childe 1936). In that people use tools in order to provide themselves with subsistence, there is obviously a connection between technological change and the form which production takes. However, it is not necessary to see this as a one-way relationship. When Marx and Engels say that 'By producing their means of subsistence men are indirectly producing their actual material life' (1970, 42), they can be taken to be stressing the materiality of human existence, rather than locating the source of social development in the subsistence economy. It is perhaps unnecessary (and increasingly unfashionable) to need to claim any lineage for one's work in the ideas of Marx, yet it could be argued that the most positive way in which the legacy of historical materialism can be interpreted does not lie in stressing the primacy of the productive forces. Instead, one could see the most important aspects of Marx's work as being the notion that being in the world precedes consciousness of the world, and the stress on relations of production as real rather than metaphysical (Heidegger 1993). These relations are situated in the real world, existing between living people and material things, and are emphatically historical in nature. At the same time, one might object to the impression that 'relations of production' need relate exclusively to the production of material things as opposed to the production of human subjects, and the reproduction of society and of knowledge. What this amounts to saying is that material production is to be located in a nexus of relations of power and knowledge which are historically situated, and are thus constituted and reproduced in radically different ways in different societies.

From this it follows that the social organisation of labour undertaken by people within a given epoch is fundamental to the understanding of their historical circumstances. Yet this may be less in the sense of the quantities of food produced and consumed than in that of how labour contributed to their formation as human subjects, and hence to the process of social reproduction. Any labour – hunting and gathering, pastoralism, agriculture, industrial production – implies a set of spatio-temporal rhythms, a discipline of mind and body which contributes to the constitution of subjectivity. People can use the same range of plants, animals and materials in order to provide food and craft goods and artworks in a multiplicity of different ways. What principally distinguishes each is the set of social relations involved (Ingold 1980), so that what is produced is of less consequence than how it is produced.

For archaeology, what is significant is the recognition that this nexus of social relationships can be constituted in different ways in different epochs. Only within capitalist societies is a separate sphere of practice recognisable as an 'economy' to be distinguished (Giddens 1981). In many contemporary tribal communities, economic activities are carried out within the framework of kinship relations (Godelier 1977). The wisdom of separating off distinct areas of study as 'economic archaeology' or 'environmental archaeology' is thus to be severely doubted, since the understanding of why people adopted the agricultural or foraging strategies which they did is unlikely to reside in the bones, seeds, snails and pollen alone. An archaeology of production must be sensitive to the need to understand the internal dynamics of a society if one is to recognise why labour was organised as it was.

DEFINING THE NEOLITHIC

The language that we use to write about archaeology at once constrains and enables what we have to say. Very often, the structure of our available language lays down the conditions for what can and cannot be said, consequentially influencing the way in which a particular debate will develop.

Writing and speech are at once made possible and constrained by the language that we use. Very often the structure of that language itself can determine the course which intellectual history will take. Words which can never quite express the concepts to which we attempt to link them fall into certain patterns, and a discourse emerges which gains a momentum of its own. So it is that when we come to discuss the term 'Neolithic', we may be referring to a chronological horizon, a stage in an evolutionary scheme, a form of economy, a set of social relations or a cultural phenomenon. As a result of this, many of the debates concerning the introduction of the Neolithic to Britain or to Europe have been characterised by exchanges which have taken place at cross-purposes, in which the antagonists have actually been referring to phenomena of a quite different order (Thomas 1993a). I would suggest that this problem is at its most acute in the work of those archaeologists (Dennell 1983; Zvelebil and Rowley-Conwy 1984; 1986) who have equated the word 'Neolithic' with 'agriculture', and proceed to discuss the developments of the period concerned as if all of the cultural and social innovations were subsidiary to the inception of farming. This is not to deny the significance of the origins and spread of agriculture. But it is important to stress that the precise mechanisms by which cultivation and herding came to be undertaken in different parts of the Old World may have varied considerably. While in some cases the availability of domesticates may have immediately brought about far-reaching changes, in others the first moves toward agriculture and pastoralism may have taken place in the context of other changes which may have been of equal or greater significance to the communities concerned.

These problems are very evident in Zvelebil's (1989) comments on the spread of the Neolithic. Zvelebil expresses the desire for a clear definition of what constitutes a Neolithic society, and agreement on how this is to be recognised in the archaeological record and on those traits which might discriminate between indigenous development and migrant populations (1989, 382). The rigour of such a project is commendable, but Zvelebil appears to want the Neolithic to be something stable and homogeneous, which can be held constant across time and space. The problem here is that the term 'Neolithic' is one which was coined by archaeologists, and which over the generations has been used as a means of describing a variety of different phenomena: tools, practices, animals, monuments or people. In the process, an expectation has been generated that 'the Neolithic' should represent a coherent entity underlain and determined by a single historical or evolutionary process. Thus, for instance, Zvelebil suggests that:

> The shift in the mode of subsistence to agro-pastoral farming remains the only process which is relatively closely defined, geographically widespread, and sufficiently archaeologically detectable to act as the signature of the Neolithic.
>
> (1996, 323)

In other words, it is assumed that in world-historic terms the Neolithic should amount to a bounded totality (Thomas 1993a), recognisable by a defined set of material traits. One consequence of this way of thinking has been the presumption that where one element of the Neolithic 'package' can be documented archaeologically, the others must necessarily also have existed (e.g. Ammerman and Cavalli-Sforza 1971; 1973). I suggest that in practice the evidence which is available to us relates to a more complex, messy and fragmented series of developments, and that any attempt to define a particular set of attributes as constituting the Neolithic will be arbitrary in the extreme. Moreover, having distinguished our check-list of diagnostic Neolithic traits and identified a range of 'Neolithic societies', it seems probable that quite different tensions and transformations were at work in each. This is not to deny that certain historical contingencies connected developments in different parts of prehistoric Europe and Asia. But it is to insist upon the importance of the local contexts within which economic and cultural innovations took place.

These rather abstract points can be substantiated by a brief consideration of what is generally portrayed as the spread of a Neolithic 'way of life' across Eurasia. In the Near East, the intensification of the exploitation of plants and animals appears to have developed in quite different ways in two different areas, the Levant and the Zagros (Redman 1977, 534). In the Zagros foothills, a heavy reliance upon herded animals seems to have developed, together with relatively small and architecturally simple settlements like Ali Kosh and Jarmo (1977, 536). In the Levant, however, the first instances of house building, cultivated barley and legumes and symbolic paraphernalia involving the use of human skulls all preceded the domestication of animals (Clark 1977, 54). In this area one can well argue that it was the development of a settled way of life and a richer ceremonial and cultural existence which fostered the domestication of plants and animals rather than vice versa. This particular chicken and egg have been discussed often enough in the past (Childe 1951; Binford 1968; Bender 1975). What needs to be pointed out at this stage is that there was no point at which an homogeneous Neolithic 'package' of economic practice and material culture ever existed. One might argue that, if the post-Pleistocene transformations of the Middle East possessed any degree of similarity, it lay in the kinds of social relationships which developed, rather than the extremely variable forces of production involved. A readiness to appropriate and manage wild species of plants and animals was emerging, and this may have been facilitated by new forms of authority, new relationships between people and place, and new kinds of claims over resources. Indeed, it might be frictions internal to society which dealt the 'first kick' towards domestication so notoriously absent from demographic and ecological explanations of agricultural origins (Bender 1975, 34).

Fundamentally, these changes were connected with the ways in which human beings classified and claimed authority over and kinship with other persons, other species, and material things. Ian Hodder (1990) has identified the beginning of the Neolithic with the 'domestication' of persons and animals, in the conceptual separation of the home from the untamed world. As he puts it, 'The building of more stable houses, the aggregation and even delimitation of settlement, the more elaborate and cultural treatment of the dead, all separate more securely the domestic from the wild' (Hodder 1987, 53). However, I would wish to resist the implication that a single universal cultural ordering of the world was dominant in Eurasia throughout much of prehistory. New material things and new forms of productive labour were doubtless connected with new cosmologies, but it can be argued that these were myriad, created and negotiated by localised communities. I am just as reluctant to see the Neolithic as the product of a determining ideological framework as I am to see it as the cultural manifestation of a single economic regime.

If these elements of the Neolithic way of life developed in a piecemeal way in the Near East, arguments have been made to the effect that their first introduction into Europe may have taken place in a more integrated form (Halstead 1996, 296). At Franchthi Cave, for instance, cattle and pigs, polished stone tools, pottery and a blade industry all appeared together (Barker 1985, 65). But as against this, sheep, goats and domesticated plants had arrived earlier at that site (Payne 1975; Hansen 1980), and there is plausible evidence for an indigenous domestication of cattle and pigs in Greece (Halstead 1996, 297). The expansion of the Neolithic into temperate Europe with the *Linearbandkeramik* (LBK) in the sixth millennium BC (fifth millennium bc) extended the pattern set up by the Balkan Neolithic. The integrated system of farming and residence in large timber houses may have been spread by colonisation (Starling 1985a, 41; but see Whittle 1996), and have been limited to a restricted set of environmental locations (Bakels 1982, 31). In terms of artefacts, architecture and subsistence practice, the LBK gives an outward impression of astonishing conformity (Modderman 1988; Coudart 1991; Keeley 1992). However, the ways in which the material resources of the LBK were put to use in everyday social life sometimes imply greater divergence: similar house spaces or pots may have held different significance within different settlements (Ilett *et al.* 1982; Keeley and Cahen 1989).

The LBK was an established cultural presence in central Europe for hundreds of years. During this time, hunting and gathering communities around the northern and western fringes of Europe were anything but static (Thomas 1996a, 123–9). The recognition of so-called 'complex hunters' (Rowley-Conwy 1983) in these areas is a reflection of the internal dynamism of these communities, and some aspects of this change may have been facilitated by the selective adoption of individual innovations acquired from Neolithic groups. These include shaft-hole adzes which passed directly from LBK and Rössen communities into northern Germany and southern Scandinavia (Fischer 1982), and the indigenous manufacture of pottery amongst the Ertebølle and Swifterbant groups (de Roever 1979), as well as the use of domesticated species (Domańska 1989). As Price (1996, 347) notes, novel foodstuffs were actually the last of the innovations to find their way from central Europe into Scandinavia.

These circumstances raise an important point. In many cases in different parts of Europe, formally 'Neolithic' traits were adopted by indigenous communities, without immediately transforming either their economic or their social structure. Zvelebil and Rowley-Conwy (1984) recognise this in their distinction between three phases in the transition from foraging to farming: availability, substitution and consolidation. Thus a community may initially make use of a novel resource without becoming dependent upon it. This scheme concentrates on the implications of change in subsistence economy, but it seems evident that late Mesolithic and Neolithic northern Europe represented a complex patchwork of communities which had elected to make use of different combinations of innovations in different ways. In some cases introductions from outside had little impact; in other cases they caused changes, but in others still the willingness to accept new artefacts or practices was conditioned by *internal* developments. It may be a mistake to argue as Finlayson does (1996, 278) that Mesolithic people would *always* be most likely to adopt innovations if these could be integrated into existing ways of life without perceptible change. This seems to presume that material culture is essentially neutral, and extrinsic to social processes. Recognising the active role of material things in the change between the Mesolithic and the Neolithic is not to imply that foraging communities were overwhelmed by an incoming tide of alien ideas and practices. On the contrary, it is more probable that new material forms provided a means of amplifying and facilitating indigenous processes of change.

So while the first contacts between foragers and farmers resulted in isolated transfers of technology and resources which had only peripheral effects, from the fifth millennium BC onwards this pattern shifted. Around the Atlantic fringe of north-west Europe, we can suggest that indigenous foraging communities combined aspects of traditional and exotic cultural repertoires in order to establish a new framework for social life (Thomas 1996c). In Britain, southern Scandinavia, the low countries and northern France, I argue that a fundamental difference existed between the mere fact of having access to domesticated resources, or pottery, or stone axes, and using these things together as a means of expressing and reproducing relationships between people, animals and landscape. This difference characterises the start of the Atlantic Neolithic, a Neolithic which was distinct in kind from that of central or south-east Europe. It was not based upon a uniform package of traits, since individual communities drew upon and elaborated the emerging cultural repertoire in quite different ways, and it was not connected with a uniform social change to facilitate agriculture, as Finlayson (1996, 272) implies. But it was integrated and it did bring about social transformations because it involved an altered relationship between people and material things. This change, although radical, should not be reduced to the stereotypical shift from hunting and gathering to agriculture.

In the Atlantic zone, the onset of the Neolithic was remarkable for its swiftness, given the extremely long period of contact between foragers and farmers which preceded it. There seems to have been very little delay between the first use of pottery and construction of monuments in the south of England, and similar developments in Scotland (Armit and Finlayson 1992). This sudden transformation over a very wide area is more easily comprehensible in terms of the adoption of a new repertoire of cultural resources by native communities than of migration or invasion (Thomas 1988a). The practical difficulties involved in the latter are familiar enough (Case 1969a). Yet while the cultural changes were clearly abrupt, the literature contains indications that the transformation of subsistence activity was much more gradual. There are hints that both interference with woodland cover and an extremely restricted use of cereals had begun in the later Mesolithic (Mellars 1976; Edwards and Hirons 1984), while the intensive pre-Neolithic use of other plant foods is well documented (Zvelebil 1994, 64). Throughout the Neolithic in Britain, environmental impacts of human activity in terms of clearance and soil erosion were both uneven and regionally variable (Shotton 1978; Bell 1982; Fisher 1982). Finally, there is a strong argument that a form of short-fallow agriculture based upon fixed plots was not fully established in southern Britain until the Middle Bronze Age (Barrett 1994, 147). While there is no sense in which economic activity can be separated from a social context, and while it is to be expected that domesticated plants and animals would have held considerable cultural significance when they first appeared in Britain, there is evidently a contrast here. The very sudden cultural change from Mesolithic to Neolithic appears to be superimposed upon a much more long-term shift from food-gathering to food-production (Figure 2.1).

I suggest that it is unhelpful to subsume the actual changes which took place in Britain around 4000 BC (c. 3200 bc) within a more large-scale or long-term process of either economic or

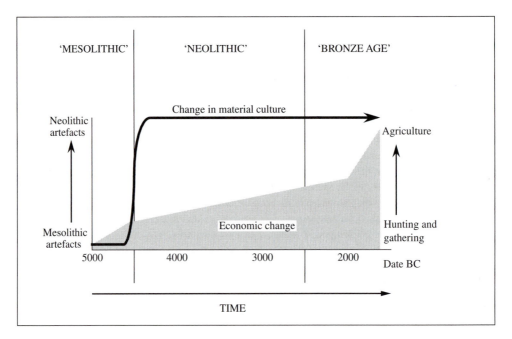

Figure 2.1 The Mesolithic/Neolithic transition

ideological transformation. The archaeologically visible traces (monuments, pottery, stone tools) are not just a reflection of some more fundamental metaphysical process: they were integral to the particular kind of Neolithic which became established in Britain. The start of this Neolithic marked a point at which a new set of cultural resources had been formulated by indigenous groups in Atlantic Europe: the ways in which they deployed these resources were highly variable. Consequently, the social and cultural formations which emerged in the early Neolithic were extremely diverse. Domesticated plants and animals were aspects of this repertoire. They may have been adopted and enthusiastically exploited by some British communities, but not necessarily by all. It is only when we presume that agriculture is the essential element of the Neolithic that we begin to expect that it will have been practised by all of these people at all times.

THE EVIDENCE OF LITHIC DISTRIBUTIONS AND LITHIC TECHNOLOGY

At the same time as an orthodox view of Neolithic agricultural and residential patterns has been developing, evidence has been gathering which might challenge it. Some of this evidence takes the form of tools and waste material of flint, chert and other stones, which occur as scatters distributed across the landscape. While these lithics have been recovered from ploughed fields by generations of amateur collectors (e.g. Laidler and Young 1938), the notion that their systematic collection (Richards 1982; 1984; 1985; 1990) and analysis (Gardiner 1984; 1987; Holgate 1984; 1988a; 1988b; Brown and Edmonds 1987) have much to tell the archaeologist is a comparatively recent one. The perceived benefit of the study of lithics is that, while the structural traces of prehistoric settlement might be minimal and fragile, stone tools are relatively indestructible, and remain locked in the topsoil, moving relatively little from their point of discard (e.g. Bradley *et al.* 1984b).

To a limited degree, stone tools and waste can provide a chronologically sensitive indicator of the inhabitation or use of particular areas. While the temporal resolution is extremely coarse, typochronology does allow a separation to be made between 'earlier' and 'later' Neolithic assemblages, in terms both of tool types and of the characteristics of waste flakes and blades. Underlying this separation is a gradual chronological decline in the standard of flint-working, resulting in a slow change from the fine blade technology of the Mesolithic to the relatively crude, squat flakes of the Bronze Age (Pitts and Jacobi 1979). Hence the metrical analysis of waste flakes may serve as an indicator of relative chronology, a proposition which has been followed to some degree of sophistication in analysis (Ford 1987a). At the same time, particular forms of arrowheads, flint axes, cores and other tools are also held to be chronologically diagnostic (Bradley and Holgate 1984; Gardiner 1984; Holgate 1988a).

These insights have been applied in Britain and abroad both to museum collections of lithics amassed by amateurs (Gardiner 1987) and to material systematically collected by fieldwalking survey (Richards 1985; 1990; Wansleben and Verhardt 1990). One way of evaluating the British material is by comparison with the European sequence alluded to in the last section. The primary Neolithic settlement of central and western Europe, the *Linearbandkeramik*, presents a major contrast both with subsequent continental developments and with Neolithic activity in Britain. Typically, small settlements of timber longhouses were located on the edges of minor valleys in the loess country (Lüning 1982, 26). It has been suggested that the plateau tops immediately above the settlements would have served as the location for fixed-plot horticulture, fertilised by domestic waste (rather than the swiddening once proposed for this phase) (Sherratt 1980; Rowley-Conwy 1981; Howell 1983a, 132). On the valley floor cattle would have been grazed.

However, as has already been mentioned, from around 4000 BC (late fourth millennium bc) onwards, the horizon at which the Neolithic was established in Britain, large timber houses are rather scarce in western Europe (e.g. Bakker 1982, 90; Howell 1983b, 64). This absence of substantial domestic architecture is a pattern which was maintained until well into the Bronze Age. Where structures are preserved by exceptional circumstances, as at Mosegården in Denmark, they may be flimsy in the extreme and the density of occupation material indicates a relatively short duration of use (Madsen and Jensen 1982, 66). Equally, in some areas it has been suggested that the early fourth millennium BC was a time when a greater dependence was placed upon domestic livestock, and cattle in particular (Howell 1982, 116). However, while this development coincided with the expansion of the Neolithic into Britain and the North European Plain, a further phase of internal colonisation was to take place in the years around 3200 BC (2500 bc) (Kruk 1980; Starling 1983, 7; etc.). This involved a change of emphasis in land use away from the water courses and towards the drier and less fertile soils, and has been connected by Sherratt (1981, 293) with the introduction of plough agriculture. This is not implausible, although these developments might constitute an essentially social and economic change played out through the medium of the introduction of new technology (Starling 1985b; Thomas 1987).

The southern British evidence has some very generalised affinities with this sequence. Those scatters of material which can be attributed to the earlier part of the Neolithic (c. 4000–3100 BC/ 3200–2500 bc) tend to be a little more discrete and to be located on light upland soils (Gardiner 1984; Richards 1984; 1990; Holgate 1988a). In contrast, later Neolithic scatters (c. 3100–2150 BC/2500–1800 bc) are often more spatially extensive and are located on a wider range of soils. This is not taken to indicate a shift of settlement from one set of locations to another, so much as an expansion from an initially relatively restricted area (Holgate 1988a, 135). However, it may be that these interpretations betray a desire to regard the dots on lithic distribution maps as surrogate 'sites'. Lithic scatters are a feature of the Mesolithic as well as the Neolithic, and result from the reduction of cores and the use and discard of stone tools, rather than necessarily from the continuous occupation of a location (Edmonds 1995, 35). In the absence of substantial architectural evidence of settlement, dense concentrations of struck lithics may relate to the repeated, sporadic frequenting of a place. The presence of lithic scatters in a given zone of the landscape is not evidence that it was 'settled', but that it formed part of the overall spatial range of human groups, whether for seasonal grazing, harvesting, food gathering or lithic procurement. Given that the last of these generates very large quantities of struck flakes, it is inevitable that lithic distributions will be to some degree skewed toward industrial activities, which may or may not coincide with domestic occupation. Moreover, if we accept that prehistoric societies were not necessarily composed of family groups engaged in continuous co-residence within a single dwelling structure, we must entertain the possibility that different elements of a community may have been engaged in different tasks or pursuits in different locations at different times of the year. The co-resident group need not have been stable, and the overall settlement pattern need not reflect the fixed locations of communities, or even their movements as bounded entities. For these reasons, lithic distribution patterns are bound to be a very blunt instrument for addressing prehistoric landscape use.

Figures 2.2 and 2.3 are the result of the author's analysis of lithic materials from Wessex and the Thames Valley held in museum collections, together with some additional locations drawn from the works mentioned above. In a major work concerned with Neolithic settlement in the Thames Valley, Holgate (1988a, Chapter 5) suggests that only those sites which have produced five or more types of stone tools should be employed for analysis. The justification for this move is that a settlement site is expected to be the locus of a variety of types of activity, using a range of tools. An immediate problem with this approach is that it assumes that the structure of Neolithic settlement would have been one based upon multi-purpose 'domestic sites' or home bases. If particular activities were carried out at special-purpose sites, using a more restricted tool kit, they

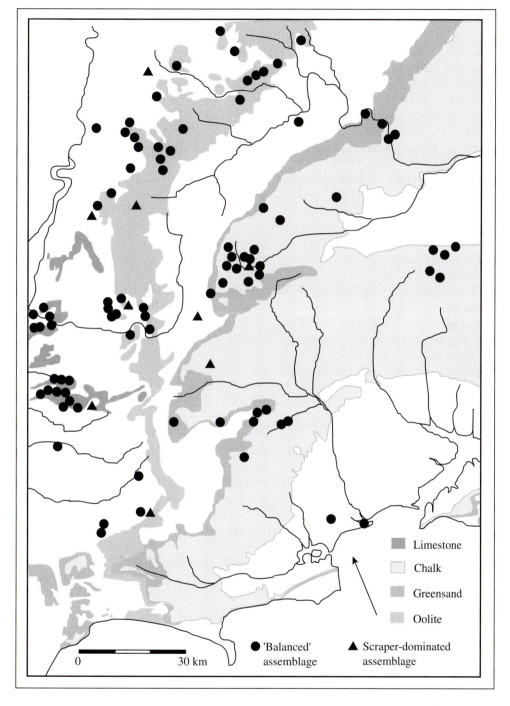

Figure 2.2 Earlier Neolithic settlement in the study area

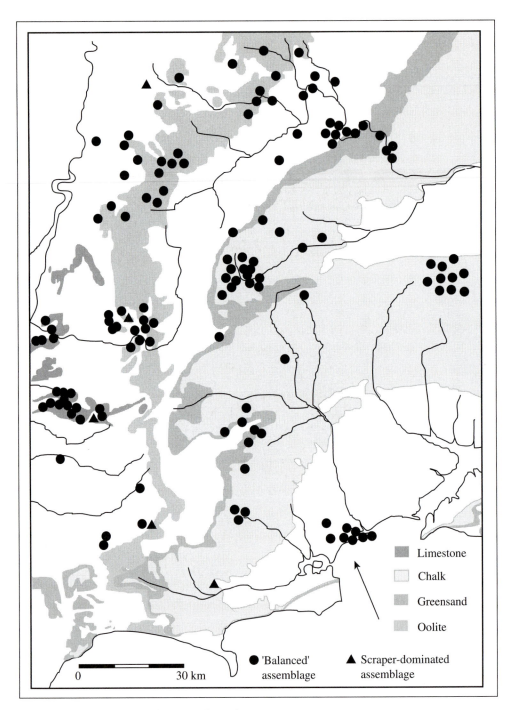

Figure 2.3 Later Neolithic settlement in the study area

might not register. For this reason, although I have performed the analysis within Holgate's strictures, I have added a small group of distinctive assemblages, in which quite large numbers of artefacts have been recovered, but these are overwhelmingly dominated by scrapers. These are generally of earlier Neolithic character, and seem to be predominantly from low-lying locations.

Broadly speaking, the distributions of earlier and later Neolithic assemblages accord with the patterns observed by other authors. As far as the chronological resolution of the evidence can demonstrate, earlier Neolithic scatters are less numerous, and appear to be more concentrated on light upland soils. Later Neolithic find-spots indicate an expansion of activity on to the clays and mudstones, together with a maintenance of activity on the limestones and an intensification of it on the chalk uplands (Figure 2.4). This last phenomenon is in part linked with the greater use of the clay-with-flints capping some areas of chalk as a location which would have afforded plentiful supplies of lithic raw material (Gardiner 1984). The precise significance of the increased number of scatters is difficult to define: a rise in population is an obvious possibility, but a change in patterns of mobility, or a more profligate use of lithic raw materials are equally plausible. Significantly, a great many of the locations involved provided diagnostic artefacts of both earlier and later Neolithic date. This need not indicate continuity of occupation. Many of these may have been places to which people continued to return, cyclically or sporadically. The overall impression is not one of a dramatic shift toward heavier soils, connected with a radically different economic strategy. Instead, a wider range of landscape zones was being used or frequented, without any indication that established locations were being abandoned. This point is brought out by the percentage figures (Figure 2.4, lower). It should be stressed, of course, that the low resolution on the chronology of these processes allows no suggestion of abrupt or revolutionary changes in land use.

As Bradley (1987a, 182) suggests, this extension into new areas can be linked to a number of other changes in the character of surface flint assemblages. As well as the increasing size and density of scatters, and the larger number of find-spots, certain technological changes can be discerned. These include the shift from narrow to broad flakes already mentioned, the use of a broader range of tools, and a decline in the use of retouched and serrated flakes. Evidently this represents a change in the way in which the raw material was regarded and used. Earlier Neolithic assemblages are characterised by the careful preparation of cores, which were often rejuvenated so as to make maximum use of the stone (Edmonds 1995, 37). Blades have been carefully removed, and often retouched for use as tools. The assemblage as a whole is one which could be put to a variety of uses: the tools are non-specific and flexible. The combination of a narrow range of tools and the careful use of cores indicates a technology suited to a mobile way of life (Edmonds 1987). Thus the character of the tools themselves gives an impression of mobility, rather than stable settlement foci.

By the later Neolithic an assemblage was in use which had a broader range of tool types, each more specific to particular activities. This might be seen as a 'less economic' use of raw material than in the earlier assemblage. However, this runs the risk of imposing a modern Western concern with efficiency on the past, and a alternative reading would be that this was a set of tools suited to a changed style of life in which portability was not at a premium. If, as Edmonds (1987, 169) suggests, the earlier Neolithic assemblage can be connected with regular, large-scale, planned movements of population, perhaps on a seasonal basis, then the later Neolithic pattern might represent the breakdown of this system, with a reduction of overall mobility. The broad spreads of tools and debitage across the landscape might indicate 'that residential locations of a fairly insubstantial nature were repeatedly moved within a well defined area' (1987, 174). In these terms, the apparent 'expansion' of settlement onto heavier soils might be explained in social terms, with less stable groups pursuing less regular movements from place to place, punctuated by events of fission and fusion.

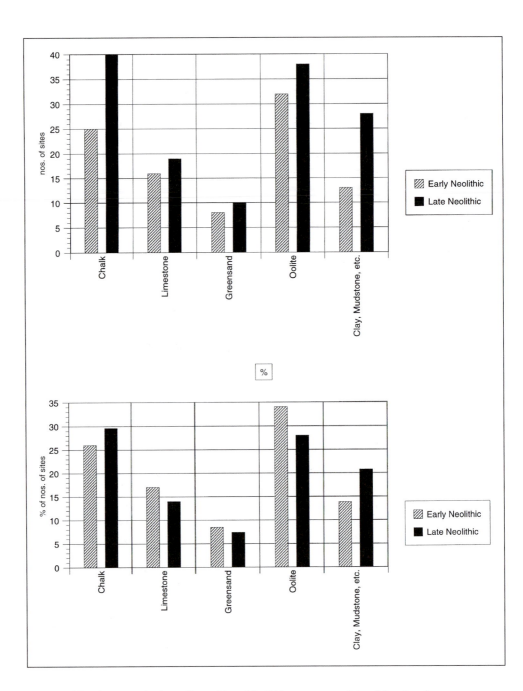

Figure 2.4 Landscape use in the earlier and later Neolithic: raw count of sites (above) and percentages (below)

The less numerous and more spatially confined distributions of lithics of the earlier Neolithic could be interpreted as having arisen from a pattern in which particular locations were of significance within a regular and repetitive cycle of movement. Some of these locations may have been horticultural plots, or year-round settlements where some members of a community awaited the return of others. But they might equally have been seasonal campsites, or the meeting-places of dispersed populations. In this sense, the scattered concentrations of earlier Neolithic chipped stone artefacts are complementary to the dispersed ceremonial monuments of the period (Barrett 1994, 136). By the later Neolithic this impression of cyclical return to known places appears to have given way to a less constrained movement across the landscape: a landscape in which larger open areas were gradually emerging. These claims might seem excessive on the basis of lithic analysis alone, but can perhaps be substantiated by placing them alongside the bioarchaeological evidence.

PLANTS, ANIMALS AND MONUMENTAL LANDSCAPES

What can be said about the crops which were grown in Neolithic Britain has tended to be rather limited, as a consequence of the very few seed impressions and samples of carbonised plant remains which have been recovered (Helbaek 1952; Hillman 1981a). The very paucity of this evidence has contributed to its being interpreted in a particular way. Thus Legge (1989, 220) suggests that 'most judgements of the importance of agriculture to prehistoric communities therefore rest, to a significant degree, on data other than that of the charred seeds, such as the size and complexity of settlements or the scale of monumental construction'.

However, it is far from clear that complex monuments, or for that matter involved ritual practices or social stratification, need to be based upon a system of sedentary agriculture with fixed fields and a dependence on staple crops. A brief consideration of North American prehistory should demonstrate this point. In the late Archaic period (1800–500 BC), a number of large enclosures were built in the lower Mississippi Valley, by communities of sedentary hunter-gatherers. The largest of these, at Poverty Point in Louisiana, consisted of six concentric rings of earthworks covering 150 hectares, and was associated with large quantities of exotic non-utilitarian material culture (Jackson 1991, 266–7). Later, in the early years AD, the massive geometric embanked enclosures of the Ohio Hopewell were constructed by people exploiting a broad spectrum of wild resources and 'cultivating a modest range of garden crops' (Braun 1986, 119). Finally, in the late first millennium AD, the massive monumental complex at Cahokia, on the Mississippi, was the product of a society which practised maize and squash horticulture in small raised gardens supplemented with many wild species (Dincauze and Hasenstab 1989, 73; Pauketat 1992). Societies like the north-west coast Amerindians had complex ceremonial cycles, yet the only crops which they cultivated were those which were used as sacraments in ritual (McMillan 1988, 183). Hunters and gatherers and those practising garden horticulture and other simple forms of cultivation often have many hours of spare time not engaged in productive labour (Sahlins 1974). There is thus no reason at all why monument-building or complex ritual should be dependent upon a large agricultural surplus. On the contrary, one might argue that it would be more likely that agricultural intensification to support urban populations in more recent epochs could be held responsible for the impoverishment of the ceremonial lives of traditional societies.

Given this evidence, it is no longer the case that any explanation for monument-building can be found in the development of an economic base, in the form of a transition from hunting and gathering to farming. A growth of territorialism resulting from the adoption of agriculture has often been cited as a reason for the first construction of monuments (Renfrew 1973b; 1976; Chapman 1981). However, if there is limited evidence for agriculture, this becomes a circular argument (monuments are the consequence of agriculture, which must exist because of the presence of monuments).

If we remove the imperative to interpret seed remains as evidence for a complex system of fixed-field crop rotation, the quality of the record is more explicable. For some time it has been recognised that 'most of the early agricultural communities continued to be substantially dependent on a wide range of wild food resources' (Hillman 1981a, 189). Substantial biases doubtless colour the representation of various species in carbonised assemblages (Dennell 1972). Nevertheless, the domination of almost all known assemblages by wild species is suggestive (Robinson and Wilson 1987, 33; Moffett *et al.* 1989), as is the general absence of weed faunas characteristic of plough agriculture (Moffett *et al.* 1989). Cereal crops certainly were grown: emmer and einkorn wheat, possibly bread wheat, and hulled and six-row barley (Hillman 1981b, 124). There is also evidence that particular crops were grown preferentially on different soils (Dennell 1976). As spelt had yet to be introduced, there would be no winter wheat, and hence only a single yearly sowing. Jarman *et al.* (1982, 142) insist that as legumes are found in rotation with cereals in the Neolithic of Europe and the Near East they were probably also present in Britain. Such a rotation fixes and replaces nitrogen in the soil, and hence is highly suitable for fixed-plot horticulture. However, the evidence for legumes in Britain is scant, and in the northern climate they might prove prone to weevil and aphid attack (Green 1981). Moffett *et al.* (1989, 254) suggest that the limited extent of British Neolithic cultivation can be contrasted with the relatively high productivity and stability of continental *Bandkeramik* garden horticulture, but it is interesting to note that the sedentary character of even these settlements can be questioned (Whittle 1996, 162).

The earliest record of the use of the plough in Britain is provided by the marks beneath the South Street long barrow, dated to 3663–3367 cal. BC (2810 ± 130 bc) (BM-356) (Evans 1971, 48). However, it is open to debate whether traces like these, or the ones from beneath round barrow Amesbury G71, genuinely reflect the use of an ard in routine cultivation (a point recognised by Evans, see Ashbee *et al.* 1979, 282). Experimental work has demonstrated that ards of the kinds found at Donneruplund or Hendriksmose will only produce scoring in the lightest of sandy subsoils, and then only after part of the topsoil has been removed by hand (Aberg and Bowen 1960; Hansen 1969). Deep marks cut into chalk like those at South Street suggest the use of a much heavier tool, a 'rip ard' (Reynolds 1981). This latter is not a tool of cultivation but of clearance, a way of turning soil matted by roots. This could easily be a means of preparing for pasture rather than tillage. Moreover, European evidence suggests that these kinds of marks might equally relate to the early stages of mound-building, and might be integral to mortuary ritual (Tarlow 1994). Indeed, there is considerable peril involved in interpreting as typical any feature found beneath a burial mound, whether plough-mark, fence-line or putative dwelling structure, as if the old land surface were a random sample of the prehistoric landscape, fortuitously preserved (Lane 1986). The artefactual evidence for cultivation is restricted to a single digging stick recovered from the Baker Platform on the Somerset Levels (Rees 1979). Nevertheless, the evidence from the continent suggests that in *Bandkeramik* horticulture no more advanced technology than hoes, digging-sticks and spades was employed (Kruk 1980; Rowley-Conwy 1981; Sherratt 1981; Jarman *et al.* 1982).

Entwistle and Grant (1989, 20) have argued that the most likely cultivation practice in Neolithic Britain was 'transient, hoe-based horticulture', representing only a part of a broader spectrum of plant foods. Hazelnuts, crab apple, raspberry, blackberry, sloe and hawthorn pips have all been recovered from carbonised assemblages, while edible roots, rhizomes and tubers are known from waterlogged contexts (Moffett *et al.* 1989, 246). Whether cereal and other domestic crops represented a dominant or minor element in the diet might have varied from place to place and time to time. Certainly, in the case of the Essex coastal site of the Stumble, collected plants maintained a predominance over cereals throughout both earlier and later Neolithic (Murphy 1990, 32; N. Brown 1997, 93). Indeed, it is interesting to speculate whether the significance of domesticated species might have been less dietary than social or symbolic, a pattern which seems quite common ethnographically (Farrington and Urry 1985). In the North American context, a strong argument has been made that the adoption of corn was initially not conditioned by dietary need, but was connected with feasting and elite activities: being a corn-eater conferred a particular kind of identity upon a person (Hastorf and Johannessen 1994). In Britain, a similar process might explain the relatively major concentrations of cereals located at 'special' sites like causewayed enclosures (Legge 1989, 218). Similarly, a small group of large timber 'houses' in Britain and Ireland like Balbridie, Lismore Fields and Ballygalley (Simpson 1996a; Cooney 1997, 27) have produced extensive caches of grain. It is worth considering whether these represent specialised storage, consumption or redistributive locations for a very special kind of food, rather than simply farmsteads.

In the past, accounts of early agriculturalists in Britain have portrayed them as tied to their fields, jealously protecting crops of cereal vital to their survival from predators and from the elements (Case 1969a). This perhaps underestimates the hardy character of primitive crops (Reynolds 1979; 1981). Equally, it is unlikely that such a degree of dependence upon a single food source was risked. Contemporary communities who combine cultivation with gathering often exhibit scant concern for their crops. Both the Ownes Valley Paiute and the Siriano of eastern Bolivia plant crops annually (in the latter case in small cleared plots, in the former with considerable effort in irrigation), returning to harvest them as part of a seasonal cycle of hunting, gathering and collecting (Farrington n.d.). Cultivation can thus be seen as a means of extending the range of crops available within a broad-spectrum regime, either as an insurance against the failure of particular species or as a means of providing exotic plants, often for ritual purposes.

If we dispense with the prejudice that only a fully agricultural society could have produced the monuments and complex artefacts of Neolithic southern Britain, the evidence for domesticated plants can best be seen as representing rather small-scale, garden horticulture, carried out on a sporadic basis. On the loess soils which then existed over much of southern England (Catt 1978), it seems likely that these plots could have been used for many years without soil decline or fall in yields (Reynolds 1979, 58–64; Jarman *et al.* 1982, 141). Even then, it is questionable whether stands of crops would have been maintained in the same location for long, rather than being opportunistically seeded in available clearings. Indeed, the environmental evidence of cultivation generally takes a form which suggests short-lived events of tillage, as opposed to the foundation of permanent fields (Evans *et al.* 1993, 188). Neolithic arable activity was often episodic, and might in some cases have represented the production of a single crop to be consumed at a particular event. The degree to which these plots would have been either weeded or supervised is a difficult question, and the relationship of horticulture to the broader pattern of mobility and settlement is better addressed in relation to other forms of evidence. Certainly, it need not have been the case that all communities in all parts of Britain had access to domesticated plants, and recent work on human bone isotope ratios both in Scandinavia and Britain has called into question the dietary role of cereals (Lidén 1995; M. Richards 1996). However, it might be unwise to take these results at face value, and replace a model of homogeneous mixed agriculture with one of universal pastoralism. It may be more prudent to view the seemingly contradictory character of the evidence as an indication of a high degree of variability, both between and within regions.

Variability is also a feature which is important in any assessment of the proxy indicators of vegetational change. As with other aspects of the evidence, the assumption of a mixed farming economy has coloured the understanding of pollen spectra and molluscan assemblages. The expectation has often been that samples taken from barrows, henges and other monuments will provide a random cross-section of the prehistoric environment. This implies that there was no positive relationship between monument-building and subsistence practice, so that the conditions recorded in ditch deposits and buried land surfaces are indicative of the landscape as a whole, which is effectively presumed to have been homogeneous. However, as Allen (1997) rightly points out, these are biased samples. By definition, monuments were built in parts of the landscape which had been cleared, even if only immediately prior to construction. The analysis is more indicative of the micro-environment of the monument than of the broader surroundings. But worse than this, if we hypothesise not a uniform landscape of fixed agrarian fields, but one in which there was considerable mobility, we might expect a very different relationship to have existed between monuments and economic activities. The monuments could represent the fixed points within a seasonal round, places of sporadic or seasonal agglomeration for population and herds. Concentrations of monuments, like those around Stonehenge or Avebury, might thus represent the foci for periodic gatherings of people and livestock, and the intensity of clearance and land use could be expected to reflect this. This problem has been compounded by the use of the term 'ritual landscape'. This is at once a very good locution and a very bad one. It aptly expresses the sense in which monuments structure and even dominate particular areas, giving a form and direction to everyday activities. But at the same time it can set up the expectation that a ritual landscape can be contrasted with a quotidian one, implying a spatial division between ritual and economic activities. If this were the case, one might expect that the environmental evidence from monumental contexts would relate to areas which were, at most, marginal to subsistence activities. I suggest the exact opposite: that areas like the chalk uplands of Salisbury Plain and north Wiltshire are likely to have seen the most intensive grazing and clearance in the Neolithic, albeit on a sporadic basis. This much may be indicated by environmental evidence suggesting very low levels of clearance in areas remote from monumental complexes (Thorley 1981; Scaife 1987; Richmond 1996).

Superficially speaking, we have a far better knowledge of the livestock component of Neolithic agriculture in Britain. The main domestic animals were cattle and pig, with sheep rather less frequently represented. Wild species are consistently found as a minor element in faunal assemblages. However, aside from red deer, the contribution of these species was more likely to have been as fur-bearers than as a meat source (Grigson in Smith *et al.* 1981). A sequence has been proposed in which cattle dominate the economy of the earlier Neolithic, being replaced by pigs in the face of woodland regeneration in the later Neolithic; renewed clearance of the downland allowed sheep to become of greater importance in the Early Bronze Age (representing 38 per cent of the sample at Snail Down barrow cemetery: Tinsley and Grigson 1981, 225). However, what one finds in a faunal assemblage depends upon the context from which it derives (Meadow 1975), and almost all of the animal remains which the author has personally studied from southern Britain come from ceremonial or mortuary contexts. Even those samples which derive from innocuous-looking pits may not directly represent the pattern of subsistence, since they may have been carefully selected for deliberate deposition (Legge 1991, 72). I have previously suggested that the predominance of pigs on Grooved Ware sites is to be connected with their use as a feasting animal rather than with environmental conditions (Richards and Thomas 1984, 206). At other sites of later Neolithic date, such as the later silts at Maiden Castle, the Peterborough Ware layers in the Dorset Cursus, or the Maiden Castle long mound, cattle continue to dominate the assemblage (Figure 2.5). If we are to postulate a return to woodland conditions in the later Neolithic, we might expect to find not only a high representation of pig, but also of wild species (Smith 1984). Wild species account for less than 5 per cent in all of the henge sites, and usually less than

2 per cent. Those assemblages which do have higher percentages of wild animals (Thickthorn Down, Wor Barrow, Maiden Castle, the Dorset Cursus) are generally earlier in date.

What is really noteworthy about the relative representation of species is the marked emphasis on cattle in the earlier Neolithic. Later Neolithic sites show varied proportions of cattle and pig, but earlier Neolithic assemblages often have more than 50 per cent cattle. Perhaps we should be less concerned with explaining the shift to pig than with the earlier pattern of cattle dominating the assemblage. Even this, though, is subject to considerable variation. Serjeantson (1996, 207) has recently pointed out the contrast between

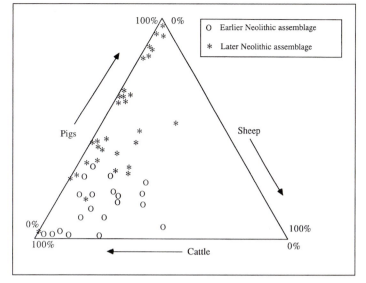

Figure 2.5 Faunal assemblages: ratio of pigs:cattle:sheep

the assemblages from earlier Neolithic sites in close proximity with one another at Staines and Runnymede, in the middle Thames Valley. At the Staines causewayed enclosure, cattle made up 78 per cent of the assemblage and pigs only 10 per cent, while at Runnymede the figures were 47 per cent and 44 per cent respectively. If the Runnymede material derived from short-term domestic habitation, this suggests that very different collections of animal bones will have been generated at different kinds of locations.

It is evident that the consumption of large quantities of meat took place at various kinds of monuments during the Neolithic. At none of these is there extensive evidence for complex bone-processing, marrow-splitting and butchery marks, although at Stonehenge Serjeantson notes that some animal bones were incomplete owing to lengthy periods of attrition prior to burial (1995, 451). More clear traces of bone-processing might be expected if the nutritional value of the carcasses were being exploited to the full. Moreover, both Legge (1981) and Smith (1966) point to the presence of articulated limbs of cattle in the ditch silts of causewayed enclosures. In a later Neolithic context, it was found that at the henge monument of Durrington Walls the different parts of the bodies of cattle and pigs had been differentially distributed between the various parts of the site, indicating not merely feasting but a very deliberate way of disposing of the debris (Richards and Thomas 1984). At all the henge monuments, and also at various other sites like the Thickthorn Down long barrow and Hambledon Hill causewayed enclosure (Sieveking's 1951 excavations, Jackson archive, Matlock Museum), relatively high ratios of bones from the meat-rich parts of pig and cattle as against waste parts (as defined by Maltby 1979, 7) were recorded. These sites all seem to have been concerned with the consumption and sometimes deliberate wasting or offering of the choicer parts of the animals. These observations, of course, are general in the extreme, and further work might address the issue of the value placed upon different anatomical parts. We should not be surprised if these were not those judged most tender by the modern palate.

Grigson (in Ashbee 1966) has noted that at certain long barrows (Fussell's Lodge, Bowl's Barrow, Amesbury 42, Knook 2, Corton, Sherrington 1 and Tilshead Lodge) the remains of bovid foot bones (metapodia, cuboids, phalanges) have been recovered in such circumstances as to suggest the burial of ox hides, often in association with bovid skulls. In addition, cattle skulls have been found in long barrow ditches, or as 'substitutes' for burials, buried beneath long mounds at Amesbury 42 and Beckhampton Road (Thurnam 1869, 132; Ashbee *et al.* 1979, 247). Closely related is the purposeful deposition of cattle skulls at the causewayed enclosures of Whitesheet Hill (Piggott 1952), Maiden Castle (Grigson in Smith *et al.* 1981, 199) and Hambledon Hill. At Stonehenge, a cattle skull had been placed on the base of the ditch, and provided a radiocarbon determination which suggested that it had been curated for some considerable while before burial (Serjeantson 1995, 449).

There is thus a close physical association between cattle bones and human remains, while in some cases the two appear interchangeable. The storage and perhaps veneration of cattle skulls also finds a close parallel in the treatment of human bones, as at Wor Barrow, where articulated human bodies were buried alongside 'bundles' of bones which may have been in circulation for some while before deposition (Pitt Rivers 1898, 66). If people moved from place to place along with cattle, and the deaths and consumption of cattle were fixed in places of human meeting and ceremonial, there is reason to presume that the lives of human communities and herds of cattle were deeply interlinked. In a sense, the herd might be perceived as complementary to the social group. If the remains of people and cattle were to some degree equivalent, the unusual treatment of cattle bones is understandable. The practice of depositing hides and skulls with burials continued into the Beaker period, with 'head and hooves' burials like those at Hemp Knoll (Robertson-Mackay 1980) and at Beckhampton (Young 1950). While this kind of assemblage can readily be recognised within a grave or a mortuary structure, it is notable that concentrations of the cuboids, metapodia and phalanges of cattle often occur at causewayed enclosures and henge monuments, alongside otherwise 'meat rich' assemblages. While this could simply represent butchery waste, it is also possible that the circulation and deposition of cattle hides, as objects of considerable symbolic significance, was more widespread than is generally appreciated.

This particular emphasis on the symbolic qualities of cattle as opposed to other species in mortuary and ritual locations needs to be put into context. As we have seen, a primary aspect of the social role of cattle is represented by the evidence for feasting. Legge (1981, 179) states that 'the majority of cattle killed at the causewayed camps are female, and . . . these animals represent the surplus available from economies based at lowland (and undiscovered) Neolithic sites'. As Grigson (1982b) points out, equal numbers of males and females must have been born, yet the young males culled soon after birth in the system presented by Legge are absent from the enclosures. This leads to two conclusions: the causewayed enclosures must have been tied in to a broader (regional?) economy, and this economy involved the movement of cattle from one place to another. Cattle seem not to have been at the enclosures at the time of year when young males were being culled. Any interpretation of the enclosures as economically independent defended settlements has therefore to be considered critically.

Sherratt (1981) suggests that the development of dairying economies before the middle of the third millennium is unlikely, since any major human dependence upon milk consumption can only take place once a biological tolerance for lactose has been achieved (see also Entwistle and Grant 1989). It must be admitted, though, that yoghourt, cheese, butter or ghee are largely free of lactose (Grigson pers. comm.), and might provide protein for a prehistoric diet. But despite this, nutritional factors alone cannot provide a complete explanation for the importance of cattle in Neolithic Britain. Arguments have in the past been made to the effect that 'wealth' in pre-industrial societies is constrained by the fact that the surplus product exists only as agricultural produce (Gamble 1981). This leads on to the expectation that such surpluses will be used to maintain craftsmen, producing prestige items. Hence the existence of craft specialisation is seen as one of the key attributes of the early state, the consequence of the ability of a managerial elite to centralise and redistribute surpluses (Renfrew 1972). As a result, craft specialisation has come to be one of the indicators of social change sought for in the Neolithic (Renfrew 1973a). Yet, as we have already noted, this notion of a material surplus may not be relevant to such a society. Monument building and the production of prestige goods hardly require a separate population of specialists. Labour may be recruited as *corvée*. Equally, food can fuel a prestige system by other means than by supporting specialists. Notably, it may be consumed in feasts (Friedman 1975). The assembled evidence indicates that cattle were killed and eaten in large numbers at special sites like causewayed enclosures. Their remains, particularly their heads, hooves and hides, seem to have been treated with some care, sometimes stored and sometimes buried as part of human funerary deposits. All of this might indicate that the eating of cattle flesh was not an everyday activity so much as something to be indulged in at particular times and in particular places. These occasions would appear to have been communal feasts. If wild plants, some cultivated plants, the flesh of lesser animals, and perhaps dairy products provided the staples of the Neolithic diet then cattle meat might have been a more highly ranked food, circulating and being consumed under different conditions.

Earlier in this chapter it was suggested that lithic analysis indicates a relatively high degree of mobility in Neolithic ways of life in lowland Britain. The botanical remains can be read to suggest no more than a partial (and perhaps seasonal?) dependence upon cultivated cereals and pulses, with considerable gathering of wild plants. The analysis of faunal remains again points to populations who were substantially mobile, or at the least who carried out different activities in different places at different times of year. It is not necessary to evoke the existence of an independent nomadic pastoralist system in Neolithic Britain (suggested, for instance, by Barker and Webley 1978; Jarman *et al.* 1982). Nomadic pastoralism is usually a form of economy which arises as the consequence of the growth of state societies nearby (Gilbert 1975), and the pastoralists usually exist as an element within a more complex regional economy. Only the Masai manage to remain entirely independent of horticulturalist neighbours, and this at the cost of drinking the blood of their animals (Goldsmitt 1979). Rather, the suggestion that cattle were actually circulating within the landscape, and that their slaughter took place in monuments remote from the settlement areas, emphasises a complex inter- and intra-community division of labour, and one which was intimately concerned with movement in space and synchronisation in time. So even if the meat of cattle was only consumed occasionally, and the importance of dairy products is unknown, the social significance of cows may have been considerable, both in symbolic terms and in the way that their seasonal movements contributed to the temporal rhythms of human groups.

STANDSTILL OR REORGANISATION?

It is now necessary to turn to the arguments which have been put forward for economic change in the Neolithic. These find their clearest expression in a pair of articles published by Alasdair Whittle and Richard Bradley in the late 1970s (Bradley 1978a; Whittle 1978). These are now quite out of date, and indeed have been renounced by their respective authors. It would be unfair to criticise them at all were it not for the influence which these arguments continue to exert, whether in textbooks, museum displays or the popular media. On the basis of pollen analytical evidence for woodland and scrub regeneration, Whittle and Bradley both proposed that 'a population grown too large on the initial riches' (Whittle 1978, 39) of clearance and cultivation fell upon a period of agricultural recession in the middle part of the Neolithic. An imbalance between population and resources led to soil decline, loss of soil stability and regeneration of clearances. It would not be until the later part of the period, with the building of the large henges and the rise of new social hierarchies associated with Beaker pottery and prestigious funerary practices that a full recovery would be effected (Whittle 1980a, 334; 1980b). Extending the model backwards in time, Mercer (1981a) suggests that the building of causewayed enclosures in Wessex could be connected with a growth of territoriality and a pressure on land in the years between 3600 and 3050 BC (2800–2500 bc).

However, it is possible that this was a model which slipped into orthodoxy on very shaky foundations. Population dynamics models were very much a part of the baggage of the ecological archaeology of the 1970s. Where it is denied that 'cold', pre-capitalist societies are as riddled with interpersonal antagonisms and internal contradictions as are modern capitalist ones, and their adaptations are considered as analogous to those of biological organisms, only their reaction to external stimuli will be considered. The idea of an agricultural 'standstill' is the consequence of not considering internally generated social change. Just as Whittle (1978, 34) rightly criticised Renfrew (1973a) for assuming that the increasing investment of effort in monuments throughout the Neolithic was a consequence of a steady and unbroken growth in population, it is necessary to criticise the assumption that all populations will inevitably rise to carrying capacity, and the Malthusian supposition that all social and technological innovations owed their genesis to the balancing of relations between population and resources.

There are other flaws in the model. It is unclear how far the hypothesised depletion of soils can be demonstrated. While valley alluviation doubtless extends back into the Neolithic (Bell 1982), there is little evidence for large-scale periods of synchronised run-off until much later (Shotton 1978; Evans *et al.* 1993, 187). Indeed, many of the soil changes which have been blamed upon Neolithic cultivation, like the inception of lessivage, may have a much earlier origin in post-glacial canopy conditions (Fisher 1982). A further complicating factor lies in exactly what is considered to have been regenerating in the later fourth millennium BC. The 'economic standstill' argument suggests an escalating onslaught on the forests from the start of the Neolithic in order to provide arable land, followed by a synchronised phase of woodland regeneration. Yet there remains considerable confusion over the character of woodland clearance in Neolithic Europe, particularly in respect of the 'elm decline'. While this has often been presented as a diagnostic signature of the onset of cultivation, associated with a 'leaf fodder regime' for feeding stalled cattle (Pennington 1974, 63–6), many different causes can be invoked, including climatic change, soil deterioration, disease and insect attack, as well as human impact (Tipping 1994, 22). Moreover, the elm declines documented on pollen diagrams in Britain are spread over 500 years or more, in contrast with the more or less synchronised adoption of Neolithic material culture. Rowley-Conwy (1982) argues that the scale of the elm decline was such that it could hardly have been entirely anthropogenic. Only woodland clearance on a massive scale could have had such a pronounced effect. Ten Hove (1968) shows that the elm decline also took place in areas which have no evidence of human occupation at the time, as in the case of northern Norway. So, if we are not clear how much of the vegetational disturbance of the early to middle Neolithic can be attributed to human agency, it is difficult to argue that the impact decreased over time. And given the arguments which have already been presented for regional and local variations in subsistence practice, we might not expect a synchronised decline in this activity in areas as distant as Wessex and the Lake District.

The notion of an abrupt felling of large areas of woodland, associated with a sudden inception of cultivation seems very much to be tied to the image of the Neolithic as a 'pioneer economy'. The language of 'land-taking' connected with clear-felling using stone axes implies a catastrophic impact upon the wildwood (Iversen 1956). This set of expectations may have influenced the inter-pretation of environmental evidence, and it is equally possible to argue that landscape change over the Mesolithic/Neolithic boundary may have been quite gradual. Clearance is not an exclusive prerogative of Neolithic communities: there are indications of forest burning to encourage game by Mesolithic groups (Mellars 1976), while natural causes of clearance include wind-throw, lightning strike and disease (A. Brown 1997, 140). Richard Tipping (1994, 9) has argued against the assumption that woodlands are unproductive while cleared land is useful. Clearings may be made for grazing, but equally cattle can browse in open woodland, which might be maintained by controlled burning (Moore 1997). The post-glacial forests of Britain were already ecologically diverse, and sporadic human and natural impacts would have meant that by the start of the Neolithic a mosaic of quite different woodland, glade and clearing conditions would have existed (Scaife 1987, 141; Moore 1997, 34). Brown (1997) suggests that this range of conditions may have been used opportunistically by Neolithic communities, grazing or planting in existing clearings. The prevention of re-colonisation by trees and shrubs caused by continued grazing, the managing of woodlands, browsing and some limited felling would have slowly increased the extent of clearance. As Brown goes on to say:

> the overall decline in total tree pollen seen in pollen diagrams from the British Isles and Ireland is not in dispute, but landscape-scale deforestation is only evident from the vast majority of regional pollen diagrams from the late Bronze Age onwards.
>
> (1997, 134)

If woodland clearance can be seen as a slow and incremental process dating back to the Mesolithic, the same could arguably be said for the cultivation of crops. Grains of what may have been cereal pollen have come from pre-elm decline contexts (Edwards and Hirons 1984). It is possible that many, or all, of these may be no more than large grass pollen (Tipping 1994, 19), but in either case the extent to which one can identify a distinct point at which cultivation began and associate it with the elm decline is lessened. Under some conditions, small localised clearances may not be detected by pollen analysis at all (Edwards 1982). At Flanders Moss in the Firth Valley, Turner argued that clearances had been too small to register (Smith *et al.* 1981, 173). So while the most spectacular impacts on the pollen record may be caused by factors other than anthropogenic ones, actual human activity may be very difficult to distinguish, and may even be 'masked' by other phenomena (Edwards 1979).

All of these points suggest that it is hard to identify a synchronised human impact on the woodlands and soils of Britain in the early Neolithic, followed by a general decline in activity. As Edwards suggests, it is 'rather dangerous to talk of a general . . . regeneration . . . unless all the sites bore a relative constant and known relationship with the human community causing the inferred impact' (1979, 263). We might also have to consider the possibility that any apparent change in human influence on the pollen record reflects not a decrease in the degree of influence so much as a change in the *structure* of that influence.

One further aspect of the vegetational record which contradicts any idea of an agrarian crisis in the middle Neolithic is the evidence of very large tracts of woodland which had never been cleared, and would consequently have been available for exploitation by any growing population (Smith *et al.* 1981, 206). The proposed selective pressure of scarce resources and limited land simply did not apply. Waton's (1982) pollen diagrams for Lewis and Snelsmore (Berkshire), for instance, show little evidence for clearance until the Middle Bronze Age and the Iron Age respectively. At Buscott Lock in Oxfordshire, Robinson and Wilson (1987, 31) report a silted stream channel with traces of later Neolithic human occupation, but with multiple environmental indicators pointing to a combination of primary and secondary woodland. Robinson and Wilson (1987, 33) go on to argue that the woodlands of the south midlands clay slopes and boulder clays remained untouched throughout the Neolithic. It is a mistake to imagine an homogeneous landscape in which clearance and regeneration might proceed at a uniform rate. A pattern of considerable variability in vegetational history is more likely, and it seems that even in the vicinity of large Neolithic monuments, combinations of open and closed conditions might have existed (Entwistle and Bowden 1991; Allen 1997).

It is beyond question that individual pollen sites document a process of woodland regeneration at some time during the Neolithic, and the same can be said of archaeological sites with mollusc faunas. However, these individual events are neither synchronised nor universal. Pollen cores which document regeneration may be found within a short distance of other sites which show no such process (Tipping 1994, 33). Some clearings, whether natural or artificial, will have gone through the expected sequence of re-colonisation by herbs, shrubs and trees, and this will have been more or less retarded by human and animal activity (Scaife 1987, 140). If we consider the likely impact of mobile communities, grazing or cropping such clearings intermittently, it is possible to imagine that a series of quite different 'histories' of clearing, maintenance and regeneration might emerge.

It is an unfortunate effect of the coarse grain of the archaeological record that we have often had very little resolution on the artefactual chronology of the British Neolithic beyond a distinction between an earlier and a later part. Within each of these two divisions, we are aware that quite different sets of material equipment and economic practice were in use. Hence it is all too easy to emphasise the discontinuity between the two, and impose some cataclysm to account for it. It is more difficult, but more rewarding, to consider the mechanisms involved in a transition. Whittle's evidence for the cessation of cultivation on the chalk is firmest for the years between 3700 and 3050 BC (2900–2500 bc). How could this be reconciled with the indication that it was in this same period that sufficient labour was available for the construction of two of the most gigantic edifices of British prehistory, the Dorset Cursus and the Hambledon Hill complex? One could hardly suggest that agricultural decline and depopulation have not taken place in the past. Nevertheless, it is to be suspected that this is an idea which has been projected back upon prehistory from more recent European experience. Agricultural depopulations did take place in England in the fourteenth and fifteenth centuries AD, but their cause had nothing to do with an imbalance between population and resources. Still less were they a consequence of the Black Death, or any other natural calamity. The late medieval period saw the birth of both agricultural capitalism and the western European mercantile world-system (Wallerstein 1974). The crisis was the result of the imbalance between the prices of cereals and wool, and the consequent shift to sheep-grazing (Slichter von Bath 1963, 164–5). All of the factors involved – market forces, capitalist reproduction, centrally organised enclosure – would have been absent in prehistory.

The evidence of the lithic distributions, we should recall, is that the more nucleated scatters of the earlier Neolithic gradually developed into more extensive and diffuse spreads, at least in some parts of Britain. I have suggested that this implies a breakdown of more repetitive and regular patterns of seasonal movement, and this might imply a degree of social fragmentation. The pollen evidence may also indicate some change in the structure of human activity within the landscape. If a wider range of locations were being used on a more sporadic basis, this might easily allow some relatively open areas to regenerate. However, it is important to note the extent to which all of these arguments make use of evidence drawn from scattered sources, using it to establish models of general applicability. In practice, it is probable that the details of landscape histories will have been extremely divergent.

CONCLUSION

A proper understanding of agricultural and residential practices in Neolithic Britain is far from complete. This chapter has attempted no more than the merest sketch of how these activities might have been organised, within one geographical area. For the moment, it is most important to be critical of traditional understandings of Neolithic settlement and economy. Although in this chapter I have stressed mobility and the continued use of wild resources, it is the potential variability of economic practice at both the regional and the local scale which has yet to be fully recognised. I have suggested two reasons why this should be the case: the belief that agriculture constitutes the essence of the Neolithic tends to promote a view of homogeneity (in other words, if people were not farming, they were not Neolithic), while the scarcity of the available evidence results in pieces of information from far-flung locations being drawn together to create hybrid models of a universal Neolithic economic regime. Some of this material may have general implications, but it seems that unique circumstances are equally likely to be presented as lucky survivals of ubiquitous phenomena.

This is not to deny that at some points during the Neolithic in Britain particular communities may have lived in substantial timber houses, or laboured in arable fields. Indeed, it is acknowledged that some form of sedentary farming system probably characterised the Neolithic communities of the Northern Isles. However, if one pattern characterised the south of England and another Orkney and Shetland, it is at present quite unclear whether the rest of Britain conformed to either of these templates, or exhibited still further diversity. But I suggest that these were the exception rather than the rule. Consequently, the notion that these people were smitten by widespread over-population and soil decline seems unlikely. My guess is that future work will begin to demonstrate the degree of idiosyncrasy involved in Neolithic subsistence patterns. This will tend to throw into relief the question of why it is that some processes of social and cultural change seem to have extended over quite large geographical areas. If contact with farming groups on the continent, and the onset of the Neolithic as formally defined made a range of domesticated species available to indigenous peoples in Britain, it seems that the extent to which they chose to adopt them, and the ways in which they chose to use them were quite diverse.

Chapter Three

Reading monuments

MONUMENTS IN SPACE

The most substantial trace of Neolithic activity which remains in the modern landscape of Britain consists of a large number of earth and stone monuments of a variety of forms. From Aubrey and Stukeley down to Daniel and Piggott, these constructions have attracted the interest of the archaeologists. However, a concern with 'monumentality' as an issue can perhaps be dated to Colin Renfrew's essay, 'Monuments, mobilisation and social organisation in Neolithic Wessex' (Renfrew 1973a). Renfrew's thesis was that monuments constituted 'the natural counterparts of other features of society' (1973a, 556). As such, their scale and complexity could be taken as an index of that of the society which created them. More recently, Richard Bradley has provided a series of contributions which together represent a concerted critique of Renfrew's position (Bradley 1984a; 1984b; 1985; 1993). Bradley draws upon Cherry's (1978) observation that large monumental constructions may be undertaken by dominant groups either at a time when they are establishing their authority, or under conditions of stress and instability. Applying this perspective to the British sequence, Bradley points to the *discontinuous* character of monument-building. Thus a massive structure like the Dorset Cursus may be constructed as the initial act in the settlement of a new area, while the large Wessex henges can be seen as a reaction to social change and conflict. For Bradley, the most important feature of monuments is their permanence. 'They dominate the landscape of later generations so completely that they impose themselves on their consciousness' (Bradley 1985, 9).

Drawing as they do on the explicitly generalising approach proposed by Cherry, these arguments still beg one major question. The domination of the landscape by monuments in the Neolithic and Early Bronze Age seems to have given way to a pattern of field systems and permanent, often enclosed settlements. This transformation of the social landscape must clearly be conceived as an historical conjuncture: a qualitative difference exists 'before' and 'after'. It follows that the monuments of the Neolithic are something specific, which relate to a society of a very particular kind. When Humphrey Case (1969a, 181) considered the role of monuments in the inception of the British Neolithic, he saw them as part of a phase of 'stable adjustment', subsequent to the initial episode of colonisation. Only when a farming economy had been in place for some generations, and a sufficient surplus had been generated, could monuments become a feature of the landscape. This view casts monuments as a kind of 'optional extra' or 'refinement', to be indulged in when conditions allow. As we have already argued, it is questionable whether food gatherers or subsistence agriculturalists should normally be expected to produce a surplus at all (Sahlins 1974, 87), and indeed the notion of 'surplus' is one which is socially defined. It is by no means clear that subsistence practice will always represent the irreducible core of a community's activities, and that ritual or ceremonial will be perceived as secondary issues, facilitated by the economic base. It may be that if we think of monuments as a display of surplus wealth or a means of prestige competition (Bradley 1984a, 20–33; Sheridan 1986) they can still be understood as 'optional'. But I will argue here that it is more consistent with the evidence to think of monument-building as a fundamental aspect of the particular kind of Neolithic existence which was established in Britain.

The starting point for such an argument lies in considering monuments (and architectural forms in general) less as objects in themselves than as transformations of space through objects (Hillier and Hanson 1981, 1). It is one of the most distinctive aspects of the Neolithic period in Britain that people had begun to dig into the earth to create pits and ditches, and to move and fashion timbers and large stones in order to create elaborate structures. Through their labour, people were creating new kinds of relationships with place and with material substances (Thomas 1999). These changes in the configuration of space would also have affected the way in which places were experienced by human beings. Thus it may be that the 'objective' fact that a monument required a certain number of worker-hours for its construction is less significant than its 'subjective' experience, an encounter perceived through the physical presence of the lived human body (Tuan 1974, 215). It follows that a major part of the importance of a monument lies in the way in which it affects the experience and interpretation of place. So-called 'humanistic geographers' have usefully distinguished between *space* and *place* (Relph 1976, 17; Tuan 1978, 10), where the former refers to a geometrical arrangement of planes and solids in relations which can be defined quantitatively, and the latter applies to the *experience* of spatiality. Places are areas of space which have been 'regioned' or identified by human activity and understanding. According to Tuan (1974, 239), the transformation from space to place involves the imposition of a conceptual order, which may involve the largely cognitive process of creating 'centres of meaning' in a landscape. This would include frameworks for the understanding of place and landscape like the Australian aboriginal 'songlines', in which the intimate knowledge of individual locations is placed in the context of the mythic wanderings of ancestral beings (Morphy 1995). However, this distinction between space and place can give the impression that we normally exist in a world of Cartesian geometry, and spread meaning or interpretation over its surface, as a secondary matter (Thomas 1996a, 86). Yet human beings do not come upon a world of shapes and forms and add meaning: their world is inherently meaningful. It is from within an existence which is already rich in meaning and experience that people choose to think of objects as having measurable extension, so that geometry is secondary rather than primary.

People live in and through experiential rather than geometric space, and they generally perceive the areas they frequent as a network of places connected by pathways and routes. For mobile, foraging people, the seasonal cycle of moving between resources usually also involves moving between landmarks which are understood in cosmological terms. Rocks, trees, clearings, rivers and mountains may be associated with particular events, or with spirits, deities and abstract qualities (Tilley 1994, 38). Something rather different is implied, though, when people alter the form and appearance of places by building structures of one kind or another. Building is an engagement which has the effect of changing the way in which a place will be experienced and interpreted in future. This kind of perspective begins to offer a means of understanding why it should be that such an emphasis on the building of monuments is characteristic of a particular phase of British prehistory. As Edward Relph suggests: 'Existential space is culturally defined and hence it is difficult to experience the space of another culture' (1976, 15). Where we become concerned less with generalised, universal explanations of monuments, and more with the cultural codes which define ways in which space is to be experienced, the opportunity for understanding the historically specific is opened up. But at the same time, once we begin to consider the 'cultural' element in a hermeneutics of space, the universal or essentialist element of 'humanistic' geography must necessarily be put aside. The experience of space is neither innocent nor primal, but socially and culturally constructed.

This cultural and historical specificity of spatial understanding can be understood in a number of ways. In materialist terms, we might link the experience of space with the spatio-temporal rhythms built up through the habitual movements that people enact in everyday life (Pred 1977, 218). If the consciousness of human subjects develops through their lived practice, the habitual use of space and time implicated in any way of life will form an element of what Foucault (1988) would term a 'technology of the self' – that is to say, a set of historically and culturally contingent social practices through which people come to recognise themselves as subjects of a particular sort. The practice of the subject is constrained by his or her movements in space and time, the performance of tasks which are repetitive or unique, habitual or strategic, and whose timing is ordered by the cycles of day and night or of the seasons. This reinforces the suggestion that the way in which hunters and gatherers become aware of themselves as beings within a world, moving seasonally through a forest or across a desert between a series of temporary camps, will be quite different from the experience of agriculturalists, continuously investing their labour in plots of land (Gell 1995) – hence, in a way, Giddens' suggestion that social control can be based on the control of people's movements in time and space (1984, 145). Cycles and patterns of movement, of encounter between body and place, generate people's understanding both of themselves and of their surroundings. Acting as 'stations' in this network of movements, features which have been constructed by human beings will have a constraining effect on the interpretive process. So a society like that of the British Neolithic, engaged in structuring a landscape through the building of monuments, is actually involved in the 'making' of human subjects and their consciousness.

Alternatively, we might argue that different ways of organising space are connected with historically situated forms of power and knowledge. In the contemporary West, architecture and civic planning can be used as repressive tools of social control, segregating and ordering social groups, as Mike Davis (1990) demonstrates in the case of Los Angeles. But we can equally often distinguish ways of organising space which form aspects of broader, cosmological understandings of the world. It is in these terms that Hirst (1985, 178) interprets the centrally planned churches of the Renaissance as 'a manifest presence and physical existence of cosmic order'. The geometry of the church was conceived as a representation of cosmic relationships, on the understanding that church architecture had a privileged position in the spiritual transformation of the human subject (see also Graves 1989). Similarly, Kus (1983, 292) describes the way that Ambohimanga, the Merina capital of Madagascar, was constructed about the cardinal points in accordance with an astronomical understanding of the cosmos.

Yet it may be a mistake to draw a categorical distinction between spatial experiences which emerge from everyday practices, and those which are conditioned by the repressive or cosmological ordering of architecture. More often than not, the same cultural schemes penetrate 'ritual' and 'domestic' contexts (C. Richards 1996a). The lived world and that of design are one and the same, so that abstract architectural divisions of space can set the conditions for everyday life, particularly within urbanised societies. But the ways in which this takes place, and the extent to which those who design and build structures desire any control over other people's movements, perceptions and activities is extremely varied. Hence Foucault (1984b, 243) writes of a shift in the locus of power in space through the eighteenth and nineteenth centuries AD, as concerns with architecture and town planning gave way to railways and electrification. Spatial control ceased to be invested in the organisation of urban space and shifted into the spheres of transportation and communications. Similarly, Cosgrove's interesting study of the relationship between economics and aesthetics in the modern era (1984) suggests a connectedness between the material order and the conceptualisation of space. Cosgrove's argument is that the symbolic appropriation of space in landscape painting is a consequence of the physical alienation of land within a capitalist economy. Only where land becomes a commodity to be freely disposed of by its owner, rather than handed down from generation to generation, can it be portrayed with a dispassionate gaze severed from the location itself. This is the view of the outsider, interpreting nature as a bounded thing behaving according to causal relationships (1984, 64). It follows from both of these examples that the cultural rules governing the interpretation of space are generated in a historical context. It may be no coincidence that Cartesian thought, so central to modernity, placed great stress on the mathematical and conceptual control of space. There is no reason to suppose that these pre-occupations should apply to European prehistory. In this chapter, we will attempt to understand how and why spaces were created and experienced in particular ways in Neolithic Britain.

THE INSCRIBED LANDSCAPE

Over the years, archaeologists and others have often made use of literary metaphors when discussing the experience or analysis of landscapes (e.g. Mitchell 1986). This 'reading' of place is generally only implied in a very broad sense, but it finds an echo in a number of recent developments within the social sciences. As Clifford Geertz (1983) argues, the recent turn away from law-like explanations and toward interpretation within social theory has been accompanied by the introduction of a series of analogies for social action and cultural tradition which are ultimately drawn from the arts. So rather than persevering in comparing social entities to organisms, machines, or systems, the metaphors of play, drama and text have increasingly found favour. The latter of these became current in archaeology with Ian Hodder's *Reading the Past* (1986), which drew upon a variety of traditions of thought, several of which were literary in inspiration. Since that time, debate has continued over the extent to which material culture can be adequately described as 'text-like'. On a number of occasions, the point has been made that in their materiality, artefacts are intrinsically distinct from the written words (e.g. Buchli 1995, 183). This is clearly correct, but it neglects that the force of a metaphor is that it implies similarities between unlike things. Material culture, landscapes and monuments are not the same things as written texts, but it may none the less be instructive to think of them as if they were. In the process, it may be possible to see them in a new light. Like Geertz's other metaphors, the use of the notion of text within archaeology is primarily heuristic.

Space, place and landscape can fruitfully be investigated using the analogy of the text (Ricoeur 1981; Moore 1986), although in practice such an analogy can be employed in a number of different ways. First, built structures can be treated as if they were elements of a symbolic language, so that they come to be generated by a structure of rules and patterns (Fritz 1978; Hillier and Hanson 1984; Hirst 1985, 175). But perhaps more radically, the landscape as a whole can be considered as a text, characterised by a 'ceaseless play of infinitely unstable meanings' (Duncan and Duncan 1988, 118). The writing of such a text is never finished, but continually altered, continually read and interpreted. Each event which leaves a mark on the landscape is the equivalent of an act of writing, each mark the equivalent of the black character on the page. This formulation places an interesting inflexion on the way that Neolithic monuments have been looked at by archaeologists. Renfrew (1976) and Chapman (1981) both saw megalithic tombs as symbols of a corporate group's claim to land and resources. Hodder (1984) saw the same structures as symbolic transformations of houses of the living into houses of the dead. Morris (1974) considered megaliths as a whole to be representations of group cosmology. All of these interpretations seem reasonable enough in themselves. What they all have in common is a recognition that the monuments had some symbolic content, and referred to things beyond themselves.

It follows from this that these monuments were at once signified things, to be referred to, and signifiers. It is not clear, though, that this signification need lead to a single fixed object or concept, so that a given monument should be expected to *mean* any one thing (Olsen 1990).

Monuments as parts of a landscape can be seen as the equivalents of written discourse; they 'inscribe' space as parts of a chain of signification. No monument should be looked on as a system of meaning closed in upon itself. Indeed, monuments are demonstrably 'intertextual', laden with nuances of mutual reference. The cursus monuments refer in their architecture to the long mound and long mortuary enclosure traditions, and may actually incorporate long mounds within their fabric (Bradley 1983). Silbury Hill, with its stepped chalk cylinders, may have been redolent of the distant passage tombs of Brittany or the Boyne valley (Thomas 1984). The way in which monuments seem to form 'traditions' which share constructional features itself indicates that the significance of a given structure is in some way conditional upon other sites.

In a pioneering study concerned with the textual character of space, Henrietta Moore (1986) places emphasis on the various ways in which the same space may be experienced or interpreted by different people. Men and women, for instance, may think about a given space in distinct ways, while some members of society may be granted a privileged position with regard to legitimate interpretation (1986, 73, 86). This can perhaps be linked to the concept of 'textual communities', social groups which cluster around alternative readings of a given text (Duncan and Duncan 1988, 117). So although meaning is invoked or produced in the physical encounter with a monument, this act of 'reading' the monument may still be open to interpretation. If we can argue that these structures had some part to play within the power relations of Neolithic communities, then it might be that the nuances of their interpretation would be a focus of struggle between persons and interest groups.

Causewayed enclosures

The arguments which have been put forward so far suggest that the monuments of Neolithic Britain structured the social landscape largely through the influence that they exerted upon the experience and interpretation of space on the part of human beings. If such spatial texts were read 'inattentively' in the course of people's everyday lives (Duncan and Duncan 1988, 123), this influence upon interpretation might have an active role to play in the processes of social reproduction and social change. The objective of this chapter is to present a picture of the changing relationship between society and monuments through time. However, at this point the argument has progressed far enough to enable us to consider one class of monuments of the earlier Neolithic, in the light of ideas concerning the construction of spatial experience and understanding.

Causewayed enclosures are among the more enigmatic monuments of the British Neolithic (Figure 3.1). Decades of debate (Curwen 1930; Piggott 1954; Smith 1965a; 1966; 1971; Renfrew 1973a; Wilson 1975; Drewett 1977; Mercer 1980; Burgess *et al.* 1988) have resulted in a variety of explanations for the function of the sites, from enclosed settlements and cattle kraals to regional fairs, exchange centres, necropoli and cult centres (Evans 1988a). Mercer (1980, 65) takes the minimal view that the term 'causewayed enclosure' cannot now be taken to suggest more than 'a constructional technique with no overall functional implication'. Barker and Webley appear equally impartial when they state that the enclosures were 'central places of some kind (or several kinds)' (1978, 161). However, their land use model for the earlier Neolithic is based upon transport cost and least-effort principles: this neglects the evidence which suggests that causewayed enclosures are in no sense central, and that they existed at the edges of inhabited areas or groups of other monuments (Bradley 1978b, 103; Gardiner 1984, 21; Holgate 1984; 1988a; Evans *et al.* 1988).

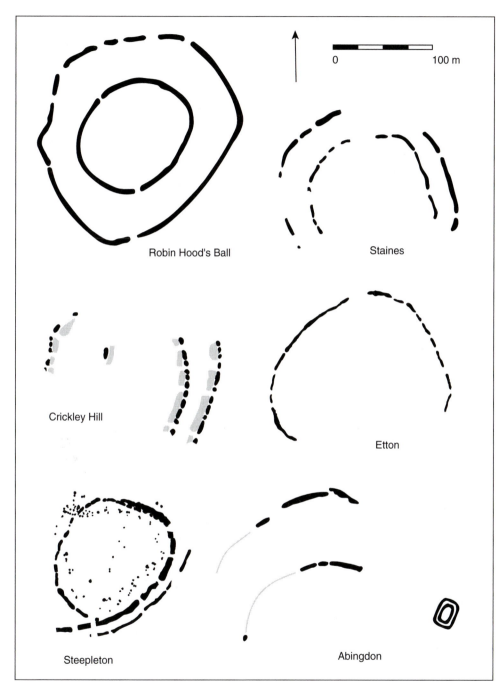

Figure 3.1 Comparative plans of causewayed enclosures

In the wake of Smith's (1965a) publication of Keiller's excavations at Windmill Hill the interpretation which came to be widely accepted was that of redistribution centre. This was taken to explain the high percentages of fossil shell and oolite in pottery from the Bath/Frome area at Windmill Hill, Robin Hood's Ball, Whitesheet Hill and Knap Hill (Peacock 1969, 145) and of gabbroic wares from the Lizard in Cornwall and of Portlandian chert at Maiden Castle, Hambledon Hill, Robin Hood's Ball, Windmill Hill, Hembury and High Peak (Smith 1971, 103). Drewett (1977, 224) summed up the problem with this view: 'if causewayed enclosures were simply trade centres, surely the foreign material would be exchanged there and then removed for use elsewhere. The discovery of such material in causewayed enclosures would suggest its use there.' Moreover, whether fine products acquired through long-distance links were redistributed from causewayed enclosures would be difficult to test using fall-off curves, since, being items that would circulate in the more highly ranked spheres of exchange, they might continue to change hands rapidly for some decades. It was the recovery of fine artefacts from the enclosures which led Bradley (1982; 1984a, 31) to suggest that they represented high-status settlements.

There are problems with this interpretation also. If, for instance, Hambledon Hill were to be thought of as the residence of an elite, it would be an elite apparently separated by several miles from the nearest concentrations of earlier Neolithic activity. As Barrett *et al.* (1991, 31) have demonstrated, the uplands of Cranborne Chase show limited evidence of earlier Neolithic occupation. It is possible that this area was peripheral to a zone of denser activity in the lower Stour Valley toward present-day Bournemouth, while Hambledon itself sits at the point where the Stour cuts through the chalk upland. The enclosure may have been located at the extreme limit of the activities of communities operating in the coastal lowlands, or on a route-way through to seasonal grazing in the vale of Marnhull. But in either case, it would be surprising to find a socially pre-eminent group located so far from its host population as to preclude day-to-day surveillance and supervision. At Hambledon, 160 acres of hilltop had been enclosed with a double ditch and palisade (Mercer 1982, 1), and grain had arrived at the site already threshed and cleaned (Mercer pers. comm.). It is hard to imagine that this degree of effort could have been mobilised by a distant elite. While causewayed enclosures may have been connected with the activities of powerful people, their peripheral locations imply that they were not constructed primarily as permanent elite residences.

Smith (1966) was originally led to the conclusion that the enclosures had not served as settlements by the absence of pits in their interiors, as at Offham in Sussex (Drewett 1977, 211). Pits *are* present in the central enclosure at Hambledon, yet these appear to have been concerned with the deliberate deposition of items like gabbroic pottery vessels (90 per cent in pits; 10 per cent in ditches), axes, red deer antler and quernstones (Mercer 1980, 23; 1988, 93). The flintwork recovered from these pits often showed a peculiar bias towards a particular tool type (scrapers or microdenticulates) (Mercer 1980: 23), while two of the pits contained post-holes. Since fragments of human bones and teeth were also found in these pits, it might be suggested that, as with the Handley Hill pit (Pitt Rivers 1898, 49), these represent one part of a multi-stage burial process: pits from which the bones were removed when defleshed. This accords with Bradley's (1984b, 24) suggestion that fine artefacts might have been involved in some stage of mortuary ritual distinct from the placing of disarticulated bones in tombs and barrows. These items might not represent 'grave goods' in the formal sense, so much as prestations necessary for the conclusion of rites of passage. Huge quantities of skeletal remains were recovered from the main enclosure ditch at Hambledon (Mercer 1980, *passim*) and there have been finds of human bones from Maiden Castle (Wheeler 1943), Windmill Hill (Smith 1965a), Abingdon (Leeds 1928), Staines (Robertson-Mackay 1962; 1987), Whitehawk (Curwen 1934a; 1936), the Trundle (Curwen 1929), Offham (Drewett 1977) and Maiden Bower (Smith 1915) amongst other sites. A range of different mortuary activities seems to be represented, since some of these occurrences represent formal burials (often in the enclosure ditches, and often women or children), some are formal deposits of bone, and some may result from more casual processes of accumulation. So enclosures were not simply burial places, but were locations which appear to have been appropriate for various practices enacted upon the bodies of the dead (Edmonds 1993, 115). These might include transitional as well as terminal phases in elaborate funerary sequences. As Thorpe (1984) shows, the proportions of males, females and children present indicate that these groups were equally eligible for these practices or processes.

At Maiden Castle the study of the material excavated by Wheeler reveals a similar pattern to that at Hambledon: flint and stone axes are concentrated in pits (7.2 and 2.7 per cent of the assemblages respectively) as opposed to ditches (3.6 and 0.3 per cent). One pit, T8, had a concentration of microdenticulates (Wheeler 1943, 86). However, all of this neglects the evidence that at Stepleton, the lesser enclosure on Hambledon Hill, a 2-acre site existed with a variety of internal features of a broadly 'domestic' nature. Occupation also clearly took place at Crickley Hill, Gloucestershire (Dixon 1988). Nevertheless, at the last site the house platforms can be tied stratigraphically to the very latest phase of a complex sequence of backfillings and recuttings of the ditches before the replacement of the causewayed camp by an enclosure bounded by a massive continuous ditch (Dixon pers. comm.). At Crickley, then, settlement appears not to have been the primary purpose for the construction of the site. The enclosure began as a relatively minor earthwork, and a change in the significance of the site over time is implied.

Another recurrent feature of causewayed enclosures is their association with lithic sources and/or stone working. At Hambledon, excavations on the Hanford spur revealed a complex of shallow mines and grubbing pits which may have provided the mediocre quality flint found in the Stepleton enclosure (Mercer 1982, 2). At Offham, far more primary core reduction waste was found than could have been needed to produce the sparse implements found on site, indicating that cores were made from the poor quality flint found on site and taken away (Drewett 1977, 217). Core preparation also seems to have taken place at Combe Hill (Drewett 1994, 10). Poor quality flint sources are also found at Robin Hood's Ball and Maiden Castle (Care 1982). At the last site large quantities of debitage were encountered, together with roughout flint axes. Edmonds (1993, 119) suggests that the enclosure was used for the finishing of axes which had been brought in from elsewhere. In other words, flint took on the form of a recognised type of artefact within the space of the monument. Significantly, in other parts of southern Britain flint axes were made in deep shaft mines, while they might perfectly well have been made from more accessible stone sources – as other artefacts were (Edmonds 1995, 63). Both causewayed enclosures and mines were distant from everyday activities, and both were spatially bounded contexts within which material transformations could take place, enabling the creation of a pre-eminent artefact, the axe. Care (1982) argued that causewayed enclosures were located so as to enable social control to be exercised over lithic resources. It may be more accurate to say that they enabled the production of particular objects to be regulated, and this finds an echo in several other aspects of the use of these sites.

First, there is an obvious contradiction between the investment of effort in the building of the enclosures and their deliberate backfilling and subsequent recutting. At Robin Hood's Ball (Thomas 1964, 11) and Hambledon (Mercer 1980, 35) the richest deposits of artefactual and faunal material actually overlay the collapse of the banks, so it is clear that at least a part of the significance of these sites did not depend upon the sustained integrity of their defences. It may be that the delineation of a separate area with an interrupted ring of pits/ditches was the most important aspect of the enclosures. But in addition, the way in which this boundary could be periodically removed and then reinstated indicates that a place possessing certain distinct qualities was repeatedly 're-made', perhaps on a cyclical basis. The nature of deposition is, throughout, particularly interesting. The material in the ditches can be of considerably greater quantity than one would expect in an Iron Age hill fort (Thomas 1964, 11) while the pottery is often un-weathered (Smith 1966) and animal bones may be articulated (Legge 1981, 173). Indeed, in Whittle's recent excavation at Windmill Hill, the sheer quantity of animal bone recovered from the ditches was staggering (Whittle and Pollard 1998). In the Wessex area at least, the ceramic assemblages from causewayed enclosures show a rather higher proportion of open or neutral bowls and cups, suitable for food consumption, and a lower proportion of carinations and beaded rims (which might allow coverings, to permit their use for storage), than contemporary assemblages from other types of sites. A similar range of vessel forms came from the 'ritual' pit of earlier Neolithic date outside the Coneybury Hill henge in Wiltshire, where large numbers of pottery sherds and animal bones had been spread across the sides and bottom of the pit (Richards 1990, 45). All the above factors seem to indicate large-scale and conspicuous consumption of food, or in other words, feasting.

Legge (1981) has suggested that the faunal remains from causewayed enclosures represent only a part of a more complex pastoral economy, involving other sites elsewhere in the landscape. Piggott (1954, 28) long ago pointed to the presence of hazelnuts and crab apples as evidence for the autumnal use of the sites, while the 'clean' grain from Hambledon could indicate occupation at a time after the harvest. The enclosure at Etton in Cambridgeshire would probably have been flooded for part of the year (Pryor *et al.* 1985). Firm evidence of seasonal occupation could only really come from a detailed analysis of a large and well-excavated faunal sample, however. To this we can add Barker and Webley's observation (1978, 173) that the soils which surrounded the enclosures were best suited to pastoral activities. Furthermore, all the enclosures in Sussex appear to have been built in areas freshly cleared of woodland (Thomas 1982; Drewett 1994, 19). In Wessex, the only two sites among the large number of molluscan assemblages studied by Evans (1971, 64) which did not show evidence of having been built in substantial clearances were causewayed enclosures, Knap Hill and Windmill Hill. All of these points argue that these enclosures were places which were visited, perhaps seasonally, rather than being subject to year-round occupation and forming the home-base for agricultural or herding economies.

Causewayed enclosures in Wessex were clearly in some way connected to channels of long-distance exchange, without necessarily representing redistribution centres in the full sense. A possible rationale for their peripheral siting lies in the character of exchange in non-capitalist societies. Where the significance of an item is vested in something other than its monetary value, some restriction of long-distance exchange may be required to safeguard the relative importance of objects passing from hand to hand. The circulation of material items within a community can form an important system of meaning, with implications for the creation of personal identity, the establishment of authority, the formation of alliances and so on (Strathern 1988, 172). The transfer of goods between distant exchange systems requires an alienation of items from their source: a dangerous and potentially polluting activity for the persons representing either system. Such exchanges will often therefore be carried out at the peripheries of social areas, within bounded spaces, surrounded by multiple prohibitions and prescriptions (Servet 1982, 23). A kind of rite of passage, allowing the movement of items between communities is achieved in the liminal state of such enclosed areas, and this kind of transaction is frequently associated with feasting and a temporary inversion of social relations emphasising the temporary nature of the arrangement (Turner 1967). This logic extends as far as the gateway communities of Meso-america and early historic Europe (Hirth 1978; Hodges 1982). In the present context it seems to be borne out by the presence of groups of monuments surrounding sources of lithic artefacts in prehistoric Britain, like the stone circles and other enclosures located in passes leading out from the Stone Age factories in Great Langdale, Cumbria (Burl 1976, 69; Clare 1987; Bradley and Edmonds 1993).

The suggestion that causewayed enclosures were originally socially neutral areas within which exchanges could be concluded in isolation from their normal social meaning begins to provide an explanation for other aspects of their use. We have seen already that the treatment of human remains in enclosures involved transitional practices like exposure, defleshing and disarticulation. These transitional states often involve a change in the character of the person, from a social being to an ancestor or a non-being (Hertz 1960; Huntington and Metcalf 1979; Bloch and Parry 1982), and as a result they too may be ambiguous and potentially dangerous. Mortuary practice involves a reclassification of people, and the end point of this process may be achieved by way of volatile liminal states (Humphries 1981). Similarly, ethnographic studies have shown that the extraction and processing of lithic materials is often carried out under conditions surrounded by prohibitions (Burton 1984). Finally, if cattle were being moved seasonally between the chalk uplands and the clay and greensand lowlands of the Wardour, Marnhull and Pewsey vales, the location of the enclosures of Knap Hill, Rybury, Hambledon Hill and Whitesheet Hill on the ecotones between the two would be significant. Here the agglomeration of herds would take place, with a consequent temporary adjustment of the conditions of ownership from the minimal to the maximal group. It is not necessary to the argument that all these activities took place on all of these sites; what is important is that they worked as a bounded space at the edge of an occupied zone, which marginalised and contained influences which could be perceived as harmful or polluting to the social fabric.

Now, it is clear that some of the enclosures were more structurally complex than others. In these cases it can often be demonstrated that the elaboration of the defensive aspect of the site, or its use for settlement, was secondary to a more modest initial construction. At Abingdon, there is evidence that the outer ditch post-dated the inner (Avery 1982; Bradley 1986), while at Hambledon the complex systems of outworks and cross-dykes were additions to the original enclosure (Mercer 1988, 101) (see Figure 3.2). Perhaps significantly, the extremely complex sites of Hambledon and Whitesheet Hill are those sites which lie on the boundary between chalk upland and clay vale. Those enclosures which were most structurally embellished and elaborated often produce the richest material assemblages (Hambledon Hill, Crickley Hill, the Trundle, Whitehawk), while the less complex sites (Robin Hood's Ball, Offham, Combe Hill) may be relatively poor. The eventual emergence of some of the sites as fortified settlements, presumably connected with elite activities, is a consequence of the purposeful appropriation of the powerful associations of these places. The liminal state is dangerous, yet powerful (Turner 1967). Gaining control over an enclosure would enable powerful groups to intercede in the processes in which the value and meaning of artefacts were created, and those in which the status of the dead was transformed. Equally, it would allow seasonal events of communal gathering, feasting and ritual to be increasingly connected with the prestige-building of these groups.

That these activities were secondary in character is demonstrated by the siting of barrows of middle Neolithic date on or near to causewayed enclosures, generally containing single, articulated burials. Oval barrows exist at Hambledon (Mercer 1980, 43), Abingdon (Bradley 1992), Maiden Castle and Robin Hood's Ball (Richards 1990), while at Whitesheet Hill a round barrow with causewayed ditch and single inhumation was set on the bank (Piggott 1952, 406). In all of these cases we can argue that an additional monument was used to appropriate and transform the original significance of the site. At Hambledon, the ditch sequence of the barrow appeared to mirror that of the enclosure, integrating the meanings of the two monuments (Mercer 1988, 98). The later use of the enclosures also involved the deposition of Peterborough and Beaker ceramics in the ditches of the more complex enclosures in particular (as at Hambledon Hill, Maiden Castle

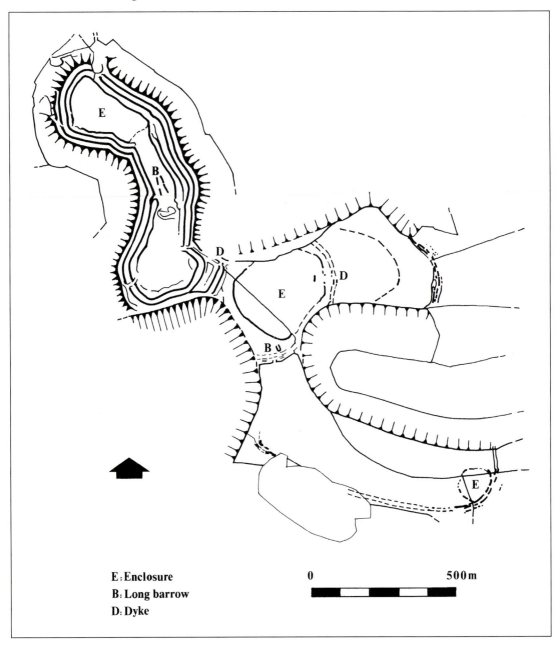

Figure 3.2 The enclosure complex on Hambledon Hill, Dorset

and Windmill Hill). At Hambledon, this involved the digging of a slot-like recut in the top of the ditch, packed with flint nodules and sherds of Beaker pottery (Mercer 1980, 37), while at Maiden Castle the enclosure was re-defined by a low bank (Sharples 1991, 256). Evidently, if the earlier histories of these monuments had involved the sporadic re-creation of the ditch circuit through acts of digging and deposition, these ancient practices were now evoked as a means of creating a special place imbued with an aura of the past. There is some similarity here with later events documented at some long barrows: ditch recuts, deposits of Peterborough Ware and Beakers, and later burials cut into the mounds or ditches at, for example, Thickthorn Down and Wor Barrow (Pitt Rivers 1898; Drew and Piggott 1936; Evans 1990). In both cases the significance of old monuments was continuing to be re-created, in contradistinction to other later Neolithic practices associated with Grooved Ware.

SHIFTING MEANINGS

Having considered a class of monuments whose meanings seem to have been altered through time, it is helpful now to return to the question of how meaning is produced out of space. This will best be achieved by looking in more detail at how space is 'read' by people. Bourdieu, in his well-known study of the Kabyle house (1970), showed the way in which cultural rules and norms were learned by growing children through their inhabitation of a space which was ordered according to a particular cosmology. The water-jars, the stable, the loft, the hearth, the loom and the rifle hidden behind it are connected both with everyday activities and with abstract values. Each is allotted its place, and gives a space to unconsidered daily routines which remind people of expected modes of conduct and cultural classifications. Without words needing to be spoken, these ways of acting and thinking are internalised by living within the confines of the house. But as Henrietta Moore (1986, 84) points out, the meanings concerned are not inherent in the space of the house, they are attributed, and knowing the meaning of a particular space is conditional upon a particular lived, social experience of that space. The Kabyle have a particular understanding of their houses, not because an abstract template has been imposed on space, but because of their shared experience of being together in their dwellings. Meaning emerges from this experience rather than vice versa: it is created in the dynamic relationship between people and physical structures.

It follows that meaning is produced within social practice, and that this social practice involves both people and things. Moore (1986, 81) suggests that it is not the actuality of past actions which is inscribed in space so much as their meaning. Indeed, we might expect the significance of past events to be continually re-created and negotiated within spaces associated with the past. On some occasions, archaeology has attempted to 'de-code' prehistoric buildings as if they represent a mapping of past social relationships. But the relationship between social space and social relations is not a mimetic one. In building structures, people are building the context of social life, rather than a reflection of an abstract social pattern. Buildings are thoroughly bound up with human existence, and we should be able to interpret them in social terms. But we should not expect them to constitute a kind of template: for one thing, this would require a form of representation which is entirely transparent (Norris 1987, 38). We in the present can produce a reading of ancient constructed spaces, because like past people we can engage with the materiality of those places. Yet our involvement will be different in quality, since it is performed on the basis of a contemporary set of prejudices and understandings (Gadamer 1975). This argument is clearly related to the conundrum which Marx presents of how it is that ancient Greek art is the product of a particular set of historical conditions, and yet affords aesthetic pleasure in the present (Easthope 1983, 25). The answer is that the pleasure which we obtain from a Greek vase is not a pleasure written in it, but the pleasure of reading.

Obtaining the 'correct' message from any statement paradoxically depends upon knowing to some extent what the protagonist wants to say before it is said. That is to say, one must know the context of the statement. Convention holds that the signified is a place at which the movement of signification comes to rest (Harland 1987, 135). However, no discourse can ever refer unproblematically to an object which is somehow located outside language, outside time and outside context (Lentricchia 1980, 189). The chance that we, existing outside the Neolithic social and cultural context, could ever present exactly the same reading of a megalithic tomb as would an inhabitant of Neolithic Britain is hence extremely slim. However, these remarks are not intended in a negative way, merely to encourage pessimism concerning the interpretation of past architectural texts. Rather, it is important to note that these same problems of the lack of fixity of meaning are ones which would have applied as much in the past as they do in the present. 'The interpretation of any signifying chain is necessarily only another chain of signs' (Lentricchia 1980, 189). I have argued already that Neolithic monuments are inherently symbolic, and refer to things other than themselves. Even in domestic space, the process through which meaning is inscribed is generally metaphorical (Moore 1986). Furthermore, symbols of all kinds always change their meanings according to context (Macdonnall 1986, 45). Where an explicitly symbolic order is in operation, it seems likely that words and things will be polyvalent (Turner 1969), and that particular nuances of meaning will have been invoked and taken on a cardinal significance at different times. So it is extremely likely that prehistoric monuments had no one single meaning, but were a means of making material a whole system of meanings. Monuments provided a technology by which people could be reminded of different rules and codes of procedure according to the context in which they were experienced.

A landscape structured through monuments could influence the ways in which people moved and held their bodies, and this might establish conditions under which they could interpret their surroundings. The probability that a number of planes of signification intersected at any monument would mean that it had a part to play in economic, ritual, juridical and spiritual issues. Given that prehistoric communities were likely to have been composed of people of different genders, different statuses and different life experiences, it is probable that they would have brought a range of different interpretive resources to these monuments, and will have understood them in a range of different ways. This implies a tension between attempts to impose homogeneous and unified systems of meaning on the landscape, and the potential anarchy of interpretation. It is to be expected that the interpretation held by those who initiated the construction of any monument would be privileged. But monuments are also distinguished as communal productions. The enormous labour effort involved in their construction sets them apart from other kinds of artefacts (Shennan 1983), and this suggests that from the moment of their inception they will represent a constellation of different, fragmented meanings. Neolithic monuments in Britain drew together materials which occurred in the landscape – stone, wood, earth and chalk – and placed them in elaborate configurations. They thus involved a kind of 'cosmological engineering', which took the elements of the familiar world and placed them in surprising juxtapositions. Each of these elements brought with it its own associations and connotations, and these might have been variously perceived amongst those who built the structure and those who used it. This will only have enhanced the instability of meaning.

A number of authors have already pointed to the significance of 'secondary' activities on established monuments (Bradley 1984a; Thorpe and Richards 1984). Dealing explicitly with this kind of phenomenon, Lane (1986, 189) described a number of Bronze Age sites in South Wales, where burial mounds had been erected over the remains of earlier structures. Lane argued that this represented the reintroduction of the past into the present in a specific guise. In broader terms, it is evident that monuments of many kinds were altered radically or subtly in order to influence the way in which they were interpreted. These acts could take a number of forms. The most straightforward example might be the structural transformation of a site, as with the addition of 'tails' to a variety of heel-shaped and circular cairns of earlier Neolithic date (Corcoran 1972, 32), both to enhance their monumentality and also, perhaps, to bring them into line with a more standardised long mound tradition. Similarly, we could point to the translation of a number of later Neolithic timber circles into stone: Moncreiffe (Stewart 1985), Croft Moraig (Piggott and Simpson 1971), the Sanctuary (Cunnington 1931), Stonehenge (Atkinson 1956; Burl 1987; Cleal *et al.* 1995), Machrie Moor (Haggarty 1991) and Mount Pleasant (Wainwright 1979a). Such structural shifts might indicate merely a more monumental form of the same 'idea', a change of function, or an appeal to the extant stone circle tradition as a means of 'rewriting' a space in the context of an already established meaning. Significantly, the rebuilding of these circles in stone often coincided with a change in the way in which they were used.

A second instance of subsequent activities which seem to aim at an alteration of the way in which a site might be interpreted can be found in the deposition of secondary burials. Numerous barrows and other monuments in Britain have had inhumations or cremations inserted into them at some time after the initial use. These acts of burial, however, are not distributed evenly through prehistory. Rather, they can be argued to have been a practice which resulted from a particular historical way of thinking about the significance of monuments. Secondary burials were very rare until the end of the Neolithic. Few seem to date from the earlier Neolithic, and to the later Neolithic inhumation tradition can be attributed only scarce examples like the two male bodies with lozenge arrowhead from the ditch at Wor Barrow, Dorset (Pitt Rivers 1898), the male burial with flint axe and jet belt slider dug into the long mound at Whitegrounds, Burythorpe, Yorkshire (Brewster 1984) and several of the burials at Duggleby Howe (Mortimer 1905). By contrast, the cremation burials of the 'Dorchester series' (Piggott 1954, 351), dating to the terminal Neolithic (Kinnes 1979), seem to have been preferentially deposited in secondary contexts. This would include the cremation cemeteries at Duggleby Howe (Kinnes *et al.* 1983), Stonehenge (Atkinson 1956) and the various Dorchester on Thames sites (Atkinson *et al.* 1951). In the subsequent Beaker horizon, secondary burials continue to be placed in earlier burial mounds like Sale's Lot, Gloucestershire (O'Neil 1966), and Thickthorn Down, Dorset (Drew and Piggott 1936). These can possibly be seen as the mobilisation of a site hitherto connected with a generalised category of ancestors in support of the claims to authority of a single person or pre-eminent group. By this logic, the sequential Beaker burials at a site like Shrewton 5K (Green and Rollo-Smith 1984) might be interpreted as the outcome of a struggle for leadership played out over the generations, each claim legitimated by the interment of a family ancestor in a significant barrow. At the same time, the deposition of bodies with Beakers at sites like the Sanctuary (Cunnington 1931), in the ditch at Stonehenge (Evans 1983) and in the bank of Durrington Walls (Hoare 1812, 170) indicates an actual shift in the kind of discourse to which the site was appropriate. So while the same kind of claim to legitimacy sanctioned by the influence of the past as is noted with secondary burials in barrows may be equally important in these occurrences, a further feature is the removal of the site from the sphere of the living into that of the dead.

It seems likely that certain aspects of the deposition of material items in monumental contexts are related to this practice of 'translation'. Axes of stone and bronze are commonly found in contexts which relate to very specific depositional practices: in rivers and in hoards (Bradley 1987b; Needham 1988). Yet very often these items are encountered deposited in significant locations in monuments, frequently in connection with the termination of activity at the site. A stone axe was found blade-down in the bank of Henge A at Llandegai (Houlder 1968, 218), another in the forecourt blocking at Ty Isaf (Grimes 1939), and others still in a disturbed stone-hole at Grey Croft stone circle in Cumbria and buried in the east entrance at Mayburgh henge (Burl 1988, 199). Bronze axes have been found deliberately buried in the extension of the ditch terminal at the Mount Pleasant henge (Wainwright 1979a) and in the forecourt blocking at Newgrange (O'Kelly and Shell 1979). Given the arguments which have been advanced that the axe represented a singularly potent symbol throughout the Neolithic and Early Bronze Age

(Hodder and Lane 1982; Kristiansen 1984), yet one which was engaged in practices largely separate from monuments and burials (Barrett 1985), these would seem to be very significant acts. They again represent an attempt to move a monument out of one sphere of discourse and into another. 'Discourse' in this case can be taken to mean practice which both comments upon and interprets an object.

The way in which a group of monuments was re-presented and reinterpreted by their continuous structural alteration can be strikingly illustrated by reference to the Dorchester on Thames complex in Oxfordshire (Atkinson 1948; Atkinson *et al.* 1951; Whittle *et al.* 1992) (Figure 3.3). Here, a complex sequence of building and rebuilding can be demonstrated (see Chapter 8 below). This sequence of changes seems to suggest that over a period of some hundreds of years a number of different spatial orders were imposed on a given area, each one transforming the way in which previous configurations could be 'read'. The exact significance of the sequence is open to question. Possibly, a single community refurbished its monuments periodically in order to come to terms with changing social reality. Alternatively, this pattern of monuments may fossilise a process of struggle over the interpretation of space played out over the centuries by competing factions, each new hegemonic group imposing its own reading of the landscape through physical alteration of the traces of the past.

BODIES IN SPACE

Because people can interpret them in a multiplicity of different ways, monuments cannot be understood as a simple instrument of social domination. Instead, they represent foci around which different social interests cluster, and through which different social strategies are played out. However, despite the argument concerning the lack of fixity of meaning, there is one strong sense in which the reading of space differs from the reading of a book. This is that the actual physical presence of the human body is required for 'reading' to take place at all (Moore 1986, 85). The encounter is a physical one, in which the kind of power relations involved are not merely discursive, but are relations of force. Architecture can be considered in terms of the mark it makes on the landscape, but at a microspatial level it can actually constrain the body's movement and attitude. The means by which the physical body progresses through a space may limit the way in which that space is experienced, and hence constrain interpretation. Objects, structures or people may be disclosed in advantageous ways, or in particular sequences which encourage an approved reading. The development of Neolithic monumental architecture can be interpreted as demonstrating increasing efforts to regulate the ways in which particular spaces were moved through, and thus experienced. This could be recognised as either a means of attempting to impose a particular understanding of place upon communities as a whole, or facilitating the reproduction of sectional knowledge amongst groups of neophytes. In some cases large numbers of people may have gathered to process through monumental structures, while in others the restricted space available *inside* monuments indicates activities which were *socially* restricted (Thomas 1993b).

The first stage in this process of change is evident in the tombs and barrows of the earlier Neolithic. Burl (1987, 28) has suggested that the eastern orientation of long mounds may often indicate a general and imprecise alignment on the rising moon. Only later were barrows aligned to the south, in an arc which Burl suggests corresponds with the part of the sky occupied by the moon at its zenith (1987, 29). While Burl's observations apply to the long barrows of the Salisbury Plain region, the same change in orientation appears to have taken place within the Cotswold–Severn tradition (on the basis of alignments quoted in Powell *et al.* 1969). The separation of 'earlier' and 'later' chambered cairns here depends upon the chronological sequence

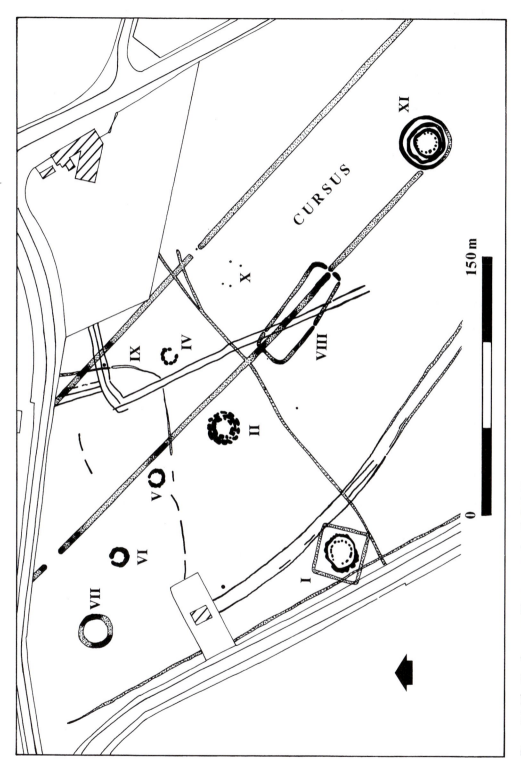

Figure 3.3 The Dorchester on Thames complex, Oxfordshire

of laterally chambered followed by terminally chambered tombs (Darvill 1982, 57; Thomas 1988b). This spatial layout is significant in itself. The earlier tombs may have up to four chambers, each approached by passages entered separately through the sides of the cairn. By contrast, in later monuments, the chamber space is reached through a single entrance in the end of the mound. Thus in the case of the transepted chambered tombs three (Wayland's Smithy), five (West Kennet, Uley) or more (Stoney Littleton) chambers can only be entered through a single entrance and antechamber. This entrance itself is set in the façade of the monument, and entering it entails crossing the forecourt area. Kinnes (1981, 84) has drawn attention to the focal role of façades within Neolithic architecture, while the forecourts of Cotswold–Severn tombs often contained hearths, pits and deposits of animal bones which may relate to ritual activities carried out in the focal area (Thomas 1988b, 550). To enter the chamber thus involved movement through a symbolically charged area containing media (pits, burnt material) which may have been redolent of boundaries and transition. These features would serve to constrain the conditions under which the space of the chamber could be experienced: it could be reached only from a certain direction, and only by the process of traversing the forecourt space. The alignment of some of these mounds on the moon at its height would place another condition on the entry to the chamber, in this case a temporal one. In this way, a degree of influence over the interpretation of space could be achieved. The movement of the body in the internal space of the monument could be prescribed in terms of direction and timing.

This desire to influence the movement of the body through space can be seen in the development of a more 'linear' aspect of monuments in the period after 3700 BC (the first half of the third millennium bc). This process is evident, for example, in the changing architecture of megalithic tombs with the emergence of developed passage tombs in Ireland, north Wales and Scotland. These tombs involve an enhancement of the linear approach to the chamber. In Ireland, Sheridan (1986) attributes the lengthening of the passage to her Stage 3, dated 3500–3000 BC (2700–2500 bc). Stage 3 also saw the development of 'roof slots' of possible astronomic significance. Several passage graves seem to have passages aligned upon celestial phenomena: the 'roof box' at Newgrange which admits the light of the midwinter sunrise, or the way that the midwinter sunset shines down the passage at Maes Howe (Moir 1981, 223). At Bryn Celli Ddu on Anglesey, five post-holes were found in an area 14 feet outside the entrance kerbstones (O'Kelly 1969, 45). These were interpreted by the excavator as evidence of 'squatting' habitation on the site after the main period of activity within the tomb (Hemp 1930). The southernmost of these posts is in direct line with the southern wall of the passage, and with a further, larger post-hole located behind the chamber (O'Kelly 1969, 27). The external posts are in some ways reminiscent of the 'A' holes at Stonehenge, which Burl (1987, 66–9) argues may have been a device for recording the risings of the midwinter moon and which thereby determine the axis of the monument. The last post erected represents the extreme rising position before the moon began to retrace its own path. It thus seems highly likely that the post-holes at Bryn Celli Ddu record a series of observations upon the rising of some heavenly body in order to ascertain its standstill position. Equally, Burl (pers. comm.) suggests that these may have represented a series of observations on the major northern moonrise. This alignment was then formalised by its incorporation into the layout of the passage and chamber (Figure 3.4). Significantly, the southern wall of the passage is straighter than the north, as if the latter had been laid out according to a series of offsets from the former. Moreover, the southern wall of the chamber appears to continue the same straight line as the passage. Intriguingly, a standing stone in the next field to the west from the monument appears to lie on almost the same alignment as the passage, to within 4° (field observation summer 1990).

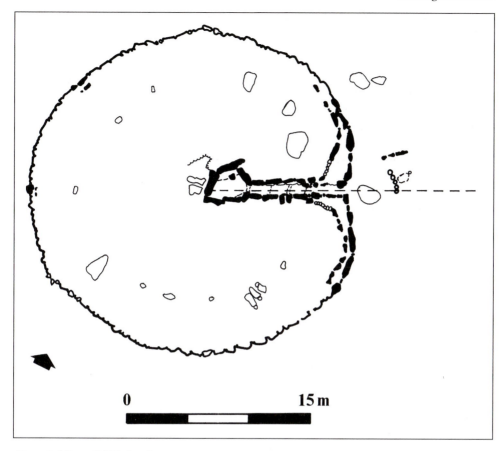

Figure 3.4 Bryn Celli Ddu: plan

As with the Cotswold–Severn tombs, then, the passage tomb tradition integrates temporal control into the control of access to the chamber. Here, though, there is more of an emphasis on the linear progression toward the chamber space. Richards (1988) has noted the difference in relative height of the passages and chambers of the Maes Howe-type passage graves of Orkney. The architecture of the Maes Howe tombs again seeks to influence a person's perception of space, and hence the way in which it is interpreted. In some cases, this might be seen as a means of intensifying an experience in the tomb interior which would be perceived as removed from everyday reality (Dronfield 1996). While resisting the suggestion that megalithic tombs were primarily constructed for the purpose of shamanic rituals involving consciousness alteration, it is plausible that this was one means of enhancing the experiential distance between the tomb's interior and exterior.

These developments seem to be largely contemporary with the emergence of another group of structures whose architecture is overwhelmingly linear, namely the cursus monuments. While Stukeley's interpretation of the Stonehenge Great Cursus as a chariot track (1740, 4) may be unlikely, it shares a conception of linear movement in space with Atkinson, who suggests that 'whatever ceremonies took place within it must have been of a processional kind' (1956, 151). Bradley (1983) has indicated a derivation of the cursus monuments from the long mounds and long mortuary enclosures, and it is possible to suggest a continuous range of variation between long enclosures which occur as early phases in the construction of long barrows, isolated palisaded enclosures (Barclay and Maxwell 1991), long ditched enclosures (Loveday 1989) and cursuses. Cursus monuments at Scorton in Yorkshire (Topping 1982) and the Cleaven Dyke in Tayside (Barclay and Maxwell 1995) have single internal mounds, indicating an overlap with bank barrows. In the case of the North Stoke monument in Oxfordshire (Case 1982a), the distinction between the two classes of monuments becomes very blurred indeed. The southern terminal of Cursus A at Rudston, the west end of the Stonehenge Great Cursus, and the Thickthorn Down terminal of the Dorset Cursus all appear to have been built on an enlarged scale in relation to the remainder of each monument, inviting comparison with long barrows (Barrett *et al.* 1991, 51).

Evidently, the connections between these different structures were not the product of gradual evolution, but involved a conscious evocation of existing monuments. In this context it is significant that both the Dorchester on Thames and Springfield cursuses had timber circles contained within their eastern ends (Hedges and Buckley 1981, 5; Bradley and Chambers 1988); all the more so in the light of Clare's recent suggestion (1987, 462) that an affinity existed between the timber mortuary structures found beneath earthen long barrows and the timber circles which stood within henge monuments in the later Neolithic. Both types of construction had as their role the provision of a focus for a larger monument, a point underlined by the presence of façades at the entrances to the two timber circles within the Durrington Walls henge (Wainwright and Longworth 1971). Although at Dorchester Site 3 the circle was clearly later in date than the ditches of the cursus, it is instructive that this structure should have been burnt, and cremations inserted into the post-holes (Whittle *et al.* 1992, 170). The cursus monument constrained movement toward a specified location, where activities took place associated with deposition, burning, and perhaps the dead. Barrett (1994, 24) has recently argued than the structure of many later Neolithic monuments can be understood as organised around the principle of processional movement toward a focal area, where architectural elements served to differentiate participants engaged in ritual activity. It is interesting to ask whether these practices were derived from the kinds of activities connected with the early Neolithic mortuary structures. Movement within the cursus might then elaborate upon processions which culminated in the deposition or removal of human remains from the mortuary structure (Lucas 1995, 140).

The construction of monuments in earlier Neolithic Britain introduced discontinuity into the landscape, by establishing boundaries around secluded and differentiated places. This was achieved by rearranging the materials which were present locally, at once drawing attention to ubiquitous substances and rendering them unfamiliar. This applies to the provision of a chamber area of stone or timber in various types of tombs (Kinnes 1975) and to the causewayed enclosures, which bounded off an area by the digging of a circuit of pits. In the period between 3700 and 3000 BC, this emphasis on the distinction between 'inside' and 'outside' was augmented by a concern with linear movement: either movement within an enclosed space or movement toward a privileged location. This is particularly evident in northern Scotland, with the shift from the bipartite and tripartite tombs of the Orkney–Cromarty tradition to the stalled cairns, which multiplied the modular arrangement of slab benches bracketed by orthostats to provide an enclosed linear space. Richards (1992) interprets the latter as a means of constraining within the chamber space a metaphorical 'last journey' of the deceased.

In southern Britain, it is very revealing that several causewayed enclosures had linear monuments erected over them. At Maiden Castle (Figure 3.5) and Crickley Hill these are represented by bank barrows (Wheeler 1943; Dixon 1988) (for discussion of the relationship between long mounds and bank barrows see below, pp. 139–40); at Fornham All Saints and Etton, cursus monuments were built through the enclosures (Hedges and Buckley 1981, 8; Pryor 1988). Earlier in this chapter it was suggested that several changes in this period resulted in a 're-interpretation' of the space of some causewayed enclosures. In their original form, these enclosures were not only associated with the dead and with ambiguous processes of value transformation, they were also open to being 'read' in a number of different ways. By drawing a linear monument across an enclosure, an attempt was being made to restrict or otherwise transform the way in which its space was experienced, and hence interpreted. In the same way, linear monuments also restricted access to and evaluation of the ritual space of the timber circles and tomb chambers. They represent an attempt to enforce some fixity of meaning upon these sites. Related phenomena may include the avenues of posts which were aligned upon the chambers or façades of some of the later long mounds, like Kilham (Manby 1976), Kemp Howe (Brewster 1968), Streethouse Farm (Vyner 1984) and Wayland's Smithy (Atkinson 1965; Whittle 1991). These in part represent an extension of the 'focusing' aspect of sepulchral architecture, but again would have involved a restriction on the way in which these spaces would have been physically encountered.

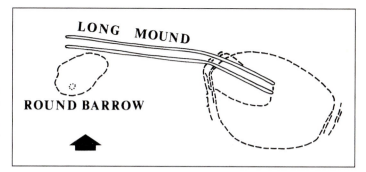

Figure 3.5 Maiden Castle, Dorset: causewayed enclosure and long mound

The simultaneous emergence of 'linear' monuments and an enhanced interest in celestial phenomena is worthy of note. The 'roof slots' and aligned passages of the passage tombs have already been mentioned, but one could add the probable astronomical significance of certain cursus monuments. While Penny and Wood's (1973) claims that the Dorset Cursus represented a complex observatory are probably overstated, the monument does incorporate a solar alignment. From the Bottlebush terminal, the midwinter sun sets directly over the Gussage Cow Down long barrow, set between the two banks of the cursus (Barrett *et al.* 1991, 50). Bradley (in Barrett *et al.* 1991) emphasises the way in which this phenomenon could only have been witnessed from within the cursus itself, indicating the exclusion of outsiders which the monument creates. Equally significant is the focal role taken on by the barrow itself, equivalent to that of the timber circles in other cursuses, so that movement within the structure becomes movement toward the dead. These alignments on the sun and moon are not to be ignored, but monuments are just as often oriented upon other monuments, or upon prominent features of the landscape. For instance, the henge monument at Old Yeavering is so oriented as to provide a view through its entrance of a notch in the hills around Kirknewton (Harding 1981, 129). This might easily be either a place of some spiritual or mythic significance, or a pass providing contact with an important group of strangers. What these orientations indicate is that astronomical phenomena were not privileged over ancestral monuments or landscape features. In the case of the Dorset Cursus, the experience of watching the sunset over Gussage Hill depended upon the momentary coincidence of chalk from the earth, the descending sun, the dead in their barrow and the surrounding forest. This does not indicate any scientific observation of the heavens, so much as a perceived unity of earth and sky, life and death, past and present, all being referenced to bring more and more emphasis on to particular spaces and places. This would tend to heighten the significance of whatever transactions and performances took place there. At the same time, it would also limit access to these spaces in terms both of direction and of timing, and would contribute to the way in which the space was experienced by promoting the impression that it stood at an axial point of an integrated cosmos.

CONCENTRIC SPACES

By the earlier third millennium BC, a new monumental tradition prevailed in much of Britain and in eastern Ireland: the henges (Figure 3.6). Attempts to seek a lineage for henge monuments in any one earlier group of sites (Wainwright 1969; Clare 1987) have proved rather inconclusive: the degree of overlap with these earlier structures can obscure the coherence of henges as a tradition (Barclay 1989). It may be more helpful to see their development as the coalescence of a variety of traits, some of them overtly evocative of the past, drawn from a common cultural pool in accordance with social needs. In terms of their organisation of space, henges elaborated the distinction between interior and exterior, and often involved a greater complexity of classification. The causewayed enclosures which preceded them sometimes consisted of multiple concentric rings, yet their central space was relatively undifferentiated. At Etton, the central area of such an enclosure was bisected by a ditch, but this kind of arrangement seems rare. We have noted that earlier Neolithic monuments are generally connected with the separation of a space from the outside world, be it an enclosure interior or a tomb chamber. With the henges, there is often a more complex arrangement of concentric spaces divided by a variety of boundaries: banks, ditches (even multiple concentric ditches in some of the Yorkshire henges), pits like those at Moncreiffe (Stewart 1985, 131), shafts like those at Maumbury Rings or Wyke Down (Bradley 1975; Barrett *et al.* 1991), and circles of posts. These are frequently combined to provide a series of spaces about a common centre, as with the henge at Milfield North, where a circle of pits was dug outside and concentric to the bank and ditch (Harding 1981, 101).

As with the architecture of earlier Neolithic monuments, it is reasonable to suggest that many of these features have as part of their role to draw attention to a particular point, the central space. At the same time, they would have had the effect of dividing up the space which a person would have to pass through on the approach to that point. Yet while the internal structure of henges can often be considered as integral to a complex experiential space, there is another aspect of their organisation which demands attention. In a number of cases, it is evident that the construction of the bank and ditch post-dated other activity on the site. At Balfarg, Mercer (1981b, 81) notes that layer U2 had been laid down before the cutting of the ditch, a layer which contains evidence for the burning of wood and deliberate smashing of pottery, some of it itself burnt. Similarly, a spread of charcoal with plain bowl pottery occurred beneath the bank at Mount Pleasant (Wainwright 1979a, 7). At Cairnpapple, an arc of stone-packed pits, some of which contained cremation deposits, focused upon a possible stone cove pre-dated the henge ditch and bank (Piggott 1948, 76–7). At North Mains, Strathallan, a number of pits and a cremation preceded the enclosure, and post ring A was constructed before the digging of the ditch, even if the interval between the two need not have been great (Barclay 1983, 126–82). We could equally suggest that the earlier phases of the two excavated timber circles within the Durrington Walls henge might precede the ditch and bank (Wainwright and Longworth 1971), and this is clearly the case at Arminghall, where the radiocarbon date of 3353–2897 cal. BC (2490 ± 150 bc) (BM-129) for the timber ring is at variance with the Beaker pottery from the ditch (Gibson 1994, 201). Finally, at Balfarg Riding School, the earliest documented evidence on the site again consisted of pits, containing deliberate deposits of earlier Neolithic pottery. Later, two rectilinear structures on the site appear to have gone out of use before the enclosure ditch was dug, Structure 2 having been covered by a low mound containing sherds of Grooved Ware (Barclay and Russell-White 1993, 60).

Cursus monuments had run across significant locations connected with the ancestral dead, had in some cases linked them together, and had laid down a processional way toward them. With henges, places which had already acquired significance were enclosed and secluded. The banks of henges, while generally unsuitable for defence by virtue of being outside the ditch (Atkinson 1951; Burl 1969), would often have restricted the visibility of actions taking place in the interior.

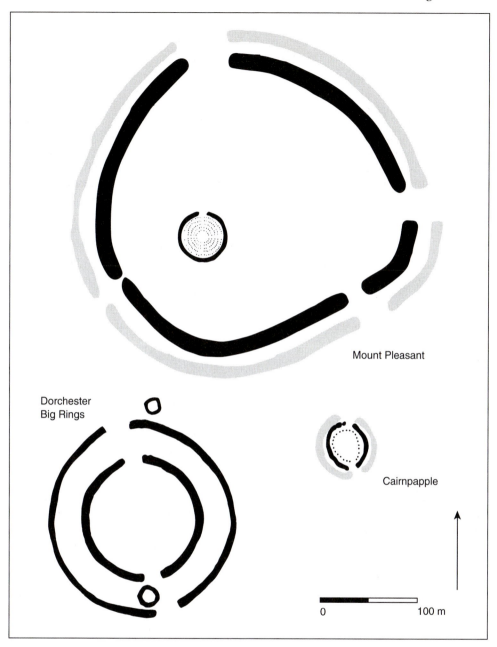

Mount Pleasant

Dorchester
Big Rings

Cairnpapple

0   100 m

Figure 3.6 Comparative plans of henges

This is especially the case with the large henges like Durrington Walls, Mount Pleasant and Avebury, although Burl suggests that a stockade may have originally surmounted the bank of Stonehenge I (1987, 51). If the interior of the henge could only be seen by those approaching along the axis of the monument, a further limitation was being placed upon the experience of that space. Barclay (1983, 182) points out that the entrances at North Mains, Cairnpapple, King

Arthur's Round Table and Arbor Low were offset from the structures within these enclosures, and this would have further limited vision and deflected movement toward the centre of the henge. Patterns of visibility and hiddenness may have played an important part in the use of many other monuments. For instance, activities in the Stone Cove at Stanton Drew would have been invisible from the interior of the nearby stone circle (Burl 1976, 105). Both this and the henge architecture suggest a social division between those who were and were not eligible to witness certain acts. At Coneybury Hill, numerous stake-holes were found within the interior of the henge, often clustered around cut features (Richards 1990, 138). Stakes were also found around the outer edge of the ditch at Moncreiffe (Stewart 1985, 130), and Barclay (1983, 182) entertains the possibility of fences having been set up between the uprights at North Mains. These points suggest that

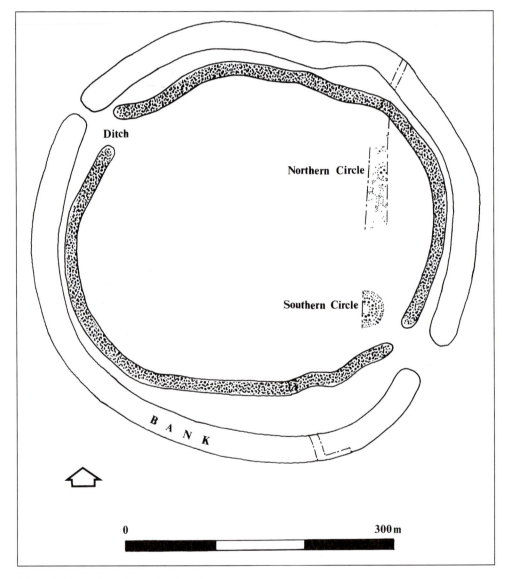

Figure 3.7 Plan of Durrington Walls, Wiltshire

substantial timber and stone uprights inside henge monuments may have been augmented by more ephemeral, perhaps temporary elements.

We have noted that one strand of continuity which can be detected between the timber mortuary structures of the earlier Neolithic and the henges lies in the provision of façades for timber circles, as in the case of the Northern and Southern Circles at Durrington Walls (Figure 3.7) (Wainwright and Longworth 1971) and perhaps the original central circle at Stonehenge (Burl 1987). It could be argued that these structures served to orient a person's movement toward the entrance to the circle, while simultaneously restricting what could be seen of activities going on inside. This possibility is borne out by a closer investigation of the Durrington Southern Circle

(Figures 3.7 and 3.8). The façade actually belonged to the first of two phases of construction of the circle (Wainwright and Longworth 1971, 27). The depths of the post-holes indicate that the posts would have risen in height towards the middle, the tallest ones flanking an entrance. As with the façades in many funerary sites, then, this structure had the effect of drawing attention to the place of entry into the monument. Durrington Walls represents a very large natural amphitheatre, and the entrance to the Southern Circle faced downhill toward the entrance to this bowl, and the River Avon. The topography thus inclines one to move toward the circle, and the architecture would then have channelled one into the interior. The disappearance of the façade in the second phase of the circle is comprehensible if we consider that this later structure was contemporary with the construction of the bank and ditch of the henge, surrounding the low ground containing the timber settings (Richards and Thomas 1984, 195). With the circle no longer 'loose' within the basin of Durrington Walls, the direction from which it would be approached was determined by the position of the southern entrance to the enclosure, which was located at the entry to the amphitheatre (Figure 3.7). The view through the entrance from outside, restricted by

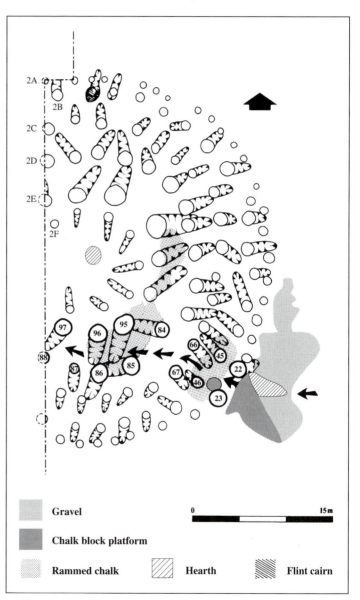

Figure 3.8 Durrington Walls: plan of the Southern Circle

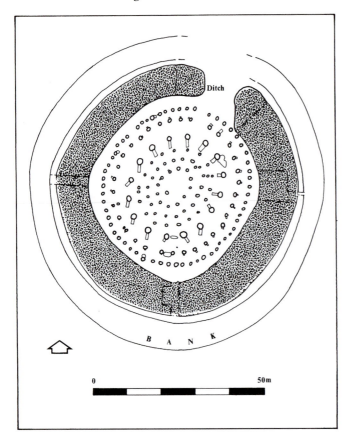

the presence of the banks, would have been dominated by the circle of upright timbers, and centred by the members set in the particularly large post-holes 22 and 23, flanking the entrance. In order to pass between these pillars, one would have to cross the rammed chalk and gravel platform. Just as with the forecourts of Cotswold–Severn tombs, this important transitional area seems to have held a hearth, and to have been a focus for the deposition of pottery and animal bones (Wainwright and Longworth 1971, 32). A further hearth was found in the centre of the concentric circles of timbers.

Crossing the platform, anyone entering the circle would have been funnelled between posts 66 and 67, only to meet head-on post 84 (Figure 3.8). At this point the progress towards the centre of the circle would have been halted, and it would have been necessary to turn aside. The spacing of the posts seems to suggest that the intended direction was left, through the setting of four large posts 85–86–95–96. This brings one between the

Figure 3.9 Plan of Woodhenge, Wiltshire

two circles 2E and 2D. These concentric circles are those between which there is the largest gap in the whole structure, and are also separated by an area of rammed chalk which could have functioned as a walkway. The inescapable conclusion to be drawn from this is that the architecture of the Southern Circle was so designed as to encourage people to progress through the outer four circles, and then to turn aside and process around the inner two circles.

Just as a social division may have existed between those taking part in activities inside the henge and those observing from outside, some distinction may have been drawn between those in the centre of the circle and those being encouraged to process around them. The presence of a hearth in the centre of the circle indicates that the central space was sometimes occupied by someone. A similar pattern of movement seems to be indicated by the nearby monument of Woodhenge (Cunnington 1929). There, the bank and ditch constrained entry to a single axis, which took the person through an entrance between the two outer circles of posts (Figure 3.9). This entrance gap did not exist in the inner circles of uprights, suggesting that a circular movement was now intended, again within the most widely spaced concentric circles of posts.

The 'linear' and 'circular' patterns of constrained movement are combined in a single recently excavated monument. At Crickley Hill in Gloucestershire, a stone platform and circle built within the causewayed enclosure were reached by a linear walkway which later provided the site of the long mound (Dixon 1988 and pers. comm.) (Figure 3.10). Advancing up this walkway towards the circle, people would eventually meet an orthostat which would have turned them aside from

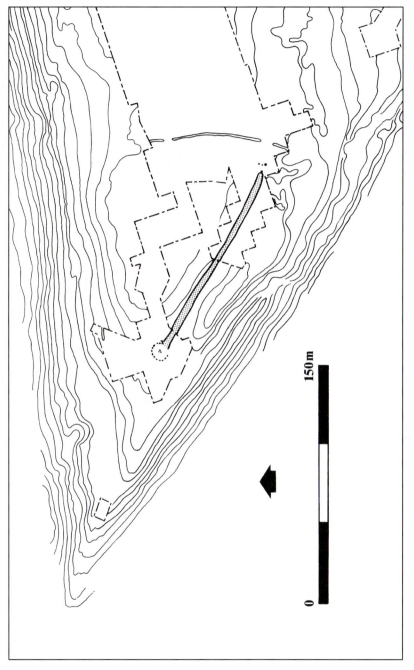

150m

0

Figure 3.10 Crickley Hill, Gloucestershire: the long mound

the centre of the circle (and the central hearth), and forced them to move clockwise around inside the circle. This same pattern of movement seems to have been recorded by wear patterns in the surface of the platform. Hence it is significant that at Balfarg, the recognition of the five lesser concentric post-circles within the henge depended upon the patterning of stones on the surface (Mercer 1981b, 110). Circular movement within the monuments of the later Neolithic may have been a rule rather than an exception. Even more than the linear monuments of the earlier Neolithic, the henges seem to have been concerned with the use of architecture to influence the movement and relative disposition of human bodies in space. Equally, the concentric division of space within henges indicates that a more complex classification was in operation than a simple inside–outside dichotomy. With the henges the ordering and division of space reached a higher degree of sophistication.

CONCLUSIONS

The monumental landscapes of the Neolithic were qualitatively different from the spatial orders which preceded and which then succeeded them. By constructing artificial landmarks which placed the bones of the ancestral dead or other symbolic media in space, an attempt was being made to influence the reading of that space. However, as with any symbolic system, the essentially arbitrary nature of this way of attributing meaning to place meant that an endless series of alternative readings was always possible. An example of this lack of fixity of meanings is provided by the causewayed enclosures. In the changing social circumstances of the period after 3700 BC, it was possible for particular elements of the meaning of the enclosures to be brought to the fore, dismissed or subverted, with a resulting reinterpretation of the monuments.

In the earlier third millennium BC, the development of monumental architecture can be seen as a response to this problem. These newer monuments acted directly upon the human body, encouraging particular spacings and timings of the encounter with particular places. This process culminated in the sophisticated architecture of the large Wessex henges at the end of the Neolithic period. However, while it seems that in the subsequent era large monuments ceased to be built (with the exception of the latest phases of Stonehenge and Mount Pleasant), a similar spatial order apparently prevailed. Space was still symbolically integrated, through smaller rather than large structures. Round barrows contributed to an inscribed landscape by a process of accretion, each one adding to a complex pattern, aligned on earlier structures and subtly shifting the overall configuration. Thus the early Bronze Age saw not a new spatial discourse, but an attempt to achieve the same effects on the landscape using labour organised on a much smaller scale. This may be indicative of social changes which took place at this time. While the henges indicate the mobilisation of colossal quantities of labour, they share with causewayed enclosures the characteristic of being ceremonial monuments rather than permanently occupied sites. The architectural elaboration which we have noted seems geared to establishing conditions for particular kinds of interaction between people (Barrett 1994, 29). A place which was already important was enclosed, and access to it at particular times regulated, while the precise experience of the location which a person could achieve was constrained. By this means, differentials would have been created or maintained in people's knowledge of the performances taking place within the henge, while the spatial relationships created between people would have contributed to the exercise of authority. But the focus on performance and event should lead us to question how far the forms of authority created within henges applied at other times and in other social contexts (Thomas 1996a, 180). It may be that a contrast between the late Neolithic and the Early Bronze Age lies in the distinction between forms of discontinuous and context-specific authority which were none the less quite extensive, and more permanent forms of authority within smaller, more closely knit groups.

A real change in the way in which the landscape was organised only came with the Middle Bronze Age, and the imposition of field systems and permanent enclosed settlements onto the land. The significance of fields, and their contemporaneity with the lapse of monument-building, is that they too restrict and constrain the bodily movements of people, but that they do so in the context of day-to-day life and of productive tasks. Monuments may have provided 'stations' in space keyed into the movement of people and animals, but field systems actually represented the locales in which labour was invested. It would be misleading to suggest that there were no monuments and no ritual in the later Bronze Age and the Iron Age. Rather, in the Neolithic, ritual and monumentality had provided the context for day-to-day productive tasks, while a landscape laid out according to the rhythms of production provided the context for ritual and monuments in the later Bronze and Iron Ages. This can be seen both in hill forts located on 'ranch boundaries' and in burials deposited in grain storage pits (Bradley 1971; Whimster 1981).

Chapter Four

Pits, pots and dirt
A genealogy of depositional practices

LAWS OF BEHAVIOUR, CULTURAL RULES

It is a commonplace that archaeology is concerned with the rubbish of past generations. Archaeologists study materials which have been discarded, abandoned or purposefully deposited by human beings at some time in the past. However, actual processes of deposition have rarely been central to the writing of prehistory. This has latterly been the case with attempts to problematise 'the formation of the archaeological record', which have generally involved the isolation of universal factors affecting or transforming archaeological materials. There has been a general failure to treat deposition as a social and cultural practice in itself. Schiffer (1972; 1976), for instance, distinguished between natural and cultural agencies which affect archaeological deposits, yet failed to see these 'n-' and 'c-transformations' as fundamentally different in their ontological status. Just as lawlike statements could be generated to predict and filter out the effects of rodent burrowing, water-sorting and transport, erosion, animal scavenging and trampling on deposits, structures and artefacts, so c-transforms were seen as universal laws governing the way in which human agency acted upon the archaeological record. Schiffer (1976, 15) gives as an example of one such law the prediction that, as settlement sites increase in size, so the distance between the use and discard locations of an artefact can be anticipated to increase.

Clearly, the aim of formulating a catalogue of potential c-transforms is to enable them to be stripped away, leaving an undistorted record of human behaviour. But the operation of what Schiffer calls a c-transform is nothing other than human social life. If it is this which the analysis is aimed at excising, one is left to wonder what remains as the object of study. Schiffer's scheme effectively places artefacts at the centre of the stage, only bringing human beings on in a subsidiary capacity to 'do' things to them. An alternative to Schiffer's behaviourism can be found in insisting that 'cultural transforms' are precisely what this name would imply, and hence that the formation of archaeological deposits is a culturally specific process. Nothing in the way in which people have conducted their lives through the millennia is necessarily stable and unchanging. It follows that depositional practices are interesting in themselves, rather than constituting an irritant, obscuring the path to the elucidation of general laws of human behaviour. If archaeological deposits are generated in accordance with cultural rules rather than natural laws (Moore 1981), one must acknowledge that these rules are arbitrary and conventional, and are open to being manipulated and reinterpreted as time goes on (see, for instance, Bourdieu 1977). Hence, the study of the way in which particular materials were being deposited, or how deposits were formed, through time, has the potential to inform us of shifts in such cultural rules and norms.

This chapter consists of an analysis of a number of related deposits which have hitherto been described as 'rubbish' or 'refuse'. Its intention will be to consider whether such a designation is appropriate, to determine whether recurrent patterns can be discerned in these deposits and their processes of formation, and to discuss whether their changing nature has anything to tell us about the preoccupations of Neolithic society in Britain. 'Rubbish' and 'dirt' are by no means categories which are common to all cultures (Moore 1982, 48). The arbitrary conceptual schemes through which people impose a system of sorts on to an inherently untidy existence can result in conceptual anomalies which may be rejected as unclean (Douglas 1966, 9; Leach 1976, 33). But equally, particular substances may be discarded, deposited or set aside without being thought of as rubbish (Moore 1986, 102). Thus Moore (1986) describes a situation in which ash, animal dung and chaff each has its own place in a conceptual scheme, each with its own set of associations and connotations which dictate that they cannot be deposited together. We ourselves may have a single category of 'dirt', but in some situations rotten material, or faeces, may not be regarded as dirty (Panoff 1970). Similarly, the sherds from broken pots may be left lying within settlements as a result of their taking on a supernatural significance (Welbourn 1984, 22). Depositional practices, then, are wholly guided by the way in which items and substances are classified. The disposal of animal bones, for instance, frequently depends upon the way in which animals are classified (Bulmer 1976). Thus different patterns of bone deposition might result according to whether animals were principally classified in terms of their habitat (Bulmer 1967), their domestic or wild status (Tambiah 1969), their conceptual distance from being 'men' (Buxton 1968), in terms of homologies with particular types of human beings (Lévi-Strauss 1969a), or according to their physical characteristics (Douglas 1957). The classification of animals may even result in their being totally avoided; thus fish may not be eaten if they are considered to be the same as snakes (Kesby 1979, 46).

Of course, none of these ethnographic examples could or should be taken as direct parallels for the classificatory schemes which we might expect to find in operation in prehistoric Britain. At most, they act as a corrective against the expectation that a single undifferentiated category of refuse would necessarily have existed throughout prehistory. Each of these examples represents the outcome of a particular set of social circumstances: the classification of the material world will not be a cultural 'given', but will exist in a state of dynamic tension created by the social actions of a community. Thus, for instance, the principle of purity which Hodder observes guiding the deposition of materials within Mesakin compounds (1982b, 162) is directly related to a transient and historical set of social relations (1982b, 168). It follows that the study of depositional practices is particularly suited to the 'genealogical' approach to archaeology outlined in the opening chapter of this book. That a rather different attitude to domestic waste from our own prevailed in Neolithic Britain has long been evident. Case (1969b, 12–15) described the burial of sherds, flints and charcoal in pits within an enclosure ditch at Goodland in County Antrim, Ireland. He suggested that this represented the scraped-up debris of settlement sites used as symbolic manure in rites of sympathetic magic designed to ensure fertility. No less striking is the use of midden material in the domestic architecture of Neolithic Orkney. The walls of the later Neolithic houses at Rinyo, Skara Brae and the Links of Noltland were all surrounded by mounds of well-rotted midden, which appears to have been curated for the purpose (Clarke and Sharples 1985, 58). Similarly, at the Knap of Howar, midden had been used to fill in the wall cores (Ritchie 1983, 58). Depending upon one's interpretation of the radiocarbon dates at the last site (1983, 57), this material could have been generations old by the time that it came to be used. While prosaic features like the thermal properties of midden material may have favoured its use for these purposes, the mere fact that the Orcadian people were happy to surround themselves with the rotted detritus of their communities is evidence enough of an attitude to 'dirt' distinct from that of the modern Occident. Beyond this, it may hint at a specific preoccupation with domestic debris, arising out of its history and symbolic connotations.

PITS

As we have seen in Chapter 2, evidence for domestic activities in the Neolithic and much of the Bronze Age in southern Britain is little more substantial than it is for the Mesolithic. House sites are few and scattered, and are often atypical of the general pattern of settlement in one way or another (Thomas 1996b). In the absence of this most basic information, more meagre resources have been drawn upon in the development of economic models. One source of information which has been exploited has been the existence of subsoil pits, containing cultural material, and often held to be the sole surviving structural component of flimsy settlement sites. It was on the basis of the distribution of these pits that Isobel Smith suggested a basic economic division between upland and lowland Britain in the Neolithic (in Field *et al.* 1964). Such a division followed Piggott's (1958) suggestion that two separate economies could be discerned in the British Iron Age, a lowland grain-producing regime and the pastoral 'Stanwick' economy of the north and west (Bradley 1978b, 29–30). In the absence of definitive evidence, then, Smith suggested that the Neolithic economy was comparable with that of the Iron Age.

As an alternative, I should prefer to emphasise the contrasts between Neolithic and Iron Age pits, which are perhaps more compelling than the similarity of their geographical distribution. On the basis of this contrast, we can go on to place the contents of the pits into the context of a number of other contemporary deposits. Differences between Neolithic and Iron Age pits can be distinguished in a number of different aspects of their morphology. Principal amongst these is shape: Neolithic pits are most often shallow, bowl-shaped forms, whilst their Iron Age counterparts are flat-bottomed and either straight-sided or of 'beehive' form. Furthermore, pits of Neolithic date are considerably smaller in size, particularly in terms of depth (Figure 4.1). Another important contrast lies in the filling of the pits. Figure 4.2 shows the numbers of layers of fill in a variety of Neolithic pits compared with Iron Age pits at Gussage All Saints and Little Woodbury (Bersu 1940; Wainwright 1979b). Such a marked difference cannot be explained purely by the lesser volumes of the Neolithic pits, and seems likely to reflect different patterns of backfilling. The Iron Age pits appear to have been used in the first instance for storage, and then to have provided a convenient repository for domestic waste. This would have built up over a period of time, although Hill (1995) has demonstrated that not all of these deposits can be explained in utilitarian terms. The more homogeneous filling of the Neolithic pits indicates a prompt backfilling.

While shallow, bowl-shaped pits might be suitable for storage of foodstuffs in a desiccating climate (see Clark's discussion of such pits at Fayum in Egypt: Clark *et al.* 1960, 211), this may not be the case in Britain. Reynolds' experiments with reconstructed Iron Age pits (1974, 126–7) indicate that to store grain effectively the pit should be sealed with clay or dung to prevent respiration. Such a seal is best achieved, and least grain wasted, if an acute angle between seal and pit wall is avoided, and hence the beehive profile has been shown to be optimal. A bowl is thus the worst possible shape for sealing. Darvill's suggestion (in Darvill *et al.* 1986, 35) that some Neolithic pits may have been hearths is only applicable in a minority of cases, since despite the presence of much burnt material in their fillings, few pits show evidence of burning *in situ* (only one amongst the 200 pits at Hurst Fen, for instance: Clark *et al.* 1960, 206).

There are particular features which occur repeatedly in pits of Neolithic and Early Bronze Age date (Figure 4.3). Almost invariably they contain burnt material: ash (Stone and Young 1948, 289; Richards 1990, 114; Rogerson 1995, 10), burnt chalk (Frere 1943, 35), charcoal (Thomas 1956, 167; Greenfield 1960, 60; Manby 1974, 11) and other carbonised organic material (Armit *et al.* 1994, 116). At Spong Hill in Norfolk, Healy noted that 'black and greasy' fills were especially common amongst those pits which contained large numbers of artefacts (1988, 6). This material may contain carbonised plant remains (Jones 1980), yet these are highly mixed in their

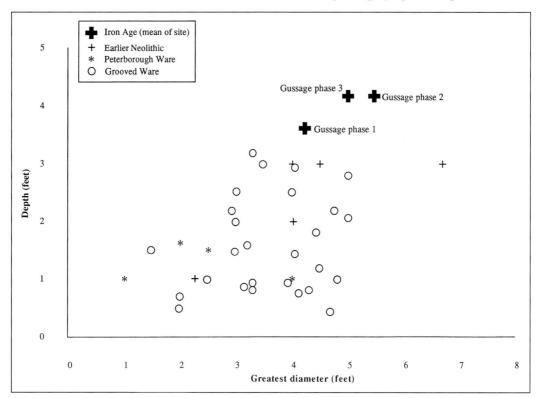

Figure 4.1 Pits: length and depth

composition and are generally dominated by wild species (Moffett *et al.* 1989), thus clearly not relating to the burning out of germinated grain. Another recurrent feature, frequently remarked upon by excavators, is that the sides of the pits are generally fresh, showing little evidence of subsidence or weathering (Calkin 1947, 30; Smith and Simpson 1964, 82). This is the case even on friable gravel subsoils (Case 1982b, 121), and confirms the impression that pits were backfilled soon after they were dug.

At a number of sites, more spectacular depositional practices alert one to the likelihood that something more complex than the routine disposal of waste material was happening. At Mill Road, in Deal (Kent), five early Neolithic pots had been carefully placed in the bottom of a conical pit and surrounded by flint nodules, a stone rubber having been left within the central vessel (Dunning 1966, 1). At Barlfarg in Fife, Feature 2430 comprised a pit which had been lined with potsherds from a number of different vessels, and then swiftly backfilled (Barclay and Russell-White 1993, 64). Similarly, at Carnaby Temple Sites 7 and 15 (Yorks), animal bones had been pressed into the pit walls. Manby's interpretation, that these objects had been pressed back by a wickerwork lining (1974, 43), seems implausible. If the pits had been lined to store plant foods, why did they already contain animal bones? The material contained within Pit 1 at Woodlands, in Wiltshire, seems to have been covered with a flint cairn (Stone and Young 1948, 289), while Pit 4 contained a deposit which resembled the contents of a basket or bag of burnt material (Stone 1949, 122–3). These complex fillings find something of a parallel at Thirlings in Northumbria, where one later Neolithic pit had had twelve stakes inserted into it from above (Miket 1976, 119).

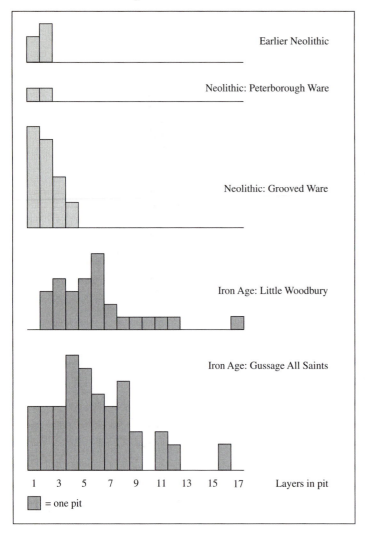

Earlier Neolithic

Neolithic: Peterborough Ware

Neolithic: Grooved Ware

Iron Age: Little Woodbury

Iron Age: Gussage All Saints

1   3   5   7   9   11   13   15   17   Layers in pit

▨ = one pit

Figure 4.2 Pits: layers in fill

The deliberate nature of these fillings is also suggested by a range of deposited artefacts which would seem to be out of character for everyday household waste. Lithic artefacts often show an unusually high ratio of tools to waste (Cleal 1984, 148; Barrett *et al.* 1991, 82). In other cases, such as the early Neolithic pit at Wingham in Kent, an assemblage entirely made up of waste flakes can be refitted back on to a core, with no tools or utilised pieces having been created in the course of the reduction sequence (Greenfield 1960, 66). The tools themselves may be fresh and un-broken, or conversely may have been broken deliberately, and may include such items as finely flaked arrowheads (Stone 1935, 60), flint and stone axes (Leeds 1934, 264; Stone and Young 1948, 290; Stone 1949), and stone maceheads (Smith 1968). At Blewbury in Oxfordshire, a flint scraper had been snapped in two, and half placed in each of two pits (Halpin 1984), while at New Barn Down in Sussex a polished flint axe had been broken by burn-ing within the pit (Curwen 1934b, 156). The disposal of these items was evidently not a function of their being worn out, and it seems equally unlikely that they were simply overlooked in the process of 'tidying up' domestic refuse. One possibility which does remain is that these were items which were discarded on account of some form of pollution or of particular connotations attached to them and which rendered them no longer suitable for use. The range of artefacts deposited in these pits extends to such items as bone pins (Leeds 1934), inscribed chalk plaques (Vatcher 1969; Harding 1988) and pottery vessels of rare and highly decorated types (Gell 1949; Chadburn and Gardiner 1985). Even the animal bones found in many pits defy simple explanations. Amongst some of the pits associated with later Neolithic Grooved Ware, like those at Larkhill (Wainwright *et al.* 1971), the Chalk Plaque Pit (Vatcher 1969) and Ratfyn (Stone 1935), the faunal assemblages may consist almost entirely of bones from the meat-rich parts of animals (author's data). Moreover, the pits at Blewbury contained bones which appeared to have been deposited as articulated joints (Halpin 1984, 1).

In contrast, Pit 418 on the King Barrow Ridge, near Stonehenge, contained an assemblage made up largely of the head and foot bones of pigs, which might have been discarded in butchery

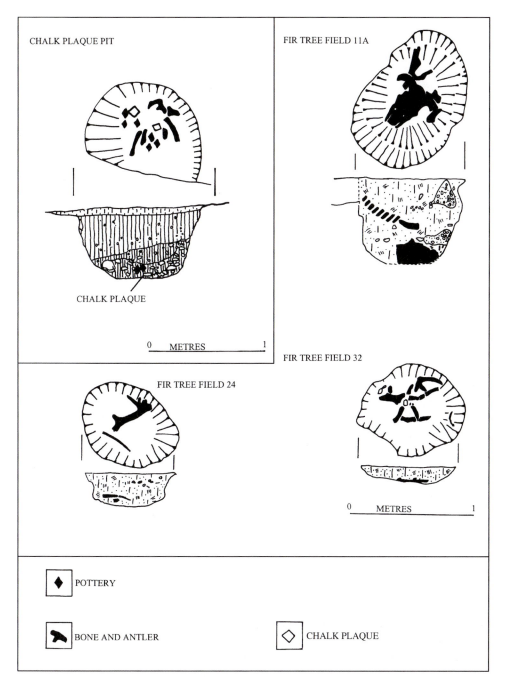

Figure 4.3 The Chalk Plaque Pit, Wiltshire, and pits at Fir Tree Field, Dorset
Source: After Cleal and Allen (1994) and Barrett *et al.* (1991)

(Richards 1990, 114), and a pit at Black Patch in the Vale of Pewsey was dominated by a large number of pig jaws (author's data). In the case of the pits at Firtree Field, Down Farm, Legge (1991, 67–8) argues that the bones included represent neither meat-rich parts nor butchery remains, but were more likely to have been selected from more substantial deposits on the surface on the basis of size and survival. Bones of brown bear have been found at Ratfyn and Firtree Field (Stone 1935; Barrett *et al.* 1991, 81), while the shells of marine molluscs have been located at a number of sites. While the presence of the numerous mussel shells in pits at Redgate Hill, Hunstanton might be explained in largely economic terms (Healy *et al.* 1993, 5), in more inland locations shells might be classed along with the fossils and exotic stones and pebbles found in some Neolithic pits as non-utilitarian manuports.

A final feature which is worthy of note is the inclusion of human remains in pit fills. These can vary from single bones to entire skeletons. At sites like Astrop, Northants (Ashmolean Museum), Barholm Pit 4 (Simpson *et al.* 1993, 25) or Sutton Courtenay Pit Q (Leeds 1934), there were no more than a few skull or longbone fragments included with an assemblage of pottery, flint tools and animal bones. Similarly, a pit alongside the terminal of the Dorchester on Thames Cursus (F3003) contained fragmentary skull and foot bones, together with a flint scraper, in a matrix which included charcoal and wood ash (Whittle *et al.* 1992, 153). At South Lodge and Handley Hill (Dorset), and in the pits within the central enclosure at Hambledon Hill, parts of human skeletons which may be the remnants of originally more complete bodies were found with stone axes and pottery vessels (Pitt Rivers 1898; Mercer 1980). Then there are more extensive deposits of articulated or disarticulated bones, like the pit graves at Nethercourt Farm, Ramsgate and Pangbourne, Berkshire, both of which contained decorated early Neolithic pots (Piggott 1929; Dunning 1966, 8). This range of variation seems to demonstrate that in practice no sharp distinction existed between the enactment of 'mortuary ritual' and the 'routine' depositing of items in pits. This rather complicates the issue of analysing pit deposits, as in some cases the presence of human bones has been taken as the basis for distinguishing between 'ritual' and 'domestic' pits (e.g. Burgess 1976). While in some cases it is clear that a particular pit represents a 'grave' in the conventional sense of the word, and any artefacts included in this context can be regarded as accompanying a human body, this is not always the case. Neolithic pit deposits suggest a number of other possibilities, where human bones may have been regarded as artefacts in themselves, or where bones may have had a secondary importance in relation to the 'burial' of an artefact. Whatever the significance of deposits buried in pits, it is clear that this was not a context in which the remains of the dead were out of place.

The foregoing discussion of a specific set of depositional practices has established the degree to which they differ from later pits which can more reasonably be claimed to have performed a storage function, and has identified some of the principles plausibly governing their filling. To summarise, Neolithic and Early Bronze Age pits are unsuitable both in size and shape for the storage of foodstuffs. They seem to have been dug and backfilled within a relatively short span of time, with a matrix of material that shows evidence of burning, but containing artefacts which have rarely been burnt. In some cases the material may have been brought to the site of the pits in baskets or bags, and in one example taphonomic analysis of the bones indicates that the material had been exposed for some time before burial (Legge 1991, 61). The faunal remains represented in pit deposits might in many cases have been selected from larger assemblages, although these 'parent' deposits might have been butchery waste, the remains of feasts or 'balanced' domestic accumulations. It is also possible that some pits contain the entire gathered-up products of a single event of consumption. Whole pots are sometimes encountered, but more often parts of a number of vessels are found, again implying that the material had been selected from more substantial deposits. The material culture associated with these pits includes a range of finely crafted artefacts, which tend to be rare as stray finds, often in pristine condition, and which were sometimes deliberately broken. Significantly, although most of these deposits diverge somewhat from what might be expected within a storage pit re-used for the casual discard of rubbish, the actual details of their contents demonstrate considerable variation. So while the practices concerned might constitute a recognisable tradition, they appear not to have been bound by a strict set of rules. This suggests that the particular contents and sequence of acts involved in the filling of a given pit were to some degree improvised, in the context of local conditions. Anticipating later discussion, we might say that if pit deposits used artefacts and substances as a material language, the particular statements being made might have been highly localised in their meaning.

What is most striking about this set of activities is that they represent a phenomenon which is temporally bounded. While some pits had been dug in southern Britain in the Mesolithic, and may have provided antecedents for those of the Neolithic (Drewett *et al.* 1988, 17), pit-digging became much more common from the start of the Neolithic. This could be seen as one aspect of an increased interest in the opening up of the earth. As a histogram of the number of pits within the study area containing pottery of sequential styles demonstrates (Figure 4.4), this is a practice which was enacted more frequently as the period went on, reaching its zenith at the end of the Neolithic with pits associated with Grooved Ware, yet rather less frequently connected with Beaker pottery. Collared Urn pits are extremely rare, and Food Vessel pits virtually non-existent. Ignoring for the moment the degree of chronological overlap between these ceramic traditions, a prosaic interpretation of this sequence might be one of a shift of economic practice away from cereals and toward pastoralism. This would present an interesting inversion of the traditional model of Grooved Ware users as having 'a pastoral economy with a little hunting which was supplemented by strandlooping and fishing' (Wainwright and Longworth 1971, 264) and of Beaker-folk as 'energetic mixed farmers' (Case 1977, 71). Arguably, once we remove the evidence

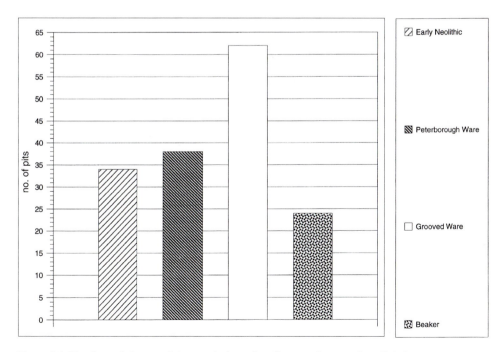

Figure 4.4 Numbers of pits containing particular styles of pottery from southern Britain

of pits from the equation, the case for any kind of abrupt change in subsistence practices through this period must be slim, at least until the advent of Deverel-Rimbury settlements and field systems.

Having demonstrated the existence of a tradition of pit deposits which were not exclusively utilitarian in character, and having shown their changing frequency over time, it may be possible to recognise temporal changes in the character of pit contents. Herne (1988, 26) identifies the use of fine plain carinated bowls as 'an horizon for the inception of the Neolithic across the British Isles', and it is striking that a high proportion of the sites which he lists as 'true' Grimston assemblages are pit deposits. Others, at Hazleton North, Gwernvale and Ascott-under-Wychwood, represent high-density scatters of material on sites which would later be occupied by chambered long cairns, the first of these being identified as an extensive 'midden' of discoloured soil (Selkirk 1971; Britnell and Savory 1984; Saville 1990). These might simply represent occupation sites, although faunal remains from the Hazleton midden suggest large-scale meat consumption (Levitan in Saville 1990, 203). Whether we define these assemblages as 'domestic' or 'ritual' in character (and the distinction may be illusory), they seem to derive from events of intense, and perhaps short-term interaction, dating from the very start of the Neolithic period, and preserved by fortune or design. Some of the early pit deposits share these characteristics. An example would be the pit beneath round barrow G.61 on Roughridge Hill in north Wiltshire. This contained sherds of at least 32 pots, roughly a fifth of them carinated vessels, in a filling of dark material including much charcoal, and which formed 'domed' surfaces suggesting basketfuls of material upended into the pit. Despite this, some of the sherds were in upright positions, suggesting careful placement (Zienkiewicz 1996, 104–6). This feature was shared by carinated bowl sherds from a pit in the forecourt of the portal dolmen at Dyffryn Ardudwy in north Wales (Powell 1973). Here, sherds had been selected from the upper parts of the five pots, as they had been in the pit at Wingham in Kent (Greenfield 1960, 66), which might also plausibly date to the primary Neolithic.

Two large, isolated pits from southern Wessex appear to date from the earliest part of the Neolithic. The Coneybury 'Anomaly' (Figure 4.5), on Salisbury Plain, contained a primary fill rich in both charcoal and soil phosphate (Richards 1990, 40). Within this layer were sherds of at least 41 plain vessels, predominantly (but not exclusively) open and neutral forms. Once again, rim sherds seem to have been deliberately chosen for inclusion, and Cleal (in Richards 1990, 53) suggests that the pottery had been made and used in a relatively short period, and may have lain exposed for a limited time before burial. The notion of selection from a larger deposit is supported by the flint flakes, which provide few refits, and the animal bones, which show some evidence of dog gnawing. The faunal remains were extensive, and probably derived from a single butchery event, in which cattle and red deer were being prepared for consumption elsewhere, while several roe deer may have been eaten on site (Maltby in Richards 1990, 60). The episodic character of this activity is mirrored at Rowden, in south Dorset, where another pit with a basal fill of ash and charcoal gave indications of a swift filling process. Joining sherds and conjoining flints were found in different layers of fill (Woodward 1991, 43). The nine pots from this pit were predominantly open and neutral carinated forms. While these pits had probably been dug with the aim of deposition in mind, at Cannon Hill in Berkshire, a charcoal-rich layer containing sherds of six carinated vessels together with flint tools and waste and some scraps of bone was located some way from the bottom of a deep shaft (Bradley *et al.* 1978).

I would suggest that these early Neolithic pit deposits make use of the act of crossing the threshold between above-ground and below-ground as a means of commemorating particular events, whether feasts, gatherings or periods of occupation. By placing representative residues of such events in the ground, a durable trace of their memory was created. This would have been less

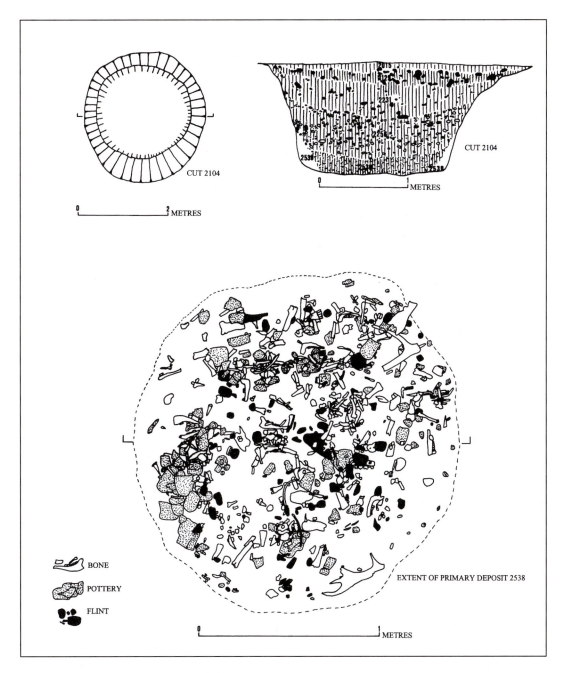

Figure 4.5 The Coneybury 'Anomaly', Wiltshire
Source: After Richards (1990)

conspicuous than a stone or earth monument, but would have had a similar effect in transforming the significance of a place, associating it with a particular practice or social grouping. Taking place at the transition between Mesolithic and Neolithic, some of these early deposits may have resulted from events which both dramatised and materialised the social and cultural changes which were taking place. In this respect, the early pits of central southern England contrast a little with the tradition of pit-digging which was to emerge in the east of England. Although there is no shortage of isolated pits of early Neolithic date in the eastern counties, there is also a number of distinctive sites composed of clusters of small pits. These are often, if not always, associated with decorated Mildenhall Ware, and it may not be coincidental that at Eaton Heath, Norwich, the two clusters of pits contained Mildenhall sherds, while 21 shafts contained plain pottery (Wainwright 1973, 7). Similarly, at Spong Hill in Norfolk five clusters of small pits contained Mildenhall Ware, while Grimston sherds were located in four further pits, all of them isolated (Healy 1988, 18).

The grouping of these pits is almost modular: the seven pits containing pottery at Loft's Farm in Essex is not dissimilar to one of the clusters of ten or fifteen pits at Hurst Fen (Clark *et al.* 1960, 208; Brown 1988, 251). Healy (1987, 12) notes that one of the characteristics of the pits at Spong Hill was that they contained relatively large quantities of flintwork, while very little early Neolithic flint could be found in the topsoil. This contrasted with the large amount of later Neolithic material throughout the profile. Healy suggests that the burial of flint might have served the straightforward purpose of keeping settlement areas free from sharp objects, although this does not explain why Mesolithic people had failed to bury their debitage, or why the practice had lapsed in the later Neolithic. As with the southern English pits, these groups may serve to render activity memorable, and to give meaning to place, although the activities being commemorated may be less epochal and more cyclical in character. Each pit may constitute a token of a mobile community's return to a given location. Consequently, it may be of importance that at Spong Hill each group of pits appeared to be characterised by pottery sherds which were distinctive in terms both of vessel form and of decoration (Healy 1988, 65–7).

Pit-digging, and the deposition of objects and substances within pits, was a set of actions which brought meaning to a locality over and above the importance of whatever activities generated the material concerned. Once these actions had been performed the location became a place of significance, and for this reason it is not surprising that pits or groups of pits have been found on sites where monuments of one kind or another were later constructed. Examples might include the group of stone-filled pits within the henge of Cairnpapple (Piggott 1948, 77), the two clusters of early Neolithic pits at Balfarg (Barclay and Russell-White 1993), the group of pits within the central circuit of ditches at Windmill Hill (Smith 1965a), and the two early Neolithic pits at Flagstones House in Dorset (Woodward 1988), as well as single early Neolithic pits in the vicinity of the henges at Coneybury, Yeavering, Llandegai A and the Pict's Knowe (Houlder 1968; Harding 1981; Richards 1990; Thomas forthcoming).

By the later part of the Neolithic, the more complex forms of material culture which were in circulation allowed more complicated 'statements' to be articulated through acts of deposition. It seems likely that the more elaborate pit contents and the increasing numbers of pits also reflect their increased social significance. Like monument-building, pit deposits formed one aspect of the continuous process in which the identities of places were created, re-created and contested. If originally these deposits were simply representative of events which had taken place in a given location, by the later Neolithic it is probable that quite specific combinations of artefacts were being used to create meanings in a very sophisticated manner. A good example of the potential of later Neolithic artefacts to facilitate this process is provided by the pair of pits exca-vated by Grimes (1960, 186–97) at Heathrow in Middlesex. These were two shallow oval features with charcoally fills, separated from each other by some 50 metres. Each contained numerous

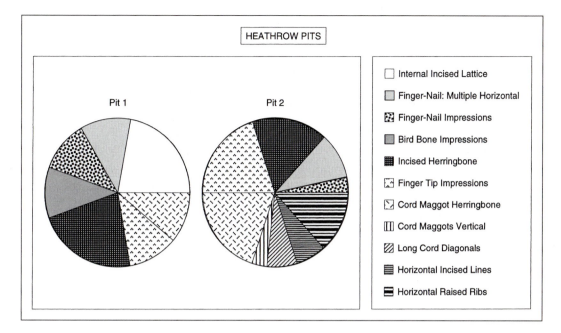

Figure 4.6 Ceramic decoration from two later Neolithic pits at Heathrow

sherds of Peterborough Ware, and a number of complete vessels was present. Although the ceramic fabrics in the two pits were indistinguishable, and there is little doubt that the features were broadly contemporary, notable contrasts between the two groups of pots can be recognised in terms of decoration (Figure 4.6). This difference may be a consequence of the contents of the two pits having been drawn from distinct assemblages used for spatially or conceptually separate activities, but it equally might represent a means of drawing attention to the difference between the two pits and their locations.

While some later Neolithic pits may have continued early Neolithic practice, drawing on material left behind after a period of occupation or a gathering of some kind, there is reason to suggest that distinct sets of practices had now been established which culminated in pit-digging and deposition. In other words, rather than the pit deposit representing an incidental outcome of the use of a location, people might now have gone to a particular place with the objective of performing a set of acts to which pit-digging was integral. Deposition became less a means of committing an event to social memory, and more of an event in itself. Hence it is significant that Holgate (1988a) is able to distinguish between pits found within flint scatters, which may be representative of generalised spreads of occupation material, and others which exist in isolation from any trace of settlement. This same distinction was repeated at a smaller scale at Firtree Field in Cranborne Chase, where the later Neolithic pits formed two distinct clusters with a single outlier (Barrett *et al.* 1991, 77). Only the northern grouping was located amidst a scatter of stake-holes which might have derived from temporary habitations, while the southern cluster was positioned closer to the Dorset Cursus. The southern pits contained more numerous artefacts and more complex deposits: decorated Grooved Ware, a high ratio of flint implements to waste flakes, exotic stones, complex arrangements of bones. Although the animal bones and artefacts in both areas show signs of having been exposed for a short while prior to burial, it seems plausible that in the case of the southern pit group objects were *taken to the location* with the intention of deposition. A similar situation may be represented at Redgate Hill, Hunstanton, where much higher densities of cultural material were found in a group of Grooved Ware pits than in the nearby palisade enclosure, which may be contemporary (Healy *et al.* 1993, 7–9). These pits rival those at Firtree Field in their elaboration: the filling of Pit 22 was divided vertically between a chalky half containing animal bones and a dark soilly half holding over 100 sherds of Grooved Ware. At the bottom of the pit lay a slab of fossiliferous calcareous mudstone (1993, 70).

A distinctive feature of the later Neolithic pits at Redgate Hill was the segregation of sherds of Peterborough Ware, Grooved Ware, Beaker and Collared Urn into separate features (Healy *et al.* 1993, 75). This is a pattern familiar from other sites, like the King Barrow Ridge, near Stonehenge (Richards 1990, 114), Spong Hill (Healy 1988, 18) and Middle Harling (Rogerson 1995, 10). It might be put down to the chronological replacement of one ceramic style by the next, or one could argue that each site had been successively visited by members of different cultural or sub-cultural groups. Both of these interpretations rely upon particular understandings of material culture: the 'chest of drawers' model of unilinear evolution and the 'pots equal people' model of culture history respectively. The probable contemporaneity of some of these ceramic traditions requires us to consider the ways in which these separate deposits may have constituted conflicting or complementary material statements, potentially linked to distinct practices or human identities.

The digging of small shallow pits and the deliberate deposition of pottery sherds, stone tools and animal bones in a matrix of burnt material was a practice which was historically circumscribed. It was engaged in by people within a particular historical epoch, and eventually it ceased. When pits began again to be dug in the second millennium BC, associated with Deverel-Rimbury settlements, they were larger, flat-bottomed and straight-sided (e.g. Drewett 1982, 332). In other words, the first digging of pits suitable for the storage of grain coincided temporally with the establishment of substantial, permanent settlements and the division of the landscape into fields. This complex of features represents the earliest sound evidence for a regime geared to intensive cereal production. By contrast, the pit-digging of the Neolithic seems to relate to a quite different set of preoccupations and conditions. In order to contextualise these deposits it will be helpful to consider a number of other practices which also involved the placing of objects and substances into the earth.

CAUSEWAYED ENCLOSURE DITCHES

Another practice which dates to the Neolithic and which involved the opening of pits of a sort (and the deposition of items in them) was the digging of the ditches of causewayed enclosures. The excavation of interrupted rings of ditch segments has been interpreted in utilitarian terms as an expedient means of quarrying material for a bank, given a labour force working in small gangs (Curwen 1930). However, the possibility that some enclosures may have had no bank at all (Evans 1988b, 133) must place this reading of the evidence in question. The ubiquity of causewayed-ditched enclosures in north-west Europe, from Poland to Ireland, suggests that some symbolic importance was attached to the delineation of a bounded area by a discontinuous perimeter. The significance of the circuit of ditch segments itself is indicated by the number of sites at which the ditches have either been cleaned out (Mercer 1988, 100) or repeatedly recut (Smith 1971, 98; Darvill 1981, 55; Dixon 1988, 81). Parts of the enclosure at Briar Hill in Northamptonshire had been recut successively up to five times (Bamford 1985, 32), while the final 'slot' recut of the central enclosure on Hambledon Hill respected all of the original causeways (Mercer 1980, 36).

The specific significance of the ditch segments is emphasised by the way in which particular deposits had been placed in their terminals at a number of sites. At the waterlogged site of Etton these include such items as rafts of birch bark, whole pots and bundles of cattle ribs (Pryor *et al.* 1985, 293). That these practices were more widespread has been demonstrated by the recent excavations at Windmill Hill, where discrete (perhaps bagged) deposits of animal bones have been located within terminals of segments of the inner and middle ditches (Whittle 1988b). Still more elaborate deposits may mark the entrances through ditch circuits. At Haddenham, an entrance was flanked by ditches containing complex structural arrangements, associated with a broken stone axe butt, human skull fragments and *in situ* burning (Evans 1988b, 134).

The presence of skull fragments at Haddenham prompts the observation that finds of human bone have repeatedly been made in causewayed enclosure ditches, either on ditch bottoms or in recuts. Their significance in these two kinds of contexts need not always have been the same. At Hambledon Hill, the interpretation of the central enclosure as a necropolis given over to the exposure of the dead gives a plausible explanation for the mass of skeletal material located in the ditches, but there are also skulls which have been placed on ditch bottoms both here and at the lesser Stepleton enclosure (Mercer 1980, 30 and 52). It could, of course, be suggested that all of the bones were actually placed in the ditches, rather than just the skulls. It need not follow that ditch deposits are representative of activities carried out inside an enclosure. Human skull fragments are also known from the ditches of several other sites, notably Abingdon, Whitehawk, Maiden Castle and Staines, the last site also boasting a sheep's skull set in one ditch terminal (Curwen 1934a, 124; Robertson-Mackay 1987, 46; Sharples 1991, 52) (Figure 4.7). Complete burials have also been recorded in ditch-butts, as at Offham, Whitehawk and the Trundle (Curwen 1929, 48; Curwen 1934a, 110; Drewett 1977, 209).

It has been noted before (Thorpe 1984, 49; Edmonds 1993, 116) that the human remains encountered at causewayed enclosures show less of a preponderance of adult males than some contemporary deposits in earthen long mounds or chambered tombs. Yet while the formal burials in ditches and in graves or pits inside enclosures are very often fully articulated women and children, a more balanced representation of age and sex groupings is found amongst the dis-articulated remains in the ditches. Moreover, these bones often occur amongst scatters of other objects and materials. At Staines, two crania, one mandible and part of a radius were found amongst two deposits in close proximity to each other in the outer ditch, which also contained 106 sherds of pottery, 121 flints and numerous animal bones (Robertson-Mackay 1987, 59). At Maiden Castle, the primary fill of the outer ditch in Trench II contained a group of bones, predominantly cranial, from one adult and two children, within a scatter of flint flakes, animal bones and a flint axe (Sharples 1991, 52). Finally, at Windmill Hill, an outer ditch deposit consisted of a child's skull, a cattle skull, cattle bones and horn-cores, and flints (Whittle 1993, 44). So while complete human bodies may have been afforded treatment which we could distinguish as 'funerary' in character, disarticulated skeletal elements might have constituted one form of cultural material amongst others. In the latter case age, gender and personal identity might have ceased to be at issue. This is not to suggest that parts of human bodies became part of an undifferentiated category of 'rubbish' in the contemporary sense. Rather, individual bones were used as a means of material signification, which also made use of artefacts and animal bones. All of these elements brought their own particular connotations and associations to the context of deposition.

While complex sequences of recutting may be specific to the enclosures, the deliberate and formal backfilling both of primary ditch cuts and of recuts provides a further link with the isolated pits. Possibly the most spectacular deposit of this kind is that found on the ditch bottom of the main enclosure at Hambledon Hill. This consisted of a mass of organic material containing animal and human bones, flint flakes and potsherds. So spatially constrained and apparently deliberately placed was this deposit that the excavator expressed the opinion that it might have

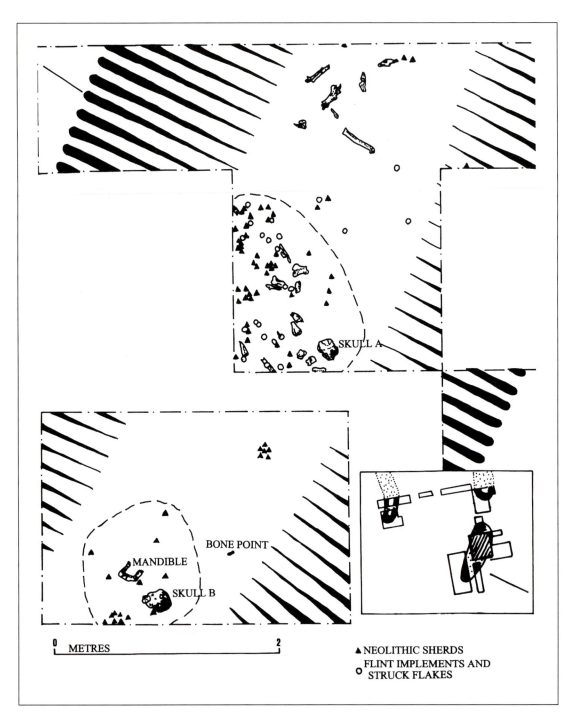

Figure 4.7 Deposits in the ditch of the causewayed enclosure at Staines, Middlesex
Source: After Robertson-Mackay (1987)

been placed there in a series of bags (Mercer 1980, 30). At a number of other sites, layers of organic and/or burnt material have been encountered in the ditches. At Robin Hood's Ball the richest of these post-dated the collapse of the bank, underlining the point that for depositional purposes it was the ditch which was of greater significance (Thomas 1964, 11). The ditches of the inner circuit at Abingdon provided a particularly instructive set of deposits. Here, dark, silty organic lenses containing a great deal of charcoal were interbedded with relatively clean gravel (Avery 1982, 17). These layers appeared to be made up of individual heaps roughly one foot across, suggested to represent basketfuls of material (1982, 17). Moreover, the excavator indicated that the organic material appeared to have been well rotted and composted before its deposition. At Briar Hill, lenses of material containing charcoal and fragments of ironstone, reddened by fire, appeared to have been sealed almost immediately after their deposition by clean layers above them (Bamford 1985, 36). All of this seems to recall Smith's suggestions that particular deposits of material in the ditches at Windmill Hill had been promptly buried (1966; 1971). It appears, then, that certain types of matter were purposefully placed in the ditch segments and buried. In many cases, such deposits involve material which had been burnt – the 'ash-filled pits' recutting the ditch at Hambledon (Mercer 1988, 96), or the scorched redeposited silts at Haddenham (Evans 1988b, 136). Great fires seem to have burnt in the ditches at Crickley Hill as part of the process of backfilling (Dixon 1988, 81). Causewayed enclosure ditches and contemporary isolated pits are thus linked by a number of similarities – the presence of a burnt soil or organic matrix, the deliberate deposition of material items, ceramic and faunal assemblages which appear to relate to the consumption or deliberate wasting of food, and the presence of human bones, particularly skull fragments. These similarities suggest that deposition in these two contexts was governed by a common set of principles, however general. Moreover, they underline the likelihood that the digging of pits and ditches, and their refilling, presumably with symbolically charged items and substances, was an important practice within Neolithic society.

Further, the opening of holes in the earth was a symbolic resource which could be manipulated in a number of different ways. These would include the delineation of an enclosed area in the case of the causewayed enclosures, but we could also note the existence of alignments of pits, often found in association with complexes of field monuments (Harding 1981; Miket 1981), and clearly involved in the process of orienting and imposing a pattern on a landscape. One such pit alignment at Bannockburn in Stirlingshire was made up of individual features which showed complex depositional histories involving silting, recutting, the insertion of stone linings, burning and filling with charcoal (Taverner 1987). The distinction between isolated pits, pit clusters and pit alignments was evidently not categorical. Bannockburn itself indicates a connection between pit alignments and 'pit-defined cursus' monuments like Inchbare, Kinalty and Balneaves Cottage in Scotland (St Joseph 1976; Maxwell 1983). In these cases, pits had been used as a means of defining comparatively large linear enclosures or pathways. Throughout the Neolithic period a number of types of monument were enclosed not by a bank but by a circle of pits. These would include some of the Dorchester on Thames monuments, where the pits were filled with a mixture of burnt and organic material (Atkinson *et al.* 1951, 119–21), or the Aubrey Holes at Stonehenge, backfilled with burnt soil and charred wood (Atkinson 1956, 27). The action of fire, then, seems to be intrinsic to the significance of these prehistoric excavations.

LONG BARROW DITCHES

A further context in which the deliberate deposition of material items has been recognised but relatively little commented upon is presented by the flanking ditches of the earthen long barrows of southern and eastern Britain. While a range of materials has been recovered from these features, there has been a tendency for only the most spectacular deposits to be acknowledged as having been deliberately placed. Thus, at North Marden in Sussex, Drewett has speculated that a collection of carved chalk objects in a ditch section at one end of the mound, and a human skull with charcoal and potsherds at the other, were ritual paraphernalia connected with the burial rite and later buried (Drewett 1986, 32, 49). Likewise, the complete ox in the ditch of the Skendleby barrow and the skull of *Bos primigenius* in that at Thickthorn Down (Drew and Piggott 1936, 82) are commented on as having been purposefully deposited. However, where clusters of knapping debris have been found in the ditches of sites like Thickthorn (Figure 4.8), Fussell's Lodge and Alfriston, these have been explained either as the 'testing' of nodules encountered in the digging of the ditch or as the consequence of its providing a shelter from wind and rain (Drew and Piggott 1936, 82; Ashbee 1966, 15; Drewett 1975, 126). These collections of flakes frequently refit to form complete nodules, without implements having been made and taken away (Edmonds and Thomas 1987, 196).

The way in which this material has been evaluated seems to depend to a great extent upon the preconceptions of the archaeologist. That which is spectacular and baffling to economic and ergonomic logic is 'ritual', that which appears more prosaic is not, even where it is recovered from the same context. In seeking to transcend this logic it is important to consider the full contents of these contexts in terms both of composition and of spatial distribution. A clear division of the evidence into the 'rational' and the 'irrational' is untenable in reference to the distribution of artefacts in the ditch of the long mound at Barrow Hills, Radley, Oxfordshire. Here, within a continuous ditch enclosing the mound, a strikingly formal pattern of deposits was located. At one end of the barrow the ditch contained groups of pottery sherds and flint scrapers, each discrete and barely overlapping. The other end contained four deposits of antler, flanked by two groups of human skull fragments (Bradley 1992). The spatial organisation of deposition thus appears to have been guided by the principle of the correspondence between, but segregation within deposition, of particular substances. Further analysis by the author of a number of other published sites confirms this impression: the cumulative patterns which emerge are ones of segregation within association. Thus, certain materials occur together repeatedly but may be kept separate from each other within particular long barrow ditches. These equivalent entities – artefacts, bones, substances – form the fundamental units of a material 'language', through which statements might be constructed contextually by means of association and separation, similarity and difference.

In brief, these deposits are commonly concentrated at the butt-ends of ditches, and the patterns of 'segregated correspondence' emerge from items either being placed in ditches on opposite sides of the barrow or at opposite ends of the same ditch. In excavated contexts, some of these patterns of segregation have been observed at a number of different sites. For instance, the bones of domesticated animals are rarely found in direct association with red deer antler: at Horslip these items were found at opposite butt-ends of one ditch (Ashbee *et al.* 1979, 214). Potsherds and antler, similarly, are often kept apart, as are antler and flint flakes, found in opposite butts of the south ditch at Kingston Deverill G1 (Harding and Gingell 1986, 11). In a smaller number of cases, potsherds had been placed in locations remote from objects of carved chalk. None of these contrasts was found throughout all of the sites studied, and it is not suggested that any of them represent absolute cultural distinctions between substances which must be kept apart in all circumstances. There may have been no fixed or universal set of oppositions determining the character of deposits. On the contrary, the material available to Neolithic people provided numerous potential contrasts and juxtapositions, which might be emphasised in particular contexts. As with both pit deposits and causewayed enclosure ditches, general principles rather than prescriptive rules allowed assemblages to be put together through an improvisatory practice

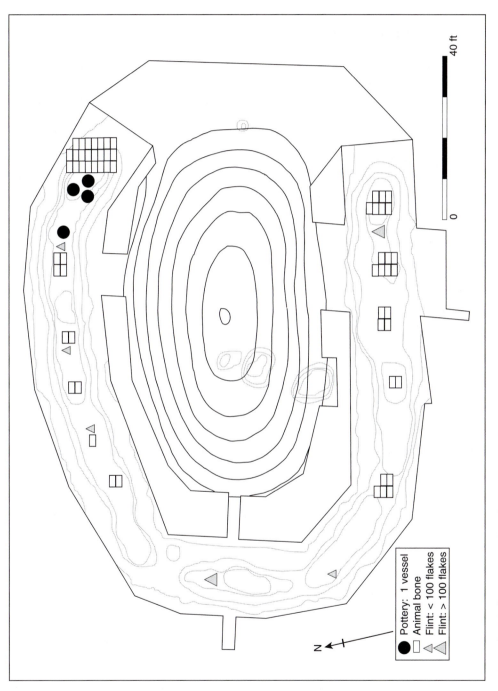

Pottery: 1 vessel ●
Animal bone ▢
Flint: < 100 flakes ◁
Flint: > 100 flakes ◀

N

0   40 ft

Figure 4.8 Thickthorn Down long barrow, Dorset: deposits in the ditch

which created specific meanings in specific locations. Long mound ditch deposits were the outcome of a creative play, or *bricolage*, which may have been a form of social strategy rather than the routine performance of a series of ritual actions.

These deposits in the primary silts of barrow ditches can be contrasted with material introduced at a much later point in the silting. A very widespread pattern is evident of burnt material, pottery, animal bones and flint tools and waste being introduced into the proximal butt-ends of barrow ditches in the later part of the Neolithic (Evans 1990). Almost without exception, the pottery concerned consisted of both Peterborough Ware and Beaker sherds, Grooved Ware being conspicuous by its absence (in contrast, of course, with pits). These deposits seem far less structured than those placed in the ditches in the earlier Neolithic, a decline in formality which is the opposite to the process observed amongst the pit deposits. This material might indicate no more than that feasts or other ceremonies were being held in the forecourt areas of the mounds, and material was finding its way haphazardly into the ditches, were it not for certain similarities both with deposits in pits and with recuts in causewayed enclosure ditches. Burnt material was being placed in the ditches, together with animal bones, pottery and sometimes fine material items (the jet belt slider at Skendleby, for instance: Phillips 1935, 71). Here, then, was another context for deliberate deposition, and one for which some kinds of pottery were, and others were not, appropriate. There is every indication that deposition in long mound ditches was one element of a broader tradition, and that this tradition as a whole was transformed as time went on, with the principles which guided it being changed in relation to new social realities. The significance of these changes can be considered once evidence concerning further contexts of deposition has been presented.

Henge monuments

The possibility that depositional practices in Neolithic Britain might have been highly structured was first discussed in a paper concerned with the henge monuments of Wessex (Richards and Thomas 1984). That this group of sites should have provided the point of entry to the question is itself revealing, for it is in the context of henge monuments that the formality of structured deposition was most pronounced and hence most easily recognised. The excavated material from the large henge enclosure at Durrington Walls in Wiltshire (Wainwright and Longworth 1971) provided the opportunity for an assessment of how objects were treated in a number of distinct contexts within a single monument. The purposeful nature of the deposition of sherds, stone tools and animal bones on these sites was underlined by the circumstances of their recovery at the Southern Circle at Durrington. Here, the concentration of artefacts at the bases of the weathering cones of the timber uprights was explained by their having been placed around the posts, 'possibly as offerings' (Wainwright and Longworth 1971, 25). Once it is accepted that the distribution of material culture within the large henges was created through purposeful acts, it is only a short step to arguing that these acts of deposition constituted a signifying practice, in which artefacts and other materials created or articulated meanings. What was placed where, in whatever pattern of association, might constitute a material 'message', lending a specificity to the location or to the activities taking place there.

Following this general hypothesis, it was discovered that the different structural elements of the Durrington monument – the Southern and Northern Circles, the enclosure ditch, the Midden and the Platform – each possessed remarkably different patterns of deposition. Pottery sherds were classified for the sake of analysis according to the presence or absence of bounded design elements and the location of decoration on or between boundaries, and the more elaborate permutations of these options were concentrated in the Platform and the post-holes of the Southern Circle.

Similar spatial and contextual variation was recognised in the numbers of flint tools, the parts of animal carcasses, and the relative proportions of bones of different animal species recovered (Richards and Thomas 1984, 197–214). At that time, the explanation provided was that material culture patterning would have shared with other aspects of communication which were highly formalised and repetitive (oratory, gesture) the role of presenting dominant messages which were effectively beyond evaluation. In this way, ritualised communication served as a means of reinforcing the authority of a powerful elite.

However, placing the analysis of Durrington Walls in the broader context of other excavated henges might lead one to modify this impression. For while the distributions of material items within these monuments frequently present striking patterns of spatial variation, there is little sense that all were determined by a formulaic and inclusive structure of rules. This depositional activity was formal and structured in the broad sense that it made use of the spatial possibilities presented by the architecture of the henges in order to develop patterns of contrast between contexts and segregation between materials. This implies a cultural order in which different classes of artefact or animal bone were marked by their difference from each other, but where no overarching classification existed to arrange this difference into a hierarchical structure. Human bones and animal bones were different from each other, but not necessarily any more different than potsherds and flint flakes. At each site, there are particular objects and types of material which appear to have been kept separate, or are restricted to certain areas. In this way, the character of the material world as a structured and yet continuous series of differences allowed particular contrasts to be established between specific contexts. In some cases we can recognise similarities in the ways that certain kinds of material have been used at different sites, and these may hint at some of the general preoccupations of the period, but there are also marked differences.

What does seem to be common to the majority of henges which have yielded appreciable quantities of cultural material in excavation is the use of a series of simple spatial dichotomies to order deposition. A penannular enclosure affords contrasts between back and front, left and right, inside and outside, and in some cases up and down, as well as distinctions between individual structural entities. This allowed the interior of a henge monument to embody a series of overlapping planes of classification, each of which might have been used to separate specific categories of material, and in the process to draw attention to distinct principles of differentiation. Because these practices drew together so many of the important aspects of the Neolithic cultural world (human bodies, animals, pottery, stone tools, monumentality, the earth) they provided the opportunity to re-order that world in microcosm. It is not surprising that each of these re-orderings should be unique: each, in effect, had a rhetoric of its own. But importantly, each made use of a relatively restricted set of elements, structured according to elementary spatial principles. Necessarily, the means by which the different elements of the classification were integrated was through the movements and dispositions of human bodies within the enclosed space of the monument. So within henge monuments depositional practice took on more than ever before a character which was performative, possessing a distinct temporal and spatial structure as a series of acts.

The elaborate distributions of cultural material inside henges are the outcome of ritualised activities which involved people moving from one position to another, placing items in particular locations. There is no guarantee that all of these people would have followed the same pattern of movement within the monument, and there are indications that the internal architecture of henges served to differentiate people according to the relative positions which they occupied (Barrett 1994, 18). Yet although the material recovered from these structures must represent a palimpsest of quite different acts rather than the imprint of a single set of repeated behaviours (Pollard 1995, 147) they none the less demonstrate very clear patterning. At the large henge of

Mount Pleasant in south Dorset (Wainwright 1979a), much of the character of deposition was influenced by the structure of the site as a four-entranced enclosure containing a smaller ditched area, Site IV. Clear differences can be recognised between the main enclosure ditch, which contained much undecorated Grooved Ware and bones of pig, and Site IV, where cattle bones and decorated pottery predominated (Thomas 1996a, 203). Throughout the depositional history of Site IV, concentrations of material appeared to emphasise the back left and front right areas of the ditch, and it is suggested that these accumulations can be attributed to a pattern of movement in which people entered the enclosure and turned left, processing around the timber circle in a clockwise direction (1996a, 203).

Pollard (1995, 148) recognised a similar pattern at Woodhenge, where a greater density of material derived from the post-holes on the left-hand side of the timber circle, where pottery sherds were generally larger but more abraded, perhaps indicating a greater density of trampling. This distinction between left and right was overlaid upon one between inside and outside. Worked chalk objects were found exclusively in the features of the interior, and worked bone only in the ditch (1995, 148). Further, the ratio of bones of pig to bones of cattle varied between the six different rings of posts, pig dominating the outer holes, cattle the inner (Figure 4.9). This pattern of cattle bones being more numerous in the centre of an enclosure and pig bones on the outside is very similar to the situation at Mount Pleasant, and in both cases the interior features contained cattle bones indicative of butchery as well as meat-bearing parts of the carcass. This might indicate either the selection of elements like skulls specifically for deposition, or the actual butchering of cattle (and their killing?) at the centre of these monuments.

The extraordinary variability of decoration on Grooved Ware ceramics meant that quite different aspects of their design could be used as the basis for establishing contrasting assemblages within henge monuments. However, as Cleal (1991, 141–2) demonstrates, one particular design element seems to have been used in a similar way at a number of different sites. Sherds bearing circular motifs, including spirals, were concentrated around the entrances to Wyke Down and the

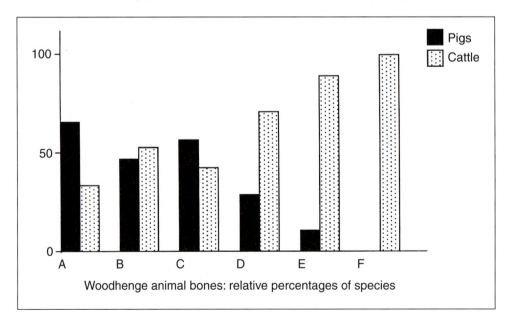

Figure 4.9 Woodhenge: ratio of bones of cattle to bones of pig in successive concentric circles of post-holes

Southern Circle at Durrington, as well as in the ditch terminals at Woodhenge. The small pit-circle henge at Wyke Down revealed a series of clear spatial patterns in the distribution of different classes of material. Carved chalk objects were found exclusively in the pits around the entrance and at the very back of the enclosure, while finds of arrowheads flanked the entrance. In the small recuts in the tops of the pits, pig bones were concentrated around the entrance, while cattle bones had a more widespread distribution. These distinctions seem to stress the polarity between the back and the front of the enclosed area, and it is suggested that the emphasis on this particular dimension can be understood as relating to the orientation of the monument, which points toward the larger and earlier structure of the Dorset Cursus (Barrett *et al.* 1991, 96). This is a good example of the way in which the deposition of objects might take on a highly localised significance, drawing attention to aspects of the immediate topography.

The Wyke Down pits were effectively small shafts, and their depth provided another potential means of differentiation (Figure 4.10). Given the evidence that these pits filled up quite swiftly, the contrasts between material buried at the bottom of each shaft, and that deposited later in the shallow recuts may be intentional. Carved chalk was found only at the bottoms of pits, and Grooved Ware only in the recuts. This use of the vertical axis to distinguish between deposits is paralleled on a much larger scale at Maumbury Ring in south Dorset. The Maumbury henge was composed of an ovoid circuit of deep shafts, each descending to as much as 35 feet (Bradley 1975). Radiocarbon dates from the site indicate that no great chronological distance separates the material deposited in the tops and bottoms of the shafts, yet these appear radically distinct in their composition (Bradley and Thomas 1984). At Maumbury, bones and antler of red deer represented 72 per cent of the assemblage in the top 15 feet of the eight shafts for which information from Gray's excavations exists, and 6 per cent of that from below 15 feet. The remainder was composed largely of domestic cattle and pig. Human bones were restricted entirely to the upper parts of the shafts, which also contained the greater number of struck flints. Potsherds, by contrast, were restricted to the lower parts of the shafts.

I have suggested that the patterns of deposition found inside henge monuments form the most developed aspect of a tradition which stretched back into the earlier Neolithic. Pits, enclosure ditches and long barrow ditches had in common the principal attribute that the context of deposition was created by digging into the earth. The shafts at Maumbury and their contents placed an even greater emphasis on the contrast between above and below ground, and something similar might be said of the uprights which made up the post circles which formed the focal element of many henges. The posts themselves mediate between earth and air, hidden and visible. In some cases, as Wainwright and Longworth suggested, objects may have been placed at the foot of the uprights, and have become incorporated into the weathering cone as the post rotted away. However, two recent excavations have indicated variations on this theme. At West Kennet, two massive palisade enclosures with smaller subsidiary post circles have provided evidence of animal bones having been packed around posts, rather than simply having fallen into the post-holes (Whittle 1997a). And in the case of a small post (pit?) circle, comparable to the British examples, at Knowth in Ireland, sherds of Grooved Ware and bones had been placed in very small recuts in the tops of the post-holes referred to as 'annexes' by the excavators (Eogan and Roche 1993).

So it seems that deposits in henges played upon the distinctions between inside and outside, above and below ground, left and right, back and front as a means of dividing up the things of the world. In some (but not all) cases these divisions were reflected in the deposited material itself. The bones of wild animals, antler picks, human skeletons, and individual human bones are sometimes restricted to the outer ditch, or the posts around the entrance into the central part of the henge. Much of the symbolism which was created and reaffirmed through acts of deposition seems to have been concerned both with boundaries and with the thresholds between them. In

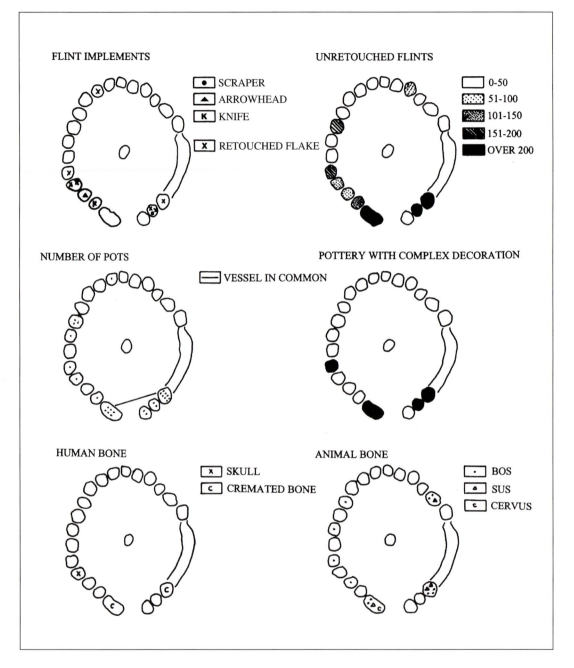

Figure 4.10 Deposits in the pit-defined henge at Wyke Down, Dorset
Source: After Barrett *et al.* (1991)

this context, it is highly significant that the classification which Colin Richards used to detect spatial patterning in the Grooved Ware at Durrington Walls was based upon two binary oppositions: bounded/unbounded and decorated/undecorated (Richards and Thomas 1984, 192–5). Each of the elements of the classification of material items which we can distinguish from the deposits in henge monuments seems to be concerned with drawing contrasts and establishing categories.

WET PLACES AND HOARDS

In the preceding sections we have suggested that the practices of deposition identified in a variety of different contexts were to some degree connected. It follows from this argument that they all represented aspects of a broader tradition of practice. However, the recognition that any depositional context one cared to mention contained the same set of items treated in the same ways would in itself tell us relatively little about the cultural categories employed by the people who put them there. This introduces a major problem concerned with representation: a deliberate act of deposition may be a means of presenting relations between things as they are, should be, or could never be. In a 'ritual' context, items could come into association which would never be mixed in day-to-day life, or could be treated in thoroughly abnormal ways (Douglas 1957). The recognition that repeated human actions have resulted in a set of archaeological evidence which is highly structured only really becomes interesting when the pattern can be contrasted with other, contemporary deposits, or demonstrated to have changed through time.

Precisely such a contrast can be recognised in another major class of Neolithic depositional practices. From the start of the Neolithic onward it is evident that certain items were deposited in wet places such as rivers and bogs. These consisted of a far more restricted range of objects than those found in pits, enclosures, henges and barrow ditches. Initially, they were restricted to pottery vessels and flint and stone axes. By contrast with dry-land deposits, the pots concerned seem to have been deposited whole, rather than as sherds, a feature which finds a parallel in earlier Neolithic bog deposits of pots containing food in Scandinavia (Bradley 1987b, 352). Finds of pottery in bogs and rivers in southern Britain are restricted to earlier Neolithic bowls and Peterborough Wares; Grooved Ware and Beaker material are entirely absent. Moreover, the earlier Neolithic vessels are exclusively carinated or shouldered bowls. Kinnes (in Coles and Orme 1979, 52), for instance, remarks that the vessel from the Sweet Track Drove site, while fitting into the Hembury style in terms of technology and finish, is of a form more characteristic of Grimston Ware. Similar vessels came from the Railway site (Coles and Orme 1976, 63), where at least one pot contained a deposit of hazelnuts. This evokes Nielsen's suggestion (1986, 242) that the very widespread distribution of the carinated bowl form in Neolithic Europe may be connected with an equally generalised set of practices involving the handling and consumption of food (see also Herne 1988).

The numerous finds of stone and flint axes from wet contexts (e.g. Adkins and Jackson 1978) have repeatedly been commented upon (Bradley 1987b, 354; Holgate 1988a, 126). Their significance as purposefully deposited items is underscored by their being larger in size than those found on land (M. Edmonds pers. comm.), and may be further emphasised by the presence of the wooden 'tomahawk' found by the Sweet track at the Drove site (Coles and Orme 1979, 49). Equally significant is the suggestion that continuity exists in deposition over a considerable period of time. There is a high degree of correlation between the areas where Neolithic axes and Bronze Age spearheads have been recovered from the Thames (Ehrenburg 1980, 5–6), while one of these areas, west of London, also shows a concentration of mace-head finds (Field and Penn 1981, 15). The types of artefacts in Bronze Age river and bog finds show a similar degree of restriction to that of the Neolithic. In the Early Bronze Age, halberds were commonly deposited in bogs (Needham

1988, 230). Of the items listed in Rowlands' survey of Middle Bronze Age metalworking (1976), those found in rivers and bogs are dominated by weapons: rapiers, dirks and spear-heads. This contrasts with the stray finds, which are predominantly axes, chisels and palstaves, and the hoards, which contain a variety of ornaments as well as palstaves.

If it can be postulated that throughout the Neolithic and Bronze Age a limited range of items was deposited in wet places, dominated by weaponry, the same degree of continuity cannot be suggested for dry-land deposits. While Grooved Ware and Beaker pits were undoubtedly contemporary with the first introduction of metalwork into Britain, none of them ever contained metal items. Equally, hoards of metalwork or stone axes are rarely found with other items: at most they may be contained inside a pottery vessel. They may be found beneath stones (Britton 1963, 311) or buried immediately below the surface of the earth (Forde-Johnstone 1964, 99), they may sometimes be located in pits as such, but animal bones, flint tools, potsherds and burnt or organic material seem to be generally absent. Hoards may often have been deposited in places of some significance, perhaps in relation to spectacular landscape features (Gourlay and Barrett 1984). This suggests that three quite different depositional traditions can be distinguished in the Neolithic of southern Britain: pits, hoards and deposits in wet places. Of these, the pit deposits seem to have declined from the later Neolithic onwards.

While Neolithic hoards of stone axes are known (e.g. Radley 1967), the practice of hoarding is one which seems to have escalated with the introduction of metal. The separateness of these traditions is emphasised both by their spatial discreteness and by the items judged appropriate to each. Burgess and Cowen (1972, 178), for instance, remark on the mutually exclusive concentrations of particular types of metalwork generally found in burials, hoards and river finds. Hoards of the major Early Bronze Age metalworking traditions, Migdale and Arreton, are largely absent from the 'core areas' of Wessex, the Upper Thames and east Yorkshire, where pit deposits are most numerous. The exclusion of metal items from pit deposits has already been noted, but equally striking seems to be the restriction of particular ceramic types to certain contexts of deposition. By the later Neolithic, Grooved Ware was suitable for deposition in the large henges of Wessex, while Peterborough Ware was not. Similarly, Peterborough Ware was appropriate for deposition in long barrow ditches and rivers, while Grooved Ware was not. Coming into this milieu, Beaker pottery was placed within a new and distinctive set of depositional contexts, being found in mortuary contexts and henges, but being absent from river finds.

COMMENTARY AND INTERPRETATION

In this chapter I have chosen to highlight certain depositional contexts, and suggest a degree of connectedness between them. This has necessarily been a selective enterprise, but it has allowed us to isolate aspects of the evidence which have often been neglected. It still remains to place these elements together and attempt to explain the historical processes from which they emerged. From the evidence of deposits located in pits, barrow ditches, enclosure ditches and henge monuments, we have suggested that cultural convention may have governed the items placed there, and their relative spatial ordering. The isolated pits, for instance, seem to have been dug specifically for the burial of particular materials, and backfilled immediately afterwards. These materials generally include a matrix which has been subject to the action of fire. While some of the items buried in these pits had been finely crafted (axes, bone pins), and seem unlikely to have been chance losses, others would not have been out of place in a domestic context. Indeed, it may be that one reason why these pits have so often been identified as the remnants of settlements is because their contents seem to us to evoke home and hearth. Yet if these communities were in many cases relatively mobile, the material concerned may derive from events of habitation rather than continuous occupation.

Some of the artefacts found in these pits may have been made for the purpose of deposition, and others were fine goods which had been in circulation for some while before they were buried. But a large proportion of the objects and substances involved was more mundane, and could easily have been selected from midden accumulations or the debris of communal feasts. In either case, two attributes of this material are worth stressing. First, as traces of the activities of the cooking, serving and eating of food and drink and of the burning of fires, the contents of pits were representative of some of the most fundamental aspects of human sociality (Lévi-Strauss 1969b; Hugh-Jones 1978). Second, items like pottery, stone tools and the bones of cattle were more than simply 'rubbish' in that they stood for a Neolithic way of life. If Neolithic societies were articulated through a changed relationship with the material world, it is to be expected that this would have been appreciated to some extent. In other words, if in the modern West artefacts are perceived as mere commodities which can be bought and sold, in Neolithic Britain material things were more evidently integral to social life. Their treatment in deposition might be expected to recognise this: in burying artefacts, people were placing something redolent of their sociality in a given location. The possibility that the deposition of material in a pit may have been a means of exerting an influence on a place is strongly suggested by some of their locations. Grooved Ware pits, for instance, are often found in or around earlier monuments. These include pits in the immediate vicinity of the causewayed enclosures at Etton (Pryor *et al.* 1985), Abingdon (Bradley *et al.* 1984a) and Maiden Castle (Wheeler 1943), and the cursus monuments at Lechlade (Jones 1976) and Sutton Courtenay/Drayton (Leeds 1934).

If depositing certain items in pits was a way of 'fixing' a connection between people and a place, this would be all the more true of a location which was surrounded by pits. Here, the act of digging the pit is itself a part of the transformation of place. With the more complex arrangements of space afforded by monumental constructions, it would have become possible to draw distinctions between items deposited in different locales, and with rings of pits broken by entrances it is possible to fix more closely a location and to choreograph activity so as to emphasise the transitional. Similarly, the flanking ditches of a long barrow, incorporating the polarity between two of the cardinal points, enable certain simple distinctions to be made between types of material deposited separately. In these cases no overriding message was being repeated: the meanings evoked by the materials involved were presumably highly localised. What was important was that the material repertoire of the Neolithic was able to serve as a 'material language' for categorising and evaluating the material world, and that in the process distinctions could be established between different areas of space.

It is arguable that the still more formal depositional practices of the later Neolithic used material things in more subtle ways in order to segregate and distinguish between people, places and things. Just as the digging of pits escalated, and the deposits within the pits became more complex, so the henge monuments of Wessex consisted of more complex arrangements of space which enabled still more distinctions to be made between things. These distinctions could be expressed as binary oppositions: cattle versus deer, inside versus outside, bounded versus unbounded and so on. But this would be to suggest the existence of a fixed cultural code, whereas Neolithic depositional activity seems to have been more inventive and performative than this would suggest. Rather than imposing a pre-existing cognitive structure on to the material world, it seems more likely that the available material things were suggesting contrasts and associations to people as they worked.

This set of practices involving the placement of materials in the ground can be distinguished from a variety of other ways in which people deposited material items. What marked these out was not so much a different set of underlying meanings, as distinct depositional locations and different assemblages of artefacts. The burial of items in graves, hoarding, and the deposition of objects in rivers and other wet places, all increased in their intensity as the pit/ditch complex declined. Significantly, they made available a rather different range of potential references and connotations from those afforded by the pit and ditch deposits. Increasingly, the items found in hoards, bogs and rivers were objects which were not elaborations of domestic artefacts, and which are rarely recovered from settlements. The eventual rise to dominance of these practices seems to have marked a major change of social and cultural orientation.

In this chapter a series of activities has been traced, gradually changing through time. However, it should not be overlooked that these traditions were maintained and transformed by the actions of people in the course of their lived experience. These depositional events were part of a broader field of human practice, doubtless elements of festivals, observances and feasts. It is the advantage (and perhaps also the burden) of the archaeologist to see these practices as dynamic phenomena, whereas to those engaged in the activities concerned they may well have seemed unchanging, unquestioned and eternal. At times, continuity will have been disrupted by innovation, or the contestation of accepted ways of doing things. Nevertheless, this should not allow us to lose sight of the way that this history of depositional practice, written as discontinuity, would have been experienced as continuity.

Chapter Five

Portable artefacts: the case of pottery

PORTABLE ARTEFACTS

Earlier in this book, current approaches which emphasise the symbolic and social significance of material culture were used as a means of assessing the changes which took place in the forms of monumental architecture produced through the Neolithic. In this chapter, a similar perspective will be applied to pottery, in the expectation that the pattern of development displayed by a form of portable artefact will be quite different in character. Perhaps more than any other aspect of the Neolithic archaeology of Britain, ceramic studies represent the preserve of a quite small number of specialists. This may be unavoidable: the study of this material requires both considerable technical knowledge and an acquired familiarity with a very large body of evidence. I would personally make no claims to this degree of immersion in the subject: my objective here is to distil what may be said concerning the social implications of ceramic production and use in the British Neolithic, and to set this alongside other classes of evidence. Pottery is only one class of artefact, and I could as easily have chosen to investigate stone axes, flint tools, bonework or carved chalk objects. However, pots have the advantages of being relatively numerous and thoroughly studied, as well as having been a form of evidence which was of critical importance to the modes of investigation of a number of different schools of archaeology. As a result, this material has been central to the construction of our understanding of the Neolithic, and has formed the backbone of a number of the canonical statements (e.g. Childe 1925; Piggott 1931; 1954; Smith 1974).

While the study of Neolithic pottery in Britain has always relied upon exhaustive empirical observation, this investigation has inevitably taken place in the context of prevailing modes of interpretation. What we choose to consider as a relevant feature of a pottery vessel is determined to a great extent by our broader conceptions of the events and processes which might be illuminated by the artefact. Thus something of the tone of Neolithic ceramic studies was set by Reginald Smith when he studied the assemblage from the pits at Peterborough. Smith (1910, 346) compared the impressed cord decoration and oval indentations on vessels from Peterborough and Mortlake with Neolithic pottery from Finland and Sweden. Moreover, he explained the similarities between these pots and the Food Vessels of the Bronze Age in terms of continuity of tradition amongst a native population driven into the west of Britain, and Ireland, by invaders from across the North Sea (1910, 351). Evidently, Smith's priorities for analysis must be understood within the emerging understanding that artefact styles might be correlated with ethnic entities in the past, and that the distributions of objects could provide an indication of folk movements in prehistory (Kossinna 1911; Trigger 1989, 163). The point here is not to berate Smith for presenting an account of Neolithic pottery which was driven by naïve conceptions of population movements in the past. Rather, it is to suggest that the study of this material has always been guided by implicit or explicit theoretical concerns. Changing the theoretical framework, we achieve a different and perhaps fresh interpretation, although this may be no more impartial or objective.

Smith's foundations were consolidated in 1931 by a pair of influential papers published by Stuart Piggott and Vere Gordon Childe. By this time Kendrick (1925) and Menghin (in Hoernes 1925) had both argued that British Neolithic pottery could be divided into two groups: an earlier, leathery 'Grimston Ware' which formed an element of Schuchhardt's (1919) 'great western family' of Neolithic ceramics, and the more profusely decorated Peterborough Wares. It is interesting that while Childe generally followed Montelius in seeing much of the cultural change in prehistoric Europe as the consequence of diffusion (Childe 1930; 1950), his discussions of the Neolithic are often dominated by migration and invasion (Childe 1925; 1940). His account of the continental affinities of British Neolithic pottery relies heavily on notions of population movement:

> The introduction of a particular ceramic technique is not, in early societies, likely to result from a mere interchange of goods, but rather implies an actual interchange of people.
>
> (Childe 1931, 50)

The comparisons which Childe established between British earlier Neolithic wares and the 'western cultures of Gaul', and between Peterborough Wares and Baltic cord-impressed pottery, thus implied two distinct phases of migration into Britain (1931, 52, 59). In his companion paper, Piggott (1931, 70) followed this line of argument, claiming that the division between earlier Neolithic Windmill Hill Wares and Peterborough Ware was sharp and distinct, and that intermediate types between the two were unknown. Each represented a separate population, with characteristic habits and landscape preferences (1931, 111). So the introduction of each of the main classes of Neolithic ceramics was characterised by discontinuity, yet, as Smith had argued, subsequent developments could be perceived as gradual changes within indigenous traditions:

> The thick, clumsy Peterborough bowls . . . stand among the obvious ancestors of the succeeding food vessels and cinerary urns of the full Bronze Age.
>
> (Piggott 1931, 73)

Childe and Piggott agreed that Windmill Hill pottery – and western Neolithic ceramics in general – had had their origins in some other medium. The 'leathery' surfaces of the vessels and their 'bag-like' profiles suggested organic containers stretched on willow hoops. The stroke ornament on rims and shoulders might then represent the stitching which held these frames in place (Piggott 1931, 81). This argument for the skeuomorphic origins of western Neolithic pottery would indicate a relatively recent adoption of potting by indigenous populations in Atlantic Europe, rather than a continuing expansion of 'Danubian' culture. The extent to which the culture-historic account of the British Neolithic relied upon influxes of population from the continent as an explanatory mechanism has been commented on before (Clark 1966), and may explain why the recognition of Grooved Ware as a distinct tradition was relatively tardy: there were no close continental parallels for this material. One problem which Childe's and Piggott's papers immediately raised was that while general affinities between the British and continental early Neolithic traditions were clear, exact parallels were much more scarce. Indeed, it was difficult to pinpoint a single continental origin for the Windmill Hill cultural assemblage as a whole, individual traits suggesting a range of different connections (Hawkes 1935, 127). A similar difficulty afflicted the notion of a Scandinavian community arriving in south-east England with cord-ornamented pots and founding a 'secondary Neolithic culture' by merging with disaffected Mesolithic folk. In practice, the parallels which had been cited for Peterborough Ware related to a number of different cultural groups: the Pitted Ware of the east Baltic in the case of indentations,

Danish *Trichterrandbecherkultur* (TRB) for cord impression. If a single group had migrated to Britain, they must presumably have toured the Baltic picking up cultural traits before they set off.

By the time that he came to write *Neolithic Cultures of the British Isles* (1954), Piggott had come to believe that some degree of continuity existed between Windmill Hill and Peterborough Wares. In particular, he argued that the carination, hollow neck, thickened rim and belly decoration of the Mildenhall Ware of eastern England might be ancestral to one form of Peterborough pottery, which he now defined as Mortlake Ware (Piggott 1954, 308). This Mortlake Ware he distinguished as characteristically British and insular, in contradistinction to Ebbsfleet Ware which had much clearer Scandinavian affinities. On this basis, Piggott continued to argue for an incursion from northern Europe in the middle of the Neolithic (1954, 315). Two years later, in her PhD thesis, Isobel Smith rejected the notion of foreign influence outright in favour of a model of continuous development from earlier Neolithic pottery to Ebbsfleet, Mortlake and Fengate Wares, and thereby into Bronze Age ceramics (Smith 1956). After publishing the results of Alexander Keiller's excavations at Windmill Hill, Smith reaffirmed this position, arguing that elements of Ebbsfleet form and decoration could be recognised emerging within the earlier Neolithic assemblage from that site (Smith 1966, 475). A relatively early radiocarbon determination from the type-site of Ebbsfleet (Burchell and Piggott 1939) appeared to confirm this argument. Another important aspect of the Windmill Hill assemblage was the presence alongside each other of pots with different fabrics and forms (Smith 1965a, 39), and since this time a number of large collections have proved to contain different components (Cleal 1992). Eventually, this would lead Smith to urge the replacement of a model of pottery 'expressing communal traditions' by one based upon trade competition between potters (1974, 111). It is interesting to note that Smith was Childe's research student, and appears to have paralleled his own gradual move away from strict culture-history and toward a greater concern with economic and social processes (Trigger 1980, 59; 154; Sherratt 1989, 178).

By the early 1980s, the pattern of change in ceramics through the Neolithic appeared to be one in which earlier Neolithic style zones (Abingdon, Mildenhall, Windmill Hill) gave way to exclusive, but spatially overlapping styles (Peterborough Ware, Grooved Ware) in the later Neolithic (Bradley 1982, 28). The issue was complicated by evidence for some degree of chronological overlap between different styles and traditions of pottery

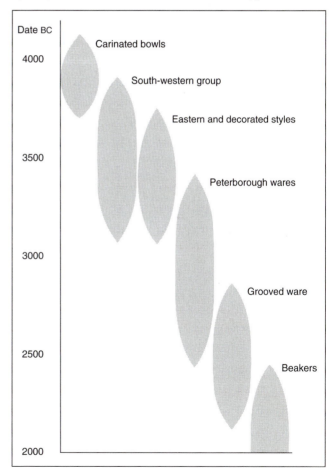

Figure 5.1 British Neolithic pottery chronology

(Figure 5.1), which challenged any simple chest-of-drawers model of cultural change. Bradley (1984b, 72) proposed an interpretation of these phenomena based upon Miller's (1982) discussion of emulation, in which each successive ceramic tradition is adopted by the dominant group within a society, and filters down to the lower orders, only to be replaced by another style as the elite seeks to maintain its hegemony over the rare and the exotic. In the context of British prehistoric studies this argument was revolutionary, since it presented material culture as being implicated in social strategies, rather than passively reflecting ethnic identities or playing an exclusively functional role. Where it might be criticised is in its implication that pottery vessels maintained much the same overall significance throughout the period, each supplanting the last in serving to express social status. In this chapter I will seek to argue that while 'pottery' is recognised as a bounded and stable category by contemporary archaeologists, it is possible that the social significance of fired clay vessels changed very considerably over the Neolithic period.

MATERIAL CULTURE, SYMBOLS AND TEXTS

Over the past two decades, there has been an appreciable shift in the way in which archaeologists conceptualise material culture, beginning with an interest in the potential role of artefacts in information exchange (Wobst 1977; Conkey 1978; Johnson 1978), and progressing to a concern with symbolism (Hodder 1982a; b) and the use of the metaphor of archaeological evidence as a 'text' to be 'read' (Patrik 1985; Hodder 1986; 1988; Buchli 1995). Perhaps by historical accident, these perspectives were initially rather formalist or structuralist in character (Wylie 1982), before developing a more interpretive aspect (Moore 1986; 1990; Hodder 1991; Tilley 1993). A consequence of this sequence of development has been a continuing tendency to present human classification processes as attributes of the internal structure of the mind, which are then imposed on to the external world. This point of view follows Lévi-Strauss in considering objects as pre-given entities which are slotted into cognitive categories (Lévi-Strauss 1966). In the realm of prehistoric pottery studies, Robin Boast seems to imply something of this sort when he argues that:

> Beakers are just pots. . . . What we must do is step back from [a] focus on 'pots as people' and look at the pots themselves. . . . We must first look at the pots as objects. . . . Objects do not inherently carry any social meaning, but objects act as a medium through which meaning is made material.

> (Boast 1995, 69)

This understanding that artefacts are in the first instance just objects, on to which meanings are grafted, is echoed in Hodder's (1986, 121) suggestion that material things have two separate kinds of meaning. The argument is that objects first of all have a significance which is functional or material, and second have a meaning which is concerned with the content of ideas and symbols. This seems to suggest a kind of stratification of meaning, and implies a version of the textual metaphor in which the object represents the equivalent of the blank page onto which a message is inscribed. However, if we accept that meaning is not a structural attribute of a thing, but is produced through an interpretive engagement (Barthes 1981), this kind of hierarchy of meanings is no longer tenable. The materiality and the symbolic significance of objects are deeply interwoven, and cannot be distinguished in the way in which they are experienced and understood. Rather than being recognised in the first place simply as material entities, and *then* afforded a symbolic significance as a secondary happening, artefacts are always experienced as meaningful things. Equally, while we might distinguish between those forms of signification which involve relationships that are internal to an artefact and those associations or connotations which spread outward from it, there is no sense in which these can be prioritised. Meaning emerges at the meeting of the two.

The opposition between material and symbolic meanings can be seen as one aspect of a more general binary structure in modern Western thought, which divides mind from body and culture from nature (Thomas 1996a, Chapter 1). As Ingold (1990, 5) argues, a consequence of this thinking is that we separate technology from society and fail to recognise that material things articulate social relationships (Kopytoff 1986, 68). Instead, artefacts are perceived as the product or end point of human activities, a manifestation of strategies and intentions which are conceived entirely in the abstract. An alternative is to picture societies as composed of both people and things (Riggins 1994, 1). Indeed, to become human at all, people must have relationships both with other people and with material things. It is hard to imagine a social being operating independently from a material world. This point is most clearly evident in non-Western societies where the circulation of objects as gifts maintains alliances and constructs social identities (Battaglia 1990, 6). Being embedded in social relationships, objects operate in ways which are similar to human beings, and they may come to have social identities (Strathern 1988, 176). Moreover, artefacts can become connected with the identities of persons and human groups, extending their presence into remote contexts (Munn 1986, 15; Battaglia 1990, 76; Mark 1994, 68). By contrast, in the contemporary West human beings are thought of as autonomous individuals who enter into relationships with others as a kind of contract for mutual benefit, whilst artefacts are alienated commodities. Both are imagined to exist in the first instance as self-sufficient things. However, in both respects this way of thinking is somewhat unusual, and is specific to our own historical and cultural context (Kopytoff 1986, 64).

Everyday engagements with material culture produce our understanding of the world, and these engagements have often been likened to the reading of a text (Patrik 1985; Moore 1986; 1990; Hodder 1988; Tilley 1989). In this respect, some particular characteristics of portable artefacts are worthy of recognition. Even in our own society, it is obvious that the economic circulation of goods is also an economy of symbols, which is facilitated by the advertising industry (Baudrillard 1988). Recently, cultural theorists have increasingly drawn attention to the dense symbolic environments constituted by shopping malls and theme parks, which produce an enveloping form of signification in which the onlookers themselves are rendered as signs to be consumed by others (Shields 1994; Gottdeiner 1995). These studies are important, but should not divert us from recognising that *everything* in the world is interpretable. When human beings transform some aspect of the world through their actions, whether by writing a letter or building a house, they change the configuration of material things and alter the ways in which they can be interpreted. But they do not introduce something of an ontologically different character into the world, as the culture/nature dichotomy might suggest. Even an entirely 'natural' landscape which has not been altered by human acts will be experienced as meaningful, since it is characteristic of humans to interpret their world (Gadamer 1975, 235). Material culture reconfigures a place, providing new possibilities for interpretation. Portable artefacts, in particular, can be juxtaposed and recombined in ways which bring particular signs and connotations to bear upon distinct events.

It has often been argued that our own culture stands out from most of human history as aberrant (Giddens 1981). One sense in which this is so is that we are literate, and this may tend to encourage us to underestimate the importance of material things in maintaining traditions and practices over long periods of time (Miller 1985, 11; Küchler 1987, 250; Llamazares 1989, 242). Objects can embody and trigger social memory, and their involvement in everyday activities as well as ceremonial events can repeatedly remind people of useful skills and accepted modes of conduct. It follows from this that artefacts can at once be instrumental tools which facilitate the operation of mundane practices, symbols which render these practices meaningful, and mnemonic devices which remind people of how to proceed. Taken together, these elements indicate that people work with things as participants in social projects, rather than simply acting upon them. The written word may provide us with new kinds of memory device, but it may also lead us to draw a more categorical distinction between words and things (Appadurai 1985, 4), and in the process cause us to believe that our designs are formulated in a cognitive realm and conveyed from person to person in language. All of this seems to be separate from the material world. As Richard Rorty (1989, 14) argues, this model of language as a 'third thing' between ourselves and the world enhances the distinction between subject and object, and obscures the character of language-use as a performative social skill.

The separation of words and things into separate realms is one aspect of Western modernity (Foucault 1970), and another is the process of alienation, objectification and commodification which renders material things as isolated objects, severed from social relationships (Miller 1987). As an estranged entity, an artefact becomes an object of contemplation: something to think about. But it follows that in non-capitalist circumstances artefacts can be indicators of the relationships which constitute them: things to think *with*. This may not have been precisely what Lévi-Strauss (1966) had in mind when he discussed the 'science of the concrete', since he was arguing that material things served as placeholders for abstract structural qualities. I am suggesting instead that 'thinking' can be a practice to which the material world is integral, rather than something carried out exclusively within the brain. Looked at in these terms, speech, writing and the manufacture and use of material culture are all things that human beings do, aspects of their engagement in the world. All require interpretation, and in the process can signify or communicate, with greater or lesser degrees of success. These different forms of discourse will be complementary, operating in different ways in different contingent circumstances, although they may employ related signs and metaphors. One form of discourse may render another explicable, or it may be possible to 'say' things through material symbols which cannot be uttered verbally (Hodder 1982b, 69).

Of course, the recognition that material culture is part of an apparatus which people use to construct meaningful worlds, rather than simply a jumble of things to be classified, does not necessarily make archaeological evidence any easier to interpret. I have suggested that artefacts are not the fixed points to which more ephemeral meanings and qualities can be attached. Rather, the network of differences and associations in which the object is embedded provides the very conditions under which it is rendered intelligible at all (Derrida 1982). Outside of this horizon of cultural intelligibility there is only abjection, non-recognisability (Butler 1993). Simply because a thing has a material existence, it does not follow that it will register as a culturally significant entity. This suggests that in order to evaluate any form of material culture, we must devise a type of analysis which attempts to construct an allegory or analogy for its past horizon of intelligibility. This, as I understand it, is what Ian Hodder (1986) means by a 'contextual archaeology'.

The enterprise of contextual analysis in archaeology is fraught with difficulties. In some cases, it implies no more than an eclectic methodology, in which the available evidence is subjected to both scientific and humanistic modes of investigation (Case 1973). However, Hodder's approach is grounded on the understanding of context as 'the totality of the relevant dimensions of variation around any one object' (1986, 139). Consequently, his contextual archaeology involves the reading of things through the device of placing them 'with their texts' (Hodder 1986, 124). This is achieved by investigating similarity and difference along a series of different axes of variation: temporality, space, depositional unit and typology. So an artefact is to be understood by placing it in relation to other temporally and spatially dispersed artefacts; by considering the kind of location and set of associations in which it was found; and by comparison with objects which share formal attributes with it. There is an immediate problem here, in that two different understandings of the word 'context' seem to be elided. Within the hermeneutic tradition, it is argued that a text or artwork becomes comprehensible within its own cultural or historical context (Gadamer 1975; Johnson and Olsen 1992). This is not the same thing as the archaeological context, which is a closed stratigraphic unit (Harris 1989). Hodder emphasises the sense in which context implies interweaving and connection (1986, 119), but the archaeological context might as easily suggest background, scene-setting or supplementarity. For Hodder:

> The symbolic meanings of artefacts are . . . not entirely arbitrary because they are bounded within contexts.

> (1992, 14)

What has happened here is that the sutured character of the archaeological context has been attributed to context in general. As Yates (1990, 155) argues, context is being used as a device which brings about closure, limiting the play of the chains of signification which extend outward from the object. The intelligibility of any artefact is facilitated by a network of relationships, whose signifying capability cannot be arrested by any kind of boundary (Barthes 1981, 33). And as Yates (1990, 154) points out, any sealed contextual unit is arbitrarily defined: someone has had to draw a line around it. However, while we might agree with Yates that there is no way to halt the endless running-on of the signifying process, so that the potential meanings of a thing are ultimately inexhaustible, we might argue that difference and relationality have a certain kind of 'geography'. While an object's 'horizon of intelligibility' will not be a bounded entity like an archaeological context, archaeological contexts might themselves be one part of the historical and cultural context of the object. So Hodder is quite right to say that it matters whether a pot is found in a grave or on a house floor. The physical location and the depositional matrix of an artefact are of critical importance. What is not clear is that this provides any kind of limit to the object's potential significance. This calls for a radical re-evaluation of context as something which is heterogeneous and unstable. Context is a network of relationships in which any definable entity is embedded, and which 'regions' itself around the thing. Thus those connections and associations which are 'closest' to the thing (in a non-geometrical sense) may be the most significant; but they provide no kind of limit for the process of signification.

In this way of thinking, there is no clear distinction to be made between the object and the context: each object forms a part of the context of others (Lucas 1995). Actions, utterances, objects and places continually recontextualise each other, and this can be seen as a part of the process by which society constantly brings itself into being (Barrett 1988a, 7). Material things may sometimes convey overt messages, but equally often they form a 'frame', conditioning the way in which verbal and gestural exchanges can proceed (Miller 1987, 102; Tilley 1989, 189). Things create the context for discourse, but are themselves 'read' and interpreted in a setting, and their potential readings may vary according to context. In structuring the context of discourse, material culture thus contributes to the creation of unconsidered or habitual attitudes through 'inattentive' readings. Material culture has a continuum of significance between 'background' and 'foreground' meanings. The ways in which items are deployed to build up a context, knowingly or not, may thus do much to give a natural or unquestioned character to essentially conventional arrangements (Shanks and Tilley 1987a, 112). As we have suggested already, the creation of a material context for society may contribute much to social reproduction. Most of the foregoing applies as much to stationary objects as to portable artefacts. But as we have also argued, what distinguishes the latter is the potential for 'play' (in both senses of the word) afforded by bringing artefacts into different configurations, in which each object is part of the context in which the others are to be interpreted. An apt example of this kind of practice can be found in Turner's study of the Ndembu Isoma ritual (1969, 39). By bringing certain objects into a ring of consecrated space, the Ndembu feel that they bring with them certain powers and virtues which they possess. By bringing these items together, the ritual makes the qualities which they seem to represent manipulable. So while architecture may provide the settings for action, artefacts can be orchestrated within these settings to provide more detailed and explicit contexts for social discourse. As Turner suggests, the play or *bricolage* of such deployment involves the evocation of particular meanings from a potentially limitless repertoire: the appreciation of a given configuration of artefacts again depends upon inculcation into a tradition of interpretation.

Just as with spoken language, material discourse is able to evoke meanings from multiple 'planes of signification' (Turner 1969) as a consequence of its ambiguity. The instability of meaning in language which Derrida describes, while it undermines the possibility of a definitive reading, actually makes communication possible. 'All forms of discourse consciously or unconsciously exploit the polysemic potential of language to transmit ambiguous, undecidable meanings' (Reugg 1979, 146). All language is consequently fundamentally metaphorical, relying upon ambiguity to provide untranslatable information (Hawkes 1972, 64; de Man 1978, 29; Ricoeur 1978, 143). The same may be true of material items, which may become associated with personal or elemental qualities through either metaphorical or metonymical connections (Ray 1987, 67). In this way material culture can act as both euphemism and mnemonic, pointing out what can or cannot be done or said by its presence. In contemporary Britain, for instance, the parliamentary mace metonymically related to the person of royalty serves as a reminder of required decorum in debate. Equally, material items may subtly alter the nature of given interactions by their presence. Thus Ray (1988, 220) gives the example of Igbo-Ukwu ware, made by women as skeuomorphs of basketry (associated with female marketing activities), thereby introducing a symbol of female economic power into male-dominated ritual contexts. Similarly, Barrett (1989) discusses the role of material things in signifying the actual presence of the person of the emperor in the Roman imperial cult.

POTTERY: DECORATION AND TRADITION

> Form and shape of pottery are often quite or very persistent.
> (John M. Tyler, *The New Stone Age in Northern Europe*, p. 159)

All of the argument that we have constructed so far applies to pottery, but ceramics as a particular form of material culture raise a series of specific issues. These are of critical importance here, since pottery was one of the principal innovations of the Neolithic period in Britain. The place of pots as an element of the Eurasian Neolithic 'package' has contributed to the argument that they are a diagnostic artefact of sedentary agricultural societies, unsuited to any mobile way of life (e.g. Burkitt 1925, 159; Childe 1936, 90; Hawkes 1940, 80; Stone 1958, 18). However, from an ethnographic point of view ceramics seem not to be restricted either to sedentary communities or to agriculturalists, even if the latter often have a wider range of vessels fulfilling more specialised functions (Brown 1989, 211–12; Hoopes and Barnett 1995, 5). As a technology for the preparation, storage and serving of food, pottery can facilitate the adoption of new foodstuffs (such as cereals) (Manson 1995, 72), but it can also enable existing foods to be used more intensively, over a greater part of the year (Ingold 1983). Pots enable more complex sequences of food production, the combination of stored and fresh foods, and the slow heating of stews, broths, porridge and weaning foods (Gibson and Woods 1990, 58; Jones 1996, 296).

While pottery is not deterministically linked with any particular economic regime, its adoption can have significant consequences. In Britain, there is little reason to believe that the manufacture of pots was limited to a particular season by climatic factors (Gibson and Woods 1990, 45). None the less, the temporal structure of potting is quite distinct from that of the production of other containers (such as baskets or leather bags). Vessels tend to be dried and fired in batches, and this means that production is episodic rather than continuous (Brown 1989, 222). So it might be that a definite place would be found for manufacture within the seasonal cycle, as Jones (1996) suggests in the case of Unstan Ware in Orkney. This has obvious implications for the patterns of mobility which might have been practised by communities. Potting skills are relatively difficult to learn, and might not be universal within communities (Hayden 1995, 261). As Vitelli (1995, 61) argues, much of the knowledge concerned involves an awareness of landscape and of the properties of materials used as ingredients and fuel, which might be acquired in the search for wild plants. In consequence, potting skills might constitute a form of socially restricted arcane knowledge, potentially distributed on lines of gender (see also Gosselain 1992, 578–9).

The past two decades have seen important advances in the study of ceramic technology. These have involved consideration of the susceptibility of vessel fabrics to thermal shock, the role of inclusions in overcoming thermal gradients and variations in expansion, and the suitability of vessel forms for different styles of cooking and other activities (Braun 1983; Steponaitis 1984). The application of these insights can produce impressive results (e.g. Howard 1981), but it may be unwise to consider the physical properties of ceramics in isolation. Pots are cultural entities, and in practice their usefulness for specific tasks is difficult to disentangle from their social significance (Hodder 1983, 215; Miller 1985; Gosselain 1992, 577). This may be all the more so where one is investigating the first adoption of pottery in a region (Marshall and Maas 1997). For this reason, the approach adopted here does not attempt to isolate technological and stylistic aspects of ceramic variability. Attributes such as vessel size and fabric composition might easily shift back and forth between 'functional' and 'symbolic' significance over time. We have already mentioned the increasing interest in a 'biographical' approach to individual artefacts, and such a perspective tends to draw together those aspects of object histories which have hitherto been kept as quite separate analyses. As Miller (1985, 173) points out, the similarity between the 'lives' of pots and those of human beings is one that has been recognised by a number of different cultures, and this is sometimes matched by comparisons between vessels and human bodies (Welbourn 1984, 20; David *et al.* 1988). Indeed, contemporary Western archaeologists routinely refer to the 'necks' and 'bellies' of pots.

Aside from the questions of why pottery should have been introduced into Britain in the first place, and of what relationship ceramics might have to other Neolithic innovations, two interrelated issues will be of particular importance in this chapter. These are the significance of decoration on pots, and the existence of relatively distinct traditions of pottery style which are comparatively long-lived. Of course, within culture-historic archaeology it was accepted practice to identify material traditions with quasi-ethnic human groups, and thus to assume decorative style to be a straightforward marker of identity (Childe 1950, 2; Binford and Sabloff 1982). Ethnographic work has demonstrated that in some cases decoration can reflect or assert the identity of an ethnic group or residential unit (Balfet 1983, 259; DeBoer 1984, 550; Gosselain 1992, 582). However, in other cases decoration has been linked to social stress (Hodder 1979), or recognised as a symbolic marker employed to bracket off defilement and pollution (Braithwaite 1982; Donley 1982), or as a means of making reference to distant entities (Ray 1987). These points argue against any attempt to generalise about the overall significance of decoration. Even a more general structural attribute of design, like the distinction between bounded and unbounded patterns (Conkey 1982; Tilley 1984), is likely to carry different connotations in different cultural contexts. For these reasons, the analyses presented here will attempt to isolate both similarity and difference, by considering contextual association and genealogical contrast.

Writing of the contemporary Shipibo-Conibo potters of the Peruvian Amazon, De Boer (1984, 557) mentions that all of the vessel forms and many of the decorative motifs currently in use can be identified in the Cumancaya ceramics of c. 900 AD. The stability of pottery traditions in Neolithic Britain is therefore not out of keeping with documented examples. However, given the plasticity of pottery as a medium, and the massive potential for making and decorating vessels in different ways, this degree of continuity is remarkable. One way of looking at this is to consider the reiterative character of tradition, whose reproduction is secured by a continual 'quotation' from the past: an active reconstruction of memory (Battaglia 1990, 10). Connerton (1989, 72) draws attention to the role of reiterated bodily practices in re-making memories of the past, while Gosselain (1992, 572) has shown how the identifiable stylistic character of pots may be owed to embodied skills which cannot easily be verbalised by the potters. None the less, given the potential range of variation that could have been generated by Neolithic potters, the main-tenance of the integrity of traditions over time seems to require a positive *exclusion* of particular forms, motifs, fabrics and decorative techniques. This point is further complicated by the way in which certain decorative motifs seem to have been shared by different later Neolithic ceramic traditions, seemingly without the distinctions between traditions becoming blurred. Some of these motifs were shared by other media (rock art, passage tomb art, carved chalk, metalwork), and all tend to be geometrical rather than representational – another point which demands consideration.

EARLIER NEOLITHIC POTTERY

The earliest manufacture and use of pottery vessels in Britain appears to coincide with the first widespread presence of domesticated plants and animals, polished stone tools, flint mines and funerary monuments, at around 4000 BC (3200 bc). These circumstances inevitably encourage an interpretation involving the arrival from the continent of an integrated 'package' of economic and cultural resources, with or without an attendant human population (Piggott 1954, 17; Case 1969a; Bradley 1984b, 9–11). However, we have noted already that it is impossible to identify a single continental source for such a package. Moreover, some of the elements of the primary Neolithic in Britain and Ireland do not appear to have existed for any long while on the continent before their presumed arrival in the islands. Examples include earthen long barrows containing linear, pit-defined mortuary structures (Madsen 1979), and plain carinated pottery bowls. This suggests less the straightforward transfer of an assemblage from one geographical area to another, and more some form of interaction between communities surrounding the North Sea and the English Channel, resulting in the formulation of new material traditions (Thomas 1996a, Chapter 5). Herne (1988) points to a group of fine undecorated bowls with a marked carination low on the vessel and a simple rim as representing the earliest pottery in Britain and Ireland. These bowls generally occur as small, isolated assemblages, often deliberately placed in deposits which may only include sherds from the upper parts of vessels and few other artefacts (Bradley *et al.* 1978; Healy 1988, 18; Thomas 1996a, 16). The pots themselves were to some degree functional, and often show evidence of heating and use for containing food (Cowie 1993, 15).

Herne describes these carinated bowls as material symbols, which, while potentially used for mundane tasks, wrought considerable changes in the cultural order of their users (Herne 1988, 26). In this respect, these vessels share with other innovations of the period the characteristic of actively promoting change. Hayden (1995, 260) and Marshall and Maas (1997) have separately pointed to the way in which pottery can be introduced to new geographical contexts for reasons which are social or aesthetic rather than strictly functional. Ceramics provide a striking contrast with traditional containers, and as well as allowing the production of new kinds of foods, they can be used to serve food at ceremonial events. Moreover, pots are breakable, and can themselves be deliberately destroyed after use, further drawing attention to the special character of conspicuous consumption. There are consequently strong indications that the first use of pottery in Britain and Ireland was as a prestigious, special-purpose artefact involved in discrete acts of consumption. Only later, according to Herne (1988, 17) did pottery find a place in everyday practices, with the emergence of plain and decorated assemblages with a wider range of vessel forms. To judge from the radiocarbon dates from the ditch of the enclosure at Flagstones House in Dorset, some of the earlier Neolithic bowl styles may have had considerable longevity, perhaps remaining current until c. 3100 BC (2500 bc) (Smith *et al.* 1997, 96). Of these, there is perhaps a case for according some chronological priority to the plain wares of the 'South-Western' (or Hembury) style. Radiocarbon dates for South-Western assemblages at Maiden Castle (primary inner ditch), Flagstones House (pre-enclosure pit), Coneybury 'Anomaly' and Rowden fall into the bracket 3900–3600 BC (3050–2900 bc), and those from Hembury are still earlier (although, being derived from charcoal, they are not entirely reliable). Several of these sites produced carinated bowls as part of more varied collections. The lugged, baggy or hemispherical vessels with simple rims of the South-Western group can be matched in northern French Chasséen assemblages (Whittle 1977, 180). This is not to argue for a wholesale transfer of Chasséen culture into south-west England, since the French assemblages contain a wider range of vessel forms, and other artefact types, such as lithics, are quite different in the two areas.

If the carinated bowl and South-Western traditions are indicative of a horizon of cultural interaction and interchange between Britain and the continent (which need not have been a one-way process), the other earlier Neolithic ceramics of southern Britain are more insular in character (Figure 5.2). The plain ware vessels of eastern England, which combine slack S-shaped or baggy profiles with heavy or developed rims (as at Broome Heath, Hurst Fen and Eaton Heath) are not easy to parallel on the continent, and seem to date to after 3700 BC (3000 bc) (Herne 1988, 15; Wainwright 1973, 9). Much the same can be said of decorated wares. Piggott's original suggestion that 'the development of decoration in southern England seems likely to be a purely insular phenomenon' (1954, 71) is probably still valid. It may be that individual decorative motifs, like the parallel vertical incised lines on the upper bodies of many Mildenhall pots, can be paralleled in continental assemblages, but it is far more difficult to match vessel for vessel. At most, we can recognise elements of a common 'language' of ceramic design and ornamentation which were drawn upon, elaborated and transformed to give increasingly distinctive styles in different regions.

Recently, Sheridan (1995, 8) has drawn attention to an interesting exception to this general pattern. In south-west Scotland and north-east Ireland, there are a number of decorated closed carinated pots which in some cases seem virtually identical to certain Castellic vessels from Brittany (see also Childe 1931, 8). These pots occur in very small assemblages, almost exclusively in funerary contexts. So it may be that from the start of the British Neolithic, very small numbers of decorated pots were used for quite specific purposes, well before the emergence of indigenous decorated traditions. In the south of England, it is arguable that the assemblage from the earthen long barrow at Fussell's Lodge in Wiltshire (Ashbee 1966) can be seen in this light. The Fussell's Lodge pots, with their early radiocarbon date, have been seen as evidence for a decorated style existing from the very earliest Neolithic. Yet the internal decoration, simple rims, and closed carinated vessels from the site are not typical of the Windmill Hill, Whitehawk or Abingdon styles. Further, the presence of decorated pots amongst the Fussell's Lodge mortuary deposit is quite out of keeping with long mound practice, which is generally dominated by plain bowls (Kinnes 1992, 109).

Most recent studies of earlier Neolithic pottery in southern Britain have argued for the coexistence of three distinct traditions: the plain carinated 'Grimston' or 'Eastern' style, the

Figure 5.2 Earlier Neolithic pottery

'Hembury' or 'South-Western' style, and the 'Decorated' or 'South-Eastern' style, composed of its regional sub-styles (Smith 1974; Whittle 1977; Drewett 1980). The problem with this scheme would seem to be that these three styles were not equivalent entities. There were not three overlapping provinces, each dominated by a single ceramic tradition. Setting aside the issue of the early carinated bowl assemblages, the south-west of England was dominated by a single style throughout the earlier Neolithic, but in the rest of the country the relationship between decorated and undecorated styles was complex, and perhaps cannot be understood at a regional scale (Figure 5.3). At many sites, both decorated and undecorated pots are present, and it has long been recognised that ornamentation seems to have been applied preferentially to vessels of specific forms, especially heavy-rimmed neutral or closed shouldered bowls (Piggott 1931, 78; 1954, 70; Whittle 1977, 86). Still more vexing is the question of the 'style zones' defined within the decorated tradition. Originally, four such groupings were recognised in southern England. Abingdon Ware, found in the Upper Thames Valley, had shouldered bowls with short necks and thickened or rolled rims, sometimes with strap handles, and sparsely decorated with stroke and pinprick ornament (Leeds 1927; Piggott 1954, 72; Smith 1956, 16). Whitehawk Ware, in Sussex, had open carinated vessels in a hard fabric, with long necks and shallow bodies (Curwen 1934a; Piggott 1954, 73; Smith 1956, 23). The Mildenhall Ware of East Anglia had shouldered bowls with elaborate rims, profusely decorated with dots, parallel incised lines and chevron designs (Piggott 1954, 73; Smith 1956, 29; Clark *et al.* 1960). Finally, Windmill Hill Ware in north Wiltshire had a distinctive form of 'thumb-groove pot', with a thin cavetto zone below the rim (Smith 1965a).

However, these sub-styles were generally defined on the basis of the characteristics of a large assemblage from a single site: in most cases a causewayed enclosure. Smith, as early as 1956, had perceptively recognised that these groups tended to merge somewhat at their edges (Smith 1956, 15). As more sites have been excavated and more collections studied, the distinctions between the separate styles have become increasingly blurred. As Frances Healy puts it, 'every decorated bowl assemblage has its own characteristics' (1995, 175). While the pottery had only been sampled at a small number of mutually distant points, it was possible to argue for a series of discrete style

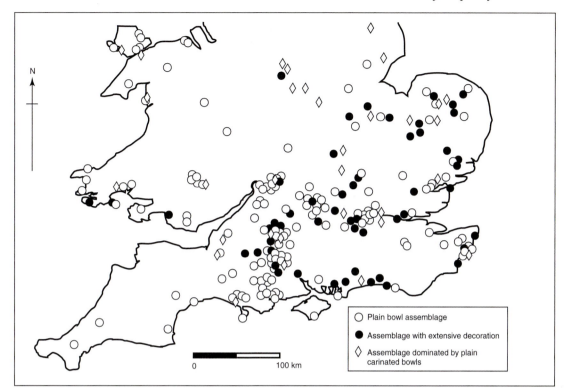

Figure 5.3 Distribution of earlier Neolithic pottery in southern Britain

zones. Increasingly, the material seems to present a continuous range of variation, without sharp boundaries dividing distinct styles. This is not to deny the existence of the characteristic regional variations in vessel form, fabric and ornament which were originally recognised, but it is to argue against the presence of homogeneous and bounded stylistic units. What this implies is that although potters from one community might have been able to distinguish their own products from others, earlier Neolithic pottery decoration was not actively used as a means of signalling ethnic difference. At the inter-regional level, this decoration would seem to have been 'isochrestic' rather than 'iconic' (Sackett 1973; 1986; Wiessner 1983; 1984), the product of unconsidered and routinised ways of working rather than an overt symbol of identity. However, I will argue below that ceramic variability was symbolically active at a much smaller scale, drawing distinctions between persons, places and practices rather than large ethnic entities.

In areas of Britain beyond the south of England, and in Ireland, there is strong evidence to support a generalised pattern of greater elaboration and geographical diversity through the earlier Neolithic, emerging from a background of more widespread ceramic forms (Kinnes 1985, 23; Sheridan 1995, 7). In the case of Scotland, Armit and Finlayson (1995, 270) present an argument for the existence of distinct styles zones from the start of the Neolithic. Unstan Ware, Beacharra Ware, Hebridean bowls and Rothesay/Achnacree Wares are each suggested to represent an emerging regional identity. This is not easy to reconcile with radiocarbon evidence which again places carinated bowls earlier than any of the decorated styles (Kinnes 1985, 23; Herne 1988, 20–1), or with the suggestion that Unstan bowls were derived from the carinated wares (Henshall in Ritchie 1983, 72).

In the post-war period, one of the most striking developments in the study of earlier Neolithic pottery has been the recognition that some vessels may have been exchanged over considerable distances (Hodges 1962; Cornwall and Hodges 1964; Peacock 1969). Gabbroic bowls from Cornwall have been recovered from a number of sites in the south-west of England, while the assemblage from Windmill Hill also included appreciable numbers of vessels containing oolite and fossil shell from the Bath/Frome area (Smith 1965a, 46). None the less, it seems that most of the pottery produced at the time was distributed over very small distances. For example, at Cherhill in Wiltshire, Trefignath on Anglesey and at a number of sites in Sussex, campaigns of thin-sectioning have demonstrated the local origins of fabrics (Drewett 1980, 26; Darvill in Evans and Smith 1983, 98; Jenkins 1986, 72). In Wessex, it seems that oolitic and gabbroic fabrics are concentrated preferentially at causewayed enclosure sites, while assemblages from pits and open sites are more likely to be of local origin (Sofranoff 1976). On the basis of the evidence from the causewayed enclosures, Smith (1971, 102) argued that gabbroic and oolitic pottery, stone axes from Cornwall and the Lake District, Portland Chert, and flint from Beer Head were all elements of a complex exchange network operating in the south-west of England. This may be so, but it is significant that these items are found largely within the enclosures themselves, and do not seem to have passed on to other locations in great quantities.

This sense that earlier Neolithic ceramic assemblages may vary according to context is supported by the evidence of vessel forms. Piggott (1931, 75) originally recognised that the various permutations of open, neutral and closed vessels with or without carinations gave a range of shapes which were differentially represented in early Neolithic traditions. Childe (1931, 47) noted in passing the total absence in Britain of the flat baking plates which are a feature of contemporary Chasséen, Michelsberg and Funnel Beaker ceramic repertoires. More recently, Gebauer (1995, 106) has pointed out that baking plates developed relatively late in the Scandinavian sequence. She argued that bread-making was not a feature of the earliest Neolithic, and that the earliest cereals in the region may have been used exclusively for brewing. In view of the reservations expressed earlier in this volume concerning the extent to which Neolithic communities in Britain were dependent upon cereal agriculture, the absence of baking plates may be significant, as may be the relative abundance of cereal remains at causewayed enclosures.

Recent ethnographic studies have drawn attention to the ways in which the shapes and sizes of vessels facilitate their categorisation, which may in turn determine the uses for which they are judged appropriate (Miller 1982; Welbourn 1984). In Miller's south Asian example (1985, 74), vessel form was shown to be only indirectly related to function. Differently shaped pots were used for distinct tasks, but this was not especially a consequence of their mechanical properties. Instead, certain forms were linked with particular foods (1985, 152). This should alert us to two points: variations in form may be indicative of differences in use and significance, but what we might judge to be the objective suitability of a vessel for a particular purpose can be only one element in our interpretation. In a significant article, Cleal (1992) demonstrated the variability of vessel form within a number of the best-known assemblages of earlier Neolithic pottery from southern Britain, primarily as a means of demonstrating the limitations of existing typologies. One point which is immediately suggested by this study is that the shapes of these pots were determined by a number of different factors. Function may be one of these, but there seems also to be a stylistic element in this variation, so that quite considerable regional preferences can be recognised in comparing assemblages.

Given these considerations, the analyses of vessel form presented in the first edition of this book have been extended, and Cleal's classification adopted, which divides pots into the categories open, neutral and closed, and simple, inflected or carinated. Cups (or very small vessels) were scored separately. 1,112 vessels from 93 sites were used in the analysis. Overall, there seemed to be

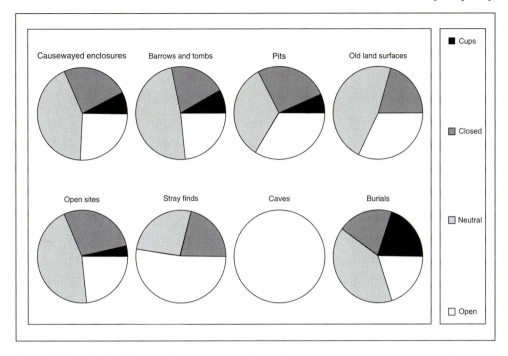

Figure 5.4 Earlier Neolithic vessel forms represented in various context types

some clear distinctions between assemblages from different kinds of contexts (Figure 5.4). Causewayed enclosures were dominated by simple forms, especially open and neutral pots, which could be argued to have been suited to the cooking and serving of food. Simple neutral forms were also common in barrows and tombs, but these also contained a high proportion of carinated vessels. Pit deposits and assemblages from the old land surfaces beneath barrows and other monuments were dominated by simple forms, especially simple open vessels. Open sites, which of all the contexts studied have the strongest claim to relate to non-ceremonial activity, contrasted with all of these, being dominated by inflected and carinated forms. Within these patterns, there seems to be a considerable degree of variation. Most notably, the composition of assemblages from causewayed enclosures was quite heterogeneous (Figure 5.5). The sites of the south-west, and also the Trundle, Abingdon and Orsett were dominated by simple neutral forms. Those from Whitehawk, Staines, Windmill Hill, Briar Hill and Etton had a wider range of vessel shapes. Part of this can be put down to stylistic variation: the South-Western tradition was dominated by simple forms. But over and above this, it appears that some of the more complex enclosures with more involved structural histories were likely to have more varied ceramic assemblages, which might be indicative of a wider range of activities being carried out at each site.

Another aspect of ceramic variation which will be considered throughout this chapter is the volume of pots. While it is possible to study vessel size by measuring rim diameters, the relationship between the sizes of rims and bodies is anything but a constant, and volume is far more likely to be indicative of the uses to which a pot might have been put. Of course, it is only possible to calculate the volume of a minority of vessels, since the technique requires a complete reconstructed profile. This will tend to skew the distribution toward smaller vessels. The analysis used throughout this chapter is a variant of what Rice (1987) describes as the 'summed cylinders

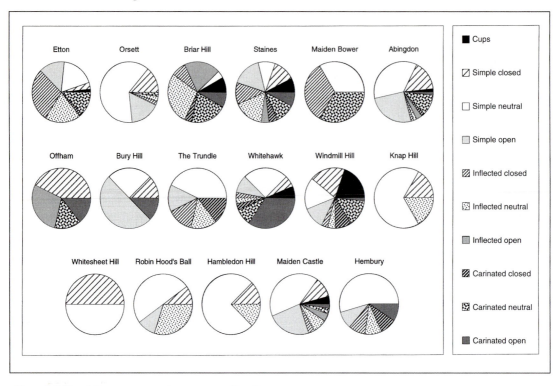

Figure 5.5 Vessel forms represented at causewayed enclosures

method'. This requires that the inner surface of the pot should be reduced to a series of cylinders, each of whose volumes can be calculated using the formula

$$v = (\pi r^2) h$$

In the analyses performed for this chapter, each pot interior was divided into a series of stacked cylinders 1 centimetre in height. This method contrasts somewhat with that used by Barrett (1980, 316), which reduces the vessel interior into a series of sub-conical geometrical forms. This latter is less laborious, but more mathematically involved: the difference in accuracy between the two is probably negligible.

The results of applying the method to 190 earlier Neolithic vessels are instructive in a number of ways. The histogram (Figure 5.6, upper) is dominated by a large number of very small pots, or rather cups, although many of these come from a small group of causewayed enclosure assemblages, and may not be entirely representative of earlier Neolithic pottery production in general. The fall-off from small to large volumes is quite gradual, with an appreciable number of vessels falling into the range of up to 8,000 cubic cm. Within this trend, there are no real indications of *quanta*: that is, peaks in the fall-off which might indicate distinct size classes. This continuous range of variation from small to large pots applies equally to undecorated and decorated vessels. This is an interesting phenomenon, given that decoration does seem to have been applied preferentially to specific vessel *forms*. Seemingly, those forms were produced across an appreciable range of sizes. In keeping with the broadly genealogical approach followed in this chapter, the precise significance of these points will become clearer as they begin to be contrasted with the characteristics of other ceramic traditions.

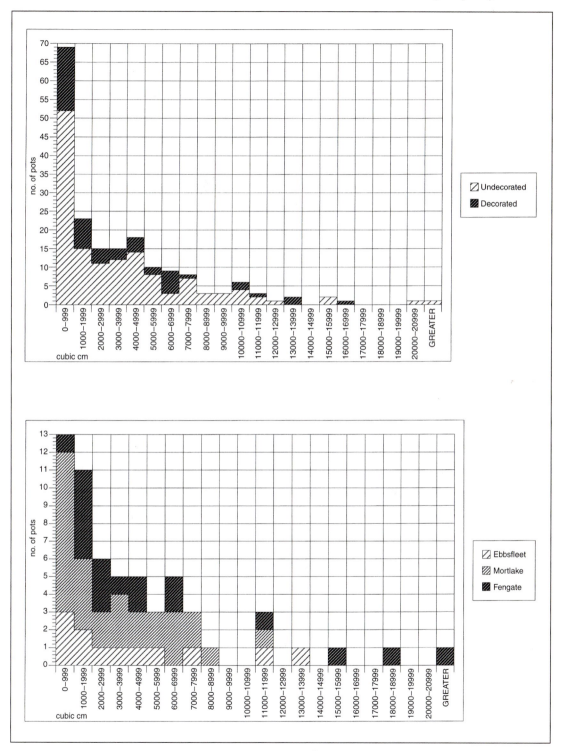

Figure 5.6 Earlier Neolithic (above) and Peterborough Ware (below) vessel volumes

PETERBOROUGH WARES

As we have seen, the relationship between the earlier Neolithic bowl traditions and the Peterborough Wares which succeed them has long been recognised as a fundamental issue. On the basis of vessel forms, decorative style and patterns of association, Smith (1956; 1966) established an influential sequence in which three successive styles of Peterborough Ware developed out of the earlier Neolithic decorated wares. Of these, Ebbsfleet Ware had marked affinities with the decorated bowls, having sparse decoration, relatively hard fabrics, and heavy rims which had not yet developed into a collar. Mortlake Ware had coarser fabrics, often with larger inclusions, considerably more profuse decoration and more developed rims, while in Fengate Ware the rim had become a collar, and flat bases had emerged, giving a more vase-like form. This sequence of change was envisaged as having taken place over a long period, since Ebbsfleet Ware was thought of as having been derived from earlier Neolithic ceramics, while Fengate Ware was believed to have taken some decorative attributes from Beakers, and was seen as ancestral to the Collared Urn series of the Early Bronze Age (Smith 1966, 475; 1974, 112). Smith also entertained the possibility that Ebbsfleet Ware had originally emerged as one of the regional styles of decorated bowls, perhaps in the lower Thames (Smith 1974, 112; Kinnes 1978) (Figure 5.7). In contrast with the other contemporary regional styles, Peterborough Ware demonstrated 'dynamic expansion and development' (Smith 1974, 113), which eventually resulted in its proliferation throughout England and Wales. However, Smith also pointed out that Ebbsfleet-like traits were present at Windmill Hill, where an argument could be made for an unbroken sequence from early Neolithic bowls to Peterborough Wares (Smith 1966, 477). In practice, assemblages which fitted Smith's criteria for 'early' Ebbsfleet (limited decoration, little cord impression, presence of plain vessels) were also present at Coombe Hill in Sussex (Smith 1956), at Whiteleaf Hill in Buckinghamshire (Childe and Smith 1954), and at a number of sites in East Anglia (Cleal 1986, 122).

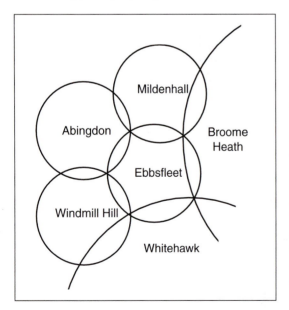

Figure 5.7 Earlier Neolithic ceramic style zones in southern Britain
Source: After Kinnes (1978)

The developments within the early Neolithic bowl traditions which have been seen as leading to the emergence of Peterborough Ware are seemingly quite widespread. At Spong Hill in Norfolk, Healy (1988, 71; 1995, 175) describes a number of earlier Neolithic vessels with coarse fabrics and deep, baggy forms, decorated with unpatterned impressions, which bear some similarity to Peterborough Wares from the same site. Many of the decorative traits which would occur on Peterborough vessels can be recognised in the various styles of decorated bowls, like the twisted fibre impressions on the rims of some Abingdon Ware pots. As far north as central Scotland, coarse, heavy-rimmed pots can be distinguished by the end of the earlier Neolithic (Cowie 1993, 17). All of this would seem to indicate that Peterborough Ware did not develop in a single region, but represents a general realignment in the ways in which ceramics were produced and used. Peterborough Wares in general seem to have had the same range of vessel sizes as did earlier Neolithic pots. On the basis of a sample of 59 reconstructible vessels (Figure 5.6, lower), there are indications of a less pronounced emphasis on very small pots, and hints of peaks at around 6,000–7,000 and 11,000–12,000 cubic cm. These might suggest the emergence of distinct size classes, but with a small sample such an inference might be premature.

By contrast, the variety of vessel *forms* was severely reduced. While some dishes, cups and hemispherical bowls are known from Peterborough assemblages, and the pottery flask from Liff's Lowe in Derbyshire can perhaps be attributed to the tradition (Bateman 1861), the overwhelming majority of Peterborough vessels are shouldered bowls. Within this category there is considerable variation, from Ebbsfleet necked jars to Fengate vases, and with some pots much deeper in the body than others (Figure 5.8). However, this does not negate the point that a Peterborough assemblage will tend to have fewer distinct vessel forms than an earlier Neolithic assemblage of comparable size. If we adhere to the hypothesis that Peterborough Wares emerged out of and eventually replaced earlier Neolithic ceramics, then it seems that one element of the original assemblage was chosen at the expense of others and elaborated through the addition of profuse decoration. Following the perspective developed in the earlier part of this chapter, this indicates some fundamental change in the practices in which ceramics were involved. Whatever activities pots were now used for demanded that all vessels should be decorated. The original arguments for Peterborough Wares being associated with a separate population with different land use preferences are now less convincing, since there is by now an overall distribution very similar to that of earlier Neolithic wares (Figure 5.9). In southern Britain, Peterborough Ware seems only to be sparsely distributed in the south-western peninsula, and this may be simply a consequence of more limited investigation.

Figure 5.8 Peterborough Ware

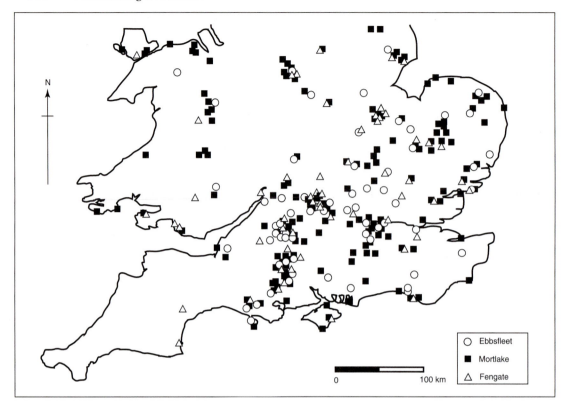

Figure 5.9 Distribution of Peterborough Wares in southern Britain

All of the existing arguments regarding the origins and development of Peterborough Ware are, however, thrown into confusion by recent radiocarbon evidence. Dates from carbonised residues on Fengate and 'Mortlake/Fengate hybrid' vessels from Brynderwen and Horton have been surprisingly early (3350–2904 BC and 3495–2925 BC respectively, combined dates), and effectively collapse the internal sequence of Peterborough development (Gibson and Kinnes 1997, 70). It is no longer easy to support a model of gradual elaboration of rim form and decoration, even if the origin of Peterborough Wares within the indigenous bowl traditions is not in doubt. The chronology could now indicate that the emergence of Peterborough Wares was quite abrupt, and that they overlapped with the plain bowl traditions for several generations. This point, and the coexistence of three more or less distinct sub-styles of Peterborough Ware (see p. 111), is something whose significance now demands consideration. It is often tempting to revert to a neat 'chest of drawers' chronology like Christian Thomsen's variant of the Three Age system, in which artefactual traditions give way to one another in an obligingly orderly manner. This would certainly render pottery more useful as a chronological indicator. However, real life is often more messy and complicated, and it might be unwise to accept a picture of the instantaneous replacement of one style by another without an explicit discussion of the social and cultural processes involved. If, as the new dates suggest, Peterborough Wares were in use by the later fourth millennium BC (c. 2600 bc), it is at least interesting that they are absent from both the early phases of Stonehenge and the ditches of the Flagstones House enclosure. At the latter site, plain bowls were evidently still in use at c. 3100 BC (Smith *et al.* 1997, 92), while there are also indications of a late date for the plain bowl assemblage beneath the bank at Mount Pleasant

(Wainwright 1979a, 7). It may simply be that Peterborough Wares spread very slowly, with some communities perhaps resisting change in their ceramic repertoire. But it seems more likely that the new style was used in some contexts and not others from the start.

At the other end of its currency, Gibson and Kinnes (1997, 67) argue that Peterborough Ware might have gone out of use before 2500 BC. This requires a somewhat parsimonious reading of the available radiocarbon dates, including the dismissal of several outliers at the younger end of the sequence. Strictly speaking this is the correct route to follow, but as Gibson and Kinnes point out, the result conflicts with other aspects of the evidence. Longworth's (1961; 1984) argument that aspects of the decoration of the Primary Series of Collared Urns can be derived from Peterborough Wares, and similar suggestions for the origins of Food Vessels (Newbiggin 1937, 202; Burgess 1974, 175) would certainly be compromised by a tight chronological horizon of Peterborough Ware use. Is it possible that particular rim forms, vessel shapes, decorative media and motifs lay 'dormant' in the final Neolithic to re-emerge in the Early Bronze Age? Given that Fengate Ware must now be seen as having originated in the mid-Neolithic, Kinnes and Gibson ask how it can be 'possible that such a specific and detailed ceramic style lasted for several centuries?' (1997, 70). The Shipibo-Conibo example (see p. 98) demonstrates the potential longevity of such traditions, as does the evident continuity of Zuni decorative structure from prehistory to the present (Hardin 1984, 584). Whether a particular pot can be unambiguously dated by radiocarbon depends entirely upon the context in which it is deposited, and whether it is associated with dateable organic material. It is worth considering whether the relatively tight horizon within which dates for Peterborough Ware can be securely identified is itself a function of the kinds of activity producing the archaeological record. The overall spread of dates associated with Peterborough Ware is rather wider, and presents an unbroken curve with obvious outliers (Figure 5.10). In this connection, it may be significant that Gibson and Kinnes rejected most dates from mixed assemblages: these might result from residuality or contamination, but they might equally result from the concurrent use of distinct material traditions.

The contextual evidence for the longevity of Peterborough Ware is complicated by a number of factors. It has been argued that Peterborough Ware and Grooved Ware were used in different circumstances, and perhaps even deliberately kept separate (Thorpe and Richards 1984; and see p. 121). This would tend to minimise the number of contexts in which the two occur together, but the argument for a rapid replacement of one style by the other would predict the same material outcome. There are also limited examples of the co-occurrence of Grooved Ware and Beakers, and these are often loose associations which might be the consequence of the re-use of a particular location. Of course, this may be significant in itself (see p. 123). In practice, there are some sites where Peterborough Ware and Grooved Ware can be found in firm association. For example, at Barholm, Pit 10 contained both Grooved Ware and Mortlake sherds (Simpson *et al.* 1993, 10). Pit F1002 at Gravelly Guy in Oxfordshire contained 24 sherds of Mortlake Ware and 11 sherds of Clacton-style Grooved Ware (Barclay *et al.* 1995, 88). In the Rudston area of east Yorkshire, Grooved Ware sherds have come from pits containing largely Peterborough assemblages (Manby 1975, 38–44). And at Firtree Field on Cranborne Chase, two Peterborough Ware sherds were recovered from a group of Grooved Ware pits (Barrett *et al.* 1991, 79). As Cleal (1991, 135) argues, it is conceivable that these sherds were residual, but the evident formality and control of deposition in these pits would render their inclusion by chance unlikely. At most it could be argued that the sherds had been curated in some way, perhaps recovered from middens because of their recognised antiquity. Such an argument might constitute special pleading, and it is perhaps better to allow the possibility of some degree of chronological overlap between Peterborough Ware and Grooved Ware.

The early dates for Fengate Ware indicate that rather than being successive stages in an evolutionary sequence, the different sub-styles of Peterborough Ware were equivalent or alternative

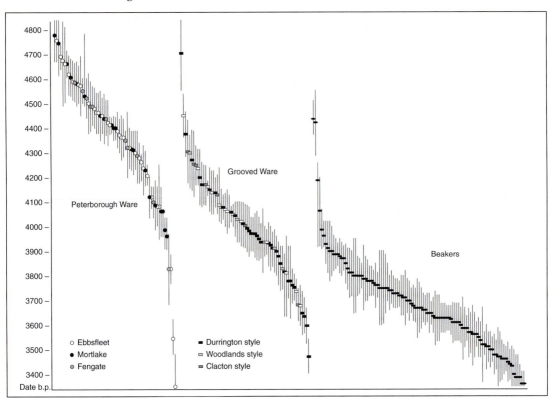

Figure 5.10 Radiocarbon dates for Peterborough Wares, Grooved Ware and Beakers (uncalibrated dates b.p.)

variations on a cultural theme. In some cases, as with the mixed Mortlake and Fengate assemblage from the ditch of the Dorset Cursus at Chalkpit Field (Cleal 1991, 149), two styles are present alongside each other, but in most cases only one style is found on a given site. Over and above this variation, there are growing indications of regional diversity. In Wales, Gibson (1995, 30) notes that while the Ebbsfleet/Mortlake/Fengate classification holds, there is a preference for bird-bone impressions and a limited use of linear motifs. In the north, the classification begins to break down. In Yorkshire there are characteristic Ebbsfleet and Mortlake vessels, but also a regional style which Manby (1967, 89) refers to as 'Rudston Ware'. These pots have a weak neck and shoulder and a distinctive T-rim, which is similar to that found on some Food Vessels (1967, 90). Manby (in Abramson 1996, 45) suggests that this style was derived from Ebbsfleet Ware, emerging alongside Mortlake and Fengate Ware. In southern Scotland and the Borders, assemblages from Meldon Bridge, Glenluce, Brackmont Mill, Thirlings and Ford are highly idiosyncratic, and each seems to demand definition as a separate style (McInnes 1969, 22; Smith 1974, 117; Gibson and Woods 1990, 62). Cowie (1993, 21) argues that the Scottish biconical impressed wares should be recognised as a development parallel to, but separate from, Peterborough Ware in England. However, if we identify the emergence of Peterborough Wares as a generalised and internally variable process, rather than the spread of an homogeneous tradition from a single area of origin, the distinction is less profound. Yet if the appearance of heavy-rimmed, highly decorated coarsewares is a single process it seems to have followed a different course in the north and the south. The southern assemblages form a number of distinct yet spatially overlapping styles, while those in the north suggest mutually exclusive regional groupings. This can be taken to indicate that pottery was being used in different ways in the two areas, and it may be that in the north decorated artefacts were involved in the definition of local identities.

The structure of decoration on Peterborough Wares was quite similar to that on earlier Neolithic vessels. The rim and upper part of the body exterior are often decorated, and the inside of the upper part of the vessel and the neck cavetto sometimes are. While Peterborough Wares used new decorative media, such as twisted and whipped cord and bird-bone impressions, and new motifs like diagonals and herringbone designs, these elaborate the basic format of earlier Neolithic ceramic decoration: the repetition of forms to fill an undivided space, presumably starting from the top of the vessel.

While we must always be concerned that the distinctions between Ebbsfleet, Mortlake and Fengate Wares are more apparent than real, and result from the way in which archaeologists have divided up a continuous range of stylistic variation, it is significant that the three sub-styles appear to have been used (or at least deposited) in distinct ways (Figure 5.11, upper). Ebbsfleet Ware is common in long mounds and in land surfaces beneath monuments, but scarce in pit deposits. Mortlake Ware is often found in ring ditches, long mounds, cursus monuments, rivers, caves, and as stray finds. Fengate Ware has a much more restricted distribution, particularly concentrated in pits. All three styles are found at open sites and causewayed enclosures, and it is notable that Peterborough Wares are often located as secondary deposits on already ancient mortuary sites. This is surprising when it is compared with the scarcity of Peterborough pottery as an accompaniment for burials. Aside from the equivocal Liff's Low flask, there are sherds of Peterborough Ware associated with a single burial at Elf Howe (Manby 1956, 5) (although this attribution has been questioned: Thorpe and Richards 1984, 72) and with round mounds on Handley Hill (Barrett *et al.* 1991, 85). Yet in neither case is it easy to make an argument for the pottery representing grave goods, as opposed to residual material or pots used in funerary performances. This indicates a preoccupation not with the recently deceased but with the ancestral dead, and with the veneration of places whose significance lay in the past. Also of note is the deposition of Peterborough vessels in wet places, most notably the lower reaches of the Thames (numerous examples in Smith 1924; Smith 1956). This again suggests a continuity of practice with the earlier Neolithic: Peterborough Wares are the only later Neolithic/Early Bronze Age ceramics frequently located in rivers and bogs, while the carinated vessels from the Sweet track (Coles and Orme 1979, 52) and the decorated Mildenhall shouldered bowl from the river Nene at Milton Ferry, Huntingdonshire (Cambridge University Museum) indicate that this vessel form had been appropriate to this kind of deposition in the earlier Neolithic.

This theme of continuity with the past in depositional practice connects with the way in which Peterborough vessel forms and decoration draw upon early Neolithic prototypes. Furthermore, in some areas there is considerable similarity between earlier Neolithic and Peterborough fabrics (Cleal 1995, 193). While Peterborough fabrics are generally coarser, there are indications that the same geological resources were being used in pottery manufacture. And just as much of the stylistic variation in earlier Neolithic pottery seems to have been significant at a very small spatial scale, so Peterborough decoration seems distinctive within rather than between assemblages. Any attempt to discriminate between the range of motifs and decorative techniques employed at different sites seems inconclusive, but within sites the variations are often striking. As we have seen, at Heathrow the decoration on the pottery from each of the two pits was entirely distinct (see Chapter 4 above). As with earlier Neolithic decorated vessels, I would argue that the ornamentation on Peterborough Ware had no specific underlying meaning, but that the *difference* that was generated through the use of a wide range of decorative motifs and media allowed separate contexts, locations, activities and persons to be differentiated.

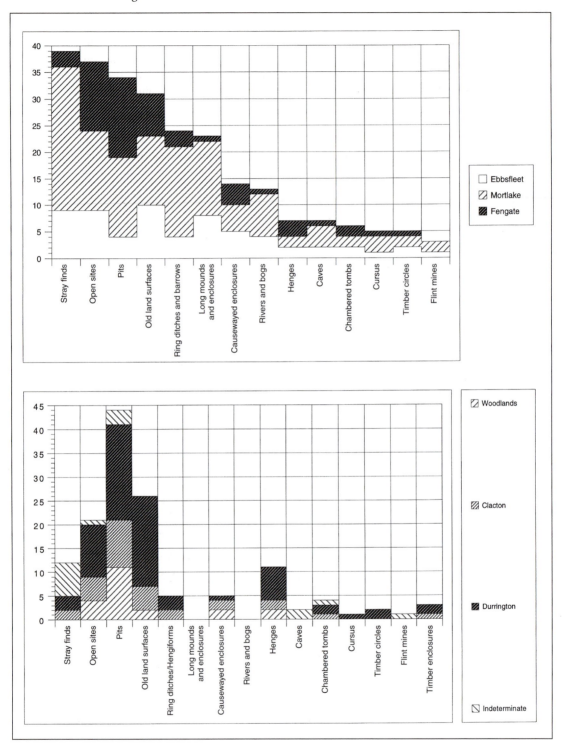

Figure 5.11 Peterborough Wares (above) and Grooved Ware (below): contexts of deposition

GROOVED WARE

While Peterborough Wares suggest themes of continuity and elaboration in relation to the earlier Neolithic traditions which preceded them, the emergence of Grooved Ware marked a profound break in the ceramic sequence of southern Britain. Grooved Ware was originally identified on the basis of its flat-based 'flower-pot' and bucket forms, upright rims, and profuse decoration executed in (it seemed at first) a limited range of media (Warren *et al.* 1936, 191) (Figure 5.12). The flat bases have sometimes been taken as an indication that Grooved Ware pots were intended to be set on flat surfaces, but it is equally likely that they facilitated the fashioning of a tall, straight-sided vessel (van der Leeuw 1976, 86). Nothing in the tradition resembles the shouldered and hemispherical bowls which had dominated southern British assemblages for more than a millennium (Wainwright and Longworth 1971, 244). The widespread distribution of Grooved Ware prompted Piggott (1954, 321) to argue for the existence of a 'Rinyo-Clacton culture', although Clarke (1970, 269) was later to contend that the northern and southern 'provinces' of this culture were actually parallel but independent developments. For Clarke, southern Grooved Ware was a specialised mutation of Fengate Ware, emerging under Southern Beaker influence. However, it is not merely the vessel shape and decoration which indicate discontinuity with existing ceramic traditions. The composition of Grooved Ware fabrics is quite distinct from either earlier Neolithic or Peterborough Wares, being less gritty, yet making extensive use of grog and shell (Smith 1956, 190; Cleal *et al.* 1994, 445; Cleal 1995, 193). Within a given assemblage, the fabrics may vary considerably (e.g. Pryor 1978, 91), and Cleal (1995, 150) notes the presence of a series of singular recipes for fillers in southern British Grooved Ware. Individual vessels may thus be quite distinctive, and the significance afforded to particular pots may also be reflected in the prevalence of repair-holes in Grooved Ware (Cleal 1988). In some cases, it seems that broken pots had been repaired, even though they might have remained functionally imperfect as containers.

Figure 5.12 Grooved Ware

In terms of vessel size, Grooved Ware stands out from any other ceramic tradition of the southern British Neolithic (Figure 5.13, upper). While the volumes of other styles peak at under 2,000 cubic cm, a large proportion of Grooved Ware pots fall into the 3,000 to 5,000 cubic cm interval. Moreover, there is an appreciable spread of pots with volumes of up to 20,000 cubic cm, and a few of up to 40,000 cubic cm. In this respect, the extremely large vessels from the henge at Durrington Walls (Wainwright and Longworth 1971, 82) do not seem to be exceptional. Indeed, at Balfarg Riding School some pots were so large that mats and baskets seem to have been used as wraps in their fashioning, leaving behind residual impressions in the clay (Henshall in Barclay and Russell-White 1993, 102). This evidence indicates a significant change in the way in which pottery vessels were being used, a proposition which finds some support in the suggestion that Grooved Ware was used in communal feasting, especially within henge monuments (Richards and Thomas 1984). Since larger vessels are less likely to be reconstructable than small, it is probable that the admittedly small sample (45) of vessel volumes gives an accurate impression that Grooved Ware was used to prepare or serve food in different ways than had been common hitherto. With the larger pots in particular, it seems likely that vessels were not intended to serve a single person.

In her thesis, Isobel Smith pointed out that southern British Grooved Ware appeared to fall into three relatively distinct sub-styles: Clacton, Woodlands and Woodhenge (later renamed as Durrington Walls) (1956, 192). While at the time these three seemed both stylistically and geographically distinct from the Rinyo style of Orkney, subsequent finds have extended the distribution of the 'southern' styles into Scotland, and have demonstrated a sharing of traits between styles (Wainwright and Longworth 1971, 243). The characteristics of the different sub-styles are easier to list than to explain. Clacton-style vessels are generally simple tubs with vertical or splayed sides and simple rims with an internal groove. They are decorated with grooved lines, dot-filled lozenges and triangles, areas of oval impressions, and multiple chevrons. Applied decoration is rare, and cord impressions generally absent (Smith 1956, 192; Wainwright and Longworth 1971, 237). Woodlands-style pots are often smaller, with thinner walls. They are generally bowls and tubs with plain and slashed horizontal or converging cordons on their surfaces, often with applied 'knots' at their intersections. Rims may be decorated with incised herringbone or plastic ornament (Smith 1956, 196; Wainwright and Longworth 1971, 238). The Durrington Walls style is characterised by large, barrel-sided vessels with closed rims. Applied cordons, grooved and incised decoration are all common, and twisted cord, comb, whipped cord, rustication and stab-and-drag are also present. The internal rim bevel is often decorated (Wainwright and Longworth 1971, 55–9). Finally, the Rinyo style has flat-bottomed truncated cone and tub-shaped vessels, rims with an internal step bevel, and decoration in the form of applied pellets and roundels, applied geometric forms, and grooved and impressed cordons (Wainwright and Longworth 1971, 242–3).

Smith pointed out that in the south at least there was little indication that the different sub-styles of Grooved Ware could be connected with distinct material assemblages (1956, 221). There is some indication of regional preferences for the different groups: as well as Rinyo Ware being characteristic of Orkney, there are large numbers of Clacton assemblages in East Anglia, Durrington Walls assemblages in Wessex, and Woodlands assemblages in the Upper Thames Valley (Figure 5.14). However, these are anything but exclusive distributions. Rather than representing distinct ethnic or social groups, this might indicate that the different sub-styles were used in different ways, which were more or less congruent with different social circumstances. This much is suggested by Cleal's observation (in Barclay and Halpin 1998) that Woodlands assemblages tend to be small, consisting of only one to three vessels (see p. 119).

Aside from overlapping geographically, the Grooved Ware sub-styles can occur together in a single assemblage. For instance, at Maiden Castle only six sherds came from a single pit, but both

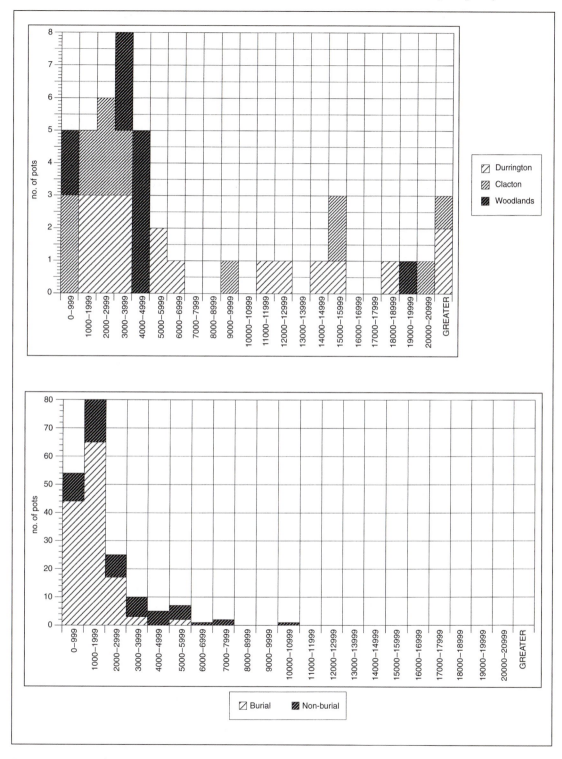

Figure 5.13 Grooved Ware (above) and Beakers (below): vessel volumes

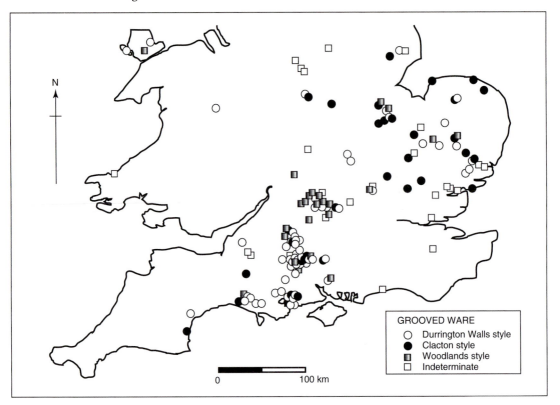

Figure 5.14 Distribution of Grooved Ware in southern Britain

Clacton and Durrington Walls traits were present (Cleal in Sharples 1991, 182). The pottery from the Coneybury henge was largely in Durrington Walls style, but with some Woodlands traits (Richards 1990, 148). And at Redgate Hill, Hunstanton, a broadly Clacton assemblage included elements of both the Durrington Walls and Woodlands styles (Healy *et al.* 1993, 50). Roughly a quarter of the Grooved Ware assemblages from southern Britain combine elements of more than one sub-style. Of these, rather more mix together Durrington Walls and Clacton traits, while the Woodlands style seems a little more distinct. Within any collection, there may be individual pots in different styles, or particular vessels may combine traits of different affinity. It seems to have been legitimate to mix elements together in creating distinctive Grooved Ware pots, and yet this does not appear to have compromised the identities of the different sub-styles, all of which seem to have been current over a long period. This is another point of contrast with Peterborough Ware, where entire assemblages can generally be identified as Ebbsfleet, Mortlake or Fengate in character.

The distinctiveness of Grooved Ware is perhaps most marked in its decoration. Colin Richards (in Richards and Thomas 1984) identified the way in which the Grooved Ware within the henge at Durrington Walls appeared to be spatially distributed according to the structure of decoration on the surfaces of the vessels. This design structure was based upon two sets of choices open to the potter in decorating a pot: between bounded and unbounded spaces, and between decorating a space and leaving it plain. The 'hierarchy' of design which Richards identified is consequently dendritic in form: each choice is set up by previous choices. This structure is most evident in the Durrington Walls sub-style, where cordons, grooves, incisions or even paired finger-nail impressions were used to define panels on the vessel surface (e.g. Shennan *et al.* 1985, 168). Moreover, pots were often divided by grooves or horizontal cordons about one-third to one-quarter of the way from the top, providing a separate design field below the rim (Wainwright and Longworth 1971, 56). In dividing space into bounded units and decorating each separately, Grooved Ware represents what Hardin (1984, 578) defines as an 'analytic' design structure: splitting up field space and manipulating it. This has consequences for the sequence of actions involved in decorating the vessel, and it may not be too extravagant to suggest a complete difference in the way in which the potter now conceptualised her or his task. Where earlier Neolithic and Peterborough Wares decorated unbounded spaces sequentially, Grooved Ware potters began by segmenting that space. This applies to Woodlands and Clacton pots as much as to the Durrington Walls style (see Richards in Barclay and Russell-White 1993, 185–6).

This break with the past in terms of the organisation of decoration was complemented by an abrupt change in decorative media, for there is little precedent in earlier traditions for applied decoration and the extensive use of cordons (Wainwright and Longworth 1971, 246). None the less, the way in which ceramic style was used socially was not dissimilar from that which we have noted in the case of Peterborough Ware, albeit more elaborate. The significance of Richards' work at Durrington Walls is that the structure of Grooved Ware decoration provided a means to classify and discriminate between spatial locations. As Cleal (1991, 141–2) has demonstrated, some particular motifs appear to have a distinct significance. At Wyke Down, Durrington Walls and Woodhenge, circular or spiral motifs were spatially associated with entrances, whether in timber circles or at ditch terminals. However, for the most part it is the *structure* of Grooved Ware decoration which is important: a 'grammar' which allowed the articulation of difference between places and practices without necessarily labelling any one with a specific material signifier. Thus, for example, Manby (in Abramson 1996, 45) notes the way in which Grooved Ware assemblages from pit groups located within short distances of each other on the Yorkshire Wolds may be quite distinct in stylistic terms. In the case of Scottish Grooved Ware, MacSween (1995, 43) suggests the operation of an overall 'syntax' of design which none the less generated vessels whose decoration was unique. So while Grooved Ware was one of the most formal and complex 'material languages' of prehistoric Britain, the way in which it was used lay in the objectification of difference.

One reason for the evident contrast between Grooved Ware and the earlier ceramic traditions in southern Britain may lie in its intrusive character. The earliest radiocarbon dates for Grooved Ware have consistently come from Scotland (Renfrew 1979, 205–8; Clarke 1983, 55; MacSween 1992, 41). This could be taken as evidence for an argument that Orkney was the place of origin of Grooved Ware, and the Rinyo style the progenitor of the southern styles. However, the actual situation may be a little less clear-cut. Recent dates for the Durrington Walls style at Hillend (2460 ± 70 bc, 3100–2920 cal. BC) (Armit *et al.* 1994, 122), and for the Woodlands style at Balfarg Riding School (2475 ± 50 bc, 3100–2915 cal. BC) are relatively early. The stratified sequence at the Orcadian site of Pool has shed some light on the issue of the emergence of Grooved Ware. Here, a first phase of activity was associated with round-bottomed Unstan Ware vessels, which were replaced in Phase 2 by 'baggy' shell-tempered vessels with incised decoration and small bases, and flat-based, angle-sided vessels, decorated with parallel lines, dots and chevrons (MacSween 1992, 269). In a final phase, there were straight-walled pots with applied decoration and scalloped and notched rim forms (Hunter and MacSween 1991, 912). The pottery from the final phase seems to have been quite insular in character, but the Phase 2 pots and the similar material from Barnhouse are classic Grooved Ware with affinities further afield. This material dates roughly to the period 3200–3000 BC (2550–2450 bc), and is thus just a little earlier than any date from the mainland.

The Pool sequence indicates both that Unstan Ware may have been earlier in inception than Grooved Ware in Orkney, and that there was 'a degree of technological and stylistic continuity' (MacSween 1992, 263) between the two. Incised and grooved lines are present on Unstan Ware, while atypical elements such as cordons, impressions and flat bases are known from Unstan assemblages at the Knap of Howar, Unstan, Taversoe Tuick and Isbister (Henshall in Ritchie 1983, 72; MacSween 1992, 263). If a new ceramic style developed in Orkney (or within a larger area of Scotland) drawing on the skills and techniques of the Unstan tradition, we are entitled to ask why such a change should have come about. Conflicting interpretations have already been proposed. Renfrew (1979, 207) argued that Unstan Ware gradually 'evolved' into Grooved Ware over a period of about 200 years, while Hedges (1984, 114) suggested the coexistence of two distinct 'sub-cultures' with characteristic pottery, funerary monuments and domestic architecture. The implication of the chronological overlap between the two traditions is that an explanation might be sought somewhere between these two. If a new style of pottery is *added* to an existing one, even if it comes in time to replace it, it is probable that it serves some new and socially defined purpose. The same might be inferred in southern Britain, where radiocarbon dates from Barholm, Bargates, Coneybury, Upper Ninepence, Wyke Down and the Chalk Plaque Pit indicate that Grooved Ware was introduced at some time between 2900 and 2800 BC (2350–2200 bc). As we have argued above, this suggests at least a century of overlap with Peterborough Ware, and perhaps more. While Peterborough Wares have a distribution which is more or less continuous over southern Britain (Figure 5.9), that of Grooved Ware is far more clustered within what Bradley (1984b, 41) would define as 'core areas': the Upper Thames, the Fen edge, Salisbury Plain, the Avebury district and the mouth of the Avon (Figure 5.14). It is unlikely that this contrast can be put down to taphonomic factors, suggesting that Peterborough Ware and Grooved Ware were not used in the same way. Consequently, it is not possible to argue that Grooved Ware simply replaced Peterborough Ware, fitting into the same contexts and practices.

Another issue which demands consideration in this context is that of regional variation. Innovation in material culture is a social process, and the adoption and abandonment of material traditions will be related to the uses to which people put artefacts. If communities in different parts of Britain had different sets of social relationships, it is to be expected that the degree to which they might cling to old traditions, or prove receptive to new, might vary geographically. So the degree of overlap between different later Neolithic ceramic styles might easily have varied from place to place. In some regions, one tradition might replace another almost instantaneously, while in another compelling reasons might exist for retaining a series of different styles alongside each other.

If the techniques employed in the manufacture of Grooved Ware had their origin in the Unstan tradition, a number of authors have pointed out that the decorative motifs have a greater affinity with the art of the Irish passage tombs (Smith 1956, 234–7; Bradley and Chapman 1984; 1986; Richards and Thomas 1984, 192–3). In recent years much debate has been concerned with similarity between passage tomb motifs and the 'entoptic phenomena' experienced by persons entering altered states of consciousness (e.g. Bradley 1989; Dronfield 1995). However, those symbols which occur on Grooved Ware as well as in the passage tombs do not seem to be the ones which Dronfield (1995, 544) identifies as diagnostic of 'subjective visual phenomena', whether induced by light-flicker, migraine or drugs. Thus although the residue of black henbane encrusted on to a Grooved Ware pot from Balfarg Riding School (Moffat in Barclay and Russell-White 1993, 109–10) is suggestive, there is no evidence that the design of Grooved Ware vessels was connected with shamanistic practices. Spirals and concentric circles provide the most spectacular link with the passage tombs, but they are actually relatively scarce on Grooved Ware. Instead, it is the variety of motifs, including lozenges, concentric triangles, bisected lozenges and triangles, zigzags and parallel lines which is convincing. While the relatively disordered art of the 'Loughcrew style' may have emerged quite early in the Neolithic (Sheridan 1986, 21), Grooved Ware has a closer affinity with the more formal and structured 'Fourknocks style' (Shee Twohig 1981, 127), and with the 'angular' and 'angular spiral' variants which Eogan identifies at Knowth (Eogan 1986; Cleal 1991, 144). These styles of decoration probably date to a period after 3100 BC (2500–2400 bc) (Sheridan 1986, 25). This is interesting, because it indicates that the art style which is most comparable with Grooved Ware is no earlier than the pottery itself. Rather than a transfer of symbols from a parietal to a mobiliary medium, we should envisage the formulation of a set of signifiers which were used in different ways in different regions. The art of the Loughcrew style was doubtless drawn on in creating this symbolic set, but it may not have been the only source.

Bradley (1982, 35) originally discussed the role of Grooved Ware in linking together different regions which had distinct monumental traditions. What is striking is that the symbols which the pottery bears appear to link it to a system of signification which extends into different geographical areas *and* into different social contexts. For instance, Grooved Ware shares many of its motifs with the carved stone balls of Scotland: spirals, concentric circles, chevrons, split herringbone, lozenge designs, zig-zags and concentric triangles (Marshall 1977, 61). Yet these designs are scarce in Orkney, and outside Orkney these objects are not found with Grooved Ware or in chambered tombs. Similarly, Isobel Smith remarked upon the similarity between the lozenge-mesh pattern of plastic ornament on the surface of some Woodlands vessels and the faceted butts of antler and stone maceheads (Smith 1956, 195). Indeed, both lozenge facets and spiral designs are known from crown antler maceheads. Yet 41 of these maceheads come from rivers and bogs, where Grooved Ware is never found, and they are concentrated in the lower reaches of the Thames, which is a gap in the Grooved Ware distribution (Simpson 1996b, 295). Recently, Cleal (in Barclay and Halpin 1999) has drawn attention to an exceptional group of Grooved Ware vessels from a pit at Barrow Hills, Radley. Of these, P33 has a complex lozenge trellis, while P39 has a pair of opposed spirals. Between them, these pots replicate the decorative motifs on the elaborate flint macehead found in a late context in the eastern passage tomb at Knowth (Eogan 1986, 146). Yet at Knowth Grooved Ware is restricted to a series of structures outside of the tomb (Eogan and Roche 1993), while Irish Grooved Ware generally lacks complex geometric motifs. All of this suggests that Grooved Ware forms one element in a complex system of material reference which served to introduce elements drawn from a broader set of signifiers into spatially dispersed and conceptually differentiated contexts. Later Neolithic society in Britain (and perhaps in Ireland) was internally fragmented, and involved practices and activities which were mutually incompatible (Thomas 1996a, 178). However, this difference was articulated by forms of signification which allowed allusions and references to be made which established relationships between segregated contexts and persons.

Context is consequently crucial to understanding Grooved Ware and its use. Overall, the contexts of occurrence of Grooved Ware contrast with those of Peterborough Ware. Stray finds are scarce, while finds from rivers, bogs and long mounds are non-existent (Figure 5.11, lower). Pits and open sites are far more common. Yet it is also clear that the different sub-styles of Grooved Ware were treated rather differently in deposition. Durrington Walls vessels were deposited in a relatively wide range of contexts, including henges, ring ditches and other monuments, while Clacton pots are generally found in pits, on open sites, and in old land surfaces. Woodlands vessels occur in a much more restricted range of contexts, particularly in pits. Although in Scotland Woodlands pots were found at Balfarg Riding School, they are absent from henges in the south. This point is illustrated by the assemblages from Cranborne Chase: the pits in Firtree Field contained Durrington Walls, Clacton and Woodlands vessels, while the nearby Wyke Down henge had only Durrington Walls and Clacton (Cleal 1991, 137). This enhances the impression that the Woodlands style was quite distinct from other Grooved Ware, and was used for rather different purposes, which perhaps involved gatherings of small groups of people.

PETERBOROUGH WARE, GROOVED WARE AND BEAKERS

As Healy (in Barclay and Halpin 1999) argues, it now seems likely that Peterborough Wares, Grooved Ware and Beakers each have distinct chronological '*floruits*' with overlapping 'tails'. As one tradition arose, another declined, perhaps over a period of several generations. However, it does not appear that each successive style was used in the same way or for exactly the same purposes as its predecessors: this was not simply a process of replacement. Consequently, the precise significance of the periods of overlap during which more than one tradition was in use remains of considerable interest. Yet any analysis is made difficult by the evident conservatism of the forms concerned, which often means that 'early' and 'late' examples of the same style are difficult to discriminate between on morphological criteria. We have seen already that Peterborough Wares (particularly Mortlake), both in stylistic terms and in use, demonstrated a strong orientation toward the past. This theme of continuity is suggested by the use of Peterborough Wares in practices which evoked the ancestral dead or made use of old monuments. Nevertheless, Peterborough Ware does not seem to have been a predominantly funerary ceramic (*contra* Burgess 1980, 41), rarely being found in association with the emergent group of single burials in flat graves, round barrows and ring ditches (Kinnes 1979). (The occurrence of Peterborough Ware with cave burials in various parts of the British Isles only serves to complicate the issue.)

We have seen that Grooved Ware in Orkney showed some signs of change through time, but elsewhere only minor traits are chronologically sensitive, and the various sub-styles persist alongside each other throughout the currency of the pottery. Reviewing the radiocarbon evidence for the Beaker pottery which began to be used in Britain after 2700 BC, Kinnes *et al.* suggest that 'the consolidated evidence casts doubt on stylistic succession as the determinant of internal chronology for British Beakers' (1991, 38; see also Boast 1995, 70). It has long been accepted that throughout the Beaker episode, individual decorative motifs survived for long periods, eventually being combined with new elements to create new styles of vessel (Lanting and van der Waals 1972, 25). However, it now seems that particular classes of Beaker, such as Clarke's (1970) All-Over-Corded and European Bell Beakers continued to be made over hundreds of years. Thus even a minimalist classification like Case's (1977) early–middle–late sequence can no longer be upheld (Case 1993). The most that can be said is that some 'early' style Beakers (such as the Wessex/Middle Rhine vessel P24 from Barrow Hills Radley: Barclay and Halpin 1999) may be associated with early radiocarbon dates, but might equally be later, while 'late' Beakers will tend to be genuinely late. Stylistic change in British Beakers therefore seems to involve a gradual increase in overall variability, and an increasing elaboration of the decoration of particular vessels.

Considered at a gross scale, the evidence indicates that in southern Britain at any given point from the middle of the Neolithic until the Early Bronze Age there would have been considerable variation both within and between ceramic traditions. As the decorated bowl styles declined, three forms of Peterborough Ware emerged. These persisted until after the Grooved Ware sub-styles were established. As Grooved Ware faded away, the range of potential Beaker styles gradually expanded. The different classes of Beaker identified by Clarke (1970) may not be indicative of the series of incursions by continental peoples which he envisaged, especially given that examples of different Beaker types may occur in the same grave (Lanting and van der Waals 1972, 29). None the less, the different styles may have constituted distinct cultural entities which were recognised as such. There is little doubt that neither Peterborough nor Grooved Ware survived into the Bronze Age (Cleal 1984, 138), but by then ceramic diversity was enhanced by the introduction of Food Vessels and Collared Urns. The only enduring theme throughout this sequence was one of *difference*, in that the cultural repertoire available at any time enabled distinctions between persons and places both to be expressed and constructed. Within the culture-historic framework, it was normal archaeological practice to identify each successive style of pottery with a distinct population group (Clark 1966, 172). However, a consideration of the contexts in which different styles were deployed might indicate that the ceramics used in the Neolithic were neither ethnic markers nor were they employed for all possible tasks, a possibility first explored by Burgess and Shennan (1976). If we accept that Grooved Ware was introduced to southern Britain from further north it is plausible that its reception was conditioned as much by its differentness from Peterborough Ware as by any particular association which it brought with it. A new style allowed new differences to be signified, and something of its identity would be clarified by its juxta-position with existing pots.

This articulation of difference through material culture would allow distinct practices to be separated from each other spatially, conceptually and materially. Such a framework might prove helpful in a traditional society undergoing a gradual and continuous process of transformation, in which different aspects of day-to-day existence might come to contradict each other. Shennan (1982; 1986), for instance, writes of conflicting ideologies based upon personal authority and communal tradition, while Thorpe and Richards contrast 'ritual authority' with 'prestige goods hierarchy' (1984, 67–8). It might not be necessary for such communities to be composed of mutually antagonistic blocs for mutually incompatible influences, resources and activities to coexist. Indeed, it is quite possible for societies to be 'complex' without this complexity involving either a unified hierarchy or bounded class groups (Ehrenreich *et al.* 1995). Where distinct or overlapping material repertoires can be identified, it is possible that they relate not to different groups of people, but to the same people doing different things at different times. We have seen that the distinction between Grooved Ware and Peterborough ceramics extends as far as their means of manufacture, and is clearest in their decorative structure. The absence of seed impressions from Grooved Ware (Jones 1980) might suggest that the pots were made at a different time of year from other ceramics, or that a deliberate attempt was made to exclude particular kinds of matter. The latter explanation fits with the use of shell as the predominant filler in Grooved Ware and the deposition of marine shells in Grooved Ware pits: an effort to include substances with distinct associations into the fabric of the pottery itself.

As with Grooved Ware, there is strong evidence to suggest that Beaker ceramics developed outside southern Britain and were only later introduced. However, it has proved very difficult to isolate a single place of origin for Beakers, and indeed the issue of origins has often come to define the 'Beaker problem' (Clarke 1976, 460). Following Sangmeister, Piggott (1963, 60) suggested that most British Beakers were the outcome of a 'reflux movement', by which ceramics which had originated in Iberia expanded into central Europe, mixed with Corded Ware elements and spread westward again. While present radiocarbon evidence gives priority to Iberian Beakers (Case 1993, 248), the continuity from Single Grave Protruding Foot Beakers (PFB) through All-Over-Ornamented (AOO) and Bell Beakers in the Low Countries seems unshakeable. Beakers in the lower Rhine form a single tradition with the Corded Ware-related vessels in both stylistic and technological terms (Lanting and van der Waals 1976, 2; van der Leeuw 1976, 108; Drenth 1990, 207), while PFB and AOO Beakers are sometimes found in the same grave (Lanting and van der Waals 1976, 8). Similarly, it is difficult to locate a place of inception for the characteristic set of items which have been associated with Beakers, and cases have been made both for the Balkans and for the west Mediterranean (Shennan 1976, 232; Case 1995a, 19). There is every possibility that tanged copper daggers, V-perforated buttons, archers' wristguards, barbed and tanged arrow-heads, stone battle axes and bone belt hooks did not all emerge within the same cultural milieu (Shennan 1977, 54; Harrison 1980, 26, 51). These points argue against the existence of a 'Beaker culture' which formed in one region and spread into others as an homogeneous entity. Instead, we might envisage the gradual coalescence of a ceramic style and an artefactual assemblage through innumerable exchanges and interactions between different communities across a huge geographical zone. Some aspects of the Beaker horizon do suggest a degree of homogeneity – the vessels themselves, and the associated trinkets. But other features are highly variable between regions. In Britain and the Low Countries, fine Beakers are matched by a 'domestic' assemblage, while in central Europe there is the plain *Begleitkeramik*, similar to Corded Ware material of pre-Beaker date (Shennan 1976, 234). In Hungary, Beakers are found with cremations, in Holland and Britain with inhumations, and in Brittany and Ireland they occur in megalithic tombs, perhaps not always with burials at all (Harrison 1980, 76). In Britain and Holland, Beakers stayed in use for generations, while east of the Rhine they went out of use quite quickly (Shennan 1986, 141). As David Clarke originally argued, there was no single Beaker phenomenon with a single explanation (1976, 461).

Clarke went on to propose a model of Beaker ceramic process in which locally produced coarse and everyday wares were complemented by fine wares which might have been exchanged over very considerable distances (1976, 462). He was able to cite the example of a Northern/North Rhine Beaker from Chesham, Bucks, made from clay from the middle Rhine Valley (1976, 466). However, recent petrological work demonstrates that the overwhelming majority of British Beakers, whether fine or coarse, were locally produced (Darvill 1986; Parker Pearson 1990; 1995). Rather than a customary element of Beaker assemblages, the exchange of fine vessels may have been episodic. While some continental vessels came to Britain in the years after 2700 BC, they stood at the head of a tradition of insular manufacture. Some of the other items of the Beaker assemblage, such as archers' wristguards and metalwork, indicate a greater role for the long-distance circulation of goods (Clough and Green 1972, 138). None the less, Barrett (1994, 94) has recently argued that the perception that a 'Beaker package' as a set of exotic prestige goods relies upon the assumption of a unified Beaker network requiring explanation at a pan-European level. Resisting such a totalised explanation, Barrett suggests that the role of Beakers can only be assessed at a local level, where their significance would have lain *within* communities, in interpersonal relations, rather than in external contacts and long-distance exchange. We can certainly agree with Barrett's point that no one living in Britain 4,500 years ago would have had any conception of the spatial extent of the distribution of Beaker pottery (1994, 97). However, I will hope to argue that the intrusive character of Beakers was important, without relying on their perceived 'value' as prestige goods.

Beakers, like other pots, were material symbols. They contrasted with the existing ceramic styles in use in southern Britain. Beakers were often visually striking, with a fine surface finish and elaborate decoration. The technology involved in their manufacture introduced several innovations (van der Leeuw 1976, 115), and they were associated with a new range of material items, which facilitated changes in social practice. Without embodying any explicit meaning or message, Beakers were inherently disruptive of established cultural categories. Beakers had a decorative structure which shared something of the formality of Grooved Ware, yet the emphasis on a series of horizontal bands indicates a rather different syntax. As we shall see, Beakers were adopted by local communities for reasons which were entirely concerned with their internal relations. In many cases, they were incorporated into 'traditional' practices. But material culture is transformative, and its adoption can have unintended consequences. In discussing the role of Beakers in Britain, Barrett suggests that 'too much of current archaeological research is directed to writing the history of things' (1994, 97). In its place, Barrett advocates a history of people and their practices. I suggest that this runs the risk of giving those people and their practices a priority over the material world which enabled and facilitated social life. Material things are not simply extrinsic 'conditions' of practice, they are integral to any human project. The history which we can write is one of the relationship between people and things. This involves the intersections of traditions of manufacture and traditions of interpretation, artefact histories and personal biographies.

It seems that recent interpretations of Beakers have been polarised between those which present the vessels as inherently valuable prestige goods (Shennan 1982; 1986; Thorpe and Richards 1984) and those which see them as mundane objects which only gained importance through their use in funerary practices and other rituals (Barrett 1994; Boast 1995). Thus Boast claims that 'Beakers on henges, like Beakers in settlements, were drawn into special practices and made special, rather than being inherently special to begin with' (1995, 78). This seems to conflict with his earlier statement that 'objects do not inherently carry any social meaning' (1995, 69). The suggestion is surely that Beakers *did* have a fixed and inherent meaning: as quotidian food containers. Boast argues that Beakers have been perceived as 'special' by archaeologists because they have been recovered from burials and henges, but it seems no more than an inversion of the same argument to claim that Beakers were *essentially* everyday items. Indeed, it could be said to introduce the contemporary Western assumption that fired clay vessels are comparatively insignificant, because they are associated with 'domestic' activities. An alternative is to suggest that Beakers were *neither* inherently prestigious nor inherently mundane, but that they were symbols which gained their meaning in their deployment, through association and connotation, or 'internal' and 'external' contextuality as Mizoguchi (1995, 177) has it. Following an argument similar to Boast's, Barrett (1994, 106) claims that the use of Beakers in henge monuments is indicative of 'an emergent elite who, whilst increasingly concerned to signify their identity by mode of dress and deployment of specific ritual items, did not achieve their position by the control of such paraphernalia'. This tends to reduce the role of the material culture involved to one of *reflecting* forms of power or authority which were created by other means. The local origin of most Beaker ceramics and the relative scarcity of the other items of the 'package' may do damage to the notion that social power could be built upon a monopoly of access to these goods. But the use of Beakers in consumption and in funerary practice would have contributed to the categorisation and construction of new kinds of human identity. To these contexts, Beaker vessels would have brought a variety of conceptual associations, and at least initially the novelty of pots which had come from a long distance away, across the sea, might have been considerable.

When we consider the contextual deployment of Beakers, it may be the patterns of association in which they occur which are most instructive. Thorpe and Richards (1984, 77) pointed out that while Peterborough Ware and Grooved Ware appear to have been 'kept separate' from one another, there is a close association between Peterborough Wares and Beakers. As Figure 5.15 demonstrates, in southern Britain as a whole the Peterborough/Beaker association is especially strong. However, this is hard to reconcile with the emerging chronology, which suggests that there was little or no overlap between the two traditions. In many cases, the associations represented in Figure 5.15 are relatively loose, where sherds of Beaker and Peterborough Ware occur on the same surface, or in different layers in the same feature. So it may be that this material relates to a series of separate events in a given location. This is not to say that the pattern is without significance, for it indicates that the two styles of pottery were appropriate for use in the same kinds of places, and perhaps in the same kinds of practices. In a sense, Beakers 'replaced' Peterborough Ware in earthen long barrows, chambered tombs, causewayed enclosure ditches and in a number of other contexts. Yet Beakers also occurred in graves and, eventually, in henge monuments. It is this

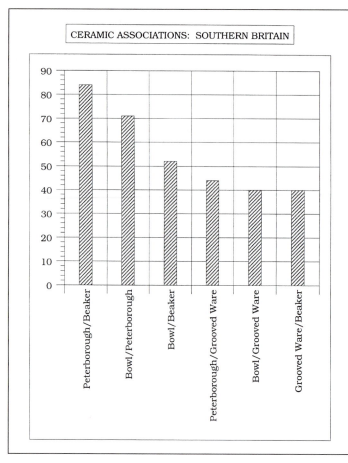

CERAMIC ASSOCIATIONS: SOUTHERN BRITAIN

Figure 5.15 Neolithic ceramic traditions: patterns of association

insinuation of a single class of material into a range of contexts which had hitherto been quite distinct from one another which signals the dissolution or at least the transformation of a later Neolithic cultural order.

Beakers were culturally disruptive as a result of their decorative structure, the contexts in which they were used, and also in their size and shape. Criticising the first edition of this book, Case (1995b, 59) argued that Beakers could not be typified as small in size. Case is undoubtedly correct to emphasise the internal variability of the Beaker tradition, which includes bowls, jars and relatively large 'potbeakers'. However, using Case's own data for burial and non-burial Beakers (Figure 5.13, lower) it is clear that *in comparison with the other traditions* of Neolithic pottery Beaker vessels are predominantly small. Particularly when compared with the range of volumes from Grooved Ware, there are strong indications of an abrupt change in the ways in which pots might be used. Beakers presented a different set of affordances from earlier ceramics, facilitated different forms of consumption and sociality, and consequently were integral to social change.

POTS THAT MATTER: A CERAMIC GENEALOGY

Artefacts are not simply arrangements of matter which can be picked up and used when required and then discarded. They are integral to society, and they have a history. The introduction of ceramics into Britain at the start of the Neolithic, and the subsequent transformations which pottery underwent do not simply reflect social changes: they were implicated in those changes. Artefacts have a historical specificity. It is important that pottery was utilised in a series of social practices through the Neolithic, but it is also significant that *particular* pots were used at specific times and places. A particular event or sequence of events is not the same if different forms of material culture are employed. That pottery changed in fundamental ways through the period is both a symptom of social change and a source of that change.

Material things are only relevant in a context. They do not first of all have a fundamental meaning, and then have a symbolic significance added to them. It is the set of relations in which an artefact is embedded which renders it intelligible. The materiality of things is revealed in practice: it does not pre-exist the attribution of significance. Consequently, archaeologists should be wary of labelling any class of artefacts as fundamentally 'domestic' or 'mundane'. In the case of pottery, although the material itself is relatively common in the archaeological record, any suggestion that vessels were used for the storage, preparation or serving of food is an inference. That they were routinely used for these purposes on an everyday basis is a further inference. In Neolithic Britain, the indications are that the earliest pottery was a rather unusual material, which transformed activities which may or may not have been mundane. In time, pottery increased in its ubiquity, but the range of practices for which it was employed is a question which remains to be answered. The implication of the variation which can be recognised in the decoration of pots is that they were significant in interpersonal relations and transactions, introducing difference and discontinuity into social life at a very intimate level. This was a pattern which intensified with the introduction of Peterborough Wares, with a restriction of vessel form yet an elaboration of decoration, and the emergence of distinct sub-styles.

Throughout the Neolithic, pottery was employed in activities which were socially significant: gatherings, feasts, funerals. Pottery lent a certain structure to these events, and the increase in variation and distinctiveness of vessels through the later Neolithic is indicative of a process in which social life itself became more complex and fragmented. With the introduction of Grooved Ware, individual vessels were more identifiable, curated and perhaps valued. But this 'value' was concerned with the symbolic associations of the pot rather than with any inherent worth. Similarly, Beakers were individually important as examples of a powerful and disruptive cultural category, rather than as prestige goods. David Clarke once argued that the later Neolithic in Europe represented a distinct horizon during which fine decorated pottery was socially important, before it was 'displaced' by metalwork (1976, 471). This may be the case only to the extent that pottery held a key place in the articulation of social relations, facilitating and constraining the performance of social life.

Chapter Six

Mortuary practice

ARCHAEOLOGICAL APPROACHES TO FUNERARY PRACTICE

It has often been noted that the evidence for funerary activity in Neolithic Britain is rather more extensive than that for everyday subsistence activities. The dead seem to be more visible than the living. Indeed, funerary monuments have sometimes been used in ingenious ways as an indirect indicator of human impact on the landscape (Atkinson 1968; Bradley 1984b, 16). It might consequently be expected that the lively and productive debate which has characterised mortuary archaeology over the past thirty years or so would have found an application in developing an extensive knowledge of Neolithic society from this material. Yet this is only partly the case. For while a very extensive battery of conceptual apparatus has been put together which could interrogate the funerary evidence, many of its individual elements are grounded in mutually antagonistic philosophies. Different schools of archaeological thought have perceived the dead in quite different ways, and have sought to extract distinct kinds of information from them. It follows that the forms of analysis which they have elaborated cannot be routinely applied without some consideration of the broader intellectual projects from which they have emerged.

Mortuary archaeology has always been carried out within some particular conceptual framework, and with the fulfilment of specific objectives in mind. Sir Richard Colt Hoare, in his *Ancient History of Wiltshire*, claimed to 'speak from facts not theory' (1812, 7), yet this professed empiricism sits uneasily with the deep influence of Romanticism on his work (Symmonds and Simpson 1975, 15). It was this sensibility which informed Hoare's fascination with 'grinning skulls' (1975: 15), and led him to identify particular funerary monuments as 'King' and 'Druid Barrows'. Similarly, Thurnam (1869, 181) turned a perception of the past fashioned by a classical education on to the problems of pits located beneath long barrows, and concluded that they had been the *bothroi* described by Homer as a means of communicating with the lower realms. With the close of the antiquarian phase of investigation, the emphasis in the study of burials changed from questions of religious belief to cultural affinity. Burials provided useful closed contexts for the mutual association of material traits, essential for the construction of grand culture-historic schemes (Chapman and Randsborg 1981, 3). Yet the theoretical orthodoxy of the time strictly denied the possibility of understanding the broader significance of past cultural phenomena in the absence of written records (Hawkes 1954).

A dramatic revision of this point of view took place with the development of the 'New Archaeology' in the 1960s. A keystone of the position adopted by Binford (1964, 1965), Flannery (1968, 1972) and their contemporaries was the proposition that culture was an extrasomatic means of human adaptation. The alternative view, that common cultural traits arose as a consequence of shared values or beliefs, was rejected as 'normative'. Hence it became a polemical exercise to demonstrate that all aspects of culture could be explained in terms of their adaptive significance. The task which Binford (1971) took on was to go to the very top of the Hawkesian 'ladder of inference', and show that mortuary practice could be understood as contributing to the adaptive success of human groups. His researches, and those of Saxe (1970) and Tainter (1978), were intended to demonstrate that mortuary practice was a system of communication through which information about a deceased person was signalled to the living. By these means, the community might realign itself to cope with its changed circumstances. These approaches made use of Ward Goodenough's (1965) 'role theory' – essentially a means for the rapid ethnographic description of social relationships – to infer that funerary rituals served to condense and articulate a series of 'identity relationships' which the deceased had developed in life. The resulting 'social persona' might thus serve as an index of the complexity of the person's dealings with others during their lifetime. Where a society was internally ranked, the expression of these social personae in mortuary practice would be expected to be diverse, in terms of the expenditure of energy or the investment of information in the treatment of the dead. Looking at an entire cemetery population, it should then be possible to 'read off' the degree of social ranking by establishing the variability of funerary practice. Clearly, this implies that the salient differences between communities are always ones which can be expressed in quantitative terms.

In the early 1980s, a critique of the Binford/Saxe/Tainter position on mortuary variability formed a distinctive element of the so-called 'post-processual' archaeologies which were then beginning to emerge. It was pointed out that for funerary remains to constitute an accurate indication of past social relationships, they would need to communicate in a way which directly reflected the living community. But this is to neglect the role of ideology in securing the misrepresentation or distortion of social reality (Hodder 1982a, 1982b; Parker Pearson 1982; Shanks and Tilley 1982). Or to put it another way, once it is accepted that the treatment of the dead in funerary ritual is a form of representation, it is impossible to argue that it will passively mirror social relationships. Like any form of discourse, mortuary practice has the potential to construct and transform relationships.

AN APPROACH TO THE ARCHAEOLOGY OF DEATH

One drawback of the generalised methodologies proposed by Binford, Saxe and Tainter is that while they advocated a comparative approach, they did not concede that death and the dead may be of varied importance to different communities. By concentrating on the single vector of rank, they presented a somewhat one-dimensional picture of past societies, which could all be placed on a universal continuum of 'rankedness'. Evidently, there is much more to human sociality than ranking, and it seems plausible that mortuary practice might be connected with other aspects of society. Furthermore, people do not bury themselves, so that funerary practice might be expected to tell us something about the relationship between the living and the dead. This might not represent a constant. While we might agree with Binford's original claim that the treatment of the dead is a social practice, it will surely be historical and cultural as well. It follows that we are entitled to ask why the dead seem to be of little consequence to some communities, and yet central to the existence of others. Certainly, if we consider British prehistory as a whole the archaeological visibility of the dead appears to vary considerably across time. The innovative contributions of the early 1980s were quite correct to point to the significance of ideology in the disposition of the dead, but again, we might ask why the bodies of the dead seem to form a more powerful ideological resource at some times than at others.

A number of quite different factors can affect the relationship between the living and the dead. Several authors have pointed out that a community's ancestors may take on a heightened significance where land and its devolution become social preoccupations (Meillassoux 1972; Harris 1982, 47). Similarly, Woodburn (1982) argues that among many hunting and gathering societies this kind of orientation upon the past cannot be recognised, and the dead are of less concern. However, it may be overly reductive to infer from this that a simple correlation can be established between particular economic regimes and an interest in the dead. Another element worthy of consideration is social reproduction. In the nation-states of high modernity, continuity from one generation to another is generally secured through the existence of institutions, such as a civil service, a judiciary, social security, the military, the police and so on. Where this state apparatus is absent, traditional authority, drawn from the past, may provide a means by which social relationships are maintained. So it may be the reproduction of power relations which leads to a preoccupation with ancestors, rather than control of resources. But even here, it is difficult to generalise. In the modern West, the factors influencing the mode of disposal of the dead are complex and varied (Tarlow 1992), while it may be misleading to imagine that 'ancestors' are always conceptualised in a uniform and homogeneous manner (Humphreys 1981, 268). It is likely that relations with the dead will be negotiated in ways which are highly culturally specific.

Reflecting on the funerary archaeology of the early 1980s, Tarlow (1992, 137) takes Parker Pearson (1982) to task for an analysis which is concerned exclusively with power and ideological manipulation, and for neglecting the subtler points of the experience of death. This is a valid criticism, but only so long as we consider power to be much the same thing as authority: a top-down notion of power as social control. Alternatively we might think of power as a relational phenomenon, a set of imbricated connections immanent in all social dealings which create knowledge, enable action, facilitate understanding and promote tastes and desires (Foucault 1978, 95). Power here is productive as much as repressive. In these terms, it may be unwise to present the 'emotive' or 'subjective' aspects of death as being disengaged from power relations. To do so is to imply that 'the individual' exists in some sense prior to the social, and is able to engage in activities and experiences which are free from political significance. Most important of all is the way in which power is involved in the materialisation of the body (Butler 1993, 15). For the human body to secure cultural intelligibility, it must perform or cite a series of regulatory norms. Thus there is no recognisable body which exists prior to the social.

This is very much what Foucault has in mind when he talks of 'the way in which the body itself is invested with power relations' (1977, 24). The human body is never merely a given thing, whose precise material character is beyond question. On the contrary, it is revealed or brought into being through its social articulation. There is no reason to suggest that this should only be the case with *living* bodies. As performances, funerals are a pre-eminent example of the way in which the human body is materialised by power, made recognisable as a person of a particular kind, and even in some cases made to disappear. As a totally subject body, a dead person is at the mercy of the living, who can treat him or her as they will. In some cases, this may mean that the presentation of the corpse in funerary ritual conforms with social ideals rather than accurately reflecting the identity of the person in life. In our own society, women are likely to be dressed for the grave in a way which is conventionally 'feminine', rather than overtly sexual or possessed of gender ambiguity. Given that the materialisation of the body takes place in the context of norms, it is deeply historical.

In studying the development of penal institutions through the eighteenth century, Foucault demonstrated the operation of a new 'technology of power' on the human body. 'Systems of punishment', he argued, 'are to be situated in a certain "political economy" of the body' (1977, 25). In the absolutist monarchical states, punishment had been a bloody spectacle, aimed at the destruction of the body, and designed to demonstrate the concentrated power of the ruler.

By contrast, the system which replaced this aimed at the punishment of the soul through the discipline of the body. Foucault (1977, 137–43) showed how a new technology of discipline and surveillance allowed a new control over the body. Institutions like schools, hospitals, factories and asylums took the prison as their model, contributing to the control of the person through supervision and through an organisation of architectural space which defined times and locations for particular activities (Hirst 1985). Within such 'panoptic' institutions, it was no longer possible for a person to be aware of whether he or she was under observation at a given time: hence a complete discipline of the workforce was achieved. The body, at once an instrument of production, an agency of reproduction and a subject of domination, became 'useful' only when subjected (Foucault 1977, 25). The point which should be recognised here is that these conditions of bodily materialisation were entirely different from any which we might expect to encounter in the Neolithic.

A number of authors (Huntingdon and Metcalf 1979, 5; Bloch and Parry 1982, 6) have made the point that mortuary practices do not merely reflect the values of a community, but are instrumental in the creation and reproduction of society. Funerary ritual represents a situation in which the body and other elements of the world can be manipulated within a bounded analytic space (Turner 1969, 39). It may be that this manipulation of the passive bodies of the dead is more significant where the institutionalised disciplining of living bodies which Foucault describes is absent. Death provides an occasion in which a socially sanctioned version of personhood is brought into being. By contrast, in a modern world where disciplinary norms permeate the body in life, the actions carried out upon dead bodies may be more secluded and 'private'. This is not to imply that pre-modern bodies were free from power and regulation. Power relations are always immanent in the body, and yet the way in which they are exercised in traditional societies may be more episodic. Anthropologists have long recognised the importance of 'life-crisis' rituals in non-Western societies (Van Gennep 1960). Marriages, initiations, circumcision and naming ceremonies provide opportunities for people to be socially categorised, and to move from one category to another. Yet they are also performances in which people are involved in self-fashioning: interpreting and producing themselves in relation to socially sanctioned norms. Only funerals impose an identity upon a person in a way which is not open to negotiation by the subject.

In ritual, human bodies are at once participants and symbols alongside other symbols. Of course, when those bodies are dead, they will undergo a series of changes, and the transformation of the body (whether by inevitable decay or by intervention in the form of de-fleshing, dis-articulation or cremation) provides a potent source of symbolism. In some cases, the rotting away of the flesh may serve as an homology for the gradual freeing of the soul (Huntingdon and Metcalf 1979, 54), but this is evidently predicated upon a particular form of eschatology. None the less, the framework of 'rites of passage', which serves to signify the change of state of a person in a variety of life-crisis rituals, is sufficiently widespread to deserve consideration in any archae-ological situation (Hertz 1960; Van Gennep 1960). In death, the body may be presented in an idealised manner, as an image of the 'correct' appearance for a person of a particular age, sex and status (a point suggested by the analyses in Pader 1982). Additionally, mortuary ritual may serve as an opportunity for the conspicuous destruction of wealth – irrespective of the actual status of the deceased person (Metcalf 1981). In contradiction to the view expressed by Tainter (1978), I should like to suggest that if mortuary ritual is a communication system, it tells us more about those who conducted the ritual than those who were buried. So while analyses of the sort carried out by Saxe or Tainter might reveal a structure in data concerning body treatment, grave goods or whatever, this structure need not indicate an undistorted map of the social relationships within the cemetery population.

The alternative is to take up the challenge of realising that the way in which the dead are projected in mortuary ritual is subject to what I will call a 'strategy of representation'. The dead are shown to us not only through a fog of time, but also through the filter of the strategies and understandings of their kin and contemporaries. This should not give us cause for despair. Nor should it mean that the rigorous analysis of mortuary remains is worthless. Rather, we should realise exactly what it is that we are analysing. That is, we are studying a representation of society, not an objective snapshot image. It follows that one cannot hope to provide a complete reconstruction of a past society from mortuary evidence alone. What one can do is compare the way in which the dead have been treated with evidence for other activities in the hope of explaining the strategy which gives rise to the representation.

Given the central role which the dead seem to have occupied in the Neolithic, it is likely that the scrutiny of the mortuary record will repay close study. This chapter will investigate in turn a series of Neolithic mortuary practices (Figure 6.1). The principal aim of these analyses will be to consider the ways in which the representation of the dead varied from place to place and through time. It is important to point out before we begin that many of these practices overlapped both temporally and spatially. This provides support for the argument that they represent alternative strategies for the treatment of the dead, rather than passive fossils of shared belief or cultural affinity.

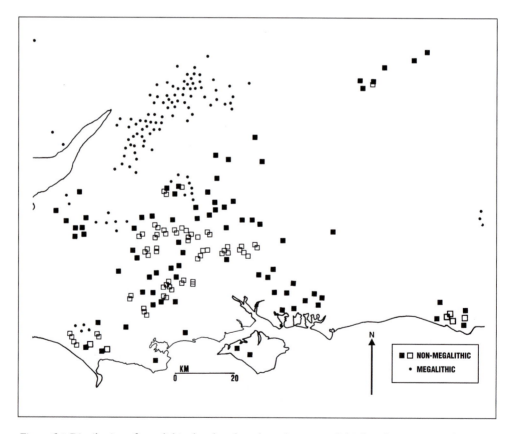

Figure 6.1 Distribution of megalithic chambered tombs and non-megalithic long barrows in southern Britain

EARTHEN LONG MOUNDS

Long mounds, long enclosures and long cairns containing the remains of the dead are a distinctive feature of the Neolithic of northern Europe, emerging in the Cerny and early TRB phases of northern France and the north European plain (Jazdzewski 1973; Kinnes 1982; Midgley 1985; Sherratt 1990). While some general connection with the long houses of the *Bandkeramik* tradition seems plausible (Hodder 1984; 1994), it may be that the appropriation of a linear organisation of space and its use in new ways marks the development of a new way of life amongst the native communities of Atlantic and Baltic Europe (Thomas 1996a, 129–33). However, in eastern Britain (particularly Wessex, Sussex, Lincolnshire and Yorkshire) and southern Scandinavia after 4000 BC, a more specific style of long mound can be recognised, characterised by a simple chamber form involving an embanked linear zone bracketed and sometimes subdivided by wooden uprights (Kinnes 1975; 1979, 58). Such 'earth graves' are familiar in Denmark, both as a part of the sequence of barrow construction, and equally often as independent self-supporting structures (Madsen 1979, 309). In Britain the evidence for non-lithic chambers remained unclear until after the Second World War. Early excavators had often failed to recognise the traces of these structures, while most of the sites investigated in the 1930s produced equivocal results (Piggott 1966, 382).

Piggott argued that the uprights of these chambers might have supported 'a tent-like gabled roof of wood' (1966, 385), comparable with the Early Bronze Age mortuary houses at Leubingen and Helmdorf. However, recent excavations like that at Streethouse Farm in Cleveland (Vyner 1984) have confirmed Kinnes' suggestion (1975, 19) that these structures were rather less complex than the ornate pitched wooden buildings envisaged by Ashbee (1970, 51). The timber and earth trough-like structure with blocked ends indicated at Streethouse (Vyner 1984, 161) would have facilitated direct access to the mortuary deposit over the flanking banks, and thus would have enabled a degree of selection and manipulation of bones prior to the construction of the mound (Figure 6.2). At Haddenham in Cambridgeshire, a similar chamber was preserved by waterlogging. Here the structure was boxlike, with roof, floor and sides composed of oak planks, again allowing repeated contact with its contents (Hodder and Shand 1988, 350) (Figure 6.3). In some examples, as at Wayland's Smithy 1, the floor of the chamber was formed by a stone pavement (Whittle 1991, 70). There is considerable evidence from the British barrows that these structures were open and accessible for some while before the construction of the covering mound. In a sense this confirms Piggott's original suggestion that the throwing up of the barrow might be seen as the equivalent of the blocking of a megalithic tomb, bringing to an end a sequence of depositional acts (1966, 387). At Kilham in Yorkshire, the linear mortuary structure was far from being axial to the trapezoid palisade enclosure, and this suggests that its construction represented a separate event (Manby 1976, 123). Similarly, at Fussell's Lodge in Wiltshire, the end pit of the mortuary structure was cut on both sides by the bedding trenches for another palisade enclosure, thus demonstrating its structural priority (Ashbee 1966). At Cold Kitchen Hill in Wiltshire, some of the timbers had evidently been in the earth long enough to be replaced (Harding and Gingell 1986, 8).

As with the Danish examples, we should not imagine that all of these linear chambers would inevitably end up underneath the eastern end of an earthen mound. At New Wintles, Eynsham, one such linear structure was surrounded by small causewayed ditches, presumably the quarries for a low gravel mound (Kenward 1982). At Aldwincle in Northamptonshire, two pairs of posts were located within a ditched enclosure, one pair bracketing the remains of two persons (Jackson 1976, 15). Furthermore, several round barrows in Yorkshire contained linear crematorium structures (Kinnes 1979, 10–15). In Scotland, the linear timber mortuary structures at Lochill

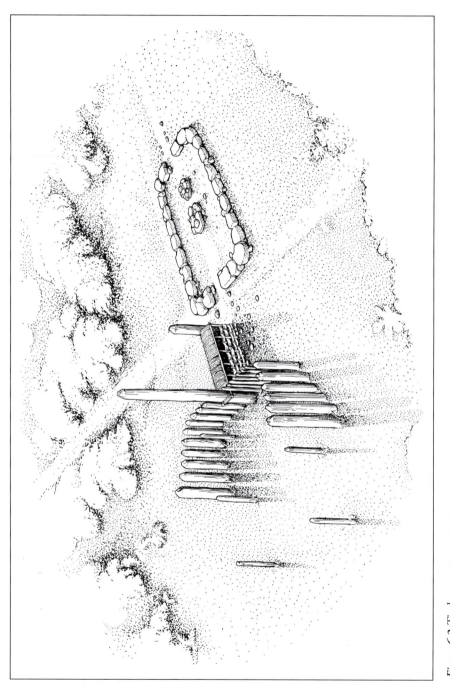

Figure 6.2 Timber mortuary structure

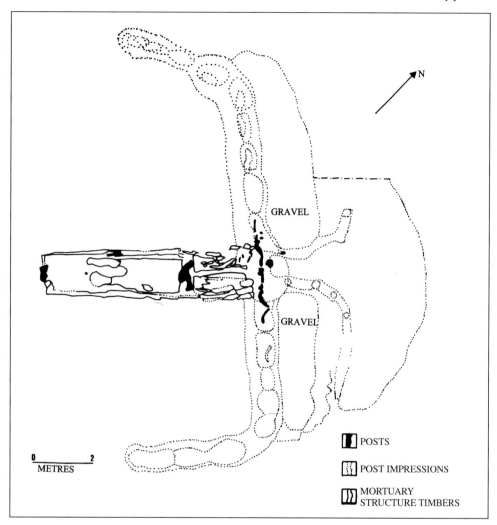

Figure 6.3 The mortuary structure at Haddenham long barrow, Cambridgeshire
Source: After Hodder and Shand (1988)

and Slewcairn were covered by trapezoidal stone cairns (Masters 1973; 1983), while the similar timber chamber at Dalladies had rotted away and been replaced by a second, stone and timber construction before this was incorporated into the side of a trapezoidal turf mound (Piggott 1973, 33).

It is noteworthy that in a number of cases the post-holes for the principal members of the mortuary structure were D-shaped rather than circular, and certainly at Wayland's Smithy, Giant's Hills 2 and Haddenham they appear to have held the two halves of a massive split tree-trunk, with the flat sides facing inward (Hodder and Shand 1988, 350; Evans and Simpson 1991, 14; Whittle 1991, 70). This indicates that the funerary deposit would have been placed between the two halves of a single cloven upright, itself fixed in the ground. Arguably, such an arrangement would have the effect of locating the place of deposition both spatially and materially.

Drawing in particular upon the evidence from Nutbane in Hampshire, Piggott (1966, 386) suggested that the timber chambers might be found in association with other pre-barrow elements: a fenced enclosure and a 'fore-building'. This latter is more often a bedded timber façade of posts, transverse to the axis of the mound, while the enclosure sometimes surrounds the mortuary zone, sometimes stands behind it, and sometimes connects with the façade to form a continuous trapezoid palisade around the perimeter of the monument. In addition to these components, there may also be short avenues of posts converging on the mortuary area from in front of the façade. These various elements provide a constructional repertoire, but it is evident that the ways in which they were combined, and the precise sequences which led up to the final long barrow were quite varied.

Often the visible earthen mound represents simply the last stage in a complex and protracted series of events. At many sites there is evidence for the use of the location even before the first traces of monument-building. A good example is Wayland's Smithy, where the old land surface beneath the mound produced fragments of stone axes which originated a great distance from the site, and a deliberately broken flint axe (Whittle 1991, 92). Seemingly in this case the timber mortuary structure and subsequent mound were set up on a location which was already associated with transactions of exchange and consumption. These kinds of activities evidently continued through the lives of the monuments. Deposits of objects which were placed before the construction of mounds include a group of quern stones concentrated in the same part of the chamber area as the human remains at Wayland's Smithy I (Whittle 1991, 70), the potsherds and cattle skull amongst the bodies at Fussell's Lodge (Ashbee 1966, 16), and the pottery vessel and 20 pig skulls at Hanging Grimston (Mortimer 1905, 103). At Haddenham, the distinction between plain potsherds found amongst the burials and decorated vessels, some of them complete, in the forecourt area (Hodder and Shand 1988, 352) suggests that one of the functions of material deposition was to draw attention to the different character of the separate spaces within the structure.

At a number of sites the timbers of the façade had been burnt *in situ*, often before the mound had been raised, as at Haddenham, Giant's Hills 2, Streethouse and Willerby Wold (Manby 1963, 177; Evans and Simpson 1991, 8; Kinnes 1992, 69). At Nutbane this burning took place between two separate phases of mound-building (Morgan 1959, 26). Sometimes the uprights of the mortuary structure had also been burnt. Indeed, in many of the Yorkshire sites the linear mortuary zones functioned as crematoria, which were often fired after the mound had been constructed, with flues having been left to allow combustion (Manby 1963, 186; 1970, 10). The closing off of the chamber, by filling with loose earth or rubble, generally took place as a separate act preceding the raising of the mound (Kinnes 1979, 58). At Fussell's Lodge the whole palisade enclosure was filled with chalk quarried from the ditches (Ashbee 1966, 2), while at Nutbane the linear chamber was surrounded by a series of small ditches, which had been backfilled before the surrounding enclosure was constructed, and this in turn was separately filled with earth and chalk before the mound was constructed (Morgan 1959, 20–2). In a number of the other Wessex barrows, the burial area was covered over with a flint cairn, often in some way associated with the skulls and hoof bones of cattle.

The separate stages in the construction of the barrow often made use of distinctive and contrasting materials: chalk, turf, timber, earth, flint, sarsen or the oak brushwood overlying the cairn at Nutbane (Morgan 1959, 24). Each element of the structure might thus be seen as a means of manipulating materials which were representative of the surrounding landscape, and introducing them into a series of physical and symbolic relationships with the bones of the dead. Since these constructional units were similar from one site to another, but the sequences in which they were assembled were not, it seems that the use of the repertoire was not entirely rule-bound,

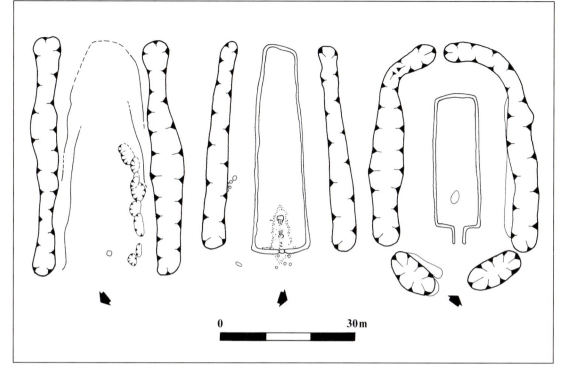

Figure 6.4 Earthen long mounds: comparative plans. Left to right: Horslip, Fussell's Lodge, Wor Barrow.

but involved a degree of improvisation. Each barrow was the outcome of a unique series of performances, which made use of the available materials. The chamber, façade, palisade and mound may have been quite stylised, but the timing of their assembly, and the group of people involved were unique. It may have been this degree of freedom in interpreting the basic design of the monument which facilitated the eventual broadening of the variability of long mound architecture (Figure 6.4).

Long mounds both in Britain and in continental northern Europe which contain the distinct structural elements discussed above tend to produce radiocarbon dates which fall between 4000 and 3500 BC (3250 and 2750 bc). As Kinnes (1985, 32) recognised, these kinds of similarities between far-flung sites are far too often considered in terms of a search for continental origins for British practices. The dates available for linear, post-bracketed mortuary structures in Denmark (2960 ± 90 and 2860 ± 70 bc for Rude; 2960 ± 100 bc for Konens Høj) are no earlier than those in Britain. We could more profitably consider that the development of a highly structured set of practices involving the deposition of human remains was part of a broader cultural repertoire whose inception coincided chronologically with the introduction of the Neolithic to the Atlantic fringes of Europe, including Britain (Thomas 1996a, Chapter 5).

The spatial relationships within these pre-mound complexes of timber features are of considerable interest. The embanked linear chamber, often the earliest element, was also the focus of the monument. Avenues of posts, like those at Wayland's Smithy I (Atkinson 1965; Whittle 1991), Kilham (Manby 1976, 126) or Streethouse (Vyner 1984), and the lesser forecourt structure at Haddenham (Hodder and Shand 1988, 351), seem to draw the attention of the onlooker in to the mortuary zone. Potentially, they might also define a path of approach toward the forecourt. Similarly, the façade trenches of sites like Streethouse, Fussell's Lodge or Willerby Wold converged on one end of the linear structure, further emphasising the importance of the depositional area. But at the same time, they separated the forecourt, the most obvious 'performative' area of the structure from any point at which direct access to the chamber could be achieved. This would seem to have established a distinction between public and perhaps 'commemorative' activities in the forecourt and the manipulation of human bones, possibly screening and secluding the latter. Equally, the digging of the flanking ditches, which provided the material for the mound, would have had the effect of limiting access to the barrow, emphasising the same axial pattern of movement implied by the post avenues.

In many of these linear mortuary structures, the burials were disarticulated, a feature which has prompted the suggestion that rites of *secondary burial* took place. The implications of such a conclusion are considerable. Where a good deal of effort has been expended in the removal of flesh from bones, for instance to the extent of burning it off (Thorpe 1984, 47), it is clear that some major distinction was being made between the two. Such a distinction has been documented amongst many different communities, and provides a good example of the way in which the human body can provide a rich resource of symbolism (Bloch 1982, 225). The distinction between a transient, rotting aspect of the body, and another, harder part which endures is of perennial interest, but the significance attributed to the two elements is by no means universal. The distinction between bones and flesh may be used as a means of expressing the divisions between order and mutability, person and community, life and death, consumption and reproduction, maleness and femaleness, and so on (Barley 1981, 149–50; Munn 1986). The separation of the two may consequently be recognised as a means by which order is achieved, and a dead body which is still fleshed may come to represent a classificatory anomaly (Douglas 1966). Practices of secondary burial are generally rites of passage which represent this anomalous state as unstable, dangerous and polluting (Hertz 1960). The separation of flesh and bones, whether by rotting or artificial means, achieves the resolution of putting the dead persons to rest, or allowing their spirit to leave the material world. Again, it is not necessary to invoke any universal belief in a soul of a particular kind to recognise the importance of this sort of transformation.

For one reason or another, bones which have been separated from flesh may come to represent some kind of absolute, removed from the complexities of the human condition. As symbols they may stand for ancestry, continuity, order, fertility or communality (Hertz 1960, 70). In different ways, control over human remains has often been perceived as important. In China, bones were placed in prominent positions as a means of gaining a symbolic control over the environment (Watson 1982, 176), while in highland New Guinea bones are kept in a 'head-house', and are seen as the means of access to the spirit of an ancestor (Strathern 1982, 117). Like the relics of Christian saints, the physical remains of the dead may be circulated and may be seen as a way of contacting ancestors and securing their intercession, or as a source of more generalised benefits. In this connection, it is worth considering the unusual patterning of bones pointed out by Shanks and Tilley (1982) in, amongst other sites, Fussell's Lodge. They saw the arrangement of skulls and longbones and the variation in the occurrence of ribs, vertebrae and phalanges as the result of a conscious process of re-ordering which served to present the dead as an undivided community, organised according to natural body symmetries. This may provide part of an explanation. But in addition, Kinnes (1975, 17) suggested that the placing of bones in barrows may in some cases have been only one stage of a more complex sequence, the final deposition of remains in the barrow being by no means an inevitable conclusion. The patterning isolated by Shanks and Tilley may thus be the end product of a long sequence of additions and removals from the burial deposit while the mortuary structure was still accessible. One aspect of the patterning at Fussell's Lodge which may be of considerable relevance concerns the division of the chamber into two by the medial post, a feature which recalls the structure of the orthostatic chambers in Clyde cairns and Irish court tombs (Corcoran 1960). Ashbee's report calls attention to 'a relative lack of ribs, small bones of the hands and feet, patellae, clavicles and scapulae' (Ashbee 1966, 62). However, it seems that this degree of selection applies more to the larger, innermost bone groups, A and B. Bone groups C and D, on the other side of the central partition, have a more even spread (Figure 6.5). The pattern might suggest the movement of bones from one part of the chamber to the other, with the gradual disarticulation of the skeleton being achieved by re-location. At this particular site, then, the spatial configuration of the chamber allowed a form of secondary burial to be played out within the confines of the mortuary area.

However, this is not to suggest that the mortuary practices associated with earthen long mounds were homogeneous. As with the construction of the monuments, the treatment of human bodies seems to have drawn on the possibilities presented by the skeleton and the monumental architecture in diverse ways which none the less indicate some recurring themes. At Nutbane, where all of the bodies were articulated, there was considerable variation in the state of preservation of the skeletons, suggesting that they may not have represented a single, synchronous deposit (Morgan 1959, 24). The child was decayed and disturbed, three of the adults slightly disordered. S4 seemed to be the last of the burials, and was undisturbed and overlaid one of the post-holes of the mortuary structure, suggesting that it had become ruinous by this stage. At Wayland's Smithy I the bones were arranged in piles. Those at the bottoms of the heaps were quite fragmentary, those above more often articulated but still never complete skeletons, and this suggests a prolonged reworking of the deposit before its final sealing (Whittle 1991, 71). Similarly, at Haddenham the chamber was subdivided in a similar way to Fussell's Lodge and only the inner compartment contained bones in any degree of articulation (Hodder and Shand 1988, 352). At Giant's Hills 2 the funerary deposit was extremely compact, and the excavators suggested that it may have represented the contents of a bag. Nevertheless, the bones concerned had undergone a variety of degrees of breakage, weathering and animal attack before burial (Evans and Simpson 1991, 16). Interestingly, the radiocarbon dates indicate that the chamber may have been in use for some considerable while before this deposit was made, and that it may have represented a final act before closure. Even at the crematorium barrow of Willerby Wold, where the burials were burnt together after deposition, the remains appear to have been disarticulated before combustion (Manby 1963, 182). Taken together, these sites suggest that some bodies may have been deposited directly into chambers, and some of these in turn may have been subject to disarticulation, re-arrangement, and even the removal of particular bones for use elsewhere. Other bones or body parts may have been brought to mortuary structures having been exposed elsewhere, or having already lain in other chambers.

At several sites burial deposits are absent or fragmentary in the extreme. This need not indicate that they had seen little use for mortuary purposes. We have argued already that defleshed bones might have had considerable symbolic significance, and their removal from a chamber would have facilitated their use in other practices and other forms of deposition. This suggests that we might think of these chambers less as vaults or ossuaries intended as the last resting place of the dead, and more as places of transition, in which dead people were transformed into another kind of being or substance, which might indeed have had none of the attributes of personhood. Alternatively, it might have been that the movement of representative bones, or the entire skeletons of specific ancestors, from one site to another was a means of cementing alliances between rival groups. Importantly, Thorpe (1984, 47) noted that different anatomical parts predominate amongst the human remains represented at causewayed enclosures and long barrows, while Ashbee (Ashbee *et al.* 1979, 83) suggests a 'reciprocal traffic' in bones between the two. So the circulation of bones

• 138 •

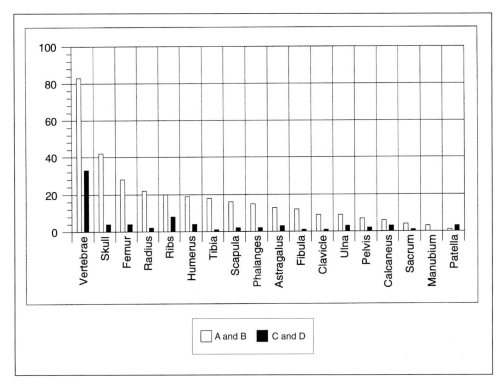

Figure 6.5 Fussell's Lodge, Wiltshire: distribution of anatomical parts

might not have been restricted to tombs and chambers. Thorpe (1984, 45) argued that many of the pits under the long barrows may be seen as the temporary resting places of burials while their flesh decayed, while the interpretation of various timber structures as exposure platforms is commonplace. At Hambledon Hill, Mercer (1980) has argued that the central enclosure was a massive centre for the exposure of the dead. This may be an overstatement, but it is evident that the processing of human remains was a major preoccupation at many enclosure sites (Edmonds 1993, 114–15). At Handley Hill on Cranborne Chase, Pitt Rivers (1898, 49–50) excavated the partial remains of an adult in a pit with ox bones and a large plain bowl (Piggott 1936, 229–30). Within the pit was a hole suggestive of an upright post, which might have been a marker to enable the remains to be recovered. It is thus clear that a number of different types of site were involved in the circulation of human remains, both within and between sites, and that cranial fragments may have held a particular significance. If such a circulation were in operation, attempts at population estimation on the basis of the number of bodies buried in long barrows (Atkinson 1968) may be flawed.

As we have seen, the long mounds which were built on the chalklands of Wiltshire, Dorset, Berkshire, Hampshire and Sussex in the period between 4000 and 3500 BC shared many of the same constructional details. However, over time even this degree of homogeneity declined. This happened in a number of different ways, but each can be understood as an elaboration of existing structures and practices which served to transform the significance of the monument and its ritual use. The first trajectory which can be isolated is that of the enhancement of monumentality. Andrew Fleming (1973, 173) once pointed out that a continuum exists between those tombs which are most effective as containers of the dead, and those which are monuments as such, and whose function is to focus the attention of the observer. Bradley (1984b, 24–5) suggests that in Britain as a whole there was a shift towards the monumental end of the spectrum as time progressed, with simple mounds becoming more elaborate. This took place in two ways. First, existing mounds were enlarged. For instance at Pentridge, an existing long mound had a 'tail' added to it to more than double its length (Bradley 1983, 16–17). At Tilshead Old Ditch, Hoare (1812, 90–1) describes a mound 'composed chiefly of white marly soil', but containing what appeared to be a circular barrow at its eastern end. At the east, too, was a mortuary area composed of flint nodules on which lay a single articulated female burial. However, another such area lay at the west end, with three further burials, seemingly a little higher than the old land surface (1812, 90–1; Thurnam 1869, 91–2). It may be that this massive long mound was the result of an earlier barrow being encapsulated by a mass of chalk rubble, with the addition of a new burial area. This would present a situation similar to that at Wor Barrow (Pitt Rivers 1898), Amesbury 42 (Richards 1990, 98), Millbarrow (Whittle 1994) and Netheravon Bake (Richards 1990, 265), where the flanking ditches were recut or replaced with new ditches, presumably in order to increase the height of the mound. The encapsulation of the small long mound at Wayland's Smithy by a massive trapezoidal mound with stone chamber presents a similar phenomenon (Whittle 1991).

Second, a new class of extremely long mounds, the bank barrows, were constructed. The relatively late date of these monuments is demonstrated by the running of the Maiden Castle and Crickley Hill long mounds across the ditches of causewayed enclosures (Wheeler 1943; Dixon 1988), and the date of c. 3496 BC (2722 ± 49 bc) (BM-1405) for the example at North Stoke (Case 1982a). Assuming the two child skeletons from a pit beneath the Maiden Castle mound to be associated with the causewayed enclosure phase (Wheeler 1943, 18–24), neither of these sites seems to have been directly connected with the disposal of the dead, but rather with monumentality for its own sake. This links the bank barrows to two contemporary phenomena: cursus monuments and the 'cenotaph' barrows at Beckhampton Road and South Street (Ashbee *et al.* 1979). Indeed, the connection with cursus monuments is emphasised by the Scorton cursus in Yorkshire and the Cleaven Dyke in Perthshire, both of which consisted of a bank mound contained within cursus ditches (Topping 1982; Barclay *et al.* 1995).

The second strand which can be distinguished is a growth of regional traditions: a point noted by Thorpe (1984, 58). The much-discussed oval barrows with single burials (Figure 6.6) (Drewett 1975; Thorpe 1984) are restricted to the south of the country, and the U-ditched examples are concentrated in, if not restricted to, Cranborne Chase (Bradley *et al.* 1984c, 94). In the Avebury area, earthen long mounds were constructed with orthostatic sarsen chambers in their terminals, a trait possibly 'borrowed' from the Cotswolds (Thomas and Whittle 1986). Bayed 'cenotaph' barrows may also have been a particular feature of the Avebury district (Ashbee *et al.* 1979). The extreme size of Winterbourne Stoke 1, Amesbury 42, Bratton, King Barrow, Old Ditch and Tilshead 7 may indicate that particularly large conventional long barrows may have been a feature of this period on Salisbury Plain, while Maiden Castle, Long Bredy and Broadmayne may indicate a preference for bank barrows in south Dorset.

The third element to mention is the shift from large numbers of disarticulated to few articulated bodies. As Thorpe (1984, 54) indicates, this is more of a general trend than a clear-cut division. It is most obvious in the case of the oval mounds containing one or two articulated bodies: Alfriston (Drewett 1975), Barrow Hills, Radley (Figure 6.7) (Bradley 1992), Moody's Down south-east (Grimes 1960) and probably the smaller long barrow on Hambledon Hill (Mercer 1980), the first two of these sites having produced radiocarbon dates later than 3500 BC. In most of these cases the burials were laid out in a simple grave, and it may be that the determinant factor in this process is a decline in the overall duration of mortuary activities prior to the construction of the mound. Rather than a prolonged phase of bone accumulation and

Figure 6.6 Burial with flint blade at Barrow Hills, Radley

Figure 6.7 Barrow Hills, Radley, Oxfordshire: long barrow

circulation, it may be that mounds were now raised soon after a single event of deposition. This would explain the situation which we have already mentioned at Nutbane, and that at Wor Barrow, where three male skeletons and three bundles of post-cranial bones, each with one skull (presumably brought from elsewhere), were found within what appears to have been an embanked linear chamber (Pitt Rivers 1898, 66; Piggott 1966, 38).

This development could be rationalised in a number of different ways. First, one could argue that particular persons, or descent groups, were becoming more important, and were monopolising a prestigious form of burial as a means of increasing their prestige. This could be seen as deriving from a change in the way in which personal identity was understood, or from an increased emphasis on the principle of endogamy, of 'keeping to oneself'. Such a development might easily manifest itself in a desire to keep all of the flesh and bones of the group within the tomb (Bloch and Parry 1982, 20), although one might also expect larger numbers of bodies in this case. However, the existence of more box-like chambers, like that at Whiteleaf Hill in Buckinghamshire, containing a single middle-aged male burial and not designed for easy access to the mortuary deposit (Childe and Smith 1954, 216), provides some support for this line of argument. But equally, we could suggest a changing relationship between the living and the dead, so that rather than engaging in intimate and continuous relations with human bones, burial became a discontinuous event. This is to some extent what Barrett (1988b; 1994) implies in his distinction between 'ancestor rituals' and 'funerals'. Bodies ceased to be disaggregated at the same time as bones ceased to circulate amongst the living. A different kind of 'ancestor' may have emerged, who was now identifiable as a named progenitor, but who was located in the past rather than remaining an integral part of the living community. Finally, given that some forms of mound were now being constructed without burials at all, the presence of the dead at all may have been of declining importance. The significance of the barrow might now lie in its outward appearance rather than its contents (Thorpe 1984, 54).

This leads on to the final point. The organisation of space within the later long barrows seems to have been very different. With the oval mounds, we have seen that the emphasis on a complex series of pre-mound activities was entirely lost, the mound seemingly being thrown up over a simple grave. However, at both Radley (Bradley 1992) and Hambledon Hill (Mercer 1980) a complex series of ditch recuts seems to have taken place after the mound was constructed. As we have already mentioned, another characteristic of later mounds is U-shaped or surrounding ditches. These two phenomena, the raising of the mound immediately after burial and the more complete enclosure of the mound, seem to have as their objective the separation of the burial deposit from the mundane world.

This point can be further exemplified by returning to the Nutbane barrow (Figure 6.8). Although this mound contained an embanked linear chamber, we have seen that the bones within it were articulated and predominantly male. Rather than focusing attention on these deposits, a massive but separate forecourt structure was built, and the mortuary area was cordoned off with a fence (Morgan 1959, 20). Kinnes (1981, 84) and Fleming (1973) both emphasise the importance of the 'business end', the focal area generally at the east of the barrow. While the monumental timber façades of the earlier barrows separated 'back' and 'front' space (Giddens 1984, 129), the decline of activities involving the manipulation of human bones would have increased the relative importance of gatherings in the forecourt. This is another indication that the world of the living and that of the dead were becoming more separate, even in the context of mortuary ritual.

We have already effectively drawn a distinction between the chamber and forecourt as locations for practice, and the mound as an object of contemplation (perhaps from a distance), or as a site of memory. But memories can slip from notice, and if the activities which preceded mound building were curtailed their significance might have dwindled. The past can become meaningless if it is not brought into the daily lives of a community (Lynch 1972, 60); places can only be kept 'alive' by involving them in practice (Relph 1976, 32). At a number of long barrows, depositional activities appear to have continued after the mound was constructed, often respecting the grading of space which had been established by the chamber and façade. At both Fussell's Lodge and Willerby Wold, the practice of depositing potsherds and animal bones in the façade area seems to have continued unabated after the construction of the mound. And at sites like Horslip, Wayland's Smithy I, Kingston Deverill and Holdenhurst the ditch deposits continued to maintain the same spatial organisation of material things, with cattle bones, pottery or stone axes concentrated in the ditch butts nearest the chamber and forecourt (Piggott 1937, 7). At Thickthorn Down and Barrow Hills this theme took a more elaborate form, with the ditch bottom used as a context in which different classes of material – flint, human bone, animal bone, antler and so on – might be distinguished between through segregation within association (Drew and Piggott 1936; Barrett *et al.* 1991, 37–8; Bradley 1992, 134–5). These activities are a further indication that the relationships between the living and the dead had changed: mounds were now being used for the commemoration of the past.

The earthen long barrows of southern and eastern Britain began as a tradition which involved a series of archetypal constructional elements, which were put to use in ways which indicate some common themes of practice. From the start, though, construction and ritual were characterised by idiosyncrasy, and local tastes and strategies gradually eroded consensus and fuelled elaboration. The coexistence of vast monumental works like the bank barrows and cursus monuments, of small oval mounds closely linked to the emerging round barrow burials, and of complex multi-stage barrows which made use of spatial divisions to classify and separate persons and artefacts, indicates the degree of divergence in practice. By this stage, there can be no suggestion that all

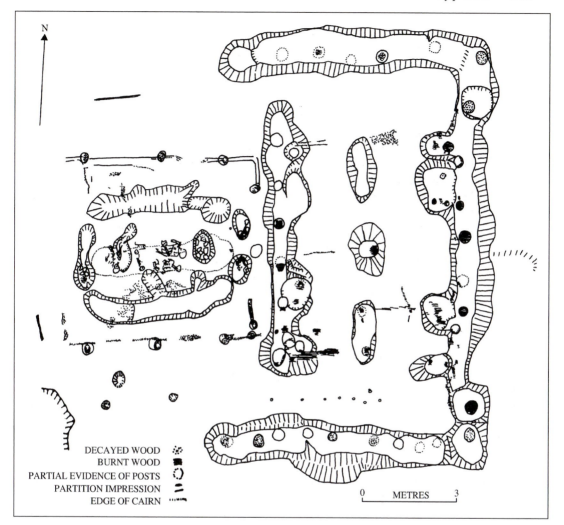

N

DECAYED WOOD
BURNT WOOD
PARTIAL EVIDENCE OF POSTS
PARTITION IMPRESSION
EDGE OF CAIRN

0   METRES   3

Figure 6.8 The mortuary structures at Nutbane long barrow, Hampshire

long barrows 'meant' the same thing. But in a sense they never did: the variation in the use and construction of long barrows is indicative of the many ways in which they were understood by the people who created them.

COTSWOLD–SEVERN TOMBS

The Cotswold–Severn tombs are a group of megalithic chambered cairns concentrated in the uplands of Gloucestershire, north Oxfordshire, north Wiltshire, Avon, Somerset and south Wales. They provide an interesting comparison with the earthen long mounds, since the two traditions share some aspects of architectural organisation and funerary practice. The principal difference between the two is that while the construction of the earthen barrows brought about the effective cessation of mortuary activity at these sites, the Cotswold–Severn tombs had chambers which remained accessible after the building of the cairn. As with the long barrows, there are strong indications that these tombs were built in locations which had already gained some significance. The excavation of sites such as Sale's Lot (O'Neil 1966), Ascott-under-Wychwood (Benson and Clegg 1978) and Cow Common Long (Rolleston 1876) revealed earlier scatters of artefacts or fragmentary structures on the old land surface. Saville (1990, 254) suggests that previous domestic occupation of a site might represent a primary criterion for tomb location. Given the presence of Mesolithic material beneath some of these tombs, it might be that some of these places represented very long-lived woodland clearances, whose importance was not exclusively as campsites, but as landmarks and meeting-places as well. That a variety of activities may have taken place in these pre-cairn locations is indicated at Hazleton North, where a large 'midden' contained the bones of numerous animals which had been slaughtered and consumed nearby, while rubbers and quernstones indicated that the processing of plants had taken place as well (Saville 1990, 241). The presence of fragmentary human remains in pre-cairn contexts at Hazleton, Gwernvale and Millbarrow implies that as well as places of temporary occupation and large-scale consumption, these were already locations where practices enacted upon the bodies of dead persons were sanctioned.

The architecture of the Cotswold–Severn group shows considerable variability. While the majority of the tombs are trapezoidal cairns with chambers approached by orthostatic or drystone passages, comparable to the long barrows in size and shape, there are also less regularly shaped mounds like Nicholaston (Williams 1940), and oddities such as the amorphous structure at Saltway Barn (Grimes 1960, 5–40). Over the years, there has been much discussion of the potential chronological significance of tomb morphology. Thurnam (1869) and Grimes (1960) both proposed 'devolutionary' sequences in which more complex chamber forms which ultimately derived from Breton prototypes declined to single cells set in the sides of cairns. Obviously, this framework is predicated upon the diffusionist postulate that human beings are generally uninventive, and that away from the 'hearths' of cultural development their creations will tend to gradually decrease in sophistication (e.g. Smith 1929, 5; Childe 1950, 9). Following Corcoran's (1972) arguments concerning the multi-phase construction of many British megalithic tombs, Darvill (1987, 63) suggested that the earliest funerary structures in the Cotswold–Severn region may have been 'rotunda graves', which were later incorporated into a number of long cairns. A strong case for such a sequence can be made for the closed cist within a circular structure inside the long cairn at Notgrove (Clifford 1936), and it may be that the 'tail' of the mound was added to a circular cairn at Sale's Lot (O'Neil 1966). However, the curved walling at Ty Isaf and Pipton seems bonded into the overall structure of the cairns (Grimes 1939; Savory 1956), while the oval structure surrounding the chambers at Nympsfield (Clifford 1938) is more probably a constructional device than a separate phase in the monument's history. It is consequently unclear how far these 'rotunda graves' represent a distinct horizon of monument-building, and how far they can be seen as one aspect of the modular construction of the cairns, also manifested in the rectilinear cells recognised at a number of sites.

Amongst the trapezoid cairns, a basic distinction exists between those tombs which have a number of chambers set laterally in the mound, and those which have a single entrance in the terminal, leading either to a single chamber or a set of transepts (Figure 6.9). On the basis of the presence of Peterborough Ware and other later Neolithic artefacts in the chamber and blocking deposits amongst some cairns with terminal transepted chambers, Darvill (1982) suggested that these might be later in date than those with lateral chambers. While some authors see this as an over-interpretation of scanty evidence, it is undeniably the case that all of the radiocarbon dates for Cotswold–Severn tombs which fall earlier than 3700 BC are for laterally chambered cairns. It remains plausible that the construction of laterally chambered tombs began a couple of centuries earlier than that of terminally chambered cairns, albeit with considerable overlap between the two.

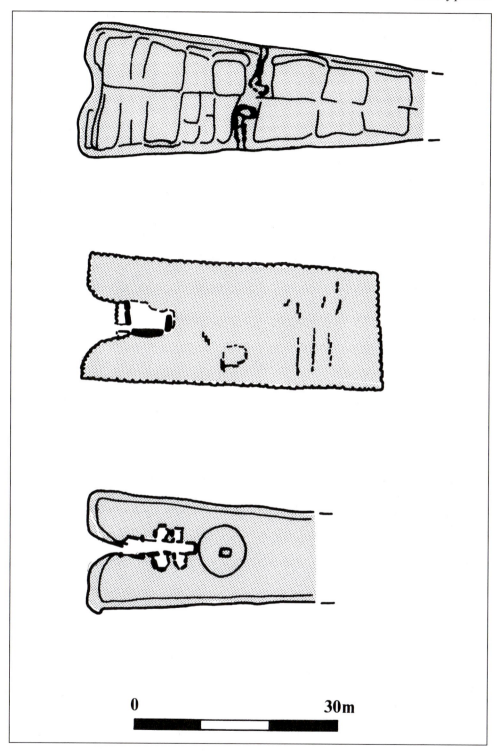

Figure 6.9 Comparative plans of Cotswold–Severn long cairns. From top: Hazleton North, Tinkinswood, Notgrove.

While the established typologies of cairn form may have had the effect of promoting interpretations which stress homogeneity (Bestley 1993), it is significant that the principal configurations of space represented within the Cotswold–Severn tradition present quite different potentials for ordering and staging mortuary practice. The recent excavations at Hazleton North demonstrated that the long cairn was flanked by two large quarries, which had provided the stone used in construction. Each lateral passage entrance opened directly toward a deep quarry pit, while quarries were absent from the east and west (Saville 1990, 23). In a manner similar to the flanking ditches of the earthen long barrows, the quarries at Hazleton encouraged an axial pattern of movement toward the forecourt, while making access to the chambers a more complex matter of moving along the outer wall of the cairn. While the forecourt at Hazleton was defined by a blank façade, it contained a deposit of animal bones, and other forecourts have revealed hearths or burnt areas, as at Luckington (Corcoran 1970), and pit deposits, as at Nympsfield and Rodmarton. Collections of animal bones, generally dominated by pig, have also come from forecourts Rodmarton, Uley and Gwernvale, and human burials were found at West Tump and Gatcombe Lodge (Witts 1881; Passmore 1938). These points indicate that these areas were architecturally defined theatral spaces, which drew people together and were used for acts of consumption and deposition. Where the chamber or chambers were accessed by a single entrance in the end of the cairn, this space would have to be crossed in any activity involving the deposition or removal of human remains. In the process, the activities of those entering the chambers and those gathering in the forecourt would have been more closely integrated. While there need not have been any great difference in the sequence of acts performed upon the dead bodies involved, the relationships between the living and the dead would have been subtly shifted by this arrangement.

Within the laterally chambered tombs, human skeletal remains are generally found in a disarticulated condition (Figure 6.10). However, at Hazleton North one complete and one semi-

Figure 6.10 Burials in the North Chamber, Hazleton long cairn, Gloucestershire

complete male skeleton were found in the entrance of the passage leading to the North Chamber (Figure 6.11). With this in mind, Saville (1984, 22) originally suggested that 'the absence of intact inhumations in the passages and chambers, particularly in the sealed North Chamber, would suggest that bodies were left to decompose in the entrance and subsequently were taken through as bones to the interior'. More recently, Saville has revised this interpretation in the light of evidence that parts of the disarticulated bodies in the chambers appeared not to have been left behind in the entrances and passages (1990, 251). Instead, it seemed probable that fleshed corpses had begun to be deposited in the chamber, each body becoming more disordered as subsequent inhumations were introduced. As the available space filled up, bodies were placed in the passage and closer to the entrance. Evidently, some of the movement of body parts had taken place before decomposition was complete, resulting in individual examples of partial articulation (1990, 251). We might note in passing that this does not fully explain the absence of articulated bodies in the northern chamber area. Somehow, all of the

Figure 6.11 Articulated skeleton in the north entrance at Hazleton long cairn

remains in the North Chamber had become disarticulated before the collapse of the passage orthostat which curtailed deposition in the North Chamber and the inner part of the North Passage (Saville 1990, 104). All of this disordering of skeletons cannot be attributed simply to 'making space' for new bodies.

Similar patterns to those at Hazleton are reported at Lanhill, where bodies in a skeletal state had been pushed to the back of the North-West Chamber before the insertion of the final burial (Keiller and Piggott 1938), and Pole's Wood East, where 'one skeleton was found undisturbed and surrounded by other human bones so disposed, and in such numbers, as to make it clear that the skeleton they had belonged to had been displaced to make room for it' (Greenwell 1877, 527). Rolleston (1876, 133) concurs that 'some if not all of the bodies had been placed in the flesh, or, at all events, when the ligaments were there'. However, the disposition of these remains cannot entirely be accounted for by the repeated clearing aside of bones. There is considerable evidence for the deliberate re-ordering of skeletal parts, whether in the form of 'placed deposits' of clustered long bones (Saville 1990, 103), or the arrangement of skulls alongside chamber walls, recognised at Pole's Wood East, Ascott-under-Wychwood and Cow Common Long. At Eyford, Rolleston notes that 'all the skulls seem to be in the south side of the cist' (1876, 133). Skulls were clustered against orthostats in the southern passage and chamber at Hazleton, while two skulls were placed on top of a collapsed orthostat in the northern entrance (Saville 1990, 125). At Penywyrlod long bones were piled up against the side walls of Chamber II, and skulls lined up against the north wall (Britnell and Savory 1984, 19). The particular attention which seems to have been afforded to skulls in these contexts is representative of a more general concern with skulls and skull fragments in Neolithic Britain.

While it may have been normal for bodies to be placed inside the tomb (whether directly into the chamber or laid out in the entrance) in a fleshed state, it seems that substantial reorganisation occurred once the flesh had decayed. Some form of transformation of the body was performed through the separation of its parts, and this does invite the kind of interpretation originally presented by Shanks and Tilley (1982), concerned with the assertion of the corporate identity of the group. Many of the Cotswold–Severn tombs have passages which are segmented by jambs or septal slabs, which serve to divide up the space leading toward the passage. At Hazleton, one pair of slabs served as a resting place for an internal blocking slab, 'a movable device, which was put in place between burial episodes, but which could be taken down when it was necessary to re-enter the chamber' (Saville 1990, 77). This would have had the effect of excluding scavenging animals from the tomb, and there is certainly very little evidence of animal gnawing amongst the bone sample (1990, 182). However, some of these constrictions are more severe than would strictly be required to enable such temporary blocking. The 'portholes' at Rodmarton and Avening (Clifford and Daniel 1940) and the 'pseudo-porthole' in Luckington Chamber B (Corcoran 1970, 43) would have made it virtually impossible to pull an articulated body into the chamber. Two points follow from this: a deliberate effort was sometimes made to establish a sequence of distinct spaces leading to the chamber, and in some cases only skeletal parts could have been passed through to the chamber interior. The implication is that both the change from fleshed to unfleshed and the movement toward the chamber were of significance.

There is, however, considerable variation both in the details of chamber morphology and in the way in which those chambers were used for the disposition of human bodies. At West Tump (Witts 1881), Cow Common Long (Rolleston 1876) and Pole's Wood East (Greenwell 1877) human remains were found within linear zones, sometimes cut into the ground surface, sometimes defined by drystone walling, and sometimes approached by an orthostatic entrance leading in from the side of the cairn. In plan, these seem rather similar to the chambers of Slewcairn and Lochill, constructed around timber mortuary structures (Masters 1983). Within these chambers, complete burials, scattered bones and piles of disarticulated remains were all encountered.

On the whole, the laterally chambered cairns show evidence for the movement and circulation of human remains which is comparable with the earthen long mounds, although the strongest evidence is for the process of reorganisation taking place within the confines of chamber and passage. However, there are also empty or almost empty chambers which imply the removal of bones. Moreover, the representation of particular body parts amongst the larger bone samples may be uneven. At Hazleton, for instance, it seems that both longbones and skulls had been removed (Saville 1990, 251), while at a number of sites there are supernumerary skulls and mandibles. The use of the transepted tombs may have been quite similar, although there are rather more complete bodies. The interment of fleshed corpses certainly seems to have taken place. Crawford writes of the 'original posture' at Hetty Peggler's Tump (Uley) as having been 'sitting or rather squatting' (1925, 104), and partially or completely articulated bodies were present in several of the chambers at West Kennet (Piggott 1962, 21) and in the undisturbed Chamber D at Notgrove (Clifford 1936). However, at Wayland's Smithy II the bones were very disordered, although the excavators saw this as evidence for sequential inhumation (Peers and Smith 1921, 190). In the case of Parc le Breos Cwm, Whittle and Wysocki (1998) present a strong case for the exposure of the bones prior to deposition. There was variation in the degree of weathering of the bones, and extensive evidence of animal biting and gnawing on those found in the chambers. However, the bodies found in the passage were in a partial state of articulation, and had not been scavenged. What is unclear about this particular site is the extent to which both weathering and animal attack could have taken place within the chambers, which might not have afforded the degree of protection evident at Hazleton. But it provides at least an indication that the architectural form of the transepted chambered mound might have been used for a variety of different mortuary practices.

In both the laterally chambered and transepted tombs spatial organisation appears to have been used in order to draw attention to differences between people, and these may have been concerned with age and gender (Kinnes 1981, 85). Given that we know so little about the organisation of gender in Neolithic Britain, it is very dangerous to draw too much inference on the basis of the differential treatment of 'male' and 'female' bodies: these contemporary categories may not have been recognised at all. For whatever it is worth, there was a predominance of female bodies in the South Chamber and males in the North Chamber at Lanhill, and there were six males in Cist 2 at Eyford. At Lugbury, no males were found in Cist A and only males were found in Cist C (Thurnam 1857), while at Notgrove an adult male was placed in the separate cist in the 'rotunda' behind the transepted chambers, with female bones scattered over the surface of its revetment (Clifford 1936). What is interesting, however, is that distinctions between young and old people are much more evident, particularly in the case of transepted tombs. Furthermore, the body treatment afforded to young people often tends to separate them out, as in the case of the cremated children in separate cists in Chamber C at Nympsfield (Clifford 1938).

The transepted chamber architecture involves a single entrance which gives access to a series of separate, but linked, spaces. At sites like Stoney Littleton and Nempnett Thrubwell (Hoare 1821; Bulleid 1941) there may be relatively many such spaces. This would seem to be the architectural equivalent of the principle of segregation within association, which we have identified elsewhere as characteristic of Neolithic depositional practices. Transepted chambers would allow different kinds of persons and substances to be deposited in juxtaposition, and in the process evaluated against each other. Interestingly, the chambers at Burn Ground, Notgrove and West Kennet appear to have been used to divide up people in rather similar ways. Young persons were deposited in the chambers to the left of the passage, particularly the front left chamber, where the bones were generally completely disarticulated. At Notgrove and West Kennet, elderly persons were found in the front right-hand chamber, articulated or partially articulated. Furthermore, at Parc le Breos Cwm, West Kennet and Nympsfield cremations were located in the front right-hand chamber (Whittle and Wysocki 1998). The possibility is that the chamber space was being used as a means of representing age classes, and that younger persons with less distinct social identities were more likely to become disarticulated after decomposition.

The evidence from tombs with single-cell chambers in the cairn terminal is even more fragmentary. These are, in any case, an architecturally diverse group of monuments. What they have in common is the provision of a single space for burial, as opposed to the multiple cells available both at laterally chambered and transepted chambered tombs. This suggests a lack of concern with classification and segmentation, which is also manifested in mortuary deposits which are often in a state of the 'utmost confusion' (Vulliamy 1921). It is uncertain whether this is a product of excarnation or disarticulation *in situ*. At Adlestrop Hill, Donovan (1938) reported the presence of the partially articulated remains of an adult male amongst a mass of bone, composed largely of the remains of children and containing a number of skulls. Yet it is unclear whether this body was intrusive, or the last in a sequence of burial deposits. A similar mass of bone at Randwick showed a scarcity of skulls and femurs (Witts 1883), again raising the possibility of bone circulation. If the simple terminal chambers are broadly contemporary with the transeptal tombs, this may be an indication that different communities had different priorities in the representation of the dead, some seeking to emphasise the undivided character of the group, others more concerned to distinguish between different classes of person.

Over the years, there has been continuing debate over the status of 'extra-revetment' and blocking material: loose, jumbled stonework found beyond the outer revetment wall and in the forecourt of many tombs. The recent meticulous excavations at Hazleton would appear to have finally settled the matter: Saville states unequivocally that 'all extra-cairn material results from the decay of the monument' (1990, 257). The downward and outward gravitational thrust of the cairn body resulted in the overbalancing of both the inner and outer revetment walls, the collapse of their upper courses, and the slippage of loose cairn material from above. It is difficult to assess how long this process of decay would have taken; however, it is to be assumed that the earliest tombs would have reached a state of dilapidation within the span of the Neolithic. On this basis Saville goes on to argue that 'it can be doubted whether any of the "blocking" claimed to exist around Cotswold–Severn tombs is deliberate and not the product of natural decay' (1990, 257). Yet it is clear that the deliberate blocking of *some* parts of *some* tombs did take place: the great quantity of material filling up the chambers and passage at West Kennet is an extreme example (Piggott 1962, 26–7). The difficulty lies in distinguishing between collapsed and placed material. This problem is compounded by the situation at the laterally chambered tomb of Gwernvale, where Britnell suggests that blocking the tomb and placing extra-revetment material against the revetment walls was a conscious act aimed at 'the "instant" production of an archaic form – a tomb which had clearly ceased to be used for formal mortuary activities' (Britnell and Savory 1984, 150). Britnell's principal evidence for this is that the forecourt blocking material included considerable quantities of quartzitic sandstone which was scarce in the rest of the cairn (1984, 64). According to this argument, laterally chambered tombs were eventually blocked, closed off and in some cases structurally altered in order to suggest great antiquity. This is a picture which fits in very well with the contemporary changes which we have seen amongst the earthen long mounds. Increasingly, the dead were being located in the past, and this past was both distant and unassailable.

At Hazleton, an estimate has been made that the entire period of use of the tomb was probably less than 300 years, and perhaps as little as half that (Saville *et al.* 1987, 115; Saville 1990, 239). This contrasts with the suggestion that the burials at Parc le Breos Cwm took some considerable time to accumulate (Whittle and Wysocki 1998). There may thus have been considerable variations in the histories of deposition and closure of particular tombs. Hazleton may be an example of a site which went through use and dereliction relatively quickly. At Burn Ground, Grimes (1960, 76) suggested that the outer revetment wall had been built within a V-shaped trench, so as to give the impression of a wall already nearing a state of collapse. Yet at Hazleton a similar feature had been caused by the gradual outward pressure of the cairn, causing the lower course of the wall to be pressed into the soil surface (Saville 1990, 50). Once again, it may be difficult to distinguish between the natural collapse evident at Hazleton, and the deliberate 'antiquation' claimed at other sites. At Burn Ground no slumping at all was visible in the *inner* revetment (Grimes 1960, 62, Figure 27), which may provide an indication that the slope of the outer wall was indeed artificial. It is interesting that the most convincing parallels which Grimes could cite for this feature were at Notgrove and Nympsfield, both also transepted terminal-chambered tombs. Darvill (1982, 47) separates those cairns at which extra-revetment was a product of erosion and decay from those at which it seems to have been a deliberate construction. All the transepted tombs considered fell into the latter category. Furthermore, the blocking in the forecourt of transepted tombs appears always to have been disturbed during Neolithic times (Darvill 1982, 59). If some of the laterally chambered tombs were altered in order to suggest great age, the transepted tombs may have actually been constructed in such a way as to indicate antiquity. This would imply that the burials contained within were from the start presented as ancient and inaccessible.

We have seen that in some of the transepted chambers, the bodies of older people were left in an articulated state – possibly because they were persons who were still remembered or venerated. Hence it is significant that the last acts carried out inside a few of the laterally chambered tombs involved the 'reconstitution' of persons from the scattered parts available. At Ascott-under-Wychwood, bones from different bodies were articulated together (Chesterman 1977, 26), while in Chamber II at Pipton seven piles of bones had been separated out, although each might contain bones from several persons (Savory 1956). In Chamber I at Ty Isaf, bones had been arranged in groups consisting of skull, mandible and one or two longbones placed against the orthostats (Grimes 1939), while at Lanhill, Keiller and Piggott (1938, 125) noted that each skull 'was furnished with a lower jaw placed in approximately the correct position, but it was subsequently proved that one of the jaws could not have originally belonged to the skull in association with which it was found'. In the same way as we have seen with the earthen barrows, specific dead people were now of importance: persons from whom descent could be claimed.

The blocking of the tombs interrupted any flow of reciprocity between the living and the dead, and separated the past from the present. Yet the tombs and their contents continued to exert an influence on their surroundings. This is demonstrated by the continued deposition of bodies and artefacts in the cairns and forecourts of the tombs. Secondary burials are often hard to date, and are thus not always of much consequence to the argument. Examples which clearly are of relevance are the child burial in a cist in the horn of Penywyrlod (Britnell and Savory 1984), the burials with leaf arrowheads in the mound at Sale's Lot (O'Neil 1966), and the female skull with Peterborough Ware sherds in front of the false portal at Gatcombe Lodge (Crawford 1925, 98–100; Clifford 1936, 45; Passmore 1938). Intrusive deposits of pots occurred in the cases of the Beaker at Sale's Lot (O'Neil 1966) and a Peterborough vessel inserted into the horn at Pole's Wood South (Rolleston 1876, 165–71; Greenwell 1877, 521–4). The deposition of a stone axe butt in the forecourt at Ty Isaf may or may not have post-dated the blocking (Grimes 1939).

SINGLE GRAVES BEFORE BEAKERS

Single burials beneath round mounds are one of the characteristic aspects of the earlier Bronze Age in Atlantic Europe (Childe 1930, 161). In culture-historic archaeology, such a practice might be presumed to be diagnostic of a particular group of people. Very often, its inception in Britain has been connected with the arrival of a distinct 'Beaker folk' (e.g. Hawkes and Hawkes 1948, 57), although the presence of typologically 'Neolithic' artefacts in some single graves threatens to undermine this interpretation. Sometimes it has been argued that 'native' people adopted the single grave rite after having come into contact with Beaker populations (Piggott 1938, 55; Stone 1958, 59). Sometimes, again, the presence of an insular tradition of inhumation and cremation burial has been acknowledged, but its significance limited to that of a cultural trait (Atkinson *et al.* 1951, 70). Until relatively recently their social implications have been somewhat neglected. Seemingly, both round mounds and burial with associated artefacts emerged quite early in the Neolithic (Burgess and Shennan 1976), although the two practices were not always mutually associated. Round barrows like Westbury 7 in Wiltshire, where a number of disarticulated skeletons

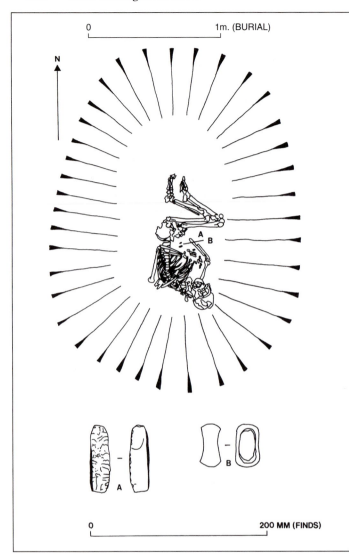

0   1m. (BURLAL)

N

A
B

A   B

0   200 MM (FINDS)

Figure 6.12 Later Neolithic single grave at Linch Hill Corner, Oxfordshire
Source: After Barclay *et al.* (1995)

were found under a mound with a causewayed ditch (Hoare 1812, 54), suggest contemporaneity with the long barrows. Other examples, like Mere 13d with its cremation inside an earlier Neolithic pot (Piggott 1931, 94–5) or the small barrow on Launceston Down containing a body with a leaf-shaped arrowhead (Piggott and Piggott 1944, 47–80), were probably early on artefactual grounds. As we have seen already, single bodies were buried beneath some of the later long mounds, as at Alfriston (Drewett 1975) and Winterbourne Stoke 1 (Thurnam 1869). This material does not argue for the revolutionary appearance of a new rite, but for the gradual emergence of the various elements of a funerary practice concerned with a single body, which became more coherent as time went on (Figure 6.12). While some of the artefacts associated with these burials, like jet belt sliders, antler maceheads, polished flint knives or transverse arrowheads occurred in a number of different graves, there was rather less standardisation in the funerary assemblage than with the Beaker graves which succeeded them.

The most extensive group of Neolithic round barrows and single graves in Britain exists on the Wolds of east Yorkshire (Harding 1997, 284), and these provided the framework for Kinnes' (1979) study of the phenomenon. In particular, the sequence at Duggleby Howe, which ran from inhumations in graves beneath a large mound to cremations inserted from above (Mortimer 1905; Kinnes *et al.* 1983, 95) enabled a seriation of grave goods to be established. The density of Neolithic graves in Yorkshire is instructive in another sense as well: these single burials were not distributed evenly across Britain, but are often found in clusters in, for example, the Derbyshire Peak District and the Upper Thames Valley. Even within these regions, the graves and barrows appear to cluster spatially, suggesting that single burial was practised by some communities but not by others.

The group of single graves and barrows in the Upper Thames is the most numerous in the south of England (see Chapter 8 below). Significantly, the area contains at least one late long barrow with articulated burials. At Radley a multi-phase oval mound covered a primary interment of two articulated skeletons, one with a polished flint blade and jet belt slider, the other with a lozenge arrowhead. The site provided radiocarbon dates earlier than 3000 BC (Bradley 1992). Nearby is the largely Bronze Age barrow cemetery of Barrow Hills, which contained a number of relatively early Beaker burials. In the same general area were a trench-like mortuary structure containing three bodies in various states of articulation, three flat graves and at least two ring ditches of pre-Beaker date (Barclay and Halpin 1999). These ring ditches appear to have established the original alignment of the linear cemetery, and it is arguable that there was some continuity in the use of the area as a place for the deposition of the dead from the middle of the Neolithic onwards. Downriver at Dorchester on Thames, Bradley has suggested that Site XI was originally a similar oval mound (Bradley and Holgate 1984, 118), aligned on Site VIII, the long mortuary enclosure. Site I also has a rather oval plan, with a line of later Neolithic recuts along one edge which would effectively correspond with the position of a façade. The remains of a primary crouched inhumation were present on the old land surface (Atkinson *et al.* 1951, 12). At both Radley and Dorchester, the oval mound served as a focus for later Neolithic mortuary activities. The cluster of monuments at Dorchester on Thames consists of a variety of round mounds and pit circles, into which secondary cremations had been dug. Presumably, others of these may have had primary inhumations on the old land surface which had not survived until the time of excavations.

According to Kinnes' seriation (1979, Figure 6.2), the cremation burials found at Dorchester, Duggleby Howe and other sites represent the culmination of the indigenous sequence of single grave burial. It is conceivable that the spread of the rite of cremation at the end of the Neolithic period was an aspect of the development of new networks of contact between privileged groups in separate regions of Britain (Bradley and Chapman 1984). Cremation burials with skewer pins are known from the Irish passage tombs (Eogan 1986, 138), while a cremation cemetery with miniature cups, bone pins and polished edge knives is known at Ballateare on the Isle of Man (Bersu 1947). However, we should not imagine that a new body treatment would be adopted if there were not compelling local reasons for such a change. In England and Wales these cremations were associated with oblique arrowheads, flint fabricators, stone maceheads, bone pins (Kinnes *et al.* 1983, 98), and to a lesser extent with Grooved Ware (Kinnes 1979, Figure 6.1). What may have been a sherd from a plain Grooved Ware vessel was found with a cremation inserted into the remains of a post-circle within the Dorchester on Thames cursus, although this attribution is not secure (Bradley and Holgate 1984; Whittle *et al.* 1992, 170). Cremations have been located in henge and hengiform monuments at Stonehenge (Atkinson 1956, 27–9), Barford (Oswald 1969), Llandegai (Houlder 1968), Woodhenge (Cunnington 1929, 29), Dorchester on Thames (Atkinson *et al.* 1951) and Coneybury (Richards 1990, 158). Generally, though, these deposits are in secondary stratigraphic positions on these sites, so that none of them need have been constructed with use as a cemetery in mind. It may consequently be unwise to cast the later Neolithic cremations as the mortuary deposits of Grooved Ware users.

Recently, Joshua Pollard has drawn attention to the spatial distribution of the cremation deposits within the ditch, bank and Aubrey Holes at Stonehenge (cited in Cleal *et al.* 1995, 153). Broadly speaking, the cremations were less densely concentrated toward the western part of the monument. Interestingly, a similar pattern can be discerned at a number of other sites. At Dorchester on Thames Sites I, II, IV, V, VI and 2 (Atkinson *et al.* 1951; Whittle *et al.* 1992) and West Stow (West 1990), the cremations were arranged around the periphery of the monument, and concentrated in the south and/or east. In several cases, the northern part of the circuit was avoided, while at West Stow and Dorchester II and III, one or two cremations were located in the centre of the monument (Figure 6.13). In the case of Dorchester Site II, one of these central

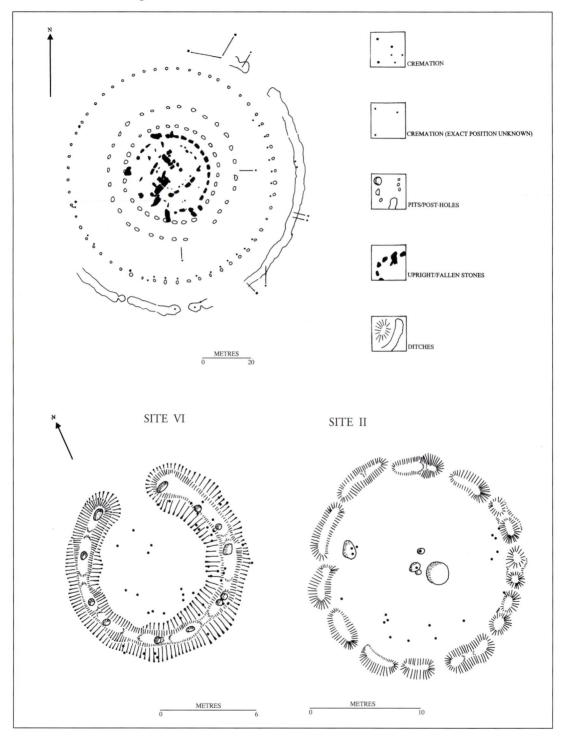

SITE VI

SITE II

Figure 6.13 Distribution of cremations within later Neolithic cemeteries at Stonehenge and Dorchester on Thames Sites VI and II

burials had the richest assemblage of artefacts within the cemetery: a bone pin, a flint fabricator, a flint flake and a fine stone macehead (Atkinson *et al.* 1951, 115). At Llandegai, cremations in the pit circle outside Henge A appear to have been arranged around a central burial, which the excavator judged to have had a 'special meaning' (Houlder 1968, 218). While no claim is made for the universality of this pattern, it does seem that circular monuments (round barrows, ring ditches, henges and pit and post circles) were preferentially chosen for re-use as cremation cemeteries, and that they afforded the opportunity for a particular spatial ordering. At Stonehenge, these was at least one case of a cremation being marked with a post (in Aubrey Hole 3) (Cleal *et al.* 1995, 155), and this suggests that although these cemeteries built up over a period of time, the positions of each deposit would have been known. Being arranged around the circumference of a circle in a particular way may have provided a means of establishing relationships amongst the dead, while the introduction of the cardinal points into this scheme suggests that it was related in some way to more general cosmological schemes.

The re-use of henge monuments as cemeteries identifies an important theme amongst the insular burial traditions of the later Neolithic: an appeal to the past and to continuity. This recalls the efforts made to place the dead into the distant past which developed late in the long mound and long cairn traditions. Duggleby Howe may have begun its history as a single grave, but the sequence of burials which built up over time indicates a concern with precedent: the use of the same location for repeated funerary performances. Much the same can be said of Dorchester and Radley: the first funerary monument sanctioned the use of the place in depositing burials of a certain kind. In Wessex, the sequence of burials in the ditch at Wor Barrow and the nearby round barrows on Handley Hill are an indication of a similar process (Barrett *et al.* 1991, 84–7), while the barrow cemetery at Winterbourne Stoke Crossroads near Stonehenge is aligned on Winterbourne Stoke 1 long mound. Barrett (1994, 123) identifies this sequential character of burial places as a means of situating a dead person historically while both drawing upon and creating memories. He also sees the development of a tradition of inhumation as a means of fixing a dead person in a landscape, in contrast with earlier Neolithic practices which repeatedly re-worked a 'place of ancestral presence' (1994, 112). The change from a set of rites which results in the disarticulation and aggregation of human bones to one which maintains the whole body, buried alone is very easy to read as an indication of the increasing role of 'the individual' (e.g. Clarke *et al.* 1985, 65). While few authors have explicitly suggested as much, the implication might be that the end of the Neolithic saw the emergence of a kind of person 'just like us': a self-contained, decision-making entity who exists in a state of reciprocal independence from his or her contemporaries. Now of course, this is a modern Western notion of individuality, and if we were to view later Neolithic and Early Bronze Age mortuary practices in isolation, we might not be tempted to think any such thing. But simply because corporate burial, which has been connected with a communal focus for society (Shanks and Tilley 1982), declined in the later Neolithic, it is easy to conclude that the new pattern was concerned with 'individuality'.

We have seen that there were two aspects to the mortuary activities enacted in long barrows and chambered tombs: a prolonged phase of transformation, followed by a discrete event of closure. The monumentality of the structures concerned indicated the extent to which these activities were connected with the creation of a place of a particular kind, a location identified by the presence of the dead. Yet we have seen that both in the long barrows and in the Cotswold–Severn tradition the role of the monument as a place of transition declined, and the monuments came to be associated with identifiable persons, whether real or fictive. At the same time, the continued use of the monuments as places of deposition maintained a relationship between the living and the dead. And as the practice of single burial developed, it too involved a series of events linked together spatially and temporally through the discontinuous re-use of important locations. Mortuary practices of this kind create and reaffirm a series of relationships: relations among the living, between the living and the dead, between people and artefacts, and between people and place (Mizoguchi 1993).

Recent anthropological work has demonstrated that the character of personal identity can be extremely variable. Persons may operate as 'dividuals', amalgams composed of parts or materials whose combination is seen as a temporary state of affairs, or as permeable entities who exchange energies and substances with one another (Strathern 1988; Coppet 1994; Busby 1997). There is no simple dichotomy between communities who lack a sense of personhood, and Euro-American 'individuals'. It is conceivable that the later Neolithic saw changes in the character of personal identity, and that these manifested themselves in, and were negotiated through, changing patterns of mortuary practice. But it is crucial to recognise that later Neolithic and Early Bronze Age funerary activities were deeply *relational*. They did not simply celebrate the achievements of individuals. If the dead were being represented in a different way, this might indicate that relations of authority, allegiance, indebtedness, kinship and mutual assistance were now reckoned between particular persons, rather than by affiliation to collective entities such as clans or age-sets. The burial of single persons as distinct events suggests that descent, rather than simply group membership, was now the most significant principle of social ordering. Social identity would then start to take on a narrative rather than an inclusive form: each person would locate him- or herself in a genealogy leading back into the past, rather than a community existing in the present. It would follow that the transactions involved in mortuary practice would enable authority to be devolved from the dead to the living, and that this might explain the stress on continuity and remembrance, although this authority might have been of a particular kind, exercised under limited conditions. One way of understanding this is to suggest that by the later Neolithic social collectivities had become less bounded and mutually exclusive, so that any particular person might operate in a number of different, overlapping contexts (Thomas 1996a, Chapter 6). A funeral is itself a gathering which brings together a distinct group of people, affirming, trans-forming or creating a particular set of relations with the deceased. It is possible that these relations were no longer congruent with membership of a particular social entity. The burial of a single person in a grave with a particular set of artefacts allowed the relationships between people, objects and a given location to be performed, but this congregation may not have been a closed community united by a common and exclusive identity.

BEAKER BURIALS

As we have seen already, culture-historic archaeology presented mortuary practice as being composed of a series of traits indicative of a particular ethnic identity. Sharing a mode of deposition and an assemblage of artefacts, Beaker burials were thus representative of a 'Beaker folk' (an interpretation which survived even Clarke's analysis: 1970). This understanding of the evidence tended to promote the impression that Beaker funerary activities were relatively uniform throughout Britain. Yet with the development of perspectives which presented the Beaker assemblage as a special-purpose 'package' of prestige items (Burgess and Shennan 1976; Thorpe and Richards 1984), it was recognised that these artefacts may have been adopted by indigenous communities in Britain, as a means of enhancing the prestige of particular persons or groups. As a result, it became conceivable that these artefacts were not used in precisely the same ways in all social or geographical contexts. We saw in the last chapter that Barrett (1994, 97) has argued that the impression that Beakers had a special status derived from their exotic character is effectively a modernist fantasy. No one in prehistory would have had any conception of the full extent of the distribution of Beaker pottery across Europe, and the same might be said of the mortuary rites with which Beakers are connected. Yet the recognition that a cultural phenomenon is novel or alien hardly depends upon a complete knowledge of its origin. Indeed, in some cases the mysterious character of an object which has come from 'over the sea' or from 'the ends of the earth' is precisely what lends it significance (Helms 1979).

I do not intend to argue that Beaker pots, archery equipment, metalwork and single grave burial had an absolute meaning which was recognised throughout Europe. On the contrary, I take it that much of the meaning which they had was created in the local context of day-to-day social conduct. But I do maintain that on their first appearance within any community these things would have been recognised as unfamiliar, and extrinsic to any local social network. What is important is not that Beaker pottery and the other artefacts associated with it were necessarily 'special', but simply that they were *different* from other, indigenous forms of material culture. In being different, they facilitated the emergence of new social practices. As Shennan (1982) suggests, the Beaker assemblage was a set of symbols, yet those symbols need not have had fixed referents. For this reason, they could be drawn into social contexts in different parts of Britain and used in entirely different ways. However, this is not to say that they were entirely malleable and mutable, or that their adoption was not itself transformational. In this section, I will suggest that Beaker funerary activities represented a set of signifying practices in which the individual objects, acts and gestures might have had little intrinsic or enduring value, but that all brought with them a range of associations, connotations and implications.

As it is conventionally recognised, the 'classic' Beaker-associated rite of burial involved the inhumation of a single person, crouched or flexed and lying on one side in a grave. Grave goods generally included the Beaker pot itself, and sometimes one or more other items drawn from a relatively standardised repertoire. A good example of such a burial is that at Hemp Knoll in north Wiltshire (Robertson-Mackay 1980). Here, a grave pit 2.4 × 2 metres was dug to a depth of 1.5 metres, and the turf stripped from the surrounding area (Figure 6.14). The grave itself formed the focus for a small round barrow thrown up on the site once the burial had been deposited. The body of a man aged between 35 and 45 was placed tightly flexed inside a coffin 1.75 metres long, possibly made of wickerwork. A European Bell Beaker was at his feet, an archer's wrist-guard on the left wrist, and a bone toggle at the waist, perhaps attached to a belt. Outside the coffin but within the grave pit were a tine of antler and, unusually, the head and hooves of an ox.

Barrett suggests that

> The inhumation tradition . . . represents a marked development in mortuary rituals, not because the corpse was occasionally accompanied by grave-goods, but because the grave, act-ing as a container, now fixed the point in the landscape where the dead were individually deposited.

> (1994, 112)

Shifting the emphasis slightly, we might say that the single grave rite involved a change from a *process of transformation* to an *event of deposition*. In comparison with earlier Neolithic funerary practices, Beaker burials were markedly episodic. Just as Barrett stresses the fixing of the corpse in space, so too these activities established a particular point in time at which a person was severed from his or her social relationships and introduced into genealogy. It would have been precisely this episodic and event-like character of funerary performances which would have rendered them memorable (see Mizoguchi 1993). A great many Beaker burials do fit the expected pattern of being deposited beneath round mounds, but a substantial number were placed in flat graves or cists which leave little in the way of an enduring mark on the landscape. These may be under-represented in the literature, being less likely to have been investigated archaeologically. It follows

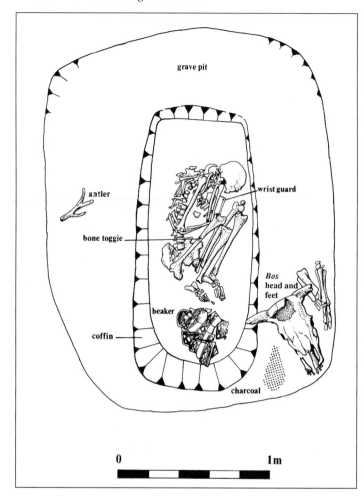

grave pit

antler

wrist guard

bone toggle

Bos head and feet

beaker

coffin

charcoal

0   1m

Figure 6.14 Hemp Knoll, Wiltshire: Beaker burial

from this that while in some cases it was desirable to create a lasting monument which brought the dead back to mind in future years, at other times the full emphasis fell upon the performance itself, and the memorability of the actions involved.

It is clear that some Beaker funerary events would have been quite spectacular. At Irthlingborough in Northamptonshire, the remains of over a hundred cattle – principally skulls – were deposited in amongst a stone cairn which overlay a burial pit (Halpin 1987; Parker Pearson 1993, 78). An appreciable number of Beaker burials represent the only interment beneath a barrow, but very many form one element in a lengthy sequence of depositional acts. For instance, at Chilbolton in Hampshire, two burials were found in a single large grave at the centre of a small round barrow. The earlier body had been placed in some form of timber chamber or coffin with an extensive collection of grave goods, and had been disturbed by the insertion of the second, after the elapse of a period long enough for the earlier corpse to have partially decomposed (Russel 1990). So, if Beaker-related burials took the form of discrete episodes, it was often the case that the effort was made to link these episodes to form a chain of events: a narrative. Where burial pits or shafts were re-opened to allow the introduction of new interments, the intention may have been to establish a connection between different generations, emphasising particular lines of descent (Barrett 1994, 124). Mizoguchi (1993) suggests that where series of Beaker burials exist in the same location, distinct 'rules' may have operated which defined appropriate relationships between primary and secondary interments. The positions of bodies in the grave, or the position of the Beaker in relation to the body, may be maintained between the primary and subsequent inhumations. While adult males were common as primary burials, secondary interments were often adult women or immature persons (Mizoguchi 1993). Mizoguchi takes these circumstances as evidence for the maintenance of the memory of the deceased and their mode of interment. Similarly, Garwood (1991, 15) indicates that at a larger spatial scale the growth of barrow cemeteries from the Beaker period onwards was conditioned by a principle of 'ordered adjacency', which implies some continued familiarity with the specific histories and contents of burial mounds over a period of time.

Beaker mortuary rituals were discrete performances which were sometimes commemorated monumentally, and sometimes drawn into historical sequences by later events. Two things follow from this. The understanding of time involved in these events would have been to some extent linear and irreversible. In placing human lives and deaths into temporal relationships with one another, this has considerable significance for the ways in which social relationships were ordered and understood. Second, although Mizoguchi's and Garwood's arguments suggest a kind of 'etiquette' involved in placing the dead, there is nothing to preclude some element of social strategy having been involved in the process. In other words, by introducing the newly dead into proximity with more revered ancestors, the living may have been constructing or negotiating histories for themselves. The kin relations implied by sequences of burial conducted on a single spot may have been, in some cases, entirely fictive. Memories of past generations may have been drawn upon selectively, or manipulated.

If this were the case, we might expect that the funeral itself would be an occasion at which a deliberate effort was made to present the dead person in a favourable light. Such an event would be of limited duration, and would involve the actual placing of the body into the ground. Necessarily, the corpse itself would be the focus of any such activity, and would be pivotal to any experience of the event on the part of the onlookers or witnesses. Under these conditions, the material setting, including the artefacts deposited with the body, would have been critically important. The grave goods did not simply reflect a social persona, they were instrumental in the performative construction of an identity for the dead person. What I hope to argue is that these artefacts constituted material signifiers whose role was to ensure that an intended reading of the corpse was made by the audience within the temporally restricted conditions of the funeral. Moreover, these were objects which would have been instantly recognisable, being drawn from a relatively restricted assemblage. This presents a contrast with the indigenous tradition of single grave burials, in which very diverse combinations of grave goods were employed. Beaker assemblages and forms of body treatment appear to have been highly conventional, even if they stopped short of being dictated by formal 'rules'.

Almost all of the British Beaker graves contain the Beaker vessel, with the exception of a few late examples. The pot itself may have served as a means by which people were categorised and identified, with more slender vessels with zoned decoration being reserved for adults (Mizoguchi 1995, 181). In the minority of cases where other objects (such as flint arrowheads, metal awls, stone or metal daggers, archers' wristguards or flint flakes) occurred in a grave, they were generally *added to* the Beaker, rather than used in its stead. Some very scarce items, such as conical jet buttons, are rarely found where both the Beaker and some other item are not also present. It seems that while the Beaker vessel was simply connected with personal identity (and perhaps had secondary connotations of eating, drinking, communality and affiliation), other objects served to qualify or add to this message. Amongst those burials which have large numbers of grave goods quite distinct assemblages can sometimes be distinguished. Humphrey Case (1977, 81–3) defined these as artisan's graves, arrowhead burials and exceptionally rich burials, amongst which could be recognised by the later Beaker period burials with antler spatulae, burials with fire-making equipment and burials with buttons or belt-rings. This may be less a direct reflection of status in life than a representation of persons in an idealised or stereotyped manner in death. There are other indications that the identity constructed in funerary practice was sometimes unconnected with reality. For example, Ian Shepherd has pointed out that one of the burials at the Borrowstone cist cemetery in Scotland was suffering from pronounced ankylosis of the spine. It had probably been many years since this person had been in any state to make use of the bow and archer's wristguard with which he was buried (Shepherd 1986, 15).

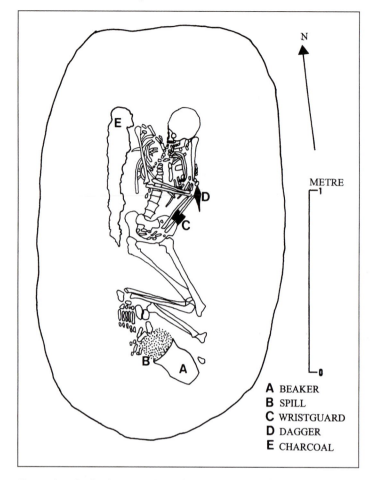

A BEAKER
B SPILL
C WRISTGUARD
D DAGGER
E CHARCOAL

Figure 6.15 Beaker barrow at Barnack, Cambridgeshire

Those few graves which contain more items than a single Beaker pot are often distinctive in other ways as well. While most grave-pits were small, shallow and oval, those which contained multiple grave goods were often larger and more rectangular. In some cases these have been demonstrated to have contained elaborate grave furniture. This would include timber coffins or chambers, as at Hemp Knoll, Irthlingborough, and Linch Hill, Stanton Harcourt (Grimes 1960, 159). At Sutton Veny in Wiltshire, a slightly later Early Bronze Age inhumation with a Food Vessel was buried with a bier as well as a coffin (Johnston 1980). It may be that these features were routinely used as a means of differentiating a minority of burials. For instance, at Barnack the excavator suggested that the primary burial in the barrow 'was probably laid out on his back with the head on a pillow and the knees drawn up, resting on a bier and probably covered with a hide or thick blanket' (Donaldson 1977, 227) (Figure 6.15). At West Overton G6b, the skeleton was covered with 'a residue of material of animal origin, probably something of the nature of a cloak or cover of furs or hides' (Smith and Simpson 1966, 127). These points suggest that in the case of these more elaborate Beaker burials a distinctive set of paraphernalia was involved in the process of transporting the corpse to the grave and interring it there. The body may have been laid out before burial, may have been visible while it was borne to the grave, and may have been on view in the grave itself, the large pit acting as an arena for its display. Until such a time as the grave was filled and any mound raised over it, a funerary ritual conducted in the open air would have represented a conspicuous drama in which the deceased was the central performer.

The impression that the corpse might have been on view at the point of interment is enhanced by the positioning both of body and of artefacts within the grave. It has often been remarked that male and female burials are generally oriented in opposed directions: males with heads to the east and females to the west in Yorkshire (Tuckwell 1975), males with heads to the north and females to the south in Wessex (Thorpe 1983, 7). This is another indication that the funerary performance involved the production of a new social identity for the deceased, here with an emphasis on the definition of sex roles which might betray either a concern over gender relations or an attempt to impose an idealised form of male and female identity on the dead. In his corpus of Beaker pottery, David Clarke defined four possible positions for the deposition of the Beaker in the grave relative to the body (Clarke 1970). Significantly, the representation of these positions varies according to age and sex, and also to the composition of the funerary assemblage. Child burials were most likely to have a Beaker positioned in front of the face, while the placing of the vessel behind the back of the head appears to have been largely reserved for men. A number of those bodies with Beakers behind their heads also have a weapon, a battle axe or a metal dagger, in front of the face (as at Woodhenge Circle 1: Cunnington 1929, 42). So the way in which the body and its attendant material symbols were arranged within the grave-pit provided the witnesses with further indications as to how to interpret the event of deposition.

I have suggested that the objects which were placed in the grave did not have fixed and universal meanings. Indeed, the performance of the funeral would have been a context in which the significance both of the grave goods and of the dead body were created anew. Yet we can argue that a particular constellation of signification and resonance was brought into play through the deployment of these particular items. The pottery vessels relate to consumption; arrowheads, wristguards and daggers are connected with violence in the form of warfare or hunting; items of dress and adornment are concerned with gender and age roles, and perhaps also directly with sexuality; antler picks evoke physical labour, and the various metal- and leather-working tools refer to craftwork. These are no more than tentative suggestions regarding what the elements of the assemblage might imply in a broad sense, and yet they have one thing in common. All relate to the human body and its activities. It was the presence of the body in the grave which rendered them intelligible as a set of related things. The grave assemblage could be recognised as a unity by the onlooker because all of the items concerned had some relation to the body. In the case of items of dress it is not the case that the objects enter the grave as a means of 'dressing-up' the corpse: the Barnack wristguard was almost certainly not attached to the arm of the burial (Donaldson 1977, 227), while at Irthlingborough and West Cotton collections of objects which in both cases included conical jet buttons were found below the feet (Windell 1989, 92). By using goods of this kind the act of interpretation on the part of the audience was inescapably drawn in to the body, as a focus of meaning.

We have noted already that the variability of Beaker funerary practice is greater than has sometimes been acknowledged. One aspect of this variation is the differing extent to which single grave burial with Beaker pottery was practised in various parts of southern Britain. Allowing for the difficulties of dating Beaker ceramics (Kinnes *et al.* 1991) those areas which contained clusters of relatively early Beaker graves very often had groups of Neolithic round barrow, ring-ditch, flat grave and cremation burials as well. It is likely that the Beaker-related funerary rite was more readily assimilated by communities which already practised the episodic interment of single bodies with grave goods. This is demonstrated by the contrast between the Thames basin and the nearby uplands of the Cotswold and Mendip Hills. In the Thames, there was a particularly dense concentration of Beaker graves in the Stanton Harcourt area, within 2 km of the Devil's Quoits henge monument, while burials with early radiocarbon dates have come from Barrow Hills, Radley (Barclay and Halpin 1999) (see Chapter 8 below). Early Beaker graves were scarce both in the Cotswolds and in the Mendips, an exception being a male burial with European Bell Beaker and possible earring inserted into the mound of Sale's Lot long cairn (O'Neil 1966). In the Mendips, few graves seem earlier than that at Blackdown barrow T5, with a 'Barbed Wire' Beaker (ApSimon 1969). Yet both areas have evidence for intensive Neolithic activity, and Beaker ceramics were certainly in use. Beaker pottery was found in the chambered cairns of Notgrove and Eyford (Clifford 1936; 1937, 161), while no less than twelve Mendip caves have produced Beaker pottery, and at Bone Hole and Charterhouse Warren Farm Swallett, this was associated with disarticulated human remains (Levitan *et al.* 1988).

The Sale's Lot burial is indicative of a broader pattern. In many cases, old and already ruinous funerary monuments seem to have provided a focus around which Beaker burials clustered, as had the burials of the later Neolithic. For instance, at Linch Hill, Stanton Harcourt, a male burial with Northern/Middle Rhine Beaker, bone belt ring and seven arrowheads was inserted into a Neolithic ring ditch (Grimes 1944, 39). Similarly, two secondary burials with European Bell Beakers were dug into the mound of the Thickthorn Down long barrow (Drew and Piggott 1936). It appears that as well as Beaker funerary practices having been more easily adopted where they tallied with established tradition, they were sometimes sanctioned by being conducted in places connected with the mortuary observances of the past.

CONCLUSION: STRATEGIES OF REPRESENTATION

In this chapter we have reviewed changes in mortuary practice in southern Britain over a period of two millennia. These changes were fundamentally concerned with the ways in which power was invested in human bodies, and how those bodies were represented – or more properly, materialised. The construction of dead bodies of a certain kind was both an outcome and a cause of social change. Over the period under study, a 'genealogy' of mortuary practice reveals several changes in the way in which the corpse was organised in death. Both in the earthen long barrows and in the Cotswold–Severn chambered tombs the body was broken down into its constituent bones. Although the aim of these practices may have been to re-position the dead in relation to the community of the living, the process was a gradual one. The tombs and barrows were places of transformation, and the change in the state of the body was brought about by a series of encounters and re-orderings. Moreover, while the end point of this process was a set of cleaned and disarticulated bones, some or all of these may have been removed from the tomb and circulated or deposited elsewhere. In this sense, a continued reciprocity existed between the community and its dead. After the blocking of chambers or the raising of mounds, there are indications that relations with the dead were maintained, although in a changed form, through performances, feasting and acts of deposition focused on the mortuary structure.

So although earlier Neolithic funerary practices transformed the corpse into something different from the living, it remained something which was integral to society. There is perhaps something to be said for the view that corporate burial is connected with corporate identity, even if only at an ideological level. And if one still maintains relationships with the community of the dead, they are still in some senses a part of the community of the living. Paradoxically, as soon as a body ceases to be simply 'one of the dead', and becomes instead a named person, it becomes more of the past than of the present. A corpse which is the body of someone who died at a certain point is located in the flow of time. Once bodies began to be left in an articulated state in tomb chambers and in graves beneath long mounds, they would have been fixed in memory in the moments of death and burial. This does not necessarily indicate the emergence of a kind of 'individuality' like that of the modern West. But it may suggest the gradual decline of bounded, mutually exclusive, corporate social units, which organised and structured a variety of different activities. Instead of seeing themselves as members of a community, composed of relations with others in the present (including the dead), people might increasingly have placed themselves socially according to the principle of descent from named ancestors in the past. The change implied is one from inclusive to 'narrative' social forms.

These circumstances might indicate that social arrangements were becoming more unstable, with affiliation and alliance becoming more strategic and negotiable. This would explain the more episodic character of funerary activity by the end of the period, and the investment of effort in the event of burial rather than the maintenance of a continued relationship with a place of veneration and transformation.

Chapter Seven

Regional sequences: the Stonehenge area

INTRODUCTION

The intention of the preceding chapters has been to question some of the accepted wisdom concerning various aspects of the Neolithic of southern Britain. In each case, the means employed has been a consideration of change through time, seeking contrasts in the evidence and hoping to establish a series of parallel accounts of different elements of social life. In the next three chapters the focus changes from temporal to spatial variability, but with the same general objective in mind. From as early as Piggott's *Neolithic Cultures of the British Isles* (1954), attempts have been made to investigate the British Neolithic on a regional basis, in his case considering primary and secondary areas of colonisation by the Windmill Hill Culture. For the most part, however, the social and cultural processes which took place in the Neolithic have been portrayed as geographically undifferentiated, perhaps because their material manifestations are superficially similar.

It is easy to see why this should be the case. Much of the fundamental research into the period was undertaken in the first half of the present century, when archaeological thought was dominated by various forms of culture history (Binford and Sabloff 1982; Trigger 1989). Characteristically, this form of archaeology proceeded under the 'normative' understanding that shared material forms (pottery styles, funerary practices, monumental architectures) were the outcome of cognitive norms and values held in common by groups of people and inculcated through tradition (Childe 1936; Binford 1965). Where similar styles of artefacts were identified distributed across large geographical areas, it was often presumed that they were the work of a single 'people' or 'folk'. Similarly, within some forms of processual archaeology, material culture was presented as the manifestation of a particular level of social evolution (Renfrew 1973a, 146–56; 1976). While prehistoric communities were understood as autonomous groups engaged in localised processes of adaptation, they were also seen as largely equivalent to one another. Variations within societies and between regions were not placed in the foreground by these analyses.

One antidote which has been proposed to the perception of past communities as homogeneous totalities is an emphasis on the 'active individual' (e.g. Hodder 1986, 6–9). However, it is not my intention here to present an account of social change in Neolithic southern England which assumes the existence of proto-modern, autonomous, alienated subjects. Instead, I will hope to suggest that Neolithic societies were heterogeneous and internally differentiated, with differently positioned persons exercising power and access to cultural resources in different ways. It follows from this that in each of the regions which I will discuss, distinct social trajectories will have emerged from the different ways in which the various cultural media of the Neolithic were deployed. In time, particular items of material culture may have come to have a quite different significance in different locations.

This project immediately raises the question of how one should define a 'region' for the purposes of study. A simple solution would be to rely upon purely physiographic features, but such an approach is almost certain to bias the account in favour of environmental determinism. Having defined one's units of analysis on environmental criteria, it would be only too easy to argue that developments within these units were different because they were based upon different ecological conditions.

How, then, should we define *social* units in prehistory? Renfrew (1973a, 552) delimited five 'chiefdoms' within Neolithic Wessex on the basis of the distributions of ceremonial monuments. However, this implies a set and constant relationship between monuments and society. While clusters of monuments may indeed relate to distinct social entities, it has to be considered that some groups may not have built monuments at all (Shennan 1981, 113). Even if a group of monuments were recognised as being associated with a particular community, this connection might take a number of different forms. In the existing literature, two different hypotheses are already current. Some authors have argued that monuments stood amongst the fields and pastures of sedentary, mixed farming communities (e.g. Smith 1984). Others have suggested that in some cases 'ritual landscapes' stood separate from areas of economic exploitation (Bradley 1978b, 103). A third possibility is suggested here: that groups of monuments may be located in areas used for periodic aggregations by dispersed or mobile populations. Such areas might be expected to have suffered unusually severe ecological impacts as a result.

It seems most unlikely that the societies of the southern British Neolithic were entirely isolated from each other, considering the widespread nature of the distributions of certain items of material culture (stone axes, particular types of pottery, etc.). Nevertheless, as Barth (1969, 9) emphasises, boundaries between groups persist despite flows of material and personnel across them. The recent interest in the uses of material culture to define social boundaries (e.g. Hodder 1978; 1982b) provides some hope of the possibility of detecting social groups from the distribution of material culture. It is with this aim in mind that DeAtley and Findlow (1984, 2) suggest that 'the groups with which people identify can often be characterised by a modal cluster of material culture and behavioural traits as well as with a central geographical, and often organisational focus'. However, this kind of approach is fraught with difficulties, assuming as it often does that cultural traits have an invariant significance (see Jones 1997, etc.). Boundary maintenance through the use of material culture is not a universal, but a strategy which arises within particular historical circumstances (Hodder 1979). Moreover, although the boundaries concerned may be those between communities, they may equally well connote age- or sex-related interest groups which transcend the local area (Hodder 1982b, 84–6; Larrick 1986). Consequently, it is not to be assumed that clusters of similar artefact types are any more of an indication of the existence of a bounded social entity than are clusters of monuments. With these points in mind, it may be wise to consider that the role of material culture in making statements about social difference is best left as an object of study, rather than taken for granted.

Empirically, the artefactual and structural evidence for Neolithic activity in Britain does appear to be clustered within a number of regions which Bradley (1984b, 41) described as 'core areas'. However, we should not imagine that these are separated by zones which are entirely bereft of Neolithic material. And to some extent, any concentration of evidence identified in the present is a product of the local history of archaeological fieldwork (Shennan 1985). While I have chosen to concentrate on three such core areas, it is not suggested that each represents a closed social entity, or that people and artefacts did not move beyond the confines of each region.

PROBLEMS OF THE EVIDENCE

The comparison of the different areas as they have been defined is complicated by differences in their histories of research. Since much of the interpretation which follows depends on differences between regions and even on the absence of particular phenomena in some areas, it is as well to make the reader aware of some of these variations. The first area which is to be considered, Salisbury Plain, received considerable attention in the nineteenth century from William Cunnington, Sir Richard Colt Hoare (1812) and John Thurnam (1869) as regards barrow digging, but seems not to have been a major focus for flint collectors prior to the activities of Laidler and Young (1938). This can be contrasted with the Avebury district, which was successively combed for flints by Kendall, Passmore, Young and numerous individuals who sold specimens to Alexander Keiller while he was in residence in the village. Despite this, the relative scarcity of Grooved Ware pits and single graves in the Avebury area in the later Neolithic cannot be entirely explained by sample bias. The history of the digging of pipe trenches and similar excavations is at least as extensive around Avebury as near Durrington, while the area has been well served by barrow diggers (Thurnam 1860; Grinsell 1957).

The combination of extensive gravel extraction and the presence of the extremely active Oxford University Archaeological Society between the wars can doubtless be held partly responsible for the unusually rich record of Beaker and earlier burials and of small pit sites with pottery in the Upper Thames Valley. This does not affect the comparative scarcity of earlier Neolithic funerary structures in the region, or explain the relatively diminutive scale of the later Neolithic monuments of the area. So while one should be aware that quite major differences exist in the ways in which archaeology has been undertaken in the various parts of the study area, it is arguable that the contrasts which are drawn here relate to genuine differences between the material practices of the communities which inhabited those regions in the Neolithic.

STONEHENGE AND SALISBURY PLAIN

Stonehenge and the landscape which surrounds it have been central to many of the accounts of Neolithic society which have been written in the past few decades (MacKie 1977; Burl 1987; Castleden 1987; Bender 1992; 1998; Barrett 1994). The recent publication of the twentieth-century excavations at Stonehenge (Cleal *et al.* 1995) has been accompanied by a series of new radiocarbon dates which radically revise the chronology of the site, bringing much of the sequence of construction back into the Neolithic rather than the Bronze Age. This in itself should be enough to encourage us to reconsider the changing relationship between the monument and its surroundings. One recent attempt to do this has been presented by Michael Allen (1997), who uses the environmental evidence to argue for a gradual process of economic intensification which escalated abruptly at the point when the stone settings at Stonehenge were constructed. Allen's article provides an excellent point of entry to the discussion of landscape change on Neolithic Salisbury Plain, giving as it does an integrated picture of the sequences from numerous sites. As he emphasises, the evidence itself is of varied quality, and this leaves considerable latitude for interpretation. So while Allen's account is an entirely reasonable interpretation of the available information, I will hope to show that a more minimal understanding of agricultural development in the region is also possible.

The keystone of Allen's argument is that dramatically increased labour power would have been necessary for the transport and erection of the stones of the Phase 3 monument, in the years after 2700 BC (1997, 140). Increased sedentism and mixed farming would have provided 'the organisational framework and a sufficiently sound economic basis to allow them, as required, to provide shelter and provision for a large and economically non-productive workforce' (1997, 125). Clearly, Allen is suggesting that the stones were set up by a group of specialists maintained by surplus production, rather than by a broader population working during the otherwise inactive periods in the seasonal cycle of labour. This can be questioned in three different ways. First, the notion of craft specialisation has been roundly criticised for importing modernist conceptions of surplus and alienated labour into the past (Welbourn 1985, 127). Second, some of the existing labour estimates for the construction of Stonehenge may have been considerably inflated. On the basis of their recent experimental work, Richards and Whitby have argued that the sarsen settings of Stonehenge 3 would have required no more than 200 people to set them up, and that all of the stones could have been transported and raised in less than two years (1997, 237). Third, one of the principal attributes of the Phase 3 monument which distinguished it from its earth and timber precursors was that it was constructed as 'a more or less organic process' over a very long period of time, with minor modifications being made by different generations, and some of the changes in design going unfinished (Cleal *et al.* 1995, 465). So rather than a separate group of people working continuously over a couple of seasons, Stonehenge 3 may have been the creation of numerous sporadic bouts of building.

The general outline of Allen's description of vegetational change on Salisbury Plain through the Neolithic is beyond question. Numerous sites have provided evidence for the gradual clearance of large areas of woodland and the inception of grazed grassland. What is arguable is the extent to which this actually documents the beginnings of mixed agriculture, as opposed to increasing grazing pressure exercised by mobile communities. In the earlier Neolithic, Allen presents a vivid picture of a vegetational mosaic involving dense primary woodland, open oak and hazel woods, patches of pasture and scrub (1997, 127). At the start of the period, the Coneybury 'Anomaly' was dug in a recent clearing, while the early Neolithic activity at Durrington Walls may have taken place on the edge of woodland. At the Lesser Cursus there was open grazed grassland. By the time of the construction of Stonehenge 1 at around 3000 BC, hazelnut shells and wood samples imply the continued existence of woodland nearby (Cleal *et al.* 1995, 65), while the later henge monument at Coneybury was built in a recent clearing (Richards 1990). At the very end of the Neolithic, the Grooved Ware pits at Ratfyn were dug in an area of scrub and long grass (Allen 1997, 132). But despite this evidence for continued landscape diversity, by the end of the Neolithic and the Early Bronze Age, indications of grazed grassland are found beneath round barrows as far apart as Boscombe Down, Earl's Down Farm, Greenland Farm, Luxenborough Plantation, and on the King Barrow Ridge (Cleal and Allen 1994).

Yet while there is considerable evidence for the progressive extension of grassland, the indications of cultivation are far more ambiguous. For instance, the disturbed stony soil profile beneath the bank at Durrington Walls does not unequivocally indicate arable activity (Wainwright and Longworth 1971, 335). Similarly, at Amesbury 42 long barrow, a phase of shady conditions in Beaker times was followed by renewed clearance and 'possible' cultivation. But this is difficult to date, since the Beaker sherds from this ditch layer were evidently re-deposited (Entwistle 1990, 108). Charred cereal remains were found in Beaker levels at Coneybury henge (Carruthers 1990, 25), but these document consumption or processing, not cultivation. Obviously, this grain must have been grown somewhere, but the indications of numerous tilled fields are not forthcoming. The ard marks beneath round barrow Amesbury G71 have frequently been cited as direct evidence of arable farming, but as we have argued already these are the product of a 'rip ard', 'the "sod buster", used on specific and unusual occasions and leaving specific and unusual evidence of its passage' (Reynolds 1981, 104). The marks may indicate that land was at some time cleared for planting, but it might equally have been prepared for pasture or barrow construction.

Finally, evidence for soil erosion and colluviation in the ditch fills at sites like Coneybury and the two cursus monuments provide only the slimmest of evidence for tillage. At Coneybury, localised colluvial layers in the ditch appear to date to the Beaker phase, and were actually cut by an intrusive feature in the northern ditch terminal containing an accumulation of animal bones with Beaker pottery (Richards 1990, 129). Yet the land mollusca from these layers are indicative of shady conditions provided by shrubs and trees, and it is suggested that the sediments were derived from 'patches of bare ground' (Bell and Jones 1990, 155). It is worth remembering that not all soil erosion is caused by arable activity, and periods of intensive grazing and trampling by cattle can have a destabilising effect (Evans 1975, 139). Seemingly colluvial layers in the ditches of the Lesser Cursus contained sherds of Middle Bronze Age pottery as well as Beaker, leaving the precise date for the inception of run-off in question (Richards 1990, 78). At the Great Stonehenge Cursus, 'possible hints of local cultivation' occurred at the base of the secondary ditch silts, and carbonised caryopses of emmer wheat were found in the sediments (Allen 1997, 129). However, the mollusc analyses indicated grazed grassland throughout the ditch sequence (1997, 129). While we might not wish to deny that any of this evidence was connected with tillage, it is at most indicative of short bursts of cultivation rather than the establishment of a sustained horticultural regime.

So it is at least open to question that the end of the Neolithic saw 'an expansion of the utilised and farmed area in which more emphasis may have been placed upon cereal cultivation' (Allen 1997, 132; see also Cleal *et al.* 1995, 169). Allen's final argument in support of this view is that the later Bronze Age field systems which cluster on the Plain may have had unenclosed precursors (1997, 136). Yet this seems to rest on the belief that field systems are essentially a means of coping with soil erosion, rather than a way of socially regulating the spatial context of agricultural production. I would suggest that prior to the construction of these fields, the horticultural activity in the area surrounding Stonehenge was limited in scale and sporadic in character. In this context, the results of Cleal and Allen's (1994) recent work on the soils beneath the round barrows on King Barrow Ridge are illuminating. The mollusc faunas here were all indicative of grassland, yet they contained subtle variations, suggesting that the pastures of the later Neolithic and Early Bronze Age may not have been homogeneous. The samples ranged from ungrazed herbaceous to short-turfed grazed grassland, and the suggestion was made that prehistoric land use may have involved cyclical grazing with periodic returns to particular locations (Cleal and Allen 1994, 81–2). This is precisely the pattern which would be generated by mobile groups gathering in the Stonehenge area at particular times of year, and dispersing farther afield.

The earlier Neolithic

Prior to the start of the Neolithic, indications of the occupation of central Salisbury Plain are scant. A microlithic flint industry has been recovered from beside the river Avon near Durrington Walls (Richards 1990, 263), and a series of large post-holes located in Stonehenge car park appear to date to the eighth millennium BC (Cleal *et al.* 1995, 43). Three of these four posts appear to line up with a tree hole, giving an interesting hint of a very early form of monumentality which elaborated on natural features. However, it is all but beyond the bounds of credibility to claim that these features first defined a special location where a monument would be built 5,000 years later.

The surface collection work carried out by the Stonehenge Environs Project has isolated a series of concentrations of chipped stone which can loosely be attributed to the earlier Neolithic. These include scatters on the King Barrow Ridge and Coneybury Hill, near Winterbourne Stoke Crossroads and the Diamond, north of the Cursus, and perhaps also on Stonehenge Down (Richards 1990, 265–6) (Figure 7.1). Cleal (in Cleal *et al.* 1995, 473) points out that the intensity of archaeological investigation has been more restricted to the west of Stonehenge Bottom, and

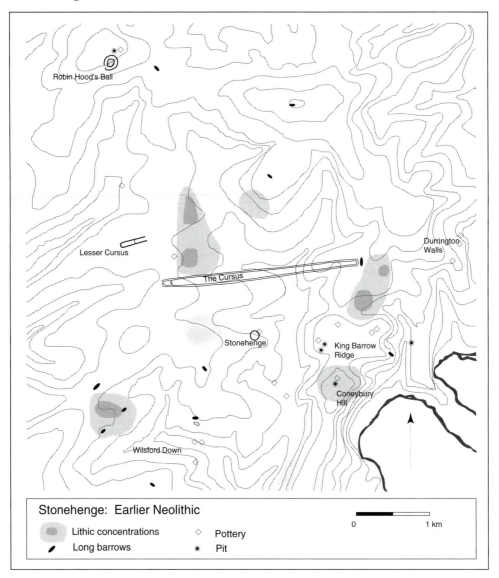

Figure 7.1 Stonehenge area: earlier Neolithic
Source: After Richards (1990) with additions

suggests on this basis that the whole of the landscape may have been densely inhabited during the earlier Neolithic. None the less, it is notable that the distributions of earlier Neolithic material in all parts of the region are rather more concentrated than those of later date, and that they are separated by areas of quite low density. Clearly, the evidence for the progressive clearance of forest cover indicates that a great proportion of this landscape was already frequented and grazed. But within this it is possible that certain locations were beginning to emerge as habitual places of camping or short-term habitation.

Interestingly, the distribution of surface finds of flint tools and waste only partly coincides with that of pottery and pit deposits, which are concentrated in a swathe along the west bank of the

Avon, from Durrington Walls down to Wilsford Down. The recovery of the latter two classes of evidence is obviously influenced by the incidence of pipeline trenches, road widening and other archaeological interventions. However, it is worth reflecting that while flint scatters are often the product of accretions of activity over a long period, pits and pre-barrow pottery deposits may result from more singular events. These two forms of evidence are therefore not always generated by the same patterns of activity. The most spectacular example of an earlier Neolithic pit deposit in the Stonehenge area, the Coneybury 'Anomaly', appears to relate to a major episode of butchery, in which several roe deer were consumed on site, but ten cattle and a pig were jointed and perhaps preserved for eating elsewhere (Richards 1990, 42–3). The pottery from the pit suggests a neatly constrained sequence of production and deliberate destruction, yet the flintwork is only a fragment drawn from processes of reduction and reworking which must have extended to encompass other locations. So while the pit is located within an area of relatively dense surface flint concentration, it gives a strong indication that different practices were being 'spread' across the landscape, nested in patterns of mobility.

This spatial dispersal of activity might be related to the notion of the 'zonation' of the Stonehenge landscape, introduced by Richards (1984, 182), and followed in the first edition of this volume. Cleal (in Cleal *et al.* 1995, 476) objects that 'the concept of "zones" is essentially static', and emphasises the degree to which people will have been moving within and beyond the surrounding region. While fully agreeing with this emphasis on mobility, it may be helpful to clarify these issues. A topography across which people and livestock move is unlikely to be homogeneous. Movement takes place between locations which each have their own significance, and which afford different combinations of symbolic and material resources. It follows from this that different kinds of activities may be judged appropriate for different places. Therefore, it is entirely possible to have a landscape composed of a series of 'zones' between which mobile populations move in order to undertake different combinations of practices: this need not imply that people or materials were in any sense static. Moreover, it is to be expected that the continued use of these places would lead to their repeated re-evaluation, and a continuous re-creation of their significance.

If the terminology of 'zonation' carries connotations of fixity and immobility, it may be preferable to describe instead a progressive process of internal differentiation of the landscape. Through the two millennia of the Neolithic, places built up sedimented histories, came to be landmarks and were transformed by deliberate human interventions. This way in which places were distinguished by the accrual of significance would not have applied exclusively to monuments, and was not achieved solely through ritual practice. Indeed, the performance of ritual in particular spaces would have been only one layer in the differentiation of place. There would not have been 'ritual places' and 'secular places', any more than there would have been exclusively 'ritual landscapes'. Rather, there would have been a variety of practices – grazing, food preparation, hunting, butchery, flint-knapping, sleeping, potting, laying out the dead – each of which would have had its own appropriate spatial range. Any combination of these activities may have applied to any particular location: what is suggested is simply that not all activities could have been carried out side by side in all locations. Within this scheme of things, it is entirely plausible that some people were excluded from particular places for some of the time. But this will surely have been the exception rather than the rule. As Bender (1992, 747) argues, there can have been no permanent separation between ceremonial and everyday activities.

One aspect of the differentiation of space in the earlier Neolithic which was first pointed out by Julian Richards (1984, 182) is the non-random distribution of earthen long barrows. Salisbury Plain as a whole contains one of the principal concentrations of long mounds in southern England (Ashbee 1970, 9), and within this a number of lesser clusters can be discerned – around

Warminster, Milston and Tilshead, for instance. To a greater or lesser extent, each of these groupings has its own distinctive character, recognisable in the details of mound construction or funerary practice. All of the barrows around Tilshead, for example, are notably large. Some of them may be multi-phase structures, and all of the excavated examples have contained multiple burials (Hoare 1812, 91; Thurnam 1869, 184, 191; Cunnington 1914, 400). The evidence from these early investigations is fragmentary and the possible reasons for any distinctiveness might reside in chronology, local preference or contingency, so too much should not be made of it. All that I wish to suggest is that the construction and use of long barrows would have both reflected and enhanced the specific character of particular locations or areas. This need not imply that each group of mounds were the 'territorial markers' of a particular group of people, or even that they were used exclusively by a specific community.

In the immediate area of Stonehenge a particularly tight cluster of six long mounds and a mortuary enclosure was gathered around the dry valley defined by Wilsford and Normanton downs. These can perhaps be distinguished from the very much more diffuse grouping which runs eastward and south from Robin Hood's Ball. As Bradley (1993, 53) implies, it is very probable that the Wilsford/Normanton mounds defined their setting as a particular kind of place, even if the straightforward distinction between an area of the dead and an area of the living does not repay scrutiny. Wheatley (1995) has demonstrated that a particular characteristic of the long barrows in the Stonehenge area is that they are preferentially located in positions from where large numbers of other mounds are visible. This lends some support to the notion of the emergence of a portion of the landscape which was dominated by the presence of these barrows and their use, if not to the exclusion of other activities. The barrows in this area show considerable variation in mortuary practice, from multiple inhumations at Amesbury 14 and Wilsford 30 (Hoare 1812, 206), to a crematorium structure at Winterbourne Stoke 53 (1812, 117), and a single burial accompanied by a 'bludgeon-shaped flint' at Winterbourne Stoke 1 (Thurnam 1869, 184; Cunnington 1914, 407).

On the higher ground to the north, at least a proportion of the remaining long mounds seem to be juxtaposed with or aligned upon the causewayed enclosure at Robin Hood's Ball. Of these, Figheldean 31 contained disarticulated human remains in a small pile, yet these appeared to derive from a single body which had been quite carefully arranged, so that the two tibiae were side by side, but lying in opposite directions, possibly within a timber chamber (Thurnam 1869, 184; Cunnington 1914, 390). Arguably these might have been the bones of a significant person which had been curated for some while before the construction of the mound. At Netheravon 6, the remains which had been disturbed by earlier investigation may have represented two adult skeletons (Thurnam 1869, 180). At Netheravon Bake, no mortuary deposit survived, but the ditch sequence documented a complex series of remodellings of the structure, reminiscent of long mounds close to causewayed enclosures at Hambledon Hill and Abingdon (Mercer 1980; Richards 1990, 265; Bradley 1992). Once again, it does not do to overstretch this evidence, but it is reasonable to argue that not all long mounds meant the same thing, and that some element of their significance derived from the position which they occupied in the landscape.

Notwithstanding Cleal's point that causewayed enclosures in Wessex were deeply involved in patterns of contact and mobility (in Cleal *et al.* 1995, 476), Robin Hood's Ball is located on the edge of the main focus of Neolithic activity. By analogy with other such enclosures, it is likely that it was used for a range of specialised activities (see Chapter 3 above), and it is to be expected that these would have contributed to the way in which the barrows in its immediate vicinity would have been understood. One notable aspect of the causewayed enclosure is that it was located in one of the more highly visible points in the local topography (Batchelor 1997, 70–1), commanding extensive views in several directions (Thomas 1964, 1). So, while Robin Hood's Ball may have been a site which was visited periodically rather than continuously occupied, it was positioned in such a way as to be noticed from a distance. This presents an interesting contrast with another monument which may have been built within a few centuries of it, the Great Cursus. For while the interior of the cursus would have been overlooked from the slopes which immediately surround it (Stone 1947, 7), it effectively runs through a region of very low overall visibility (Batchelor 1997, Plan 9). One of the reasons for this is that it lies in a obvious pathway which runs between the River Till and the basin of Durrington Walls above the River Avon, crossing the Fargo and King Barrow Ridges and Stonehenge Bottom where their slopes are least pronounced. There is thus reason to believe that the cursus formalised a pre-existing routeway.

At the same time, the layout of the cursus was closely connected with the positioning of the local long mounds. The only radiocarbon date from the monument is relatively late, yet this came from an antler found in a 'recess' in the southern side of the south ditch, which probably represented an intrusive feature (Stone 1947, 14; Richards 1990, 96). There are strong indications that, as with the Dorset Cursus (Barrett *et al.* 1991, 56), the Stonehenge Cursus was constructed at a time when long barrows were still being built and used. At its eastern end, the terminal of the cursus runs parallel with the large long barrow Amesbury 42. To the north, long barrow Durrington 24 appears to align itself either on this mound or the cursus terminal, while Figheldean 31 lies on the same alignment. Amesbury 42 is itself a two-phase structure, the second, much larger ditch documenting a massive elaboration of the mound (Richards 1990, 98). No burial deposit was found in the barrow, yet the remains of four or five oxen were located beneath the mound by Thurnam (1869, 182). In a terminal of the primary ditch, a cluster of flint debris was located, which seemed to be the product of *in situ* knapping rather than dumped waste (Richards 1990, 98). At its western end, the ditch of the cursus was surprisingly deep, and Christie suggested that along the terminal the bank must have risen up, looking very like a long barrow (1963, 372). It is possible to argue that the western terminal and the rebuilt mound mirror one another, and represent parts of a single design. Moreover, all of the cuttings which have been made into the cursus ditch have encountered concentrations of knapping waste, again emphasising connections with the long barrows (Stone 1947, 14; Christie 1963, 372). Finally, at the western end the long barrow Winterbourne Stoke 1 aligns on the cursus terminal, suggesting that it post-dates the construction of the cursus. This is entirely in keeping with the single burial at Winterbourne Stoke 1, which suggests a relatively late date. The alignment of the oval mound Amesbury 14 is less clear, but it too may point toward the western terminal.

The Stonehenge Cursus monumentalised a pattern of east–west movement across the landscape, while having an integral place within the local sequence of long mound construction. Simultaneously, the cursus would have served to inhibit the movement of people and livestock between north and south. I suggest that one effect of this imposition on the landscape would have been to further separate and distinguish the group of long barrows in the Wilsford/Normanton area from those to the north. Some of the latter, I have argued, were intimately connected with the activities which took place in the Robin Hood's Ball enclosure. In this way, the construction of the cursus provided something of the context for that of Stonehenge, immediately adjacent to the former group of mounds. The precise relationship between these processes and the construction of the Lesser Cursus seems unclear. Bender (1992, 748) argues that the monument was quite short-lived, much of the ditch having been backfilled soon after it was dug. In a sense, it may be that the Lesser Cursus existed as part of a single event or happening, which drew upon local traditions of monument-building and deposition for its efficacy. The Lesser Cursus shared a form and was located close by the Great Cursus, had two phases of ditch construction which are chronologically indistinguishable at 3640–3044 BC (2690 ± 100 bc) (OxA-1405), and had a 'formal arrangement' of antlers deposited on the bottom of the Phase II ditch (Richards 1990, 77). As we will see, this last represents one element of the local micro-tradition of monument use.

THE FIRST STONEHENGE

Stonehenge was a peculiarly long-lived monument, which went through a series of modifications and reconstructions (Figure 7.2). Bradley (1991, 214) has cited the circle as an example of the role of ritual in maintaining social stability, operating as a focus of continuity as its surroundings underwent successive social changes. What this means in practice is that as a location Stonehenge represented a powerful symbolic resource, whose significance could be repeatedly remade by placing new elements into the context of established traditions and sedimented histories. Even the earliest activity at Stonehenge drew upon the past. While the timber uprights which probably stood in the Aubrey Holes find little precedent in earlier monuments, the ditch of Stonehenge 1 was dug in segments, like that of a causewayed enclosure, and surrounded an internal bank (Cleal *et al.* 1995, 64). Five chalk objects, similar to those found in some causewayed enclosures, were recovered from the ditch, but on the whole the material assemblage was much poorer than that from the earlier enclosures. The earliest filling in this ditch was a chalky mud, which contained numerous flint flakes in distinct concentrations, like those in the long barrow and cursus ditches (Cleal *et al.* 1995, 68, 370).

While the ditch was dug at some time in the period between 3015 and 2395 BC, a number of placed deposits of animal bone on the ditch bottom came from animals which had died 70–420 years earlier (Bayliss *et al.*, 1997, 48). These included two cattle mandibles, a deer tibia and an ox skull, all located near to the two southern entrances of the enclosure. The jaws had lost their teeth, and so had been deposited some while after death, yet the surface of the bones was good, indicating that they had been well cared for (Serjeantson 1995, 442). We have already seen that the bones of human beings may have been curated and moved around for lengthy periods before their final deposition. Here there is an indication that equivalent treatment was applied to animals, and particularly cattle. Moreover, the placing of bones derived from these ancestral animals (the progenitors of existing herds?) was being used to sanction the layout of the enclosure. This recalls the presence of cattle bones as equivalents or substitutes for human burials at Amesbury 42 and other Salisbury Plain long barrows.

The north-east entrance to the enclosure was flanked by traces of great fires in the ditch, and also by concentrations of antlers, a high proportion of which came from hunted animals (Cleal *et al.* 1995, 109). As well as providing another link with the depositional practices associated with the cursus monuments, this starts to underline the emphasis which was being placed upon entering and leaving the monument. There is little indication of any structure having existed in the centre of Stonehenge at this point, and none of the artefactual or faunal evidence which one would connect with feasting or occupation. In this connection, Darvill's (1997, 179) suggestion that the entrances of the Phase 1 monument echo the NE–S course of the Avon is interesting, although we might wish to infer no more than a general correlation with the surrounding topography. One possibility is that the earliest monument at Stonehenge was a place to be moved through, a stage on a journey, a means of orienting movement within a landscape. The Aubrey Hole timbers would render the structure highly visible, while the deposits of animal bone and other materials would give meaning to the act of passing through the enclosed space. It may be significant that the south-western entrance, later closed by the digging of ditch segment 22 (Cleal *et al.* 1995, 109), would have led most directly to the long barrows of Wilsford and Normanton. Just as the new monument drew upon the past in its form and its deposits, so its location related to an existing group of funerary monuments.

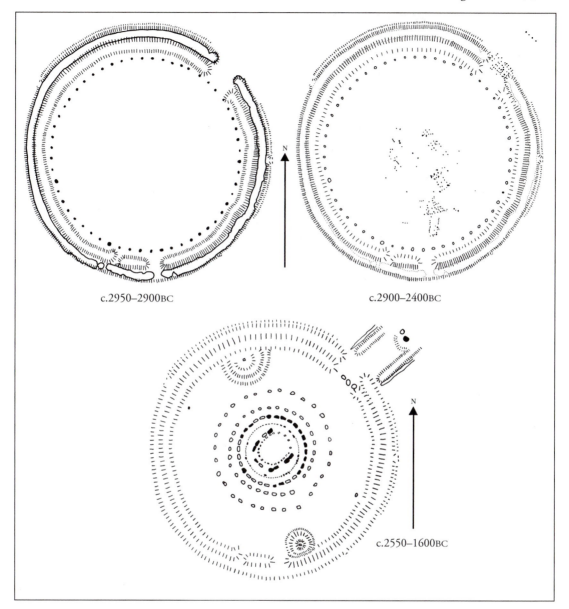

c.2950–2900BC

c.2900–2400BC

c.2550–1600BC

Figure 7.2 Stonehenge: main phases of construction
Source: After Cleal *et al.* (1995)

Strictly speaking, Stonehenge 1 was a 'middle Neolithic' monument, neither quite a cause-wayed enclosure nor a henge, and built during a period when Peterborough Ware was in use. However, despite the recovery of Peterborough Wares from several locations nearby, including immediately to the west on Stonehenge Down, none has been found at Stonehenge. Similarly, the two closest parallels for the monument, the Flagstones enclosure in Dorset and Llandegai henge A, both of which have internal banks and have produced early dates (even if in the latter case these relate to an internal 'fire trough' rather than the enclosure itself: Houlder 1976, 59) have no trace of Peterborough Ware either. The currency of particular forms of material culture did not guarantee their use in all contexts dating to a given period. The exclusion of certain objects from given locations is another indication of the heterogeneity of the Stonehenge landscape.

This earliest use of the Stonehenge enclosure may have been relatively short-lived. The primary silting in the ditch was succeeded by a layer of organic material including burnt matter, above which there are the first traces of deliberate backfill (Cleal *et al.* 1995, 112). The backfilling of the ditch appears not to have been a single coherent operation throughout the circuit, but a series of events which were interspersed within the gradual accumulation of secondary silting. Radio-carbon samples from articulated animal bones within these secondary silts have provided dates of 3300–2920 BC (2455 ± 30 bc) (OxA-5982) and 2920–2660 BC (2270 ± 35 bc) (OxA-5981). As well as animal bones, which included a high proportion of wild species, the secondary deposits contained disarticulated human remains including skull fragments, which were concentrated around the enclosure entrances (Cleal *et al.* 1995, 122–4). This presents an interesting combination of change and continuity with the initial monument: the introduction of the remains of the dead into the enclosure ditch, but with a structure of deposition which maintained the emphasis on entrances.

Some while after the first episodes of backfilling in the ditch, a number of small recuts were dug, some of them containing sherds of Grooved Ware and groups of animal bones. Later still, human cremations began to be inserted into the ditch, the bank and the Aubrey Holes, from which the timber uprights had by now been removed (Cleal *et al.* 1995, 115). This sequence of activity, now designated as Phase 2 of the monument's history, had a markedly episodic character. It was composed of innumerable minor acts of various kinds: the throwing in of backfill, sometimes in quantities so small as to be little more than symbolic; the placing of human bones; the digging and filling of recuts; the burning of human bodies on pyres near the ditch; the burial of cremated bodies. These acts brought quite different substances and associations to bear on the enclosure, as if on numerous occasions attempts had been made to redefine its meaning through practice. Another indication of the unresolved character of Stonehenge during Phase 2 is the profusion of post-holes in the centre of the monument, which might be interpreted as resulting from a series of distinct structural arrangements. Within this, screens, façades, a 'passageway' leading southwards, and an entrance structure leading to the north-east causeway have been identified (Cleal *et al.* 1995, 150). At the north-east entrance, further post structures have been interpreted as a series of enclosed corridors (1995, 146), which may have incorporated a lunar alignment (Ruggles 1997, 216). Arguably, then, the Stonehenge site emerged from a somewhat confused period as a monument strongly associated with the dead, but with a continued stress on entrance and leaving, procession through space. This movement seems to have been increasingly restricted by the structural arrangements, or alternatively increasingly secluded, while the progress of the living into the centre of the enclosure and out again was set against the arrangement of the dead around the eastern periphery.

THE DEVELOPMENT OF THE LATER NEOLITHIC LANDSCAPE

As far as the resolution of the evidence allows, there are indications that in the period after the construction of Stonehenge the immediate area saw an intensification of occupation. There was no radical change in the areas of the landscape which were frequented. The lithic scatters located by the Stonehenge Environs Project are a little more extensive, and some places, like Wilsford Down, the Diamond, Stonehenge Down and the area north of the Cursus have flint assemblages containing an 'industrial' component (Richards 1990, 24). This should not be taken to suggest the establishment of an exclusively industrial landscape to the west of Stonehenge Bottom, so

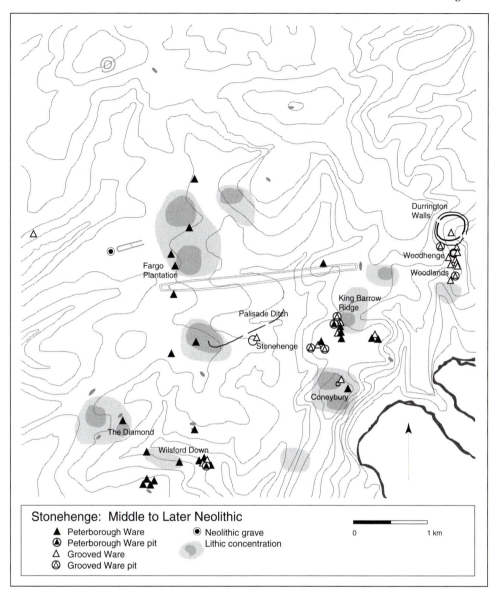

Figure 7.3 Stonehenge area: middle/later Neolithic
Source: After Richards (1990) with additions

much as that flint core production was carried out, alongside other practices, in some parts of the region and not others. Richards points out (1990, 271) that this activity is associated almost exclusively with Peterborough Ware, located as topsoil finds and in the old land surfaces beneath later round barrows (Figure 7.3) (Stone 1938; Vatcher 1961; Grimes 1964; Smith 1991). In this respect, Cleal *et al.*'s diagrams (1995), which identify Peterborough Ware as 'middle Neolithic' and Grooved Ware as 'late Neolithic' may be misleading, giving the impression that first the Durrington area, and then the region at the west end of the Cursus were effectively abandoned. As we have seen in Chapter 5, while Peterborough Ware, Grooved Ware and Beakers can no longer be seen as contemporary throughout the greater part of their currency, there were substantial periods of overlap between successive ceramic styles, and this recognition is necessary in order to understand the Stonehenge landscape.

One of the striking conclusions of the Stonehenge excavation report is that the Palisade Ditch, a linear timber structure which ran for more than a kilometre immediately to the north and west of Stonehenge, was probably contemporary with Phase 2 of the monument (Cleal *et al.* 1995, 161). The Palisade Ditch elaborated the themes of spatial restriction and seclusion on a prodigious scale, echoing the timber façades which formed a part of the Phase 2 structure, and limiting the ways in which Stonehenge could be approached from the north. At the same time, the Palisade would have screened the view northward from the monument, re-emphasising the north–south division of the landscape which had been established by the Great Cursus.

To the east of Stonehenge, the King Barrow Ridge and Coneybury Hill saw continued occupation into the later Neolithic, with flint scatters which seem to lack the industrial element. Within an overall spread of lithic material, there were distinct concentrations which contained large numbers of tools (Laidler and Young 1938; Richards 1990, 109). Core reduction sequences here suggest a greater degree of curation of lithic raw material (1990, 270). The small henge monument at Coneybury was roughly contemporary with Stonehenge 2, and presents an interesting contrast. At Coneybury, there was an assemblage of Grooved Ware derived largely from pits in the interior, and it is even possible that the henge ditch was a later addition to an unenclosed arrangement, one of the internal features having produced an earlier radiocarbon date (3340–2707 BC, 2430 ± 90 bc) (OxA-1409). There is far less evidence of funerary activity here (a single cremation in the ditch), while the faunal remains emphasise the consumption of meat throughout the use of the site (Richards 1990, 138–49).

Amongst the general scatter of occupation evidence along the King Barrow Ridge, cut features containing both Peterborough Ware and Grooved Ware have been found. While they are seldom recovered from the same context, there is no particular spatial segregation between the two ceramic styles (Cleal and Allen 1994, 69). Some part of this pattern is doubtless chronological, but it is noteworthy that the character of deposition in these features is quite distinct. The contents of the Peterborough Ware features, such as the hollows surrounded by scatters of stakeholes in Area L, have little to distinguish them from casual discard (Richards 1990, 114). However, those of the Grooved Ware pits appear more formal in composition. One pit from the area south of King Barrow Wood contained two chalk plaques inscribed with designs similar to those on Grooved Ware, accompanied by pottery and animal bones (Vatcher 1969; Harding 1988). Pit 418 from the Wessex Archaeology excavations contained the skulls and foot bones of four pigs, together with sherds of Woodlands-style Grooved Ware, while 'Feature A' from the 1968 electricity cable trench appears to have held a post, and has been compared to the Aubrey Holes at Stonehenge (Cleal *et al.* 1995, 107).

To the west of Stonehenge bottom, the entire excavated assemblage of Grooved Ware amounts to no more than 20 vessels and 75 per cent of these come from a single site, Wilsford barrow G52 (Smith 1991, 35). No Grooved Ware pit deposits have been located in this area at all. Eastward from the King Barrow Ridge, between Ratfyn and Durrington Walls, Peterborough Ware is entirely absent, and finds of Grooved Ware are numerous. Much of this material has come from pits, whose contents appear still more carefully deposited than those on King Barrow Ridge. At Woodlands, to the south of Durrington Walls, four pits contained a wide variety of flint tools, including unused axes and flint balls (Stone and Young 1948, 290). Pit 4 contained a pair of antlers placed leaning against the side of the cut (Stone 1949, 123). The deliberate character of these deposits is further emphasised by the appearance of Pit 4 as 'a basketful of material deliberately placed upside down' (Stone 1949, 123) and the capping of Pit 1 with a flint cairn (Stone and Young 1948, 289). This group of pits had seemingly not formed part of an occupation, since there was no scatter of lithics in their vicinity (Richards 1990, 270). At Ratfyn, one of four pits was sealed by a shell-filled layer (Stone 1935, 60), and it is notable that many of the pits in this area contained marine shells, items which must have been brought some considerable distance, and which may have constituted symbolic tokens of connections with far places. Still more pits containing richly decorated Grooved Ware were identified beneath the bank of Woodhenge, suggesting that these deposits may have extended over a considerable area (Pollard 1995, 141).

Broadly speaking, Grooved Ware declines in density of distribution westwards from Durrington Walls, while Peterborough Wares fall off as one moves eastwards from Wilsford, Normanton and Fargo. These ceramic traditions may or may not have been used alongside each other in the Stonehenge area for an appreciable period of time. We have seen already that arguments have been put forward suggesting that the whole region was intensively occupied, if only intermittently, from the earlier Neolithic onwards. It is thus unlikely that this pattern emerges from phases of abandonment of portions of the landscape. Evidently, different kinds of pottery were appropriate for use in different locations, whether simultaneously or sequentially. I suggest that by the middle and later Neolithic, the area west of Stonehenge and that around Durrington Walls had developed distinct identities, emerging from different histories of human activity, and that increasingly these were influencing the ways in which people were conducting themselves in these locations.

THE ARRIVAL OF THE STONES

We have seen that Phase 2 at Stonehenge was a period in which conflicting cultural resources were employed within the enclosure, perhaps even one in which the meaning of the site was contested and struggled over. Finally, though, the cremation cemetery came to make up the principal use of the monument. The cremations were evidently deposited over some period of time, since several of their pits were recut on at least one occasion (Cleal *et al.* 1995, 153). It was while this funerary activity was still taking place that the first stone setting was erected on the site, composed of Bluestones set in the Q and R holes (1995, 154) (Figure 7.2). Significantly, the change from wood, a material which grows, to stone, which was used elsewhere for the chambers of funerary monuments (Whittle 1997b, 152) took place at the point when Stonehenge had been redefined as a place of the dead (see also Parker Pearson and Ramilisonina 1998). The precise character of the stone setting seems unclear. Concentric pairs of stones in 'dumb-bell' shaped holes were present in the eastern part of the monument, but this pattern appears to break down further west. Potentially, the structure might have represented an unfinished circle, or a curved façade facing south-west, toward Wilsford and Normanton (Cleal *et al.* 1995, 188). A few of the sarsen stones might also have been in place at this time: Stone 97 and the Heelstone outside of the entrance, and the Station Stones within the enclosure (1995, 268).

It now seems beyond question that the Bluestones were brought to Stonehenge from south and west Wales by human action, rather than by glacial transport (Green 1997, 265; Scourse 1997). The original arguments in favour of considering the Bluestones as glacial erratics involved the range of variation amongst them, and the lack of selection 'for structural properties such as strength, durability and ease of dressing' (Thorpe *et al.* 1991, 149). This implies that the stones were chosen on purely functional grounds. However, just as stone axes were exchanged over long distances to areas which had entirely adequate sources of flint axes, it may be that the Bluestones gained much of their significance from having come from a distant and largely unfamiliar place. Indeed, the similarity of some of the stones to Group XIII axes from Prescelli might have been recognised by some people. Most Neolithic monuments made use of locally occurring materials:

they reconfigured locations by digging subsoil out of the ground, raising stones, placing posts in holes and opening pits and ditches. All of this involved presenting the component parts of a landscape in unfamiliar ways, putting its substance on view and enabling entry into the earth itself. In this respect Stonehenge 3 stands apart from all of its precursors. By floating and dragging the Bluestones to Salisbury Plain, it was possible to bring with them something of the spirit of another place. Stonehenge became a hybrid location, which stood apart from its surroundings by being 'somewhere else'. This sense of occupying a unique place would have been enhanced by the growing astronomical significance of the monument. From the start of Phase 3, Stonehenge incorporated a solar orientation, and particular sunrise and sunset effects would have observable by people who stood inside the inner parts of the structure (Ruggles 1997, 218, 225).

As far as one can tell, it seems that this first stone structure at Stonehenge was relatively short-lived. By around 2580–2480 BC (c. 2050 bc) the Sarsen circle had been constructed, and it is probable that the sarsen trilithons were set up at the same time. The Bluestones were removed from the Q and R holes, and may have been placed in a new arrangement which involved at least two Bluestone trilithons and a tongue-and-groove pair, the shaped stones from which survived in later settings (Cleal *et al.* 1995, 206–7). Over the period in which the principal elements of the familiar form of Stonehenge came together, a series of other changes took place in the surrounding landscape. The destruction of the Lesser Cursus dates to 2890–2147 BC (2050 ± 120 bc) (OxA-1406), and this is very similar to the date for the supposed intrusive feature at the Great Cursus. It is conceivable that the latter relates to an act of destruction rather than the construction of the cursus, so that at the same time as the stones of Stonehenge were being raised, efforts were being made to erase the two linear monuments from the face of the land.

At much the same time again, intensive activity was going on at Durrington Walls. Durrington forms a large natural amphitheatre rising up above the River Avon, at the point where any axis of movement defined by the Great Cursus reaches the river. It had evidently been in use for some considerable while, since concentrations of plain bowl pottery were found beneath the bank of the henge. The dates associated with this material fall in the later fourth millennium BC, again raising the question why Peterborough Wares should be absent from particular contexts. By around 2600 BC (c. 2050 bc) Durrington had become one of the largest henge monuments of southern Britain, but there are indications that this enclosure lay at the end of a long sequence of development. The Midden beside the southern timber circle produced a very early date of 3255–2611 BC (2330 ± 95 bc) (NPL-192), so material may have been accumulating here over a very long period. The Southern Circle itself was a two-phase structure. The second phase produced radiocarbon dates equivalent to those from the ditch, while the first phase is effectively undated. Scatters of post-holes and a gully, associated with Grooved Ware, were found beneath the bank in successive excavations (Stone *et al.* 1954; Wainwright and Longworth 1971, 15). There is thus every indication that a complex series of free-standing features existed before the ditch was dug at Durrington Walls. This being the case, we could argue that the south-east entrance to the henge monumentalised an existing pattern of movement up from the river, into the natural bowl and into the entrance of the southern circle (see Chapter 3 above).

The emergence of Durrington Walls as a massive enclosed space ran side by side with the development of the stone settings at Stonehenge. So stones were not necessarily perceived as 'better' than or superseding upright timbers, and the two forms of monumental architecture were being constructed simultaneously in different locations. Like Coneybury Hill before it, Durrington Walls contrasted markedly with Stonehenge. As Whittle observes (1997b, 150), the sparse deposits of artefacts at Stonehenge are characteristic of stone circles. Durrington, however, has produced rich assemblages of ceramics, lithics and faunal remains, which argue both for conspicuous public consumption and profligate deliberate deposition (Richards and Thomas

1984). While there is a large collection of Grooved Ware from Durrington Walls, and none from Phase 3 contexts at Stonehenge, the occurrence of human remains at Durrington is very limited. Three fragments from a single skull were found in post-hole 79 of the Southern Circle, while a tibia came from the bottom of the henge ditch near the south-east entrance (Wainwright and Longworth 1971, 191). These remains are far from insignificant, and were placed in important locations within the site, but they are probably better understood as one element in a set of depositional practices which made use of varied substances and materials rather than as funerary activity as such.

So by the end of the later Neolithic, two different enclosures were in use on Salisbury Plain which made use of a common architectural heritage in different ways. For although the materials used in the stone settings were distinctive, their layout, and the techniques used in jointing the trilithons were similar to those employed in timber circles (Richards and Whitby 1997, 231). Durrington Walls was characterised by consumption on the part of the living, and the spatial segregation and classification of material things through deposition. This activity was eventually separated from the surrounding landscape by the construction of the ditch and bank (Braithwaite 1984, 99). Yet at Stonehenge the ditch had been deliberately backfilled, and served as only a formal boundary to the site. The use of the site as a cremation cemetery had provided the context for the reorganisation of the monument and the introduction of the stones, and we can argue that this set the conditions for its subsequent development.

BEAKER-AGE ACTIVITY

At Stonehenge, the earliest evidence for the use of Beaker pottery came with the removal of the Bluestones from the Q and R holes (Figure 7.2). There are also Beaker sherds from the stoneholes of the sarsen circle and trilithons (Cleal *et al.* 1995, 168, 354). This demonstrates that Beakers were in use at Stonehenge appreciably earlier than at Durrington Walls, again drawing attention to the different material assemblages which were used on each site. However, since there were probably no more than 10–15 Beaker vessels deposited at Stonehenge over a period of some hundreds of years (1995, 354), the prevailing impression is still one of a sparing use of artefacts, at least for depositional purposes.

Beaker ceramics are plentiful in the Stonehenge area, both in old land surfaces and as topsoil finds, to some extent reflecting the resistant character of their fabrics. However, this material is much more common to the west of Stonehenge Bottom than on the King Barrow Ridge or around Durrington Walls (Figure 7.4). The same pattern is evident in the surface concentrations of lithics: 'Early Bronze Age' types are scarce in the eastern part of the area (Richards 1990, 273). Beaker burials, whether in flat graves or under round mounds, are more numerous around Wilsford, Normanton and the west end of the cursus. Those on the King Barrow Ridge and Coneybury Hill are on the western side, overlooking Stonehenge. While the visibility of Stonehenge does not appear to have been the overriding influence over the location of barrows which it became with the Wessex cemeteries, the monument was increasingly coming to serve as a focus for mortuary activity in the area, to a greater extent than other structures (Woodward and Woodward 1996, 287). The relationship between Stonehenge and the emerging funerary aspect of the landscape is underlined by the presence of Bluestone fragments in several Beaker and Early Bronze Age graves, such as Amesbury 51 and Fargo Plantation at the west end of the cursus (Stone 1938; Ashbee 1976, 1; Bender 1992, 746), and Amesbury 4 nearer to Stonehenge (Pitts 1982, 126). Just as the Bluestones themselves had originally evoked a connectedness with a far-off place, so the pieces derived from their reworking connected discrete funerary events with a monument which had been implicated in the treatment of the dead over generations. When the burial of a

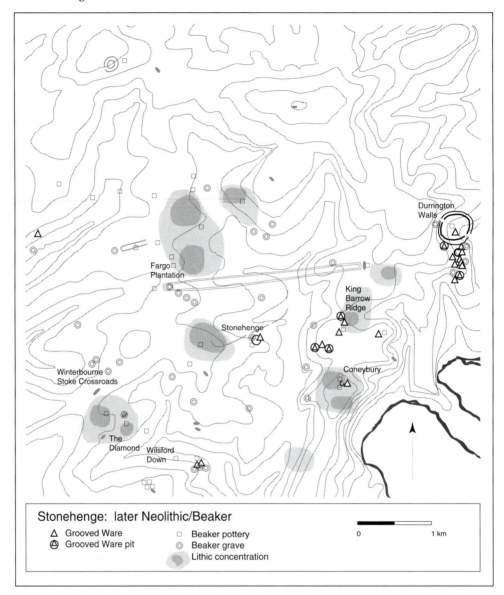

Figure 7.4 Stonehenge area: later Neolithic / Beaker
Source: After Richards (1990) with additions

young man, who may originally have been accompanied by a Beaker pot as well as an archer's wristguard, was deposited in the ditch at Stonehenge, three pieces of Bluestone were placed in the grave (Evans 1983, 15).

Successive remodellings of the stone structures at Stonehenge involved the rearrangement of the Bluestones into a concentric oval and circle, eventually transformed into a horseshoe and circle. At the north-east entrance, a series of uprights including the Slaughter Stone replicated the original timber entrance passageways. Eventually, the Avenue was added, leading across the King

Barrow Ridge and down to the Avon (Cleal *et al.* 1995, 274–7, 485). As Barrett (1994, 43) suggests, these gradual modifications can be seen as permutations of a basic pattern involving restricted access to an enclosed space, within which the view of the outside world was severely limited by the interlocking circles of stones.

While these incremental changes of form were carried out at Stonehenge, the kinds of activity taking place around Durrington Walls remained distinctive. At Woodhenge, another henge monument with internal post settings was constructed in the period around 2480–2039 BC (1867 ± 74 bc) (BM-677). In a similar way to Coneybury and Durrington Walls, the Woodhenge ditch enclosed an area which had been of significance for some considerable while. Dense deposits of cultural material were located under the bank, and a number of cut features seem to have pre-dated the henge (Cunnington 1929, 5–11). Woodhenge appears to have been used in a very similar way to Durrington Walls, with spatially ordered patterns of material deposition integrated with formalised ways of moving around the enclosure (Pollard 1995, 152). Human remains were present, in the one burial and isolated skull fragments in the ditch, and one cremation silted into the post void of post-hole C14 (Cunnington 1929, 29; Pollard 1995, 145). However, these do not seem to have represented a dominant element in the use of the site. In the ditch, groups of antler picks were deposited in interleaved bundles (Pollard 1995, 145), an echo of now ancient practices. Cunnington (1929, 9, 18) pointed out certain structural similarities between Woodhenge and Stonehenge. Given that it is now recognised that the two sites were contemporary, these are perhaps worthy of reconsideration. The entrance of Woodhenge faced down towards Durrington Walls, but shared a solar alignment with Stonehenge. Cunnington suggested that the four inner rings of posts at Woodhenge had the same diameters as the four principal sarsen and Bluestone settings at Stonehenge. The similarity is perhaps not precise, but is close enough to indicate an explicit relationship between the two monuments. So Woodhenge continued the Grooved Ware-associated traditions of Durrington Walls, arguably on a more modest scale (Thorpe and Richards 1984, 79), yet the details of its construction made a kind of reference to Stonehenge. Conversely, the construction of the Avenue seems to have taken place at around the same time as the digging of the Woodhenge ditch (Cleal *et al.* 1995, 327), and would have had the effect that Stonehenge, like Durrington Walls and Woodhenge, would have been approached from the Avon. In the process, the symbolism of water, rivers and connectedness to the sea would have been introduced to Stonehenge (Richards 1996b).

While there is little evidence of non-funerary Beaker-related activity around Durrington and Woodhenge, Beaker burials are present in the area. Woodhenge Circle 1, for instance, consisted of two concentric ring-ditches surrounding a grave containing a male burial with a Beaker vessel and a perforated axe-hammer (Cunnington 1929, 42). Similarly, a flat grave covered by a sarsen stone immediately to the west of Durrington Walls contained a burial with a flint dagger, a whetstone and a conical button; a small round barrow immediately beyond the south-east entrance of the henge contained a female burial with a Beaker, and one of the barrows at Totterdown Clump (south of Woodhenge) may have held another Beaker burial (Hoare 1812, 170–2; Stone *et al.* 1954, 164; Wainwright and Longworth 1971, 5). This conforms to the familiar pattern of burials gravitating toward monuments of an earlier date. What is surprising is that non-funerary depositional activities involving Grooved Ware appear to have continued for some considerable while in the Durrington area. The comparatively late dates for the construction of Woodhenge are complemented by dates from Grooved Ware pits at Ratfyn and Durrington Married Quarters. Elsewhere in the Stonehenge region, a further late date for Grooved Ware came from the small hengiform enclosure Winterbourne Stoke 44 (Green and Rollo-Smith 1984, 316).

DISCUSSION

Throughout this chapter I have been at pains to emphasise the ways in which different parts of an intensively, if sporadically occupied landscape gained distinct identities and were used in different ways. The particular connotations and histories which places acquired served both to limit and facilitate the kinds of activities which took place within them subsequently. In the earlier Neolithic, Wilsford and Normanton Downs gained a particular association with the dead through the construction of a series of long mounds. The building of the first monument at Stonehenge took place against the background of this understanding of the immediate past of the landscape. While mortuary practice had no part to play in the initial use of the site, the deposition of already ancient animal bones in the ditch betrays an orientation on the past. Although a variety of different symbolic elements was used in the many attempts to redefine the enclosure which followed, death and the past appear to have been recurring themes.

Through the Neolithic period, a series of enclosed sites were constructed and used on central Salisbury Plain: Robin Hood's Ball, Stonehenge, Coneybury, Durrington Walls, Woodhenge. As we have seen, a number of different elements distinguished their locations: visibility, proximity to other monuments (including long barrows), proximity to the river. These differences were then enhanced by the details of the construction and use of each enclosure: timber as distinct from stone architectural elements, backfilled ditches as distinct from open ditches, mortuary practice as distinct from the conspicuous consumption of food and artefacts, the use of distinct artefactual assemblages. The enclosure of these sites served to define them as places of particular interest, pre-eminent locations within which activities of heightened importance could be focused upon. The emphasis on the regulation of movement and the staging of social interaction which are particularly evident at Stonehenge, Durrington and Woodhenge underline this point. However, these were not simply ritual spaces within a secular landscape. The kinds of practices and symbolic associations evident inside each monument spilled out into its surroundings. The deposition of Grooved Ware and other associated materials was concentrated in the whole area surrounding Durrington Walls. The connection between the upright stones at Stonehenge and the dead was carried out into the landscape through the burial of Bluestone chips in Beaker graves. The people who inhabited this landscape engaged in different activities in different places at different times. Distinct architectures, modes of conduct and material assemblages attended these practices. The burial of the dead, the extraction of flint from the earth and the gathering of a community for feasting may simply have been incompatible activities (Thomas 1996a, 178–82). Some acts will not have been appropriate for a place of the dead, and others will have been avoided in proximity to running water. These patterns of located action, which became more elaborate as the period progressed, would have held contradictory aspects of social life apart, while segmenting and structuring the lives of persons and groups.

In a similar way, the patterns of movement which led people through the monuments were extended outward by the cursus monuments and the Avenue. In this sense, each of the highly ritualised activities which we can isolate in the context of the monuments had a broader currency, and was intertwined with the conduct of everyday life. Furthermore, the astronomical or cosmological elements which can be identified at Stonehenge and Woodhenge identify particular times as events during which it would have been important to occupy certain symbolically charged locations, but these periodic or cyclic observances would have been integrated into the cyclical patterns of herding, hunting, gathering, harvesting and craft production. The internal differentiation of the landscape which is suggested by mortuary practice, public monuments and depositional activity was complemented by the emergence of distinctive places for camping, working flint cores, gathering plant foods and other resources. So we should imagine that the historical process by which places gained and lost their identities was one in which ceremonial and quotidian activities were thoroughly imbricated in one another. In these terms, the many sporadic remodellings and rebuildings of Stonehenge are best seen as one part of the rhythm of this landscape: a particular activity conducted in its rightful place and time.

Chapter Eight

Regional sequences: the Upper Thames Valley

INTRODUCTION

The Neolithic occupation of the gravel terraces of Oxfordshire and Gloucestershire provides an interesting contrast with that of central Wessex. While the monuments of Wessex form regional concentrations on the blocks of chalk downland, those of the Thames Valley make up a number of smaller complexes running at intervals along the course of the river. We have seen that in Salisbury Plain extensive areas of grassland gradually emerged, but there are indications that in the Upper Thames basin the scale of clearances may have been somewhat smaller. The patchwork of lime, elm and other woodland which covered much of the valley at the start of the Neolithic was opened in a number of places in the course of the fourth millennium BC, principally those where groups of monuments were constructed (Robinson and Wilson 1987). The pollen site at Daisy Banks, close to the Abingdon causewayed enclosure and the barrow cemetery of Barrow Hills, Radley, provided indications that lightly or seasonally grazed grassland had been established early in the Neolithic. Moreover, there appear to have been cereals grown in the area throughout much of the period (Barclay *et al.* 1996, 6). Across the river at Thrupp, mollusc samples from a ring ditch suggested further open country in the later Neolithic. At Dorchester on Thames, another group of monuments was set in permanent grassland, and open conditions were also present at Yarnton, Drayton, Stanton Harcourt and Gravelly Guy (Barclay *et al.* 1995, 67).

However, these results from the monumental foci can be deceptive. At Yarnton the ditch deposits preserved waterlogged remains of alder (Hey 1997, 110), while clearances at the Yarnton mortuary enclosure and the Drayton cursus appear to have regenerated very quickly. The implication is that stands of woodland and scrub must have existed close by. This seems to be corroborated by the continued presence of shade-loving species of snails at Stanton Harcourt and other sites, which must have survived in refuges. At pollen sites like Sidlings Copse and Spartum Fen, there was little trace of clearance until the end of the Neolithic, and upstream at Buscott Lock woodland cover was unbroken until later prehistory (Robinson and Wilson 1987; Barclay *et al.* 1996). Faunal samples throughout the period are dominated by cattle, with very little evidence for the presence of sheep, while the plant remains from Gravelly Guy, Barton Court and Yarnton show a preponderance of wild foods, with cereals generally present only in very small quantities (Hey 1997, 109). Moreover, there was very little build-up of alluvium in the Thames Valley throughout the Neolithic (Evans *et al.* 1993, 187). The overall picture is one of small clearances arranged like a string of beads along the river Thames, particularly at the confluences with its tributaries, containing grazing, stands of cereals and groups of monuments.

THE EARLIER NEOLITHIC

Addressing the Neolithic settlement of the region, Holgate (1988a) suggests that the river gravels saw relatively little activity in the earlier part of the period. At North Stoke, Ford (1987b) has demonstrated the presence of small surface scatters of earlier Neolithic chipped stone, but this fits into an overall impression that traces of occupation are highly ephemeral. Despite this, it is clear that the Upper Thames was frequented by earlier Neolithic communities, since considerable numbers of monuments were built on the gravels. However, all of the constructional traditions represented – causewayed enclosures, cursuses, oval barrows, mortuary enclosures, ring ditches and bank barrows – are ones which fit into the middle of the Neolithic, rather than the very beginning of the period. Moreover, the plain carinated vessels which are characteristic of the earliest Neolithic are entirely absent from the Upper Thames (Barclay *et al.* 1996, 14). This suggests that the intensity of activity on the gravels may have increased as the period progressed. It is striking that the earlier Neolithic monuments of the valley and its surrounding uplands have all but mutually exclusive distributions (Figure 8.1). Megalithic chambered tombs are found on the limestone hills of the Cotswolds, to the north (Lambrick 1988, 112), while earthen long mounds are concentrated on the Berkshire downs. Cursus monuments, oval barrows and mortuary enclosures are clustered along the stretch of river between Eynsham and North Stoke, while an unusually dense grouping of causewayed enclosures is found upriver from here (Barclay *et al.* 1996, 15). One argument which might be raised to account for these distributions is that each cluster of sites relates to a separate ethnic group with its own diagnostic tradition of monument-building. However, it is significant that as well as being distinct in form, these structures were also used in very different ways. In this sense the concentrations of monuments are complementary, and may have been used at different times by the same people, for different purposes. The obvious corollary of this is that in the earlier Neolithic the Upper Thames was visited sporadically by mobile populations, quite possibly moving between lowland and upland on a seasonal basis. This might help explain the limited evidence for habitation on the valley floor.

The causewayed enclosures of the western part of the Upper Thames basin, which extend onto the gentle southern slopes of the Cotswolds, include Aston Bampton (Benson and Miles 1974, 39), Little Clanfield (1974, 33), Signet Hill, Westwell (R. Hingley, pers. comm.), Eastleach (Palmer 1976), Down Ampney (R. Hingley, pers. comm.) and Langford (Palmer 1976), with a further possible site at Eynsham (Lambrick 1988). All of these sites are relatively small, and while several of them have multiple circuits of ditches, they show little evidence of the defensive elaboration which distinguishes some enclosures in Wessex and Sussex. Aside from the enclosures, traces of earlier Neolithic activity in the area are very scarce. In part, this can be explained by the limited extent of gravel extraction, by comparison with the land around Oxford and Abingdon (Benson and Miles 1974, 76). Lithic scatters are scarce, and the only other indication of an early Neolithic presence is a comparatively large number of flint and stone axes. Another possible causewayed enclosure was discovered at Gatehampton Farm, Goring, where the Thames cuts through the uplands to the south. Here, a crouched juvenile burial was found in the upper silting of a flat-bottomed ditch, and dated to 3095–2890 BC (BM-2835) (2410 ± 45 bc) (Allen 1995, 26). This site and the enclosure at Abingdon are located on either side of the area dominated by cursus monuments. Some of these may have been quite early in origin, since the Drayton Cursus has produced a radiocarbon date of 4000–3538 BC (HAR-6477) (3040 ± 100 bc). However, these linear monuments were not always the first trace of Neolithic activity at a given location. Sometimes they incorporated earlier sites or places of importance within their plans: the Dorchester Cursus ditch cut across those of Site VIII, a rectangular 'mortuary enclosure' (Atkinson *et al.* 1951), the North Stoke bank barrow butted on to a similar enclosure and

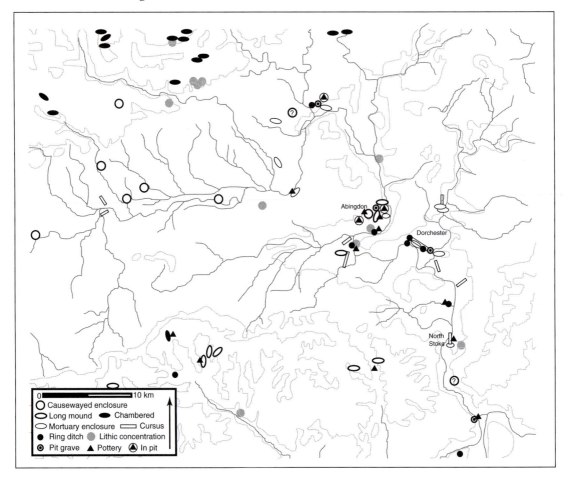

Figure 8.1 Upper Thames Valley: earlier Neolithic

narrowly avoided a presumably earlier ring ditch (Bradley and Holgate 1984, 102), whilst the Drayton/Sutton Courtenay Cursus was built over an area which may already have held two or more pit graves. It is in this zone, south of Oxford, that traces of earlier Neolithic activity are most dense, including ring ditches, burials, mortuary enclosures and finds of pottery (Figure 8.1). Again, this may reflect the intensity of archaeological investigation around Abingdon and Dorchester on Thames, but the concentration of cursus monuments suggests a real contrast between the south-east and north-west parts of the Upper Thames basin.

The Abingdon causewayed enclosure seems to differ from those further to the west in having a relatively complex structural history. While the radiocarbon dates from charcoal samples at Abingdon suggest an early foundation for the enclosure, these have been queried on the grounds that they may relate to old wood (Bradley 1986). The earliest reliable date would then be that of 3680–3340 BC (BM-352) (2760 ± 135 bc), from the middle fill of the recut inner ditch. The site was evidently a two-phase construction, the outer ditch having been added to enlarge the area enclosed (Avery 1982, 15). In the first phase the ditch and bank appear to have been relatively insubstantial structures, and the filling of the inner ditch consisted of deliberately placed deposits of fully rotted organic material, interspersed with spreads of clean gravel (1982, 17). The closest parallel for this is from Wessex, in the organic deposits carefully placed in the ditch segments at Hambledon Hill (Mercer 1980, 30). If the ditches at Abingdon were essentially quarry pits for a simple dump rampart, it seems likely that their filling with organic layers alternating with sterile lenses is a consequence of the periodic, or cyclical, collection and burial of material which derived from activities which took place, also on a cyclical basis, within the enclosure. The ditch deposits contained large quantities of pottery and animal bones (including several articulated limbs), several axe fragments, and two pieces of human cranium. Much of this material was fresh and unweathered when it was deposited. While Avery argued that this material resulted from a single episode of 'tidying up' before the construction of the outer ditch, Bradley (1986, 184–5) has drawn attention to the formal character of the inner ditch filling, and contrasted this with the evidence from the outer ditch. What this suggests is that in its earlier phase the use of the enclosure involved very deliberate and repetitive depositional practices, but that with the re-organisation of the site the character of activity changed somewhat. The outer ditch was more substantial than the inner, and the rampart here was probably revetted with turf (Case 1956, 14). In a manner comparable with Crickley Hill on the northern Cotswolds (Dixon 1988), the Abingdon causewayed enclosure may have become a defended site. The position of the enclosure between the steep slopes of two stream channels would have facilitated this development.

To the east of the enclosure, the oval mound at Barrow Hills, Radley was roughly contemporary with this later activity. The radiocarbon dates which range between 3370–2935 BC (BM-2391) (2550 ± 50 bc) and 3350–2605 BC (BM-2390) (2350 ± 130 bc) were taken from antlers in the two concentric ditches surrounding the barrow. However, the earliest phase of the monument may have been a rectangular enclosure, and is effectively undated (Bradley 1992, 132). A central grave contained two burials: an adult female with a polished flint knife, and an adult male with a jet slider. Bradley suggests that these were deposited at the start of the structural sequence, which consisted of five separate phases of ditch-digging. This would be rather early for these particular grave goods, although the carbon dates taken from the skeletons seem, in contrast, very much too late (Garwood in Barclay and Halpin 1998). As at the causewayed enclosure, the ditches contained highly structured deposits of antler, human bone, flint and potsherds, placed on a number of different occasions (Bradley 1992, 134). The link between the two sites is compelling: in both cases the observed pattern was the outcome of numerous discrete events of construction and deposition. The Barrow Hills mound is also a good parallel for middle Neolithic barrows at Hambledon Hill, Whitesheet Hill and Maiden Castle. In each case, a conspicuous burial was linked to changes in the use of a causewayed enclosure, perhaps related to the rise to pre-eminence of a particular social segment.

However, the oval mound did not exist in isolation. A possible second long mound lay to the north, while three flat graves dated to the later fourth millennium BC and a linear mortuary structure containing several bodies was also excavated at Barrow Hills (Barclay and Halpin 1998). So while the causewayed enclosure was still in use, Barrow Hills was already being used as a location for the burial of the dead. In this respect, Abingdon conforms to a broader pattern of long mounds and other linear monuments forming small groupings. Pairs of oval enclosures exist at Stadhampton and Stanton Harcourt (Barclay *et al.* 1995). Several of the monuments at Dorchester on Thames (Atkinson *et al.* 1951) can be interpreted as oval mounds (Bradley and Chambers 1988). The bank barrow at North Stoke, dated to 3640–3370 BC (BM-1405) (2622 ± 49 bc) appears to run between a 'mortuary enclosure' similar to that at Dorchester and a peculiar arrangement of ditches at the north end (Case and Whittle 1982). More isolated to the north was a linear enclosure at New Wintles, Eynsham (Kenward 1982), which can be interpreted as a simple mortuary structure similar to those under Wayland's Smithy I (Atkinson 1965) and Haddenham (Hodder and Shand 1988).

These long and oval structures do not form a homogeneous group, and the great variability of earlier Neolithic mortuary practice is emphasised by the presence of ring ditches with Abingdon Ware in their primary ditch fills at Corporation Farm (Bradley and Holgate 1984, 120) and Thrupp Farm (Thomas and Wallis 1982, 184). A ring ditch at Newnham Murren, Wallingford, with a crouched female burial, is also perhaps dated by a sherd of Abingdon Ware in the grave fill (Moorey 1982).

A further element of mortuary practice which seems to have persisted throughout the Neolithic in the Upper Thames was the deposition of human skeletal remains in pits. At Dorchester on Thames, near the south-east end of the cursus, a pit with human bones (largely cranial) was excavated, and dated to 3940–3196 BC (OxA-119) (2850 ± 130 bc). Another element of the Barrow Hills complex was pit 5352, which contained the remains of one articulated male and two disarticulated females (Barclay and Halpin 1999). Similarly, Pit F at Sutton Courtenay contained the bones of a woman and two children (Leeds 1923, 151–2), and Pit V ten skulls, all but one of which may have been male (Leeds 1934, 267). The chronological relationship of these pits to the cursus is unclear. At Tolley's Pit, Cassington, a pit containing six skeletons appears to be of rather later date, as maggot-decorated sherds were found in the fill (Leeds 1940). There were two pit graves at Mount Farm, one with a burial dated to 3380–2900 BC (HAR-4673) (2500 ± 100 bc), with Peterborough sherds and a flint knife (Barclay *et al.* 1995, 107). Another pit at Barrow Hills, F483 contained two fragmentary bodies, with transverse and barbed and tanged arrowheads in the fill (Barclay and Halpin 1999).

Some of these examples attest the existence of a tradition of simple inhumation. Indeed, there are very few clear instances of the kind of corporate mass burial characteristic of Wessex and the Cotswolds anywhere in the Thames basin. Others, on the analogy with pit graves in Cranborne Chase (Pitt Rivers 1898), may have constituted one element of the cycle of bone processing, and it is possible that the use of human bones as portable objects of symbolic importance was of particular significance in the Upper Thames region. Sutton Courtenay V and Dorchester both show the deposition of skulls in areas which would later be the sites of cursus monuments. Skull fragments have also been reported from the inner ditch at Abingdon (and also from the enclosure at Staines, downriver: Kinnes 1979, 120), in the ditch of the Barrow Hills over the mound (Bradley 1992), in one pit and one ditch segment at New Wintles (Kenward 1982, 51), in the ditch of Dorchester Site VIII (Whittle *et al.* 1992), with later Neolithic material in Sutton Courtenay Pit Q (Leeds 1934), and with Fengate Ware in pits at Astrop, Northants. (Ashmolean Museum). We have seen that skull fragments were recovered from the Abingdon causewayed enclosure, and in addition a human pelvis was located in the outer ditch (Case 1956). It seems unlikely that all of these cases can have been the result of carelessness on the part of the Neolithic population. The interpretation suggested here is that the deposition of parts of ancestral human bodies, and particularly the skull, in significant locations was regarded as a means of introducing the influence of the dead into the landscape.

LATER NEOLITHIC INTENSIFICATION

The overall distribution of monuments and material culture indicates a continued intensification of human activity in the Upper Thames after 3000 BC, particularly in the area north of Oxford, around Yarnton, Cassington and Stanton Harcourt (Figure 8.2). Holgate (1988a) was able to point to an increased number of flint scatters which included diagnostically later Neolithic elements. As we have argued already, this does not mean that people were occupying the river gravels for the first time, but it may indicate that they were spending longer on the valley terraces, and engaging in activities likely to generate lithic waste. Just as the barrows and long enclosures of

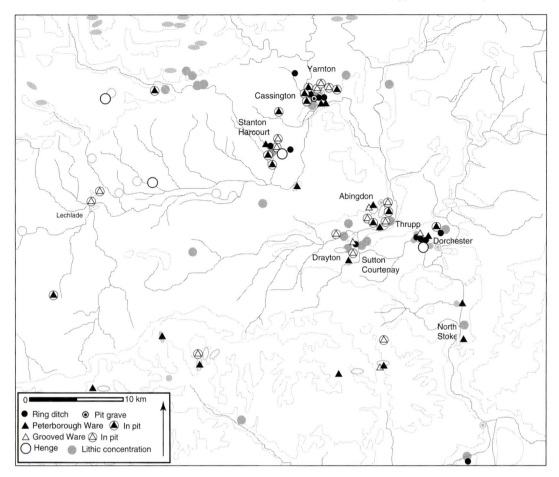

Figure 8.2 Upper Thames Valley: middle /later Neolithic

the earlier Neolithic had formed small groupings, the ring ditches, henges and pit deposits of the later Neolithic demonstrate the emergence of a series of distinct foci spaced at 5–15 km intervals along the river. Bradley (in Bradley and Holgate 1984, 130) has pointed to the small scale of monuments in the Thames Valley by comparison with Wessex. The number of structures is also worthy of consideration. Cranborne Chase, for instance, had one very large cursus while the Thames had at least seven small ones. Such a pattern could be explained in a number of different ways. The diminutive size of the Upper Thames Valley monuments need not be a reflection of a smaller population. Instead, the multiple centres could indicate less centralised communities, circumscribed at a lower level. Alternatively, one could point to the structure of activity on these sites, which continued to be episodic, involving the input of relatively small amounts of labour. This would not support the notion that the use of each complex was the prerogative of a single social group. Instead, the later Neolithic might have seen the formalisation of a series of significant *places*, which groups of people continued to occupy on a cyclical or sporadic basis.

Mortuary sites of later Neolithic date are numerous in the Upper Thames Valley. The complex associated with the Dorchester Cursus contained a large proportion of these, but other examples are scattered along the gravel terraces. At Linch Hill Corner, near Stanton Harcourt, a double ring ditch surrounded a central grave, containing a female burial with jet slider and flint knife (Grimes 1944, 34). Nearby at Gravelly Guy, ring ditch IX, 1 consisted of a deep revetment trench holding upright posts. A sherd of Mortlake Ware was found in the lower silts (Barclay *et al.* 1995, 84–8). Other ring ditches with Peterborough Ware associations have been excavated at Stanton Harcourt and Cassington (Case 1963). At Barrow Hills, Radley, the oval mounds and flat graves were succeeded by a group of ring ditches, although it is not clear whether all of these were used for funerary purposes. One of these was a characteristic segmented ditch, while ring ditch 801 was stratigraphically earlier than a group of Grooved Ware pits. Probably the most interesting was ring ditch 611, which enclosed a very small central area. Two cattle limbs and a group of antlers had been placed on the ditch bottom, and these provided a date of 2870–2200 cal. BC (2000 ± 80 bc) (BM-2713). In the secondary ditch silts were sherds of a Grooved Ware bowl, which appears to have been smashed *in situ* (Barclay and Halpin 1999).

The Barrow Hills ring ditches illustrate the ambiguity of the small ditched or mounded burial sites in the Upper Thames, which can easily be confused with a number of other classes of monument (Figure 8.3). These latter include a variety of non-funerary hengiforms, such as City Farm, Hanborough (Phase 1); Stanton Harcourt Sites X, 1 and XXII, 6; Corporation Farm, Abingdon (Case 1986); and also timber circles, such as Gravelly Guy IX, 2 and Dorchester 3. What complicates the issue is that an individual monument may have been rebuilt on a number of occasions, changing from one kind of structure to another. This need not mean that the different constructions were interchangeable: they were clearly used in different ways, and a change of form implies a change of significance. But it is characteristic of the Upper Thames that distinct activities and material traditions were not segregated into remote parts of the landscape. Instead, discrete episodes of construction and deposition served to repeatedly transform the character of prominent locations. This could be taken to imply that the occupation of these places was discontinuous, episodes of settlement being marked by ritual events.

The gradual intensification of activity in the Upper Thames is also attested by numerous finds of pottery. Peterborough Wares are often found in a loose association with mortuary sites, although rarely as grave goods as such. For instance, Peterborough sherds have been found in the ditch fills of mortuary enclosures at Dorchester on Thames and Yarnton (Hey 1997, 106). More often, both Peterborough Ware and Grooved Ware are located in pit deposits. Some of these appear quite structured, like a pit at Barton Court Farm which contained a Mortlake vessel inverted over a deposit of carbonised plant remains (Barclay *et al.* 1995, 109). But as Healy points out (in Barclay and Halpin 1999), many small bowl-shaped pits with nondescript contents have also been excavated on sites on the gravels. While these may be connected with the transient occupation, it is difficult to assign them a domestic function. Rather, they might be seen as a relatively informal way of marking and memorising a human presence. Whether for cultural or chronological reasons, Peterborough Ware and Grooved Ware are rarely found in the same closed context (Pit F1002 at Gravelly Guy being an exception). However, the spatial separation between traditions found in Wessex does not seem to apply, as in East Anglia, where pits with Peterborough, Beaker or Grooved Ware sherds are frequently found in the same general location (Healy 1984, 104). As with the funerary monuments, the general impression is one of repeated material interventions which added to or transformed the history of a place. Recent excavations at Yarnton have added to this pattern, demonstrating that distinct but related ceremonial, funerary and occupation areas were maintained over a lengthy period (Hey 1997, 106–7).

There have been many finds of Grooved Ware in the Upper Thames, although it has not been recovered from the large henge monuments at the Devil's Quoits, Dorchester Big Rings or Condicote on the northern Cotswolds (Saville 1983). At smaller monuments like Barrow Hills 611 and Corporation Farm, Grooved Ware deposits may have been involved in changes in the

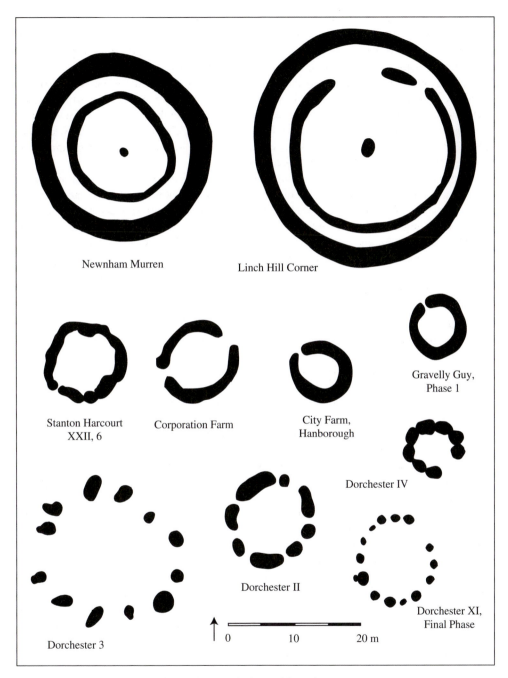

Figure 8.3 Comparative plans of Neolithic ring ditches and hengiforms

significance of existing structures. One pit at Gravelly Guy produced sherds in the Clacton style (Barclay *et al.* 1995, 88), but most of the other material from the region is either of Durrington Walls or Woodlands style. There are hints that these two sub-traditions were treated in slightly different ways. At Abingdon Common a pit was found isolated from any other prehistoric material, lined with stones and containing very large sherds of six Durrington Walls Grooved Ware vessels (Parrington 1978, 31–3). Stanton Harcourt Vicarage Field Pit A (Thomas 1955, 4) contained a highly decorated Durrington Walls vessel inverted on the floor of the pit, in a matrix of dark soil. The only other finds were six flint flakes. A quite separate pair of pits nearby contained much smaller sherds in the Woodlands style (Case 1982c, 103). Another complete Durrington Walls vessel was found in pit F1039 at Gravelly Guy (Barclay *et al.* 1995, 89), and sherds in the same style came from a further isolated pit at Thrupp Farm (Thomas and Wallis 1982, 184).

Woodlands-style Grooved Ware has also been found in pits, but these generally occur in clusters, and are often associated with standing monuments. At Barrow Hills, ornate Woodlands sherds were found in pits located amongst the barrows, burials and ring ditches (Barclay and Halpin 1999). Similar pits were excavated at Barton Court Farm, and near Cassington Mill, where a number of pits were again found in an area rich in ring ditches and Beaker graves (Case 1982b). At Lechlade, pits with Woodlands sherds, burnt soil, charcoal, flints, animal bones and a deposit of antlers were found at the Loders and Roughground Farm, close by two cursus monuments, a pit alignment and post-hole arrangements (Jones 1976, 2; Darvill *et al.* 1986; Allen *et al.* 1993, 9–10). The relationship between Grooved Ware pits and earlier monuments was particularly close at Sutton Courtenay (Leeds 1923; 1927; 1934), where it seems that the pits with the most complex fillings were those located between the cursus ditches. Two consistent elements can be detected in the filling of pits with Woodlands pottery: burnt organic soil and animal bones. At Blewbury 'the animal bone had evidently been deposited as joints, as articulated shaft and knuckle bones were apparent' (Halpin 1984, 1). These bones (kindly shown to me by Claire Halpin) include roughly equal proportions of pig and cattle, and are largely from the meat-rich parts of the animals. At Cassington (Jackson 1956) pig bones predominated.

THE DORCHESTER ON THAMES COMPLEX

We have seen already that in the Neolithic of the Upper Thames any one style of artefact or earthwork is less significant in isolation than in the context of the complex sequences of activity which were played out at a number of focal locations. For the sake of illustration we can consider the set of structures at Dorchester on Thames. These monuments were constructed over some hundreds of years, representing a series of ways in which a particular space was reconfigured rather than the playing-out of a single coherent design. The available evidence can sustain a number of different interpretations of the structural sequence (Atkinson *et al.* 1951; Bradley and Chambers 1988; Whittle *et al.* 1992), depending upon whether stratigraphy, alignment, material associations or parallels with other sites are given greater weight. The account presented here will differ in some details from all of the published versions. However, which of these interpretations is favoured is less important than the overall pattern of episodic transformation.

The earliest structural phase at Dorchester on Thames arguably consisted of an arrangement of oval and oblong enclosures and mounds (Figure 8.4). Site VIII, the long mortuary enclosure, was recognised by Atkinson (1948, 66) as an early element, since its ditch had entirely silted up by the time that the cursus was dug through it. Some hundreds of metres to the south-east of this was a D-shaped enclosure, Site 1, which was later to be incorporated into the cursus (Bradley and Chambers 1988, 279). Site 1 in turn cut the pit containing human bones mentioned above

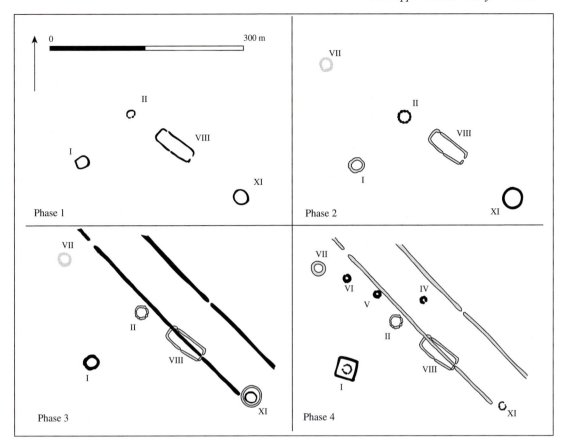

Figure 8.4 The Dorchester on Thames complex: sequence

(1988, 280). The mid-fourth millennium BC date from this pit provides a *terminus post quem* for the entire complex. The relationship between the two long enclosures is complicated, since Site 1 is aligned toward Site VIII, whose eastern entrance faced back to Site 1 (Whittle *et al.* 1992, 196), yet which had a slightly different orientation.

Bradley (in Bradley and Holgate 1984, 118) pointed out that Ditch II of Site XI, which was arguably its earliest structural unit, was distinctly oval in plan, and that it and Site II shared the alignment of Site VIII rather than that of the cursus. When the first, causewayed ditch of Site II is separated from the plan it also appears ovoid, with its long axis aligned toward Site I. It was originally claimed that Site II Phase 1 had never been finished, and that the ditches had been backfilled before any silting had taken place (Atkinson *et al.* 1951, 23). However, this assumes that the material on the ditch bottom (a fine black soil) was a product of the destruction of the monument. Were this so, one might expect the matter which filled the ditch segments to be similar to that which had been taken out. If alternatively the ditch segments had been quarries for a central mound, Zeuner's findings (in Atkinson *et al.* 1951, 121) that 'the dark fillings of the pits and ditches are debris from fires mixed with other organic refuse and varying proportions of natural soil' are illuminating. It may be that at these sites, and at others like the round mound at Newnham Murren (Moorey 1982), activities involving the burning of fires had taken place on or around the barrow, at a time before much silting had taken place into the ditches. This suggests that some period of time might have elapsed before the circular ditch of Phase II was cut.

Site I, upon which Site II was aligned, was another oval structure in its earliest form. The original ditch was U-sectioned and produced sherds of Abingdon Ware. Later recuts containing Fengate Ware were clustered along the west side of the ditch. The large sherds in these recuts, contrasting with the small scraps of pottery elsewhere in the monument, are indicative of purposeful deposition. Despite the distortions in plan which have resulted from this recutting it is possible to suggest that this edge originally constituted something akin to a façade trench. A parallel for such a monument might be found in Grendon, Northants., a sub-rectangular ring ditch with façade, dated to the earlier fourth millennium BC (Gibson 1985). At Dorchester Site I, the remains of a crouched burial were found on the old land surface (Atkinson *et al.* 1951, 12). This suggests a similarity to the Barrow Hills oval mound, also with crouched burials in a shallow grave.

It is possible that a second major phase of activity at Dorchester involved the construction of a series of circular mounds. At both Site II and Site XI an oval monument was 'converted' into a round one. The break in the cursus's south-west ditch to avoid the outer ditch of Site XI indicates that this probably occurred before the construction of the cursus. In the outer ditch of Site XI, Ditch III, Ebbsfleet sherds were found in a layer of dark soil which overlay a primary silting. Ebbsfleet sherds were also recovered from the upper silting of Site VIII. Sites II and IX preserved the orientation of the mortuary enclosure. Another ring ditch, Site VII, lay on the same axis. Rather little has been published about this monument. It contained a cremation with a Collared Urn and a bronze awl, and its morphology suggests a bell barrow (Atkinson *et al.* 1951, 60). However, it remains a possibility that the Bronze Age barrow replaced an earlier mound. At the south-east end of the cursus, the southern ditch again stopped short of another (unexcavated) ring ditch. By analogy with Site XI, this too may be earlier than the cursus.

The cutting of the cursus ditch is dated by a piece of antler from the ditch base at 3510–2920 BC (BM-2443) (2560 ± 100 bc). The cursus extended the alignment of Site 1, but slighted that of Site VIII, actually cutting across the mortuary enclosure and running up to the perimeter of Site XI, incorporating the small monuments into a greater structure in a way also seen at North Stoke and Drayton. This combination of incorporation and destruction is characteristic of the way in which the Upper Thames monument complexes were re-worked and modified over time. However, the cursus itself represents an unusually large investment of effort, joining two separate groups of monuments together and imposing a single spatial ordering upon them all. Ditch I at Site XI, which contained transverse arrowheads and was dated to 3309–2667 BC (BM-2440) (2370 ± 90 bc) was clearly later than the digging of the cursus. Whittle *et al.* (1992, 166) argue that the sequence at Site XI can best be understood as the progressive enlargement of a round mound, so that Ditch I would be the earliest of the concentric ditches, and the whole monument would post-date the cursus. It is quite likely that a round mound might be located within an entrance through the cursus ditch, but this neglects the point that Ditch I appears to cut Ditch II. Ditch III was relatively deep, and would have provided the material for a mound of appreciable size, while the relatively shallow Ditch I might be explained as having been cut from a higher level, through such a mound. Ditch I, in turn, was cut by a series of pits, making up a monument of a different kind.

At Site I a similar circle of pits was dug, again cutting the earlier oval ditch, and changing the alignment from NE/SW to E/W. A single sherd of Grooved Ware from the top of the oval ditch might be connected with this episode of activity (Whittle *et al.* 1992, 196). The square ditch which encloses the site shares the orientation of the circle of holes, which aligns with Site XI. So despite the Abingdon Ware in the square ditch, it too was dug late in the sequence. Allen's mention of a round barrow within a square ditch at Limlow Hill, Cambridgeshire, indicates that the feature need not be early in date (Allen 1938, 170). The penannular settings of pits within Sites I and XI are very similar to another group of features, Sites IV, VI and VI. Gibson (1992, 85–6) argues that these were all post circles, whose uprights were dug out before a series of cremation burials were deposited within and around the sockets. Nearer to the south-east end of the cursus a larger post circle, Site 3, had had its uprights burnt *in situ* rather than extracted. On this evidence we could tentatively argue that in the early third millennium BC the character of the Dorchester complex was fundamentally altered, with the construction of at least six post circles. Unlike any of the preceding monuments, these were not obviously funerary structures. The destruction of the circles by fire and the removal of posts, and the subsequent insertion of large numbers of cremation burials indicates a further change in the way in which the location was used.

The cremation cemeteries which replaced the timber circles at Dorchester have produced a series of secure radiocarbon determinations. Inside the south-east end of the cursus, ring ditch 2, which contained 28 cremations, was dated to 2922–2628 BC (BM-4225N) (2280 ± 50 bc). The burned post-circle, Site 3, and its cremations produced a series of dates commencing at 3018–2393 BC (BM-2164R) (2170 ± 120 bc), and ending at 2280–1530 BC (BM-2165R) (1600 ± 130 bc). One of the post-holes on this site, F2012, produced a large sherd which might be either plain Grooved Ware or Collared Urn (Whittle *et al.* 1992, 170). If the latter, then the latest carbon date could indicate that further cremations were introduced to the circle in the Early Bronze Age. This would involve an astonishing degree of continuity.

In all, 128 cremations were recovered from the Dorchester sites excavated by Atkinson, Piggott and Sanders (Atkinson *et al.* 1951) and a further 31 in the more recent excavations by the Oxford Archaeological Unit. Interestingly, T.H. Gee's notes (Ashmolean Museum) indicate that a cremation in a pit was located 10 yards south-east of Site I in 1956. Others might have been present. Some form of spatial expression of differences between the burials is certainly indicated at Site II. This introduces a serious problem into any assessment of the Dorchester complex: most of the individual sites were excavated in advance of gravel quarrying and on the basis of their recognition on aerial photographs. A consequence of this was that large open areas were not excavated in the earlier investigations. While larger areas were opened at the south-east end of the cursus, the work was different in character from that at Barrow Hills, where the entire barrow cemetery and its surroundings were stripped. With this point in mind, it is still interesting to note the scarcity of Beaker barrows and flat graves, and of Grooved Ware pits from Dorchester, a circumstance which contrasts both with Barrow Hills and Stanton Harcourt. Garwood (in Barclay and Halpin 1999) makes the attractive suggestion that much of the activity at Dorchester on Thames might fit into the chronological hiatus between the earlier Neolithic mounds and flat graves and the Beaker cemetery at Barrow Hills. This suggests a degree of complementarity between the two complexes. In practice, sporadic acts of pit-digging may have continued at Barrow Hills over this period, while within the levels of confidence which can be assigned to the radiocarbon chronology it is possible that both the Grooved Ware pits and the earliest Beaker graves at Barrow Hills overlapped with the Dorchester cremation cemeteries. In any case, the indications are that two significant locations separated by less than 10 km were used in quite distinct ways throughout the Neolithic. This might be conceived in terms of an ebb and flow in the intensity of activity between the two places, or of the performance of different practices at either. Evidently, the maintenance of grassland clearings at both sites indicates that neither was ever entirely abandoned. If Dorchester and Barrow Hills were in any sense interlinked, this would lessen the force of any territorial model which would present the clusters of monuments as the 'central places' of distinct groups of population.

THE UPPER THAMES HENGES

The large henge monument of Big Rings would seem to fall late into the sequence at Dorchester on Thames. The pottery from Atkinson's excavation was Beaker (Clarke 1970, 493), although this was small in quantity and does not provide a reliable date of construction. Like the other henges of the Upper Thames, Big Rings produced very little material culture, and had little in the way of complex internal structures, in contrast with the great Wessex henges. A notable feature of the site is the pair of ring ditches, one located near either entrance. Site XIV, in the southern entrance had a cremation associated with a stone axe deposited in its ditch (Whittle *et al.* 1992, 166). Given that this structure may have been incorporated into the bank between the two concentric ditches of Big Rings, it would seem to have been earlier than the henge, and imply that the latter post-dated the cremation cemeteries. Site XII, by contrast, was located outside of the henge, and contained one of the few Beaker inhumations in the Dorchester complex, buried with a Beaker vessel, tanged copper dagger, riveted knife and stone wristguard. A separate pit within the ring ditch contained the remains of a possible wooden bier, suggesting that the funeral of the person concerned had been relatively elaborate. Each of the two ring ditches lay on the left-hand side as one entered the henge, and suggest an emphasis on entering and leaving the monument, as opposed to any activities which might have taken place inside.

The large henge of the Devil's Quoits at Stanton Harcourt is in many ways comparable with Big Rings. Here, hearths had repeatedly been burnt on the floors of the ditches on either side of the entrances (Barclay *et al.* 1995, 20). Small quantities of human and animal bone were associated with these hearths, but finds were otherwise very sparse. Two post-pits in the southern terminal of the eastern entrance add to the impression of an elaboration of the entrances of the henge at the expense of internal features. The Devil's Quoits contained traces of a slight timber structure, and an internal setting of stone uprights. Hearth F156 in the south terminal of the east entrance produced a date of 2890–2200 BC (HAR-1887) (2060 ± 120 bc), while the antler pick from stonehole F203 gave 2920–2570 BC (OxA-3689) (2005 ± 65 bc). Given that fragments of conglomerate similar to the uprights were found associated with Beaker sherds in layer G of the secondary ditch fill (Barclay *et al.* 1995, 45), it seems probable that the stones were added a generation or so after the construction of the earthwork.

Neither Big Rings nor the Devil's Quoits produced the kinds of evidence for large-scale gatherings and the conspicuous consumption of food and artefacts which characterise Durrington Walls or Mount Pleasant. They were perhaps more comparable with the earlier phases at Stonehenge, where structures and placed deposits drew attention to the entrances as opposed to the interior of the enclosure. This suggests that although enough labour could be organised to build very large monuments in the Upper Thames, these were not often used as gathering-places for very large groups of people. Both Big Rings and the Devil's Quoits were located in the midst of complexes of other features, which included mortuary structures and burials of earlier and later Neolithic date. At Dorchester, the cursus represented another massive manifestation of corporate labour, but both sequences seem to have involved the playing-out of distinct and contradictory influences and principles in relation to one another. Because monument-building and acts of deposition in the Upper Thames were bounded and discrete events, which might actually have been separated by the movement of communities to other locations, each new occupation might involve the re-evaluation, modification or destruction of existing structures. The existing landscape and the material traces of past history provided a means by which continuing social tensions and antagonisms could be worked out. At different times, different understandings and practices might have dominated, with the effect that at sites like Dorchester on Thames each phase of activity involved not simply structures of different forms, but arrangements which implicated people in very different kinds of performance.

BEAKER GRAVES

We have seen already that the practice of single burial, often with grave goods or within a separate ring ditch, was a feature of the Neolithic of the Upper Thames from an early date. Perhaps unlike much of Wessex, these burials were an integral element of the developing monumental complexes (Figure 8.5). This pattern continued into the Beaker phase, and had important consequences. If the communities who used the Thames gravels were already attuned to conducting elaborate funerals, and thereby establishing a connection between genealogy and place, the cultural dislocation experienced as a result of adopting a new material repertoire might have been limited. Resistance to change might have been minimal, and continuity in the use of locations might be expected. This much is indicated by the sequence at Barrow Hills, where there were at least three Beaker flat graves, and Beaker-age burials in ring ditch 201, barrow 4a and barrow 12 (Barclay and Halpin 1998). Of these, flat grave 919 probably contained some of the earliest Beaker vessels and metalwork in Britain (Healy in Barclay and Halpin 1998). Two separate episodes of burial, both involving the remains of children, produced dates of 2860–2140 BC (OxA-1874) (1980 ± 80 bc) and 2870–2290 BC (OxA-1875) (2040 ± 80 bc). The earlier of these inhumations was interred

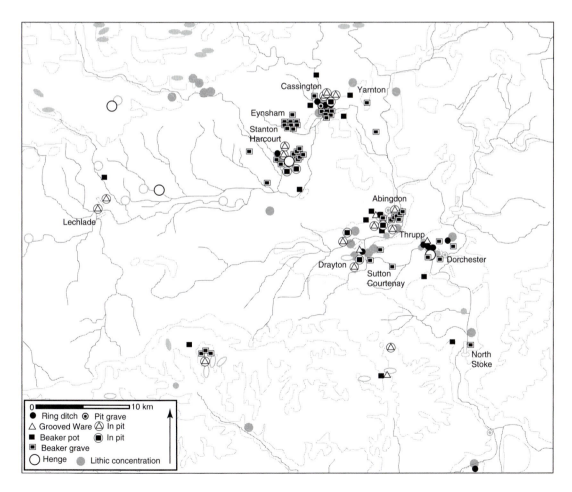

Figure 8.5 Upper Thames Valley: later Neolithic/Beaker

with a 'barbed-wire' decorated Beaker and three sheet copper rings. These earliest burials must have been very little later than the Grooved Ware pit deposits on the same site, if not actually contemporary.

Similarly, at Stanton Harcourt Vicarage Field, a series of Beaker flat graves was found in close spatial proximity (if contextual separation) to more Grooved Ware pits, and relatively close to the Devil's Quoits henge (Barclay *et al.* 1995, 80). Accepting established typologies, some of the graves too might have been comparatively early. Continuity in the location of funerary practices from the Neolithic into the Beaker era is suggested at the double ring ditch X, 6 at Stanton Harcourt, which contained two Beaker burials cutting an earlier grave, while the outer ditch of the monument contained sherds of Peterborough Ware (Barclay *et al.* 1995, 90), and at Linch Hill, where the Neolithic double ring ditch was cut by a smaller Beaker monument. Moreover, the Beaker flat grave cemeteries which arguably fall late in the sequence, at Cassington and Eynsham (Case 1977, 82) indicate no major departure from the focal areas of the Neolithic.

DISCUSSION

A series of themes emerge from the discussion of the Neolithic sequence in the Upper Thames Valley which point to its distinctive character. At the start of the period the river gravels may have constituted a complementary landscape zone, visited and used for seasonal grazing by communities who also frequented the surrounding uplands. The presence of large quantities of chalk flint at sites like Abingdon, Barrow Hills and Stanton Harcourt is a further indication that throughout the Neolithic people were moving between the Thames basin and the downs (Healy in Barclay and Halpin 1999). The construction of monuments in the valley may not have begun until some centuries into the period, and immediately began to create a series of distinct clusters of earthworks. The individual structures were generally smaller than those of Wessex, but were often subject to multiple rebuildings. The focal areas within which monuments were built, which in most cases represented clearances maintained over lengthy periods, continued to be used over hundreds of years. The kinds of structures built, and the practices carried out around them changed considerably, but the locations remained stable. This suggests that while the events which occurred in a place transformed its significance, the accumulated history of the location remained of importance.

Chapter Nine

Regional sequences: the Avebury district

INTRODUCTION

The chalk downs of northern Wiltshire have seen some of the most significant field research on Neolithic sites in Britain, including Maude Cunnington's excavations at the Sanctuary, Alexander Keiller's work at Windmill Hill and Avebury, Stuart Piggott's at the West Kennet long barrow, Richard Atkinson's at Silbury Hill, and Alasdair Whittle's recent campaign of fieldwork (Cunnington 1931; Piggott 1962; Smith 1965a; Whittle 1993; 1997c). These investigations have contributed much to our understanding of the period, and at the same time have been instrumental in constructing a particular image of the British Neolithic. This is unavoidable, but it may have had the effect of masking some of the singularity of the Neolithic sequence in the Avebury district. Many of the monuments of the area are unique, while the ways in which particular artefacts were used and deposited appear to have been equally distinctive.

The great henge monument of Avebury, which contains part of the modern village, lies in the valley where the River Kennet now rises. It is situated within a block of chalk upland from where the land slopes away to the north and west, into the Thames and Avon vales. The chalk rises somewhat to the south, onto the Bishop's Cannings Downs, before dropping into the greensand Vale of Pewsey, while to the east are the higher Marlborough Downs. There are traces of short-lived Mesolithic occupations in north Wiltshire immediately west of Avebury (Evans *et al.* 1993, 151–3) and at Cherhill (Evans and Smith 1983, 107), although Whittle (1990a, 107) has suggested that in the Mesolithic the main focus of settlement had been on the lower reaches of the Kennet around Hungerford. The Avebury area would then have constituted a peripheral zone, sporadically visited for hunting and flint extraction. This pattern might have been responsible for a relatively late commencement of Neolithic activity in the area (Whittle 1993, 39). However, Holgate (1988a) inferred from distributions of stone tools that a shift of population on to the downs around Avebury had already begun by the end of the Mesolithic, as part of a general move away from the damp lowlands and onto the chalk of Hampshire and Wiltshire and the Upper Thames terraces.

Certainly, by the middle of the fourth millennium BC there had been clearances of the primary woodland at West Overton, Avebury, Cherhill, South Street, Horslip and Easton Down (Evans *et al.* 1993, 186). However, there is little indication that these episodes amounted to a unified horizon of deforestation. Some cleared areas may have begun to regenerate quite quickly, and there are suggestions that activity on the higher ground surrounding the Kennet Valley may have been quite sporadic and spatially restricted (Whittle *et al.* 1993, 232). Smith (1984, 103) pointed out that earlier Neolithic faunal assemblages from north Wiltshire generally contain a higher percentage of sheep than collections from elsewhere in southern England. This may be an indication of the existence of appreciable areas of grassland from an early date. Several of the earlier Neolithic monuments appear to have been built in grassland, including the barrows at Beckhampton Road, Millbarrow, Horslip, South Street, West Kennet and Easton Down (Whittle 1993, 39; Whittle *et al.* 1993, 219). However, the composition of the surrounding vegetation varied very considerably, and in some cases woodland or scrub was evidently close by, allowing clearings to be invaded very swiftly (Whittle *et al.* 1993, 228). So the earlier Neolithic landscape may have contained numerous small clearances, sustained for varying amounts of time. At Horslip, South Street, and Easton Down, and beneath the bank at Avebury there were indications of cultivation, whether in the form of disturbed soil profiles, or the plough marks beneath the South Street barrow. However, this activity appears to have been short-lived and episodic, and in all cases had been replaced by grass before the monuments had been constructed.

Other earlier Neolithic sites, like the causewayed enclosures at Windmill Hill and Knap Hill, and the group of pits on Roughridge Hill, were located in woodland or scrub. Moreover, at Easton Down, West Kennet, Cherhill, Millbarrow, Windmill Hill, and South Street there was some regeneration of wood or scrub in the later fourth millennium BC (Whittle 1994, 31). This might be taken as evidence for a general decline of activity, but it is clear that there was no equivalent regeneration on the valley floor (Evans *et al.* 1993, 189). The grassland beneath the later Neolithic bank at Avebury was mature, while the turfline under Silbury Hill was indicative of a herb-rich grassland maintained by grazing (Whittle 1997a, 24). The turf-stack at the core of Silbury, presumably derived from a broader area, suggested a more complex combination of mature grazing, grass which had formed over cultivated areas, disturbed ground, and woodland (1997a, 36). One way of explaining this would be to say that as the network of small early Neolithic clearances began to regenerate, activity became more concentrated on the valley bottom, producing larger and more sustained clearances – or indeed a cleared corridor along the valley floor. Toward the end of the Neolithic or the start of the Bronze Age there are indications of a further change in the character of land use. Renewed clearance, cultivation, or ploughing, are documented at Cherhill, West Overton, Easton Down, South Street, the West Kennet long barrow ditch, the outer ditch at Windmill Hill, West Overton G19, and at several locations on the Marlborough Downs (Whittle *et al.* 1993, 232). This activity is not generally precisely dated, often only being associated with Beaker sherds, so that its synchroneity is not assured. Moreover, as with earlier indications of tillage, episodes of Beaker cultivation in the Avebury area may have been short-lived and transient, even if they contributed to an appreciable increase in alluviation (Whittle 1997a, 5).

EARLIER NEOLITHIC OCCUPATION

The density of earlier Neolithic chipped stone in the Avebury area is not generally high (Whittle *et al.* 1993, 227), although the material forms small discrete scatters at a number of locations, complementing the dispersed pattern of the funerary monuments. Some of these finds are concentrated along the south-facing escarpment of Milk Hill, Tan Hill, Golden Ball Hill and the Bishop's Cannings Downs, overlooking the Vale of Pewsey, while others cluster on the valley floor and the lower slopes surrounding Avebury village (Figure 9.1). These latter are associated with a number of small assemblages of earlier Neolithic pottery. Of these, only the sherds from Waden Hill came from a pit context (Thomas 1956, 167). Further to the west, groups of pits at Roughridge Hill and Hemp Knoll are characteristic of earlier Neolithic depositional practice. The Roughridge Hill pits contained sherds of carinated bowls, which might arguably be early in date, as well as human cremations (Proudfoot 1965, 189). The five oval pits at Hemp Knoll formed a rough alignment, and held a very large quantity of flint waste, and sherds of twelve

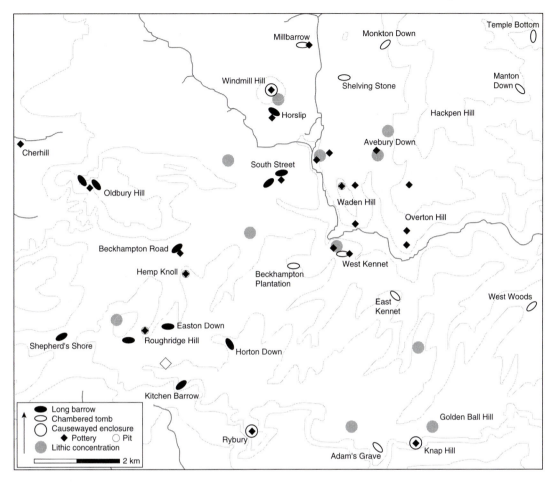

Figure 9.1 Avebury: earlier Neolithic

pottery vessels in five different fabrics (Robertson-Mackay 1980, 126–9). While the distinctive form of the Roughridge vessels and those from the old land surface beneath the South Street long barrow could be accounted for on chronological grounds, it is noteworthy that the earlier Neolithic pottery of north Wiltshire is unusually diverse. The pots from Waden Hill, the pre-enclosure pits on Windmill Hill, and from beneath round barrow Avebury G.55 fit reasonably well into the plain 'south-western' tradition of Wessex and the west, while the sparsely decorated assemblages from Hemp Knoll, West Kennet and the Rybury and Knap Hill causewayed enclosures are not entirely out of keeping with Wessex, even if they have affinities with more northerly traditions. The more extensive decoration at Windmill Hill is more difficult to parallel on the chalkland, and is perhaps more akin to assemblages from further east.

North Wiltshire also stands out from the rest of Wessex in having the three causewayed enclosures of Windmill Hill, Rybury and Knap Hill concentrated in a relatively small area, while the fourth, very large (and possibly later) enclosure of Crofton lies immediately to the south in the Vale of Pewsey. This pattern finds a closer parallel in the Upper Thames Valley. In view of the arguments for the liminal status of enclosures developed on pages 42–5 above, it is significant that Knap Hill and Rybury lie on the southern edge of the concentration of long mounds and chambered tombs surrounding Avebury, and on the edge of the chalk escarpment, while Windmill Hill is to the north-west of the focal area of the Kennet valley. Located on this periphery of the Avebury landscape, it is arguable that Windmill Hill played a role in regulating the movements of people and things into and out of the area. The site consisted of three concentric circuits of interrupted ditches, which effectively created a hierarchical division of space, and possibly of any congregation of people entering the monument (Evans 1988c, 92). The most likely entrance route lies to the north-west, where the slope of the hill is steepest and where the ditches are most closely set in relation to each other (1988c, 90). At this point, the stranger admitted to the site would be most able to appreciate that he or she was entering a nested series of concentric spaces defined by banks and ditches. The ditches themselves represented more than a mere quarry for bank material, constituting receptacles for the highly formal and structured deposition of cultural materials.

One of Smith's (1965a; 1966) most interesting conclusions from the Windmill Hill excavations was that the numerous deposits of animal bones in the ditches, including articulated limbs and associated with unweathered sherds of pottery, implied that communal feasting had taken place. Deposits of waste and organic material would have been placed in the ditches and immediately covered over with raked-down bank material (Smith 1971, 97). More recent excavations (Whittle 1988b; 1990b; Whittle and Pollard 1998) have demonstrated the deliberate and repetitive nature of these deposits. One group of material on the top of the primary rubble of the outer ditch consisted of a human child's skull and the butchered skull of a young ox, associated with two cattle horn cores and bones of deer (Whittle 1988b, 2). Other deposits consisted of bundles of bones either tied up or perhaps placed in the ditch in bags (1998b, 5). The 1988 excavations also illustrated the sheer density of animal bones in the ditches, a feature not immediately clear from the earlier reports. This material occurred in spreads or dumps, generally derived from more than one animal, and dominated by cattle (Whittle 1993, 41). Across the site as a whole there was a decline in the density of cultural material from the inner to the outer ditch circuit. There were also differences in the character of assemblages from the different ditches, with articulated animal bones, human bone and heavy-rimmed pottery vessels most common in the outer ditch (1988b, 44). Discrete groups of animal bones were most common in the inner ditch (Whittle and Pollard 1998, 238). It is suggested that these acts of deposition served to enhance the symbolic importance of the ditch circuits as an ordering of space. A cultural repertoire which included potsherds, animal bones and human skull fragments was deployed in order to distinguish and identify particular locations within the enclosure. The awareness that these were remnants of past meals and gatherings, and of dead people, would have served as a means of eliciting a particular understanding of a place. Whittle and Pollard suggest that the variation in the composition of individual deposits within the enclosure indicates that many different people were involved in sporadic acts of deposition (1998, 244). It is equally possible that each separate deposit drew upon and combined symbolic elements in novel ways, creating new, locationally specific meanings.

While the excavations at Windmill Hill have produced prodigious quantities of cultural material, it may be that the principal occupation of the site was quite short-lived (Whittle 1993, 44). This activity, however, fits into a longer history of the use of the site. Features which pre-dated the enclosure included not only the pits located by Keiller (Smith 1965a), but also a series of post-holes and an adult male burial in a pit below the outer bank (Whittle 1990b). Considerable quantities of later Neolithic and Beaker pottery and other material came from the upper parts of the ditches, by which point silting had almost finished. This later activity might have involved no more than sporadic visits to the site, yet the deposition of a number of stone axes and maceheads indicates that it remained a location which held some importance.

Further to the west, the enigmatic site of Cherhill demonstrates some affinities with the causewayed enclosures. The earlier Neolithic ditches were amorphous and did not form an enclosure, yet they produced evidence for acts of deliberate deposition. One of the pits dug into the bottom of Ditch 1 contained a large pottery sherd sealed beneath five slabs of calcined sarsen, while another had further sarsen slabs positioned about its edge (Evans and Smith 1983, 55). On the bottom of the ditches were placed groups of pottery, stone, flint and animal bone, all of which may have been deposited in a single event, while a large sarsen boulder had had thirteen smaller stones grouped around it. The ditches were deliberately backfilled from the northern side, where the spoil had presumably been piled. Like the ditches at Windmill Hill, the Cherhill site involved a series of acts which created their own memorial: the construction of a temporary landscape feature as the setting for some kind of performance which resulted in the discard of considerable quantities of cultural debris. Backfilling this feature sealed and memorialised the traces of action.

LONG BARROWS AND CHAMBERED TOMBS

Just as the causewayed enclosure at Windmill Hill represents only one stage in the Neolithic activity on the site, so a surprising number of the funerary monuments of the area have provided indications of having been constructed in locations which were already of some significance (Whittle 1993, 43). The old land surfaces beneath the long mounds at South Street and Horslip have both produced traces of Mesolithic activity. While Smith (1984, 114) saw this as an indication of a Mesolithic involvement in early agriculture, this may be making too much of rather ephemeral evidence (Whittle 1990a, 103). It may none the less be an indication that the barrows were constructed on sites which had been known and frequented for generations. Something similar is suggested at Beckhampton Road, where a large sarsen boulder had been incorporated into the south-east corner of the mound (Ashbee *et al.* 1979, 242). The way in which the lateral fence which formed part of the mound construction had to swerve in order to accommodate the stone indicates that it was not simply an opportunistic inclusion. Arguably, the barrow may have been deliberately built in this particular place so as to include an existing landmark, which might easily have held a series of cosmological associations. The old land surface beneath the mound produced a radiocarbon date significantly earlier than that from the ditch, providing further evidence that the site had been in use for some while. At South Street five more large sarsens were found within the mound, although in this case it was suggested that the stones had been moved aside during a phase of cultivation (Ashbee *et al.* 1979, 264). Other traces of pre-mound activity included flint-knapping debris, patches of charcoal, groups of stakeholes and patches of fine chalk rubble. At Horslip a series of intersecting pits was located beneath the long mound (1979, 211), while at Millbarrow ten post-holes and five pits contained fragments of earlier Neolithic pottery and human bone (Whittle 1994, 18). At Easton Down the indications of human activity prior to the building of the barrow were more limited, but the mound had been constructed in such a way as to incorporate a small natural knoll (Whittle *et al.* 1993, 200). This might have been as much a way of subsuming a noted landscape feature as of saving effort in the raising of the mound. In general, the long barrows of the Avebury area appear to have elaborated upon a landscape which was already composed of significant locations, whether natural landmarks or places associated with particular events or practices.

The earlier Neolithic funerary monuments of the Avebury area show considerable diversity, again causing the region to stand out from the rest of Wessex. North Wiltshire has earthen long barrows similar to those found to the south, but it also has mounds with stone chambers, more comparable with the Cotswold–Severn tombs (Barker 1984). The two kinds of structures have mutually exclusive distributions, chambered mounds to the east and unchambered to the west (Figure 9.1). This pattern is influenced, but not determined, by the availability of locally occurring sarsen stones, and its full significance is unclear. The best-known of the chambered tombs, and the long mound which produced the most spectacular results on excavation, was the West Kennet long barrow (Piggott 1962). Here, it is possible that an original mound of modest proportions was elongated at some stage, producing a monument which dominates a prominent ridge crest above the Kennet valley floor (Thomas and Whittle 1986, 136). The barrow appears to have been built in the mid-fourth millennium BC (Atkinson and Piggott 1986). Initial burial deposits included both articulated bodies and clean bones, and it seems that skeletal parts were taken out from the chambers as well as placed in them (Thomas and Whittle 1986). Seemingly the chambers were entered and used over a long period, with their contents being repeatedly reorganised. If the deposition, removal and repositioning of human remains were not casual activities, then the spatial configuration of the chambers would have limited the numbers of people who could have been present and witnessed these events. So even if access to the tomb were not generally limited, this kind of ritual activity would have generated a form of socially restricted knowledge. From the earliest, it seems that the five separate chambers leading off from the central gallery were judged appropriate for the deposition of the bones of different kinds of person. While we remain largely ignorant of the ways in which people were categorised in the Neolithic according to gender and age, in modern terms the westernmost chamber, excavated by Thurnam, was dominated by the bodies of adult males, while there were many young persons in the south-east transept. We can suggest that the initial deposition of human remains in the interior of the monument served to establish an ordering of space, in which the separate chambers took on distinct associations with particular classes of person. This use of spatial segregation as a means of categorisation would be both reproduced and transformed by subsequent activities, but it would have had the effect that any object which was brought into the tomb would have been evaluated in the context of the established significance of the location in which it was placed.

At some time during the centuries which followed the mortuary activity at the West Kennet long barrow, a series of secondary deposits was introduced into the chambers, consisting of alternating layers of clean chalk and burnt material with a higher organic content (Piggott 1962, 29). The dark, organic layers in particular contained large quantities of broken pottery, stone tools and waste, and human and animal bones. The precise character and meaning of these deposits is of no small importance to our understanding of the social development of the Avebury area in the Neolithic. A number of different interpretations have been offered. Piggott, the excavator, noted the diversity of the cultural material in the secondary deposits, and the presence of sherds of Grooved Ware and Beaker pottery at the base of the sequence. Parts of individual vessels were widely horizontally and vertically distributed within the chambers, and this gave the impression that they had been filled as a single act (1962, 29). Piggott considered, and rejected, the notion that the different ceramic traditions represented in the secondary deposits were indicative of a number of different cultural groups which had coexisted in Neolithic north Wiltshire. Instead, he argued that the material must have accumulated over a lengthy period, before being placed in the tomb. This interpretation required that the artefacts must originally have been deposited in some other location, which Piggott hypothesised to have been an 'offering-house', which:

> would receive ritual or votive offerings including pottery, and contain the debris of ritual meals including animal bones and the ashes of the hearth.
>
> (Piggott 1962, 75)

Aside from the absence of earlier Neolithic pottery in the secondary filling, Piggott argued that no chronological sequence could be recognised in the West Kennet deposits (1962, 29). Case (1995c, 11) built upon Piggott's account, suggesting that the material in the chamber filling had been derived from a midden, and that it had been deposited from above by pulling the capstones aside. This helped to explain the particular configuration of the stratigraphy, which might have been generated by the dumping of basket-loads of matter. Case (1995c, 14) went on to argue that the removal of the midden from its original location and the closing of the tomb could both be connected with changes in land use in the Beaker period. Obviously, for the secondary filling to constitute a single event of deposition, both Piggott's and Case's interpretations require that they must have been introduced to the chambers at a time when Beaker pottery was already in circulation.

Both of these arguments rely on the understanding that the artefacts within the secondary layers lacked any spatial or chronological structure. However, this may not be the case. It has been pointed out that the Peterborough Ware which represents the dominant element in the assemblage appears to be internally differentiated, such that different decorative motifs pre-dominate in each chamber (Thomas and Whittle 1986, 143). While it might be objected that such a pattern could be generated fortuitously, the vertical distribution of different ceramic traditions is more conclusive. For although individual sherds of the later styles are found in the lower layers, the overall pattern is one in which earlier Neolithic pottery is succeeded by Peterborough Ware, Grooved Ware and Beaker in chronological order (Figure 9.2). If this is the case, it remains to explain the fragments of Grooved Ware and Beaker which occurred low in the profile. Case (1995c, 10) suggests that as a highly experienced excavator Piggott would have recognised any animal burrows which might have displaced sherds within the stratigraphy. However, there are other reasons why artefacts can move down through a soil profile. Siiriänen (1977, 352) has documented the effect of gravity in displacing objects within rockshelter sediments, while Rowlett and Robbins (1982, 73) have shown how artefacts can move both upward and downward in archaeological deposits without leaving any appreciable trace in the soil. Furthermore, if we were to hypothesise that the West Kennet secondary filling was not laid down in a single episode, but resulted from a series of repeated events, it might be expected that trampling and other disturbances would have had a further effect in causing vertical displacement

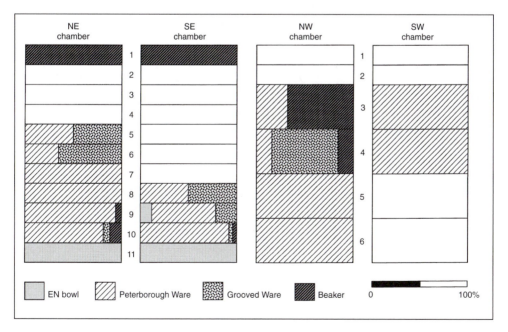

Figure 9.2 West Kennet long barrow: composition of ceramic assemblages in the secondary chamber deposits

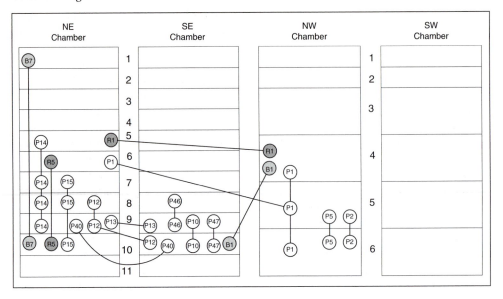

Figure 9.3 West Kennet long barrow: vessels found in more than one context in the secondary chamber deposits

(Schiffer 1987, 125). These suggestions are strengthened by the way in which individual sherds of Grooved Ware or Beaker pottery which were found low in the stratigraphy generally join with other sherds higher up (Figure 9.3).

The alternation of clean chalk and burnt organic layers at West Kennet is reminiscent of the ditch deposits at causewayed enclosures like Abingdon and Windmill Hill, where acts of deposition were repeated sporadically over lengthy periods. Moreover, the way in which small potsherds and human bones had been carefully placed within the angles of the chamber walls and amongst the drystone walling is indicative of the care with which the material was positioned (Piggott 1962, 29). This does not accord with a picture of midden material or the scrapings from the floor of a cult house being poured into the chambers. The secondary deposits were created by a set of activities whose social importance can best be understood by comparing them with the earliest performances which took place within the tomb. We have seen that in the earlier part of the Neolithic, dead bodies were introduced into the chambers, in many cases in an articulated state. These bodies were then allowed to rot, parts of them were removed, and the remaining elements were reorganised in varying ways. It follows from this that the interior of the West Kennet long barrow was a location in which human bodies were transformed. In this respect there was a structural similarity with the later deposits. Although there were fewer human bones here, the way in which the artefacts had been treated mirrored the operations conducted on the human remains. The bodies had been brought into the chambers whole, and had been broken down into their constituent parts, which were then spatially disaggregated. In the same way, the pottery vessels in the secondary deposits had been broken, and the parts scattered. Like human bodies, the integrity of the pots had been compromised by this 'breaking', as had their facility as containers of liquids. The distribution of sherds of particular pottery vessels, in particular Piggott's (1962, 38–40) P12 and P15, suggests that they might have been deliberately smashed against the forecourt and passage orthostats before individual sherds were introduced into the chambers (observation based upon material and notebook in Devizes Museum). Moreover, many of the sherds from the chambers have fresh breaks (Thomas and Whittle 1986, 145).

This deposition of large numbers of sherds of Peterborough Ware, together with animal bones, may well be connected with feasting activities in the immediate vicinity of the tomb, but the important point here is that it involved a conscious evocation and remembering of the founding events which had taken place within the tomb. The significance of the alternating layers within the chambers is that they represent a series of repeated performances in which the past was brought to mind, and the manipulation and spatial categorisation of artefacts served to reconstruct the categories of personhood which had been established in mortuary practice. Interestingly, the bones, pots and flints within the secondary deposits appear to have become more spatially concentrated over time, eventually coming to emphasise the north-east chamber. It may be no more than coincidental that the original burials in this chamber had been of mature adults. In any case, this spatial restriction of the material 'play' within the tomb interior suggests one of the themes which we will see repeated in the Avebury sequence: a growth in the complexity of ritual and other practices, combined with a concentration into a smaller number of spaces, and a more restricted part of the landscape.

While the West Kennet long barrow provides the richest set of evidence, other long mounds in the Avebury district illustrate both the distinctiveness and the variety of local practices. At Millbarrow, north of Windmill Hill, Whittle's recent excavations showed another mound with a stone chamber whose size was increased at some point in its history. Millbarrow was flanked by two separate sets of ditches, presumably indicating that a primary mound had been added to, with the inner ditches having been partially backfilled when the outer ones were dug (Whittle 1994, 11). A stone kerb had probably been set up around the mound at this point. The site had been virtually destroyed in historic times, but in the stone-holes of the chamber there were numerous struck flints and sherds of Peterborough Ware, suggesting that a chamber filling like that at West Kennet may have existed at one time (1994, 47).

The evidence for mortuary practice from the long mounds of north Wiltshire is sadly fragmentary, but suggests a degree of contrast with southern Wessex. Only King's Play Down (Cunnington 1909) bears direct comparison with the rite of single inhumation practised in some later long mounds. At Oldbury Hill, a male and two female adult skeletons were recovered from chalk-digging (Cunnington 1872), and at Shepherd's Shore five disarticulated burials were excavated (including three adults and one child) (Cunnington 1927). Easton Down also contained disarticulated burials, two adult males and two children (Thurnam 1860). The disturbed chamber at Millbarrow produced indications that at least nine bodies had been present at one time (Whittle 1994, 44). At two sites it is possible that burials had been removed: the chamber at Temple Bottom contained only a few teeth and hand and foot bones (Lukis 1867), whilst that at West Woods was empty save for a deposit of 'black material' (Passmore 1923). When compared either with southern Wessex or the Cotswolds, these numbers of burials appear rather low. This might indicate that long mound burial was a more socially restricted privilege in north Wiltshire. However, the earthen long mounds at Beckhampton and South Street contained no primary burials whatsoever (Ashbee *et al.* 1979), and at Horslip only a single femur head was recovered while two post-holes provide only equivocal evidence for the existence of a timber chamber (1979, 212). One explanation for this might be that it was the monumental aspect of the barrows, rather than their funerary role, which was of greatest importance. Confusingly, though, Wheatley (1995) has demonstrated that the long mounds of the Avebury region were not located in such a way as to secure a high level of intervisibility. Instead, each appears to have a separate visual envelope, which may reflect their construction on the edge of distinct areas of clearance (Whittle *et al.* 1993, 231).

The South Street and Beckhampton Road long barrows had no trace of a chamber, and were built in a distinctive 'bayed' fashion, in which the mound was divided up into a series of cells defined by axial and lateral fences. This arrangement is reminiscent of the internal structure of some Cotswold–Severn cairns (Saville 1990), and may have been shared by West Kennet, where a line of six stones running off from the axial sarsen core of the mound may have represented a bay division (Piggott 1962, 11). At Beckhampton Road the bays had been filled individually, often with quite distinct materials. Three cattle skulls had been placed beneath the mound on the axis of the barrow, while five antler picks had been deposited in two neat piles (Ashbee *et al.* 1979, 247). At South Street the bays had separate fills of chalk and turf, thick bands of chalky mud, coombe rock and chalk, while a distinct zone of chalk rubble was found at the front of the mound (1979, 268). Six fragments of deer antler and four cattle scapulae had been deliberately incorporated into the mound, in every case placed in the coombe rock or chalk rubble. Evidently, great care had gone into building these mounds in a very particular way, with particular substances and materials placed in quite specific combinations. It is likely that these materials had distinct meanings and associations, and that manipulating them in this way was perceived as a means of intervening directly in the cosmos.

A similar explanation may account for the incidence of fragments of imported stone in the fabric of the north Wiltshire long mounds. This is best known in the case of West Kennet, where the drystone walling between the uprights of the passage and chambers employed pieces of Corallian from near Calne, and Great Oolite from the area between Bradford on Avon and Frome (Piggott 1962, 14). Also notable at West Kennet was the use as orthostats of sarsens which had previously been employed for the sharpening of stone axes (1962, 21). Foreign forms of oolite, sandstone, forest marble and other stones have also been found at Kitchen Barrow and Adam's Grave, and in the unchambered mounds of Easton Down, Shepherd's Shore and Horslip, where they could not have had a constructional role (Piggott 1962, 58; Ashbee *et al.* 1979, 212; Barker 1984, 19). Moreover, similar stones were recovered from the ditches of the Windmill Hill causewayed enclosure (Smith 1965a). If the construction of these monuments represented a form of 'cosmological engineering' in which the elements employed built the meaning of the structure as well as its physical presence, then the incorporation of materials which had been brought over long distances might be especially significant. The physical manifestation of contacts with far-off places would enhance the importance of a monument, just as disposing of goods which had been exchanged over a distance might enhance the social standing of a person.

The earlier Neolithic of the Avebury region seems to be distinguished from the rest of Wessex by a greater degree of cultural heterogeneity, to some extent facilitated by long-distance contacts. As we have seen, there are chambered long mounds as well as unchambered, and these find their closest parallels in the Cotswold–Severn region. However, the chalk mounds, flanking ditches and cuspate forecourts distinguish the north Wiltshire barrows from the Cotswold cairns (Barker 1984, 29), while mounds with chambers set laterally are entirely absent. All of the Avebury chambered mounds have either simple or transepted chambers positioned in their terminals. Taking the laterally-chambered tombs to be relatively early in date (see Chapter 6 above), we could argue that a style of chambered tomb which emerged in the west was introduced to the Avebury area some centuries later. Indeed, neither Millbarrow nor West Kennet, the two north Wiltshire chambered barrows which have been radiocarbon dated, fall in the first half of the fourth millennium BC. The complex ceramic assemblage at Windmill Hill and the foreign stones incorporated into a number of long mounds add to this impression of cultural diversity and long-distance contact.

LATER NEOLITHIC CULTURAL PRACTICES

The distinctiveness of north Wiltshire became considerably more marked in the later Neolithic, although we can argue that this character was founded in the developments of the earlier period.

One feature which sets the area apart is the emergence of an unusual range of depositional practices. Single grave burials are rather rare in north Wiltshire, the most likely example being West Overton G.19 (Whittle 1993). Similarly, later Neolithic pit deposits are scarce, although we could mention the assemblage of Fengate Ware from a pit beneath West Overton G.6a (Smith and Simpson 1964), or Pit 1 at the West Kennet Avenue, which contained sherds of Grooved Ware (Smith 1965a, 212). What is striking is that the segregation of later Neolithic and Early Bronze Age ceramic traditions found elsewhere is barely recognisable in the Avebury area. While the West Kennet palisade enclosures provided 'pure' Grooved Ware assemblages (Hamilton in Whittle 1997a), most of the local Grooved Ware came from locations which also produced Peterborough Wares and/or Beakers. Whether one's view of the ceramic chronology encourages one to see this as an indication that different styles were used consecutively on the same site, or simultaneously, it is doubtless significant.

Three unusual sites have provided indications that material culture was treated in rather distinctive ways in later Neolithic north Wiltshire. When the round barrow Avebury G.55 was under excavation, such a richness and diversity of artefacts was discovered beneath the mound that it was speculated that this might have been the site of the 'offering house' which had provided the contents of the West Kennet chambers (Smith 1965b, 41). This material was concentrated within a radius of about 50 metres around the barrow, and included earlier Neolithic pottery, Fengate Ware, Grooved Ware and Beaker pottery. Most of the finds were unstratified, although it was presumed that it must have been held in the old land surface. However, the Beaker material mostly came from seven pits, which also contained residual elements from the earlier 'occupations' (1965b, 32). In addition to the artefactual assemblage, there was also a Beaker flat grave, which was evidently earlier than the barrow.

Another round barrow, West Overton G.6b, produced an assemblage as diverse as that from G.55. This included sherds of fifteen Windmill Hill vessels, twenty-four Grooved Ware pots, twenty Peterborough bowls (including Ebbsfleet, Mortlake and Fengate styles) and thirteen Beakers, yet the total lithic assemblage amounted to only one leaf arrowhead, one borer, four scrapers and 125 flakes (Smith and Simpson 1966, 152–5). The Grooved Ware sherds were relatively fresh, and some retained traces of a carbonised deposit. The largest earlier Neolithic sherd and the arrowhead were contained within slight hollows in the subsoil, but there was little other indication of the context in which the material had been deposited. If the site had been a settlement the lack of chipped stone is surprising. Finally, on the line of the West Kennet Avenue, a so-called 'occupation site' was excavated by Alexander Keiller in 1934, covering an area of 150 × 50 metres. This produced very large quantities of pottery, stone tools and flint waste. Much of the material came from the subsoil, but there were also two pits and a number of 'holes', which contained large quantities of charcoal, but had not held posts. The ceramic assemblage was dominated by Peterborough Ware, but there was also Grooved Ware. Pit 1 contained three Grooved Ware vessels and a Peterborough sherd, and a small Beaker sherd in a layer of silt at the top of the pit, as well as a complete ox skull (Smith 1965a, 212). Smith (1965a, 212) argued that the site had been contemporary with the construction of the Avenue, perhaps representing a camp for the workforce, on the grounds that one of the stones was missing at the densest part of the occupation, opposite stone 30a. A recent radiocarbon determination from the site gave a result of 2990–2760 cal. BC (2310 ± 80 bc) (HAR-9695). Since there is no independent date for the stones of the Avenue this is difficult to evaluate, but it could be taken as an indication that the site is considerably earlier than the Avenue, if not entirely unconnected with it (Pitts and Whittle 1992, 204).

Precisely how the material from these three sites might have accumulated seems rather problematic. It is increasingly unlikely that all of the major ceramic styles from earlier Neolithic bowls to Beakers were in circulation simultaneously, so that these assemblages must have been deposited over a period of at least 600 years, and possibly longer. If these sites had been settlements, it is difficult to imagine how the pottery would have survived, in the absence of some mechanism for burial. It has often been pointed out that Neolithic and Bronze Age pottery does not survive well on the surface, and is therefore only found in fieldwalking under fortuitous circumstances (Holgate 1988b). This is partly a consequence of modern mechanised farming practices, but climatic conditions also play a part, while the trampling which sherds would undergo in a domestic site would be considerable. Moreover, the notion that such a domestic site would have been continuously occupied for more than half a millennium implies a degree of residential stability which is not supported by other evidence. One possibility is that the cultural material from these sites did not lie on an unprotected surface, but was contained in a midden of some kind. This invites comparison with the midden at Durrington Walls, which contained sherds both of Grooved Ware and Beaker pottery, yet which produced a very early radiocarbon date, suggesting that it had accumulated over a period of some hundreds of years (Wainwright and Longworth 1971, 38–40). If this were so, it still seems remarkable that waste material should be deposited in the same place over such a long period. Even in the case of a highly sedentary community, it would seem unusual for the same midden to be maintained over such a period. In the case of people who appear to have been relatively mobile, it is a phenomenon which requires some explanation.

We have argued already (Chapter 4 above) that the deposition of Neolithic material culture did not involve its loss of importance or meaning. When they were placed in pits or ditches, objects and substances might have ceased to be used, but they continued to be significant, and their presence imbued a location with a particular character. In the case of West Overton G.6b, Avebury G.55 and the West Kennet 'occupation site' the mode of deposition was different, but the significance would surely have been as great. For people to return to a location over some hundreds of years in order to add to a growing mass of cultural debris indicates that some degree of conscious curation was involved. This impression is strengthened by the subsequent histories of the three sites. G.55 provided the location for a Beaker grave, which must have been dug into or beside the area where the pottery and other material was deposited. This use of a midden as a funerary space is, on the face of it, unexpected. Later, both G.55 and G.6b were the sites of further burials, with round mounds raised over them. The West Kennet site, by contrast, lay in the path of the stone Avenue: something which may not have been fortuitous, and which may have involved a conscious incorporation of a powerful location. This compares with the way in which cursus monuments were built over long mounds, enclosures, pits and other structures (Chapter 3 above), or indeed with the construction of the Carnac stone alignments across a variety of earlier monuments (Thomas and Tilley 1993).

LATER NEOLITHIC OCCUPATION

As well as the composition of their artefactual assemblages the three sites which we have just discussed have in common that they were all located on the low slopes surrounding the Kennet Valley bottom (Figure 9.4). We have seen already that the environmental record indicates some relaxation of clearance on the higher ground in the middle of the Neolithic, but a maintenance or even expansion of grazing on the valley floor. At West Overton, Evans excavated a series of sarsen lines on the valley bottom which date to this horizon, and whose function seems obscure (Evans *et al.* 1993, 187). In general the surface distributions of lithics show little change in the locations which were frequented in the later Neolithic, but it seems that the scatters on the low country surrounding the Avebury henge were now larger and less clearly defined, often spreading over

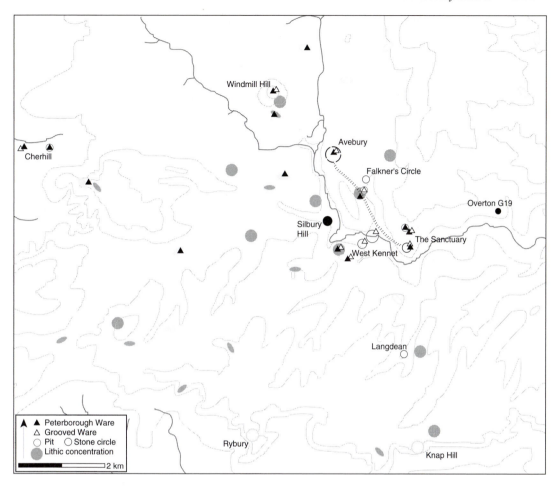

Figure 9.4 Avebury: middle/later Neolithic

extensive areas. The distributions of Peterborough Wares, Grooved Ware and certain later Neolithic stone types (transverse arrowheads, maceheads and stone axes) also seem to emphasise the Kennet corridor, adding weight to a picture of activity becoming more concentrated on the lower ground.

One aspect of the period which stands apart from this trend is the increasing evidence for flint extraction in the area to the north and west of Avebury, on Hackpen Hill and the Aldbourne Downs. Polished discoidal and plano-convex knives are present in the material from Hackpen, while the flint collector Passmore (n.d., 19) mentions numerous axes and arrowheads as having come from Stock Lane and Stock Close. Surface collection suggested that this material was concentrated along the line of intersection of the chalk and the clay-with-flints (Holgate 1988a, 92). The country around Avebury represents the extreme northward extension of the Wessex chalk. In areas to the north and west of here, flint would only have occurred in drift, river and beach deposits. It is probable that north Wiltshire and the Berkshire Downs would have been the source of considerable quantities of flint which were carried or exchanged into the Thames Valley, the Cotswolds and Mendip. This much appears to be documented by finds of chalk flint cores in these regions (Saville 1982; Grinsell 1985). This need not suggest that north Wiltshire had developed a quasi-industrial exploitation of flint. It is more likely that the extraction and circulation of cores played a part in maintaining relations between different communities in the south and west of Britain, equivalent to or complementary with the circulation of limestone and sandstone which we have already discussed.

THE LATER NEOLITHIC MONUMENTAL COMPLEX

The shift of focus toward the valley floor was particularly marked in the building and use of monuments. As the chambered tombs and long mounds were blocked up and fell into disrepair, there is little evidence that new ceremonial structures were built to replace them on the high downs. There were perhaps small stone circles at Langdean and Clatford, although their date is uncertain (Whittle 1993). There is also little indication of later Neolithic activity at the causewayed enclosures of Rybury and Knap Hill. Instead of a great many small and dispersed monuments, the later Neolithic saw the creation of a complex of much larger structures, considerably more concentrated spatially, and eventually more thoroughly integrated with one another.

The central element in this pattern was the great henge monument at Avebury itself. It has generally been argued that the earthwork enclosure at Avebury and the stone circles which it contains must have been contemporary with each other (Smith 1965a, 248). Originally, it was held that a third small stone circle, matching the two inner ones within the outer circle, spanned the northern bank and ditch, thus pre-dating them. This has since been shown not to have existed (1965a, 248). One structure which may have pre-existed the henge has recently been revealed to air photography: a double-ditched rectangular enclosure with a central pit or grave, rather similar to the oval barrow at Barrow Hills, Radley, located immediately to the west of the northern inner circle (Bewley *et al.* 1996). Smith (1965a) perceptively suggested that it would have proved difficult to erect the stones of the outer circle if the great ditch had already been cut, and argued that the lower chalk which was used to pack several of the stoneholes must have been quarried from the deeper part of the ditch. However, only one stone was unequivocally erected from the ditch side, while there are other potential local sources for lower chalk (Pitts and Whittle 1992, 206). Moreover, it seems that the bank of the enclosure was a two-phase structure: a turfline within the bank can just be made out in the section from Gray's excavation (Gray 1935, 130), but is far better seen in photographs from the Vatchers' Avebury School site excavation (Pitts and Whittle 1992, 206). This earlier bank might be matched by a primary ditch, which survived as a distinct step on the inner edge of the ditch sectioned by Keiller in 1938, filled with a chalk rubble which was quite distinct from the silting of the main ditch (Pitts and Whittle 1992, 210).

If Avebury was a long-lived and multi-phase monument, the difficulties in dating it become much more profound. As at Stonehenge, the multiple refashionings and the consequent redistribution of cultural material mean that redeposition and residuality are worthy of consideration. Pitts and Whittle's (1992) exhaustive search for bone in the excavation archives produced a series of radiocarbon dates for Avebury, but these are quite difficult to interpret. Three of the dates came from the old land surface beneath the bank, but the youngest of these, 2920–2660 cal. BC (2240 ± 90 bc) (HAR-10500) came from below the later part of the bank. Another roughly equivalent date came from the material of the bank itself. A sherd of Grooved Ware was recovered from underneath the bank, but again from the later part of the structure. The only indication of a date for the primary bank is that it is probably later than the charcoal from the old land surface in Gray's excavation, which gave a determination of 3150–2910 cal. BC (2430 ± 80 bc) (HAR-10063). All of these dates seem to conflict with the figure of 3050–2800 cal. BC (2350 ± 90 bc) (HAR-10502), from an antler from the primary fill of the henge ditch, although it may be that this was residual, perhaps ultimately derived from the first-phase ditch. The two dates acquired from the stone-holes are in no better agreement, being separated by more than 250 radiocarbon years. One date would suggest that the stone circles are contemporary with the second-phase bank and ditch. The other is ostensibly the more reliable, being derived from bone rather than charcoal, and gives 2510–2230 cal. BC (1920 ± 90 bc) (HAR-10327). Overall, the radiocarbon series can be read to give a 'short' sequence to the site, in which the primary bank was simply a marker, and the whole structure was built at around 2700 BC, or a longer sequence in which a primary bank and ditch were built after 3000 BC, and enlarged at around 2700 BC, while the stones were added at about 2350 BC.

The case for a longer sequence at Avebury is somewhat strengthened by the presence of what appears to be a timber circle, revealed on a geophysical survey of the NE quadrant of the site (Ucko *et al.* 1991, 227). This suggests that at some stage in its history the Avebury henge may have been more directly comparable with the southern Wessex enclosures of Durrington Walls and Mount Pleasant. As at Stonehenge, the stone settings may have replaced a number of timber structures.

If the sequence at Avebury were to have involved both timber and stone phases, it would be directly comparable with that at the Sanctuary on Overton Hill, which was directly linked to the henge by the West Kennet Avenue. Piggott's (1940) interpretation of the site as a series of successive timber buildings, eventually with stone uprights standing inside the hut, may have been unnecessarily complex. If some of the timber circles of the later Neolithic could not possibly have supported roofs (Mercer 1981b, 157), it is arguable whether any did. Pollard (1992, 215) has pointed out that the post-holes could form a single-phase aisled structure, very similar to Site IV at Mount Pleasant. A very wide range of ceramics was represented at the Sanctuary, with Beaker sherds coming from the post-holes of the Ten Foot and Bank Holiday Rings (Smith 1965a, 245), but these were consistently high up the profile (in weathering cones?), while only Mortlake, Fengate and Grooved Ware sherds occurred in the lower fills (Cunnington 1931, 322–3; Pollard 1992, 215). This would be consistent with an interpretation of the Sanctuary as a later Neolithic monument at which activity continued into the Beaker phase. Pollard (1992, 217) argues that the close interconnection between the plans of the timber and stone circles implies that they represent a single structure. Certainly, at least the stumps of the timbers must have been visible for the stones to have been erected in circles which had the same central point. However, Cunnington (1931, 309) pointed out that if the lithic and timber elements were contemporary, the Stone and Post Ring would have had only a 3-foot-wide entrance, with the rather untidy arrangement of an orthostat on one side, and a post on the other. These observations lead to the conclusion that the Sanctuary was a two-phase structure, in which stones were added to a setting of concentric timber circles while they were still standing.

Another important point made by Pollard is that the West Kennet Avenue and the outer stone circle of the Sanctuary both appear to have been constructed in ways that acknowledge the existence of the other. Stones 1 and 42 of the stone circle were set at right-angles to the other stones, conforming with the Avenue, while the intervals between the Avenue stones decline as they approach the Sanctuary (Pollard 1992, 217). This amounts to an indication that the Avenue stones and the Sanctuary stone circles are parts of a single episode of building, which post-dated the timber phase at the Sanctuary. By analogy, it is possible to suggest that the Avenue was also contemporary with the stones and later than an earth and timber phase at the Avebury henge, supporting the case for a longer chronology.

EXPERIENCING AVEBURY

Beaker pottery was associated with the later activity at the Sanctuary, while one of the upright stones within the Avebury henge produced a radiocarbon date which corresponds with the period when Beaker pottery was in use. We have seen that the final deposits in the chambers of the West Kennet long barrow involve sherds of Beaker ceramics. At the end of a long period of use, the interior of the tomb was blocked off by the erection of three extremely large sarsens across the entrance (Piggott 1962, 17; Barrett 1988b, 34; 1991). The stone-hole of one of these, stone 45, contained fragments of a cord-ornamented Beaker vessel, sherds of which were also found in the chambers. Paradoxically, this blocking would have had the effect of enhancing the appearance of the façade, making the monument still more imposing when seen from a distance. In this connection we can distinguish again between the internal and external significance of the monument (Thomas and Whittle 1986, 135). The actions and understandings evoked by the tomb would differ depending upon whether a person viewed it from a distance, or took part in ritual activities in the forecourt, or was granted access to the tomb interior and intimate knowledge of the chamber contents. The division between the inside and outside of the monument would effectively set up a graded field of knowledge, within which different people would have gained distinct understandings of the tomb and its meaning. Evidently, the importance afforded to these different perspectives shifted through time, so that the tomb eventually became a monument to be looked at rather than entered, whose external significance was privileged over a hidden and inaccessible interior.

This development at the West Kennet long barrow is best understood in the context of its position in relation to the Sanctuary, the West Kennet Avenue and Avebury. The tomb sits on a ridge crest which is visible from the Sanctuary entrance, as one faces along the line of the Avenue and down into the valley bottom. With its huge façade stones now in place (Figure 9.5), it would have represented an imposing landmark as one set off toward the Avebury henge. We have seen that later Neolithic activity in the Avebury area was concentrated in a cleared area along the Kennet Valley, and it may be that many of the monuments were constructed in such a way as to be visible as one moved down this open corridor. At the end of the Neolithic, the building of the West Kennet Avenue, which amounted to a processional way composed of paired upright stones, tied and defined the route to be taken down the valley more closely. Entering from the east, the Sanctuary would have represented a distinctive mark of the start of the progress toward the henge. As a circle of stone and timber uprights *without* a ditch, it may have been intended that one moved through it in a particular way (Pollard 1992), but its unbounded character suggests that its role was to admit rather than to exclude. From here, the Avenue prescribes a path around Overton Hill, in sight of the West Kennet barrow and Silbury Hill, before turning northwards toward the henge. As such, it acts as a guide to the approved way of moving through the valley (*not* carrying on west to Silbury), insinuating rather than forcing a particular passage.

For much of the course of the Avenue, the Avebury henge is invisible. Along the stretch which leads past the east side of Waden Hill, the bank of the monument is effectively hidden by a low ridge which rises to the east of the Avenue. Only when the Avenue begins to rise up above about 540 feet OD does the bank suddenly become visible. It is at precisely this point, about 400 m from the entrance to the henge, that the Avenue abruptly changes its direction, swinging round to the west. This path takes one on to a flank about 250 m outside of the south entrance to the henge. Moving in this direction takes one across the entrance, and if one turns one's head toward the monument, very little can be seen of the interior. Much is hidden from here by the protruding eastern bank terminal. About 85 m outside of the entrance, the course of the Avenue again swings to the right, back towards the entrance. Possibly, given the relatively distant spacing of the stones at the change of direction an option exists between carrying on around outside the monument, or turning and entering. If the latter course is taken, one now has the first opportunity to look in through the entrance to the henge. However, one's view is restricted by the particularly close-set banks, and beyond this is impeded by the especially large stones 1 and 98 of the outer circle. It is

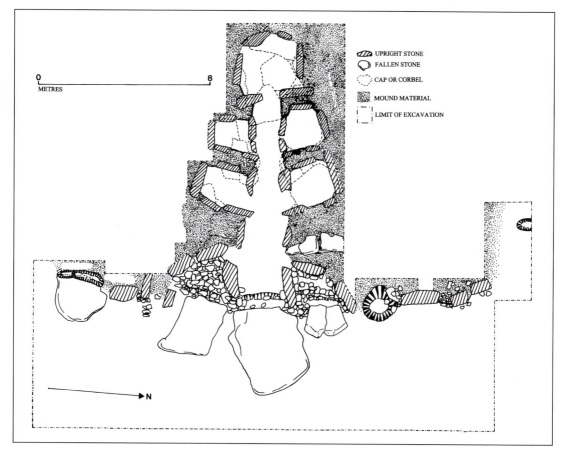

UPRIGHT STONE
FALLEN STONE
CAP OR CORBEL
MOUND MATERIAL
LIMIT OF EXCAVATION

0   8
METRES

Figure 9.5 West Kennet long barrow: entrance and forecourt area

particularly notable that these two stones and the uprights of the southern inner stone circle effectively shield the Obelisk from view from the Avenue and entrance. If one today stands at the site of the Obelisk and looks south, the whole of the area between the bank terminals is obscured by standing stones. Entering between banks, ditches and stones, one would now face the southern stone circle. Ahead and to the right would be the Ring Stone, or perhaps a rather larger stone which originally stood in the same socket (Smith 1965a, 102–3). If this constituted a barrier of any sort, one would again have been faced with the same choice as on entering the earthwork: enter the circle or carry on past on the left-hand side. At the focus of the south circle stood the Obelisk, a monolith of considerable size (Smith 1965a, 198). To the north of this upright were a number of small pits, of prehistoric date but with no artefactual contents. If the digging of these pits (and deposition of organic materials?) were to have been part of ritual practices undertaken within the circle, they would have been hidden from the view of anyone entering the henge from the Avenue by the Obelisk itself. Passing by the circle, its uprights would now only partially impede vision, but inside this and surrounding the Obelisk was another, more angular and more close-set arrangement of uprights. The Obelisk thus stood at the centre of a series of nested spaces, separated by barriers which impeded rather than totally closed off access, and which rendered activities at the centre obscure and partial to the gaze rather than totally invisible. The impression one gains is again one of access to spaces and to knowledge being graded rather than there being a binary division within society.

North from here stood the northern stone circle, again focused upon a central stone setting. Here the central feature was a cove of three large stones, defining three sides of a box open to the north-east. Approaching from the south entrance, and particularly from having passed by the southern circle, vision into the Cove would be restricted by the stones of the circle and of the Cove itself. Interestingly, Burl (1990, 7) suggests that stone coves may derive from the orthostatic chambers of megalithic tombs. Just as the arrangement at West Kennet sets up a distinction between the restricted chamber space and the forecourt, the 44 square metres of the Cove represent the most restricted space within a hierarchy of zones (Cove<Northern Circle<Inside Henge<Outside Henge). Thus the Avebury henge serves to draw in far more people than the chambered tombs through its sheer size, but at the same time its architecture functions to classify them more rigorously through their movements and access to knowledge and performance. As with the tomb, the architecture of the monument allows a complex set of practices to be carried out at a given time, in such a way as to simultaneously produce an impression of social unity and yet reproduce differential access to knowledge.

MONUMENTS OF THE VALLEY FLOOR

In their final form, Avebury, the Sanctuary and the Avenue represent parts of a unified design. However, there were other monuments in the Kennet Valley which would have been visible along the Avenue, but which stood apart. Today the most conspicuous of these is Silbury Hill, the largest mound of human origin in Europe. Allowing for the probability that the experimental radiocarbon dates from vegetal matter in the primary turf mound are unreliable, it is likely that Silbury was built as a more or less continuous process in the period between 2800 and 2000 BC (Whittle 1997a, 25). The construction of the monument involved a number of distinct stages, and it is unclear to what extent each of these would have constituted a recognisable structure in its own right, and how far the final form would have been anticipated when the work was begun. The three major phases were distinct in character, and the final mound covered over the quarry ditch of the second. The excavator believed the building to have been an uninterrupted process, on the grounds that no turfline had formed over the mound at any point in the sequence (Atkinson 1970). However, it is not clear that such a turfline could have developed on the side of a mound which stood at an angle of 30° (Whittle 1997a, 25). Although there may have been no appreciable hiatus in the creation of the mound, it remains a possibility that the different phases involved changes in design, which might themselves indicate changing priorities or even conflicts over the form the work was to take. Revealingly, the dates from the antler picks from the ditch of the final monument (2456–2280 and 2280–2047 BC, 1899 ± 43 and 1802 ± 50 bc) (BM-842; BM-841) fall into the same general bracket as we have suggested for the stone phase of Avebury, the Sanctuary and the West Kennet Avenue.

When completed, Silbury would have had an imposing appearance, with stepped concentric revetment walls of chalk blocks, infilled with rubble (Whittle 1997a, 25). The connotations of this architecture are arguable. It may be that the various remodellings were attempts to draw upon quite different traditions derived from different places. In this way the earlier mounds find parallels in the Hatfield Barrow inside the Marden henge, the nearby Marlborough Mound (if indeed it is Neolithic in date: Whittle 1997a, 169–70), the Conquer Barrow in southern Dorset, and the large round mounds of Yorkshire. The final phase, by contrast, may be modelled on the passage tombs of the Boyne Valley and Brittany, traditions whose use had long lapsed by the time that Silbury was completed. Whittle (1997a, 147–9) suggests even more far-flung prototypes for the great mound. Whichever is the case, the general point is that Silbury Hill can be seen as another example of the process begun in the earlier Neolithic whereby the Avebury district absorbed and modified cultural forms which had developed in other areas.

Despite its imposing size, it is notable that the position of Silbury to the south-west of Waden Hill is by no means prominent (Whittle 1997a). It could easily have been placed in a more suitable location to dominate the surrounding country. Although a series of investigations has been undertaken over the past two centuries, no funerary deposit has ever been found beneath the mound. In these respects Silbury recalls the late long barrows of Beckhampton Road and South Street, neither of which contained burials and both of which were located on the valley floor to the south and west of Avebury. It may be that, like Beckhampton Road, South Street and the later phases of the West Kennet long barrow, Silbury Hill is a monument which was intended to attract the eye of the onlooker from a distance, as he or she passed up the valley. Moreover, Silbury was so positioned that it could not be seen from all directions at once: it is actually invisible from much of the area north and west of Waden Hill. As we have argued already, by the end of the Neolithic the monuments of the Avebury area were intended to be seen in sequence rather than simultaneously, forming a kind of spatial narrative, each structure revealed in turn. Intriguingly, the very top of Silbury Hill would have been visible from the Obelisk, the large upright stone inside the Avebury henge (Devereux 1991, 895), prompting the question of whether activities in the stone circle and on top of the mound were intended to be intervisible (Barrett 1994, 31).

The final element in the later Neolithic monumental landscape of Avebury was the pair of large palisaded enclosures on the valley floor at West Kennet, immediately to the north-east of the long barrow (Whittle and Smith 1990; Whittle 1997a). These have produced a series of dates in the interval 2600–2100 BC (2000–1800 bc), which again places them in the same general chronological range as Silbury and the stone monuments of Avebury. The larger of the monu-

ments, Palisade Enclosure 1, was surrounded by a double concentric circuit of timbers, while Enclosure 2 contained three smaller structures (Figure 9.6). These three lesser enclosures reproduced the styles of construction and deposition of the main enclosures, although while their outer palisades were identical, the arrangements inside were subtly different (Whittle 1997a, 153). The wooden posts which made up the palisades were set in deep trenches and packed with sarsen stones, while animal bone and sherds of fresh and unweathered pottery were packed against the posts (1997a, 61). Further indications of formal deposition came from Structure 2 within Enclosure 2, which contained an extremely rich concentration of fine flint arte-facts and Grooved Ware (1997a, 93). As at other Grooved Ware sites

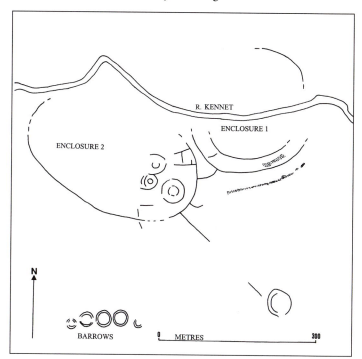

Figure 9.6 West Kennet palisade enclosures

in Wessex, animal bones were numerous and dominated by pig, the majority of which appear to have been young animals. There were few butchery marks and few traces of marrow-splitting, indicating the large-scale consumption of meat in a somewhat profligate manner (1997a, 119–20). However, the context from which much of this material was recovered suggests that it was generated before or during the construction of the palisade enclosures, rather than during their use.

Whittle argues that the two palisade enclosures were used in sequence, although the presence of a radial palisade ditch which links the two provides a case for contemporaneity. In either case the activity on the sites came to an end when the posts were burned, seemingly deliberately. Like the Avebury henge, the West Kennet enclosures seem to display an emphasis on concentricity, with enclosed spaces nested inside each other. This might betray a concern with secrecy and seclusion, but the provision of a number of separate bounded spaces of different sizes suggests that multiple social performances were being undertaken, whether sequentially or simultaneously, involving constituencies of different sizes. The structurally distinct interiors of the three smaller enclosures imply that the activities which went on inside them were differently organised, and may have involved the reproduction or transfer of different knowledges.

If the West Kennet palisade enclosures were contemporary with the complex of stone monuments, the implications are worth considering. Unlike the other monuments, the palisade enclosures produced no Beaker pottery, despite their dates being indistinguishable from those of the Beaker burial at Hemp Knoll (2453–1979 cal. BC/1975 ± 135 bc, NPL-139). At a time when other timber monuments were being replaced by stone, these new structures were built in wood, and activities within them made exclusive use of a Grooved Ware ceramic assemblage. While artefacts and animal bones are sparsely distributed within the ditch and internal features at Avebury, and at the Sanctuary, the palisade enclosures have much stronger evidence for feasting and deliberate deposition. We have seen that the Avebury complex was laid out in such a way as to facilitate processional movement across a landscape, but the enclosures lack this kind of linear spatial organisation. These contrasts suggest the coexistence of two entirely different sets of ceremonial practices, conducted in locations which must have been to some extent intervisible. These would have required quite different patterns of movement and ways of using material things. They might easily have involved the exercise of different forms of authority: a point which argues against the interpretation of later Neolithic Avebury as a hierarchical theocracy (MacKie 1977, 148). Most importantly, the West Kennet enclosures were used for acts of conspicuous consumption on the part of the living, performed in structures made of a living substance, wood. Avebury and the West Kennet Avenue were made of dead stone and, as we will see, were directly associated with the burial of the dead.

BEAKER POTTERY AND BEAKER BURIALS

The available radiocarbon dates are not adequate to tell us whether Beaker pottery was introduced to the Avebury area earlier or later than elsewhere in southern Britain. Beaker sherds were deposited in 'traditional' contexts at Windmill Hill (Smith 1965a, 80), the West Kennet long barrow (Piggott 1962), Knap Hill (Connah 1965) and in the stone sockets at the Sanctuary (Cunnington 1931, 323), suggesting that the new ceramic style was accepted for uses other than the accompaniment of single burials (Figure 9.7). Beaker burials which might arguably have been early in date occurred in flat graves at West Lockridge and Smeath Ridge, Ogbourne Down (Grinsell 1957) and the barrow Roundway 8, which contained an elderly man with Wessex/ Middle Rhine Beaker, tanged copper dagger, copper racquet pin, stone wristguard and two barbed and tanged arrowheads (Annable and Simpson 1964, 38). All of these are somewhat remote from

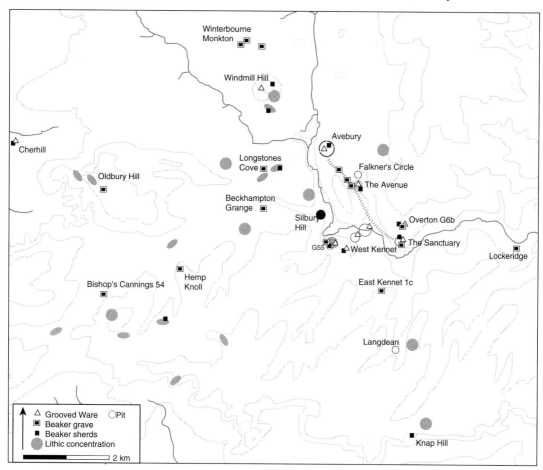

Figure 9.7 Avebury: later Neolithic / Beaker

the main Avebury monuments, but another group of burials was intimately connected with the stone structures. At the Avebury henge, stone-holes 41 and 102 contained human bones, in the former case associated with Beaker sherds (Smith 1965a, 204). The body of a juvenile person with a 'barbed-wire' decorated Beaker was buried at the foot of stone C12 at the Sanctuary (Cunnington 1931), while another Beaker burial was found at the Longstones Cove, which may have formed part of a possible Beckhampton Avenue (Clarke 1970, 501). On the West Kennet Avenue, burials with Beaker vessels were found by stones 25a and 29b, a body with a decorated bowl of uncertain affinity was by stone 22b, and further human remains beside stones 18b, 5b and 25a (Smith 1965a, 209–10). Given the limited proportions of Avebury and the Avenue which have been excavated to date, this suggests that a considerable number of people were buried under or beside the upright stones. It is not clear whether these burials were interred at the time when the stones were erected, or later, with the stones temporarily supported by timbers (Pitts and Whittle 1992, 210).

In any case, the Beaker phase in Avebury saw the development of a close association between sarsen stones and the dead. This pattern is perhaps manifested in the large blocking stones at the West Kennet long barrow, and certainly in the case of the Beaker graves beneath large sarsens at

Winterbourne Monkton (Annable and Simpson 1964, 39). In all of these examples the stone was visible above the surface while the remains of the dead were hidden beneath the earth. Burl (1979, 197) suggested that the Beaker graves at Avebury might have been the 'dedicatory' burials of sacrificial offerings, but another interpretation is possible. While single graves are customarily seen as evidence for the development of personal authority and prestige, at Avebury they appear to have been integrated into the overarching structure of the monumental complex. If the stones were recognised as an indication of the presence of human remains below the ground, it is possible that they amounted to a manifestation of the presence of the dead in the landscape. The Sanctuary, the Avenue and the Avebury henge might have become a landscape peopled by the dead, and the procession up the valley from Overton Hill might have been conceived as a journey in the company of the past generations. All of this would have been in contrast with the practices conducted at the West Kennet palisade enclosures, where the dead, stones, and Beaker pottery were conspicuously absent.

The later Beaker burials of the Avebury area seem more often to have been deposited beneath round mounds, and flat graves and burials beneath stones may have declined. However, the central burial at West Overton G.6b, which was deposited with a particularly rich funerary assemblage, indicates that the connection between stones and the dead survived. Here, the central grave both contained and was surrounded by a series of sarsen boulders (Smith and Simpson 1966, 127).

CONCLUSION

In the final chapter we will investigate the contrasts between the three regions which have been considered in detail. For the moment it will be enough to point out the distinguishing features of the Avebury sequence. What marks Avebury out above all is the way in which the scattered traces of activity in the earlier Neolithic gave way to a marked concentration on the Kennet Valley floor. It seems that the building of monuments was focused in this area, but also that temporary or more sustained occupation was also nucleated around these structures. The monuments of Avebury were more closely integrated than those elsewhere, and while the West Kennet palisade enclosures and the henge and avenue complex reveal quite different uses, they remain parts of a closely interconnected landscape. Moreover, they continued a tradition of incorporation, in which artefacts and buildings of exotic kinds were introduced to the Avebury region, contributing to a pattern of cultural diversity. Silbury Hill, we have seen, could only be compared with large mounds in Ireland, Brittany or further afield, and perhaps the best parallels for the West Kennet Avenue lie with the stone alignments of the Morbihan. The Avenue introduces another of the central themes which can be recognised in the Avebury material, the enduring significance of place. The West Kennet Avenue drew together the existing, and perhaps already ancient, sites of Avebury and the Sanctuary, while running across and incorporating the 'occupation site'. In this, it recalls the way in which the long mounds of the earlier Neolithic incorporated traces of human occupation and natural landmarks. These places were important, and yet some of them were abandoned in the process of convergence in which the tight grouping of monuments on the valley bottom became one of the landscapes most densely packed with symbolic media in Neolithic Britain.

Chapter Ten

Conclusion

INTRODUCTION

As an exercise, this book has involved the isolation of a series of different aspects of the Neolithic of southern Britain, which have then been investigated in parallel: pottery, monuments, depositional practice, subsistence economy, funerary practice and regional variability. The separation of these elements has been largely arbitrary, and is primarily heuristic. Every element of Neolithic culture potentially has its own story (see Pitts 1996, for example), and tracing each through time can lead us to unexpected conclusions. This 'genealogical' approach can help to break down our preconceptions, but we should not imagine that putting the parts back together will create a definitive or final account of the Neolithic. At some points the different fragments which I have presented will converge, but it is equally possible that various aspects of the evidence will conflict or contradict one another. As an outlook, genealogical history is opposed to 'totalising' accounts of the past which attempt to impose a premature finality. I hope that some of what has been written here challenges orthodox views of British prehistory, and suggests interesting alternatives, but this is intended as a contribution to continuing debate rather than an end point. Necessarily, then, in drawing together the different strands of my argument this chapter will be somewhat provisional and speculative. The intention is to suggest future directions for investigation rather than bring about any kind of closure.

Even this task is complicated by the very distinct character of each of the sources of evidence which I have considered. Each gives us access to a different aspect of Neolithic society, and yet it is sometimes difficult to place them alongside one another. For instance, pottery, stone tools and environmental evidence are conventionally assigned to chronological horizons in quite different ways, and may have different degrees of temporal sensitivity. If we use a very coarse temporal resolution in order to compare different sequences of change – 'earlier' versus 'later' Neolithic for instance – we can easily create a spurious impression of synchroneity. One of the benefits of a genealogical approach lies in demonstrating that different aspects of cultural change may have had a degree of autonomy from each other. So in this chapter we will seek dissonance and contrast as much as homogenisation.

WHAT WAS THE NEOLITHIC LIKE?

One single question informs much of what has been investigated in this book: what kind of a phenomenon was the Neolithic? Much of the recent literature portrays the Neolithic as an economic system, or at least as having been founded upon a particular kind of subsistence economy. For this reason, we first addressed the issue in a chapter concerned with economic change. At a global level it may by now be impossible to give a definitive answer to this question, since the social and economic processes which characterised the Neolithic period in different parts of the world increasingly seem to have been quite distinct. In the case of southern Britain there is a stronger case that some identifiable transformation occurred at around 4000 BC, but it is surely primarily in the local context that this must be evaluated. Moreover, it is arguable that at this time changes overtook a number of different cultural practices, ranging from mortuary activity to the processing and serving of food. I have suggested that previous accounts of the period have presented the new forms of material culture which emerged at the start of the Neolithic as subsidiary to changes in economic practice or ideological structure. In place of these arguments I have tried to demonstrate that subsistence activity, social relationships and cultural meanings all varied across space and time. The British Neolithic consisted of a set of material resources, including pottery, polished stone tools, monuments and domesticated animals. Different communities could use this technology in order to create and reproduce economic regimes, social systems and interpretations of the world (Thomas 1997). Yet while the Neolithic repertoire could be used in very different ways, it was also fundamentally transformative. Although in the present we may perceive Neolithic material culture as a set of *things*, their real significance lay in the ways in which they were used, or performed. Utilised in performance these artefacts and resources intervened in social life, transforming everyday activities. Indeed, many of the consequences of adopting Neolithic material culture will have been unintended ones. Much of what we have discussed in this book has concerned the ways in which the elements of the Neolithic assemblage were modified and elaborated in tune with local conditions and strategies.

In the case of food production and acquisition, previous accounts have tended to argue that a homogeneous Neolithic economy (that is, mixed farming) provided the conditions under which cultural innovations could be introduced. So, for instance, agricultural surplus was required before monument-building or craft specialisation could be undertaken. I have argued precisely the opposite: Neolithic communities in Britain practised a variety of different economic regimes, ranging from hunting and gathering to herding and horticulture. However, the understanding that the 'Neolithic revolution' was based upon an epochal change in subsistence practice has promoted the expectation that all Neolithic communities should have practised a single economy. It follows from this that any piece of evidence relating to Neolithic agriculture has been adopted as representative of the whole. In consequence, isolated and perhaps atypical phenomena have been cobbled together to construct a uniform image of 'the Neolithic economy'. This has generally involved the combination of sedentaryness, a stable domestic community co-resident in a permanently occupied structure, the cultivation of cereals in defined and continuously cropped fields, the keeping of a variety of domestic animals at individual farmsteads, and a proprietary or territorial relationship with land.

This model can be contested on a number of grounds: 'Neolithic houses' in mainland Britain are much more scarce than those attributed to later periods, and many of the structures identified as houses may not have been lived in; episodes of clearance, woodland regeneration and soil erosion were less intense than those experienced in later periods, and were not synchronous; samples of carbonised plant remains have generally been dominated by wild species, while faunal assemblages almost always relate to ceremonial activities rather than everyday diet. Where cultivation has been identified, it appears to have been episodic, rather than representing the establishment of long-lived agrarian landscapes. Those few field systems which have been isolated seem to have been composed of paddocks used for stock management, rather than ploughed fields. Much of the environmental evidence for the Neolithic has come from the ditches and old land surfaces associated with ceremonial monuments. These may not have been characteristic of entire landscapes. If we postulate that many Neolithic communities practised a form of 'tethered mobility' involving periodic returns to a number of fixed points (Whittle 1997c), it is reasonable to assume that large monuments (as places of occasional population aggregation) would have seen the most intense of human impacts on soils and vegetation. Away from the 'core areas' like Stonehenge and Avebury, the extent of Neolithic deforestation may sometimes have been very slight.

This is not to deny that the issue of economic change has been raised in the traditional literature. However, in many cases the character of change is understood as quantitative rather than qualitative. Very often, population growth is seen as the principal motor of landscape development. This may have taken the form of continuous growth and increasing sophistication, so that the achievements of the Iron Age appear to have been based upon millennia of gradual development. Alternatively, a scenario of 'boom and bust' is postulated, in which population rose repeatedly to the carrying capacity of the land, resulting in a number of catastrophic collapses. In either case, only changes in the *scale* of a fundamentally unchanging structure are considered. In this book I have argued that the economic practices of later prehistory were not fully established until the middle to late Bronze Age, and that the ways of life which preceded this horizon were different in kind. By contrast, changes in subsistence activities and residential patterns *within* the Neolithic are quite difficult to assess. Both the composition of lithic assemblages, and their distribution in the landscape indicate shifting patterns of mobility and residence. Furthermore, faunal collections dating to the later Neolithic are less often dominated by cattle. On the whole, though, there seems to have been no single pattern of economic change through the British Neolithic, more a general tendency toward diversification.

MONUMENTS AND PLACES

Once we relinquish the idea that a uniform economic transformation was the necessary condition of cultural change, we may come to recognise that monuments had a more fundamental role in the British Neolithic. In several parts of north-west Europe the construction of monuments may have begun as early as any other manifestation of 'Neolithicisation'. For example, in Brittany the large menhirs may date to the earliest Neolithic (Giot 1988). The decoration of several such stones with representations of hafted axes, cattle, shepherds' crooks and possibly boats may indicate that the various elements of the Neolithic cultural assemblage were being publicly introduced to the landscape (Thomas 1990). Similarly, chambered tombs located the remains of the dead generations in places where communities would routinely encounter them. In this way, monuments as an aspect of Neolithic culture served to continually remind people of a series of relationships, between the living, the dead and the land. Like other elements of the Neolithic, monuments were performative. Their construction involved the bringing together of large numbers of people and the co-ordination of their efforts, and this may have involved the creation and manipulation of indebtedness, affiliation and alliance. Monuments also brought together materials and substances drawn from the earth. They were often used as the settings for ritual activities, in which communities were gathered together, but also segregated and categorised. This was a fundamental characteristic of the British Neolithic: cultural innovations allowed relationships between people, animals, artefacts and places to be founded and strengthened, but at the same time enabled them to be classified and separated.

At a larger scale the building of monuments brought about a transformation of landscapes and the ways in which they were inhabited. The presence of tombs and enclosures influenced the movements of people from place to place. As the Neolithic period progressed, greater effort appears to have been expended in attempting to regulate the character of the physical encounter with monuments, by the means of more elaborate architectural organisation. This is significant because, just as human groups constructed monuments, so monuments created people – in the sense that they promoted a particular set of experiences and understandings of the world. This again was characteristic of all Neolithic material culture. Neolithic artefacts and resources transformed social reality and social conduct in fundamental ways, changing the whole matrix of perceptions and expectations through which people learned their place in the world. Effectively, the Neolithic created different kinds of human being. This is a theme to which we will return.

Locally, we can also recognise ways in which particular monuments acquired 'histories' of their own, as sequential acts of construction and deposition drew on new associations and transformed the physical form of structures. While we often talk of 'monuments' as an undifferentiated class of phenomena, it seems that a given site could function in quite different discourses at different times in its history. Very different activities might have been appropriate to the monument at these different junctures. Some of the depositional episodes that are evident at these sites may have constituted acts of 'translation', by which a location was redefined. In this way the introduction of burials into a monument hitherto used for feasting or exchange transactions might remove the place into a new sphere of practices defined as being 'of the dead'.

DEPOSITION AND SIGNIFICATION

These episodes introduce the question of depositional practices as such. While monuments, mortuary practice, material culture studies and the like have long been recognised areas of investigation within Neolithic archaeology, the question of deposition is one which has been neglected; indeed, it has only recently been recognised as an object of study in itself. It is particularly instructive to consider deposition in relation to monument-building. Both phenomena appear to have been implicated in the creation of the identities of places. Putting objects and substances into the ground seemingly served as a kind of contextualised classificatory statement. A number of different context types (pits, causewayed enclosure ditches, long barrow ditches, henge ditches and interiors, and so on) were employed, each having attributed to it a distinctive assemblage of items which could legitimately be deposited. This means of fixing classificatory schemes in space employed both direct association between materials and segregation *within* association. So a number of items brought together into a closed space or set of spaces could be manipulated in order to highlight either similarity or opposition. In this way the burial of a collection of items could be at once a means of transforming and/or commenting upon the significance of a particular place, and of disposing of particular artefacts (or at least of removing them from circulation), and, in addition, of presenting a statement about the nature of certain metaphysical relationships, and of making those relationships manifest in space. Put simply, depositional practice was a means of using the material world in order to create meaning. It did not so much repeat a series of fixed distinctions between cultural categories as make use of the cultural repertoire of the Neolithic in order to make context-specific material statements.

It is particularly important that the character of depositional practice changed through time. While the placing of objects into the ground was a symbolically significant form of action from the start of the Neolithic, the frequency with which small, isolated pits were dug for the purpose of deposition appears to have increased in the later Neolithic. Furthermore, while earlier Neolithic pit contents may have been derived from materials generated in various kinds of social performance, and may have served to memorialise these events, by the later Neolithic the digging and filling of a pit may have constituted an event in itself. It seems that in this period, also that in which the definition of space and deposition of material culture within monuments reached its peak, a particular emphasis was being placed upon the classification and identification of objects, places and persons. In the succeeding Bronze Age, quite different depositional regimes came to dominate, largely concerned with the use of bronze artefacts. However, there do seem to have been strands of continuity which linked elements of these practices to the deposits of pottery and stone axes found in rivers and bogs in the Neolithic. In a sense, then, bronze metalwork came to fit into the pre-existing structures of classification established in the Neolithic, yet in the process transformed them. That Bronze Age transformation had the effect of selecting one element of depositional practice and privileging it. By contrast, in the Neolithic a very wide range of media had been employed in depositional activities, drawing in a wide variety of potential symbolic references.

POTS AND CATEGORIES

These studies of deposition show how Neolithic material culture fundamentally changed the means by which the world could be rendered meaningful. In a modern existence where objects circulate as alienated commodities it is difficult to appreciate the extent to which material things can serve as a network of reference through which meanings are created and articulated. Contemporary conditions tend to promote a perceived separation of subject and object, in which a disembodied mind contemplates worldly things from which it is entirely separate. It may be more accurate to conceive of 'thinking' as an activity which takes place in a material world. Thought is not an abstracted preparation for action, but a part of our physical engagement with things. As much as thinking *about* things, we use things as tools to think *with* (Thomas 1998). We have suggested already that the new range of artefacts and resources which became available in Britain from the start of the Neolithic transformed social conduct. If we recognise that material things are implicated in thinking, it is clear that these artefacts would also promote new ways of classifying and understanding reality. As one of the forms of material culture which were entirely novel at the start of the Neolithic, pottery vessels provide a particularly appropriate window on Neolithic materiality.

Pots transform the ways in which foods can be combined, cooked, stored, presented and consumed. Their production is episodic rather than continuous, and promotes a punctuated use of time. In these ways, the inception of pottery production would have had an immediate impact on the rhythms of social life. To begin with, pottery may have been employed in a relatively restricted set of transactions (Herne 1988). These may have expanded as the Neolithic period progressed, but I have attempted to warn against the assumption that baked clay vessels were always ubiquitous and mundane. Like all material things, pots only gain significance in a context: they do not have a primary, functional meaning to which a secondary symbolic meaning is added. It is the set of relationships within which an artefact is embedded which renders it intelligible. In Neolithic Britain it seems that one of the most important roles of pots lay in the articulation and objectification of difference. Although ceramic styles like the decorated bowl traditions of the earlier Neolithic, Peterborough Ware and Grooved Ware have often been interpreted as the identifiers of ethnic groups of sub-cultures, the contrasts and variations of pottery decoration appear to have been most distinct at a very localised level. The implication is that the use of differently marked vessels worked as a means of drawing distinctions between different activities, different locations and different classes of person.

As decoration became more profuse in the later part of the Neolithic, the range of vessel forms in use declined, while the continuous range of vessel volumes may have been replaced by an emphasis on more distinct size classes. This could indicate that within particular ceramic traditions there was a smaller range of vessel categories. If so, it may have been that pots were again being used for a more limited set of activities. Whether or not Peterborough Ware and Grooved Ware shared any degree of chronological overlap, it is evident that they contrasted in terms of vessel shape and size, decorative structure and media, style of use, patterns of association and contexts of deposition. We argued that these contrasts were indicative of the continuing use of ceramics in order to articulate difference. In this respect, one of the ways in which Beaker pottery may have proved instrumental in social change may have lain in undermining established cultural categories.

CLASSIFYING THE DEAD

If much of the significance of Neolithic artefacts derived from their status as a ready-made matrix of categories and differences, it is also important that the period saw a considerable increase in the emphasis on the spatial and classificatory placing of the dead. Funerary rites from the start of the period rendered human remains manipulable, in much the same way as other classes of artefacts. In some cases this enabled different kinds of person, or different body parts, to be segregated. Equally often, body parts were jumbled together, suggesting that no universal conceptual scheme dictated the character of mortuary practice. At a general level, earlier Neolithic funerary rites often involved some form of physical transition (exposure, defleshing, cremation) followed by rearrangement and sometimes an act of closure (deposition, mound construction, tomb-blocking). The disaggregation of the body is a rich source of metaphors, and would doubtless have been open to multiple interpretations. All that I wish to stress here is that like other artefacts, earlier Neolithic bodies were subject to circulation: their parts were moved from place to place, and combined with other materials in acts of deposition. Bodies, in other words, formed one element in a generalised *economy of substances* (Thomas 1999). In particular, there seems to have been a general preoccupation with skulls and skull fragments, which continue to be found in pit deposits, buried land surfaces, causewayed enclosure ditches, river sediments and the post-holes of monumental structures.

This encourages us to conceive of megalithic tombs and earthen long barrows as places of transformation rather than vaults or graves. Yet this involvement of dead bodies in patterns of reciprocity appears to have declined over time, gradually being replaced by the rite of single grave burial. Explanations for this phenomenon have ranged from the arrival of new populations with distinct cultural traditions, to a change in ideology toward the naturalisation of personal power (Shennan 1982), the emergence of individual identity, or a growing emphasis on the inheritance of land between close kin (Barrett 1994). I have chosen instead to emphasise the gradual decline of bounded and inclusive social entities (such as 'tribes' or 'clans') and their replacement by more fluid and overlapping groupings. Under these conditions personal identity and kin relations might cease to be recognised through affiliation or group membership, and patterns of descent or genealogy would take on a greater importance, particularly as far as the devolution of authority would be concerned. This is to say that a pattern of being-alongside others (including the ancestral dead) was slowly replaced by an emphasis on being-descended-from. These two principles are contradictory, although they can coexist within a community. Significantly, though, they imply very different relationships with the dead. In the former case human beings may cease to be alive in the modern biological sense, but their 'death' does not involve their removal from society. They are transformed into another kind of being, their bones continue to circulate, they maintain an influence in the present. By contrast, an emphasis on descent and genealogy may mean that the identities of the dead as named progenitors are preserved, but paradoxically they are placed firmly in the past. Social relations extend vertically backward into the past, rather than horizontally through the present.

These kinds of changes explain a number of the developments of the middle to later Neolithic. We have seen that a number of chambered tombs were finally closed off, rendering their contents inaccessible, while earthen long mounds began to be enclosed by ditches. The distance between the living and the dead was increased. The bodies of the dead were now buried whole and fleshed, while in some cases attempts were made to 'reconstitute' entire bodies from disarticulated body parts. Eventually, the practice of cremation emerged as an alternative form of funerary activity which focused entirely on the moment of 'social death' and its memorialisation. Cremation cemeteries, in which quite formal spatial relationships were established between deposits of burnt bone, may have served as a means of physically representing relationships of descent. They also demonstrate another aspect of the same process: a growing preoccupation with the past. Cremation cemeteries were inserted into existing henges, ring ditches and round barrows, just as deposits of cultural material and secondary burials were introduced into the ditches of long barrows and causewayed enclosures, and the chambers of megalithic tombs. In a real sense, the past came to be of greater importance in the later Neolithic.

REGIONAL NARRATIVES

We have seen that it is possible to generate a series of parallel accounts of the Neolithic using different sets of evidence – economic and environmental data, monumental structures, cultural deposits and mortuary remains. None the less, each of these consumes the available material in ways which can limit our appreciation of regional variation. The principal aim of the three case studies presented in Chapters 7 to 9 has been to demonstrate the extent to which the Neolithic cultural assemblage was deployed in quite different ways in different settings. While all of the three areas investigated were drawn from central southern England, it is to be anticipated that comparable differences would distinguish other areas with extensive evidence of Neolithic activity, such as East Anglia, east Yorkshire, the Peak District, eastern or south-west Scotland, or the Orkney Isles.

Particular aspects of each of the regional sequences proved to be quite distinctive. In the Stonehenge area the most important process which was identified was the progressive differentiation of the landscape: the construction of monuments and the use of artefactual assemblages gradually created a series of defined locations which were reserved for different kinds of activity and the exercise of distinct forms of authority. In the process, different material traditions were often kept quite separate from one another. The area saw extensive clearance of tree cover for pasture, but cultivation may have been quite limited in extent, and discontinuous. The monuments of the region were quite large, and were highly diverse. Stonehenge itself was used as a cremation cemetery at one stage in its history, but there were otherwise rather few single grave burials in the later Neolithic. Beaker graves were much more numerous, but these were spatially concentrated in the western part of the area, conforming with long-established patterns of landscape segmentation.

In the Upper Thames Valley the clearance of woodland took on a very different pattern, with a series of smaller openings in the canopy arranged along the course of the river. Within these islands of clearance, areas of pasture and tillage could be found, as well as complexes of monuments. These latter were rather smaller than those of Wessex, and within the region as a whole monuments tended to be replicated, so that there were numerous similar causewayed enclosures, cursus monuments, ring ditches and henges. There were also numerous single graves, both in the later Neolithic and the Beaker phase, suggesting that a pattern of small, overlapping social units developed relatively early. While the valley floor was frequented from the start of the Neolithic, it is suggested that activity became more intense in the later Neolithic. This use may none the less have been highly transient, and both monuments and areas of occupation give indications of multiple, discontinuous phases of activity.

The pattern in the Avebury area was again very distinct. Here, the emphasis was on cultural diversity, the maintenance of long-distance contacts, and a progressive concentration of activity on the Kennet Valley bottom. While the earliest Neolithic saw a number of small clearings being established in north Wiltshire, many of these seem to have gradually regenerated, and a more extensive open area emerged on the lower country. Cleared areas were dominated by pasture, although there was a series of sporadic events of cultivation. Patterns of deposition were quite different from those in south Wiltshire or the Thames, with a variety of artefact traditions sometimes being used together in a single location. The exception to this pattern was the exclusive use of Grooved Ware in the West Kennet palisade enclosures at the very end of the Neolithic, a time when Beakers were already being used elsewhere. It was suggested that this was connected with the emergence of the Avebury henge, the West Kennet Avenue, the Sanctuary and the West Kennet long barrow as components of a processional landscape primarily associated with the dead, while the timber enclosures were used for a separate set of activities involving conspicuous consumption on the part of the living. Later Neolithic single graves were again scarce in the Avebury district, and Beaker burials were more numerous, although many of them were to some extent integrated with the complex of stone monuments. These monuments themselves were exceptionally large, and in some cases (Avebury, Silbury Hill, the Avenue) both unique and exotic.

Neolithic people

These regional variations owed very little to differences in ecology or topography. For the most part they can be attributed to the ways in which Neolithic material culture was utilised and transformed by local communities. These artefacts and resources always realised their potential in the context of power relations, and the multitude of strategies through which people sought to promote their interests. However, it is a reasonable criticism that much of this book has represented a history of practices, and that the people who carried out those practices are less easy to identify. I have argued throughout that we should not separate material culture from society. History is never concerned exclusively with people or things, but with the relationships between them. People make artefacts, but artefacts make up the material world in which people learn culturally specific ways of being human.

Of course, the people of Neolithic Britain are dead and gone, but the material things which they have left behind them are more than a reflection of their way of life. Neolithic material culture was a technology through which people created meaning, crafted identities and developed understandings of the world. The Neolithic made new ways of being human possible, and these possibilities were exploited in different ways as time progressed. In the context of the issues raised in this chapter, we can start to spell out some of the characteristics of Neolithic personhood.

First, we have suggested that from the start of the Neolithic people found themselves involved in a series of cycles of circulation: seasonal movements from place to place which articulated with productive labour and the availability of resources; the movements of livestock between pastures; the circulation of gifts between affines and communities; the cycles of extraction, transformation, breakage and deposition implicated in the 'lives' of artefacts like pots and stone axes; the disaggregation of bodily substances in mortuary practice and the circulation of bones between persons and places. These were central realities of Neolithic life, all of which involved material things, and they suggest that the principles of exchange, performed transaction and circulation were of cardinal importance. There are also indications that these different cycles were perceived as either interconnected or parallel with one another: human bones and cattle bones were sometimes treated in similar ways; pottery vessels were sometimes treated like human bones; human bones were sometimes treated like other artefacts in deposition; and so on. All of this suggests that Neolithic social life involved a series of equivalent or interlocked flows of substance: human bodies, animal bodies, earthly materials. We can easily imagine that this framework would encapsulate sexual activity, the consumption of food and relations between gift-givers and gift-receivers.

I do not wish to imply that there was a single, universally accepted understanding of personal identity in Neolithic Britain, but it seems likely that it would have been within this picture of flows and connections that people gained their sense of humanity. That is, they might conceive of themselves as beings whose substance was absorbed from animals and other humans, and dissipated through exchange, sexual activity and the eventual disaggregation of their body after death. They might be persons networked to many patterns of circulation, through whom flows of substance or energy washed, rather than the bounded 'individuals' of the modern West.

We could go on to suggest that the changes in material reality which took place through the Neolithic would have proceeded alongside changes in human self-understanding. If earlier Neolithic life involved a series of synchronised and interlinked temporal cycles, there are suggestions that this pattern began to break down after 3000 BC. While many communities maintained a degree of mobility, the character of their yearly cycles may have been less repetitive and more opportunistic. The growing diversity of material culture suggests that more effort was being spent on differentiating people from one another. However, the use of distinct assemblages for different activities in separate locations indicates that, rather than reflecting the development of 'ranking' or 'social stratification', new statuses or prerogatives were emerging which could be exercised in specific and limited social circumstances (Thomas 1996a, Chapter 6). Rather than an all-encompassing set of social relations constrained within an overall group identity, the later Neolithic saw the development of multiple social contexts in which people might act in different ways. In this book we have seen the very different contexts for action which existed in the Stonehenge area by the later Neolithic as well as the two complementary monumental complexes of Avebury.

Later Neolithic people operated in multiple, fragmented spheres of sociality. The communities with whom they might interact would change according to context, and this suggests that their sources of self-identity would have gradually shifted. As we have seen, the single grave rite embodied both a growing orientation toward the past and the commemoration of a single dead person from whom descent could be claimed.

Bibliography

Aberg, F.A. and Bowen, H.C. 1960 Ploughing experiments with a reconstructed Donneruplund ard. *Antiquity* 34, 144–7.

Abramson, P. 1996 Excavations along the Caythorpe gas pipeline, North Humberside. *Yorkshire Archaeological Journal* 68, 1–88.

Adkins, R. and Jackson, R. 1976 *Neolithic Axes from the River Thames*. London: British Museum.

Allen, G.W.G. 1938 Marks seen from the air in the crops near Dorchester, Oxon. *Oxoniensia* 3, 169–70.

Allen, M.J. 1997 Environment and land-use: the economic development of the communities who built Stonehenge (an economy to support the stones). In: B. Cunliffe and C. Renfrew (eds) *Science and Stonehenge*, 115–44. Oxford: Oxford University Press.

Allen, T. 1995 *Lithics and Landscape: Archaeological Discoveries on the Thames Water Pipeline at Gatehampton Farm, Goring, Oxfordshire 1985–92*. Oxford: Oxford University Committee for Archaeology.

Allen, T., Darvill, T.C., Green, S. and Jones, M.U. 1993 *Excavations at Roughground Farm, Lechlade, Gloucestershire: A Prehistoric and Roman Landscape*. Oxford: Oxford University Committee for Archaeology.

Ammerman, A.J. and Cavalli-Sforza, L.L. 1971 Measuring the rate of spread of early farming in Europe. *Man* 6, 674–88.

Ammerman, A.J. and Cavalli-Sforza, L.L. 1973 A population model for the diffusion of farming into Europe. In: A.C. Renfrew (ed.) *The Explanation of Culture Change: Models in Prehistory*, 343–58. London: Duckworth.

Annable, F.K. and Simpson, D.D.A. 1964 *Guide Catalogue to the Neolithic and Bronze Age Collections in Devizes Museum*. Devizes: Wiltshire Natural History and Archaeological Society.

Appadurai, A. 1985 Introduction: commodities and the politics of value. In: A. Appadurai (ed.) *The Social Life of Things*, 3–63. Cambridge: Cambridge University Press.

ApSimon, A. 1969 1919–1969: Fifty years of archaeological research. *Proceedings of the University of Bristol Speleological Society* 12, 31–56.

Armit, I. and Finlayson, W. 1995 Social strategies and economic change: pottery in context. In: W.K. Barnett and J.W. Hoopes (eds) *The Emergence of Pottery: Technology and Innovation in Ancient Societies*, 267–75. Washington: Smithsonian.

Armit, I., Cowie, T. and Ralston, I. 1994 Excavation of pits containing Grooved Ware at Hillend, Clydesdale district, Strathclyde region. *Proceedings of the Society of Antiquaries of Scotland* 124, 113–27.

Ashbee, P. 1966 Fussell's Lodge long barrow excavations, 1957. *Archaeologia* 100, 1–80.

Ashbee, P. 1970 *The Earthen Long Barrow in Britain*. London: Dent.

Ashbee, P. 1976 Amesbury barrow 51: excavation 1960. *Wiltshire Archaeological Magazine* 70/71, 1–60.

Ashbee, P. 1978 *The Ancient British*. Norwich: Geo.

Ashbee, P., Smith, I.F. and Evans, J.G. 1979 Excavation of three long barrows near Avebury. *Proceedings of the Prehistoric Society* 45, 207–300.

Atkinson, R.J.C. 1948 Archaeological notes. *Oxoniensia* 13, 66–7.

Atkinson, R.J.C. 1951 The henge monuments of Great Britain. In: R.J.C. Atkinson, C.M. Piggott and N. Sandars, *Excavations at Dorchester, Oxon.*, 81–107. Oxford: Ashmolean Museum.

Atkinson, R.J.C. 1956 *Stonehenge*. London: Hamish Hamilton.

Atkinson, R.J.C. 1965 Wayland's Smithy. *Antiquity* 39, 126–33.

Atkinson, R.J.C. 1968 Old mortality: some aspects of burial and population in Neolithic England. In: J.

Coles and D.D.A. Simpson (eds) *Studies in Ancient Europe*, 83–94. Edinburgh: Edinburgh University Press.

Atkinson, R.J.C. 1970 Silbury Hill, 1969–70. *Antiquity* 44, 313–14.

Atkinson, R.J.C. and Piggott, S. 1986 The date of the West Kennet long barrow. *Antiquity* 60, 143–4.

Atkinson, R.J.C., Piggott, C.M. and Sandars, N. 1951 *Excavations at Dorchester, Oxon*. Oxford: Ashmolean Museum.

Avery, M. 1982 The Neolithic causewayed enclosure, Abingdon. In: H.J. Case and A.W.R. Whittle (eds) *Settlement Patterns in the Oxford Region*, 10–50.

Bakels, C.C. 1982 The settlement system of the Dutch Linearbandkeramik. *Analecta Praehistorica Leidensia* 15, 31–43.

Bakker, J.A. 1982 TRB settlement patterns on the Dutch sandy soils. *Analecta Praehistorica Leidensia* 15, 87–124.

Balfet, H. 1983 Production and distribution of pottery in the Maghreb. In: H. Howard and E. Morris (eds) *Production and Distribution: A Ceramic Viewpoint*, 257–69. Oxford: British Archaeological Reports S120.

Bamford, H. 1985 *Briar Hill*. Northampton: Northampton Archaeological Monograph 3.

Barclay, A. and Halpin, C. 1999 *Excavations at Barrow Hills, Radley, Oxfordshire. Vol. 1: The Neolithic and Bronze Age Monument Complex*. London: English Heritage.

Barclay, A., Gray, M. and Lambrick, G. 1995 *Excavations at the Devil's Quoits, Stanton Harcourt, Oxfordshire, 1972–3 and 1988*. Oxford: Oxford Archaeological Unit.

Barclay, A., Bradley, R.J., Hey, G. and Lambrick, G. 1996 The earlier prehistory of the Oxford region in the light of recent research. *Oxoniensia* 61, 1–20.

Barclay, G.J. 1983 Sites of the third millennium bc to the first millennium ad at North Mains, Strathallan, Perthshire. *Proceedings of the Society of Antiquaries of Scotland* 113, 122–281.

Barclay, G.J. 1989 Henge monuments: reappraisal or reductionism? *Proceedings of the Prehistoric Society* 55, 260–3.

Barclay, G.J. 1996 Neolithic buildings in Scotland. In: T.C. Darvill and J.S. Thomas (eds) *Neolithic Houses in Northwest Europe and Beyond*, 61–75. Oxford: Oxbow.

Barclay, G.J. and Maxwell, G.J. 1991 Excavation of a Neolithic long mortuary enclosure within the Roman legionary fortress at Inchthuthill, Perthshire. *Proceedings of the Society of Antiquaries of Scotland* 121, 27–44.

Barclay, G.J. and Maxwell, G.J. 1995 The Cleaven Dyke: a Neolithic cursus monument/bank barrow in Tayside region, Scotland. *Antiquity* 69, 317–26.

Barclay, G.J. and Russell-White, C.J. 1993 Excavations in the ceremonial complex of the fourth to second millennium BC at Balfarg/Balbirnie, Glenrothes, Fife. *Proceedings of the Society of Antiquaries of Scotland* 123, 43–210.

Barker, C.T. 1984 The long mounds of the Avebury region. *Wiltshire Archaeological Magazine* 79, 7–38.

Barker, G.W.W. 1985 *Prehistoric Farming in Europe*. Cambridge: Cambridge University Press.

Barker, G.W.W. and Webley, D. 1978 Causewayed camps and early Neolithic economies in central southern England. *Proceedings of the Prehistoric Society* 44, 161–86.

Barley, N. 1981 The Dowayo dance of death. In: S.C. Humphreys and H. King (eds) *Mortality and Immortality*, 149–59. London: Academic Press.

Barrett, J.C. 1980 The pottery of the later Bronze Age in lowland England. *Proceedings of the Prehistoric Society* 46, 297–319.

Barrett, J.C. 1985 Hoards and related metalwork. In: D.V. Clarke, T. Cowie and A. Foxon, *Symbols of Power at the Time of Stonehenge*, 93–106. Edinburgh: National Museum of Antiquity.

Barrett, J.C. 1988a Fields of discourse: reconstituting a social archaeology. *Critique of Anthropology* 7 (3), 5–16.

Barrett, J.C. 1988b The living, the dead, and the ancestors: Neolithic and Early Bronze Age mortuary practices. In: J.C. Barrett and I.A. Kinnes (eds) *The Archaeology of Context in the Neolithic and Bronze Age*, 30–41. Sheffield: Department of Archaeology and Prehistory.

Barrett, J.C. 1989 Conclusion: render unto Caesar . . . In: J.C. Barrett, A. Fitzpatrick and L. McInnes (eds) *Romans and Barbarians in North-West Europe*. Oxford: British Archaeological Reports S471.

Barrett, J.C. 1991 Towards an archaeology of ritual. In: P. Garwood, D. Jennings, R. Skeates and J. Toms (eds) *Sacred and Profane*, 1–9. Oxford: Oxford University Committee for Archaeology.

Barrett, J.C. 1994 *Fragments from Antiquity*. Oxford: Blackwell.

Barrett, J.C., Bradley, R.J. and Green, M. 1991 *Landscape, Monuments and Society: The Prehistory of Cranborne Chase*. Cambridge: Cambridge University Press.

Barth, F. (ed.) 1969 *Ethnic Groups and Boundaries*. Boston, MA: Little, Brown and Co.

Barthes, R. 1981 Theory of the text. In: R. Young (ed.) *Untying the Text*, 31–47. London: Routledge and Kegan Paul.

Batchelor, D. 1997 Mapping the world heritage site. In: B. Cunliffe and C. Renfrew (eds) *Science and Stonehenge*, 61–72. Oxford: Oxford University Press.

Bateman, T. 1861 *Ten Years' Digging in Celtic and Saxon Grave Hills in the Counties of Derbyshire, Stafford and York*. London: John Russell Smith.

Battaglia, D. 1990 *On the Bones of the Serpent: Person, Memory and Mortality in Sabarl Island Society*. Chicago: University of Chicago Press.

Baudrillard, J. 1988 *Jean Baudrillard: Selected Writings*, ed. M. Poster. Cambridge: Polity.

Bayliss, A., Bronk Ramsay, C. and McCormac, F.G. 1997 Dating Stonehenge. In: B. Cunliffe and C. Renfrew (eds) *Science and Stonehenge*, 39–59. Oxford: Oxford University Press.

Bell, M. 1982 The effects of land use and climate on valley sedimentation. In: A.F. Harding (ed.) *Climatic Change in Later Prehistory*, 127–42. Edinburgh: Edinburgh University Press.

Bell, M. and Jones, J. 1990 Land mollusca from Coneybury henge. In: J. Richards (ed.) *The Stonehenge Environs Project*, 154–8. London: English Heritage.

Bender, B. 1975 *Farming in Prehistory*. London: John Baker.

Bender, B. 1992 Theorising landscapes, and the prehistoric landscapes of Stonehenge. *Man* 27, 735–56.

Bender, B. 1998 *Stonehenge: Making Space*. London: Berg.

Benson, D. and Clegg, I. 1978 Cotswold burial rites? *Man* 13, 134–7.

Benson, D. and Miles, T. 1974 *The Upper Thames Valley: An Archaeological Survey of the River Gravels*. Oxford: Oxford Archaeological Unit.

Bersu, G. 1940 Excavations at Little Woodbury, Wiltshire, part one: the settlement as revealed by excavation. *Proceedings of the Prehistoric Society* 6, 30–111.

Bersu, G. 1947 A cemetery of the Ronaldsway culture at Ballateare, Jurby, Isle of Man. *Proceedings of the Prehistoric Society* 13, 161–9.

Bestley, N. 1993 Type and typology and writing the past: the case of the Cotswold–Severn monuments. *Archaeological Review from Cambridge* 12, 91–103.

Bewley, R., Cole, M., David, A., Featherstone, R., Payne, A. and Small, F. 1996 New features within the henge at Avebury, Wiltshire: aerial and geophysical evidence. *Antiquity* 70, 639–46.

Binford, L.R. 1964 A consideration of archaeological research design. *American Antiquity* 29, 425–41.

Binford, L.R. 1965 Archaeological systematics and the study of culture process. *American Antiquity* 31, 203–10.

Binford, L.R. 1968 Post-Pleistocene adaptations. In: L.R. Binford and S.R. Binford (eds) *New Perspectives in Archaeology*, 313–41. Chicago: Aldine.

Binford, L.R. 1971 Mortuary practices: their study and potential. In: J.A. Brown (ed.) *Approaches to the Social Dimensions of Mortuary Practices*, 6–29. New York: Memoirs of the Society for American Archaeology 25.

Binford, L.R. and Sabloff, J.A. 1982 Paradigms, systematics and archaeology. *Journal of Anthropological Research* 38, 137–53.

Bloch, M. 1982 Death, women and power. In: M. Bloch and J. Parry (eds) *Death and the Regeneration of Life*, 211–30. Cambridge: Cambridge University Press.

Bloch, M. and Parry, J. 1982 Introduction: death and the regeneration of life. In: M. Bloch and J. Parry (eds) *Death and the Regeneration of Life*, 1–44. Cambridge: Cambridge University Press.

Boast, R. 1995 Fine pots, pure pots, Beaker pots. In: I.A. Kinnes and G. Varndell (eds) *'Unbaked Urns of Rudely Shape'*, 69–80. Oxford: Oxbow.

Bourdieu, P. 1970 The Berber house or the world reversed. *Social Science Information* 9, 151–70.

Bourdieu, P. 1977 *Outline of a Theory of Practice*. Cambridge: Cambridge University Press.

Bradley, R.J. 1971 Stock raising and the origin of the hillfort on the South Downs. *Antiquaries Journal* 51, 8–29.

Bradley, R.J. 1975 Maumbury Rings, Dorchester: the excavations of 1908–13. *Archaeologia* 105, 1–97.

Bradley, R.J. 1978a Colonisation and land use in the late Neolithic and early Bronze Age. In: S. Limbrey and J.G. Evans (eds) *The Effect of Man on the Landscape: The Lowland Zone*, 95–103. London: Council for British Archaeology.

Bradley, R.J. 1978b *The Prehistoric Settlement of Britain*. London: Routledge and Kegan Paul.

Bradley, R.J. 1982 Position and possession: assemblage variation in the British Neolithic. *Oxford Journal of Archaeology* 1, 27–38.

Bradley, R.J. 1983 The bank barrows and related monuments of Dorset in the light of recent fieldwork. *Proceedings of the Dorset Natural History and Archaeological Society* 105, 15–20.

Bradley, R.J. 1984a Studying monuments. In: R.J. Bradley and J. Gardiner (eds) *Neolithic Studies*, 61–6. Oxford: British Archaeological Reports 133.

Bradley, R.J. 1984b *The Social Foundations of Prehistoric Britain*. London: Longmans.

Bradley, R.J. 1985 *Consumption, Change and the Archaeological Record*. Edinburgh: Department of Archaeology.

Bradley, R.J. 1986 A reinterpretation of the Abingdon causewayed enclosure. *Oxoniensia* 51, 183–7.

Bradley, R.J. 1987a Flint technology and the character of Neolithic settlement. In: A. Brown and M.R. Edmonds (eds) *Lithic Analysis and Later British Prehistory*, 181–6. Oxford: British Archaeological Reports 162.

Bradley, R.J. 1987b Stages in the chronological development of hoards and votive deposits. *Proceedings of the Prehistoric Society* 53, 351–62.

Bradley, R.J. 1989 Deaths and entrances: a contextual analysis of megalithic art. *Current Anthropology* 30, 68–75.

Bradley, R.J. 1991 Ritual, time and history. *World Archaeology* 23, 209–19.

Bradley, R.J. 1992 The excavation of an oval barrow beside the Abingdon causewayed enclosure, Oxfordshire. *Proceedings of the Prehistoric Society* 58, 127–42.

Bradley, R.J. 1993 *Altering the Earth*. Edinburgh: Society of Antiquaries of Scotland.

Bradley, R.J. and Chambers, R.A. 1988 A new study of the cursus complex at Dorchester on Thames. *Oxford Journal of Archaeology* 7, 271–90.

Bradley, R.J. and Chapman, R.C. 1984 Passage graves in the European Neolithic: a theory of convergent evolution. In: G. Burrenhult (ed.) *The Archaeology of Carrowmore*, 348–56. Stockholm: Institute of Archaeology.

Bradley, R.J. and Chapman, R.C. 1986 The nature and development of long-distance relations in later Neolithic Britain and Ireland. In: C. Renfrew and J.F. Cherry (eds) *Peer–Polity Interaction and Socio-Political Change*, 127–36. Cambridge: Cambridge University Press.

Bradley, R.J. and Edmonds, M.R. 1993 *Interpreting the Axe Trade*. Cambridge: Cambridge University Press.

Bradley, R.J. and Holgate, R. 1984 The Neolithic sequence in the Upper Thames Valley. In: R.J. Bradley and J. Gardiner (eds) *Neolithic Studies*, 107–35. Oxford: British Archaeological Reports 133.

Bradley, R.J. and Thomas, J.S. 1984 Some new information on the henge monument at Maumbury Rings, Dorchester. *Proceedings of the Dorset Natural History and Archaeological Society* 106, 132–4.

Bradley, R.J., Over, L., Startin, D.W.A. and Weng, R. 1978 The excavation of a Neolithic site at Cannon Hill, Maidenhead, Berkshire, 1974–5. *Berkshire Archaeological Journal* 68, 5–19.

Bradley, R.J., Chambers, R.A. and Halpin, C. 1984a *Excavations at Barrow Hills, Radley*. Oxford: Oxford Archaeological Unit.

Bradley, R.J., Cleal, R.M., Gardiner, J., Legge, A.J., Raymond, F. and Thomas, J.S. 1984b Sample excavation on the Dorset Cursus in 1984. *Proceedings of the Dorset Natural History and Archaeological Society* 106, 128–32.

Bradley, R.J., Cleal, R.M., Green, M., Gardiner, J. and Bowden, M. 1984c The Neolithic sequence in Cranborne Chase. In: R.J. Bradley and J. Gardiner (eds) *Neolithic Studies*, 87–105. Oxford: British Archaeological Reports 133.

Braithwaite, M. 1982 Decoration as ritual symbol: a theoretical proposal and an ethnographic study in southern Sudan. In: I. Hodder (ed.) *Symbolic and Structural Archaeology*, 80–8. Cambridge: Cambridge University Press.

Braithwaite, M. 1984 Ritual and prestige in the prehistory of Wessex c. 2000–1400 BC: a new dimension to the archaeological evidence. In: D. Miller and C. Tilley (eds) *Ideology, Power and Prehistory*, 93–110. Cambridge: Cambridge University Press.

Braun, D.P. 1983 Pots as tools. In: J.A. Moore and A.S. Keene (eds) *Archaeological Hammers and Theories*, 107–34. London: Academic Press.

Braun, D.P. 1986 Midwestern Hopewellian exchange and supralocal interaction. In: C. Renfrew and J.F. Cherry (eds) *Peer–Polity Interaction and Socio-Political Change*, 117–26. Cambridge: Cambridge University Press.

Brewster, T.C.M. 1968 Kemp Howe. *Annual Reports on Excavations* 1968, 8.

Brewster, T.C.M. 1984 *The Excavation of Whitegrounds Barrow, Burythorpe*. Wintringham: John Gett.

Britnell, W. and Savory, H. 1984 *Gwernvale and Penywyrlod: two Neolithic Long Cairns in the Black Mountains of Brecknock*. Cardiff: Cambrian Archaeological Association.

Britton, D. 1963 Traditions of metalworking in the late Neolithic and Early Bronze Age of Britain. *Proceedings of the Prehistoric Society* 29, 258–325.

Brown, A. and Edmonds, M.R. 1987 *Lithic Analysis and Later British Prehistory*. Oxford: British Archaeological Reports 162.

Brown, A.G. 1997 Clearances and clearings: deforestation in Mesolithic/Neolithic Britain. *Oxford Journal of Archaeology* 16, 133–46.

Brown, J.A. 1989 The beginnings of pottery as an economic process. In: S.E. van der Leeuw and R. Torrence (eds) *What's New? A Closer Look at the Process of Innovation*, 203–24. London: Unwin Hyman.

Brown, N. 1988 A Late Bronze Age enclosure at Lofts Farm, Essex. *Proceedings of the Prehistoric Society* 54, 249–304.

Brown, N. 1997 A landscape of two halves: the Neolithic of Chelmer valley/Blackwater estuary, Essex. In: P. Topping (ed.) *Neolithic Landscapes*, 87–98. Oxford: Oxbow.

Buchli, V. 1995 Interpreting material culture: the trouble with text. In: I. Hodder, M. Shanks, A. Alessandri, V. Buchli, J. Carman, J. Last and G. Lucas (eds) *Interpreting Archaeology: Finding Meanings in the Past*, 181–93. London: Routledge.

Bulleid, A. 1941 Notes on some chambered long barrows in north Somerset. *Proceedings of the Somerset Archaeology and Natural History Society* 87, 56–71.

Bulmer, R. 1967 Why is the cassowary not a bird? A problem in zoological taxonomy. *Man* 2, 5–25.

Bulmer, R. 1976 Selectivity in hunting and in disposal of animal bones by the Kalam of the New Guinea Highlands. In: G. de G. Sieveking, I. Longworth and K. Wilson (eds) *Problems in Economic and Social Archaeology*, 169–86. London: Duckworth.

Burchell, J.P.T. and Piggott, S. 1939 Decorated prehistoric pottery from the bed of the Ebbsfleet, Northfleet, Kent. *Antiquaries Journal* 19, 405–20.

Burgess, C. 1974 The Bronze Age. In: A.C. Renfrew (ed.) *British Prehistory: A New Outline*, 165–232. London: Duckworth.

Burgess, C. 1976 Meldon Bridge: a Neolithic defended promontory complex near Peebles. In: C. Burgess and R. Miket (eds) *Settlement and Economy in the Third and Second Millennia BC*, 151–80. Oxford: British Archaeological Reports 33.

Burgess, C. 1980 *The Age of Stonehenge*. London: Dent.

Burgess, C. and Cowen, J.D. 1972 The Ebnal hoard and Early Bronze Age metal-working traditions. In: F. Lynch and C. Burgess (eds) *Prehistoric Man in Wales and the West*, 167–88. Bath: Adams and Dart.

Burgess, C. and Shennan, S. 1976 The Beaker phenomenon: some suggestions. In: C. Burgess and R. Miket (eds) *Settlement and Economy in the Second and Third Millennia BC*, 309–31. Oxford: British Archaeological Reports 33.

Burgess, C., Topping, P., Mordant, C. and Maddison, M. 1988 *Enclosures and Defences in the Neolithic of Western Europe*. Oxford: British Archaeological Reports S403.

Burkitt, M. 1925 *Prehistory*. Cambridge: Cambridge University Press.

Burl, H.A.W. 1969 Henges: internal structures and regional groups. *Archaeological Journal* 126, 1–28.

Burl, H.A.W. 1976 *Stone Circles of the British Isles*. New Haven, CT: Yale University Press.

Burl, H.A.W. 1979 *Prehistoric Avebury*. New Haven, CT: Yale University Press.

Burl, H.A.W. 1987 *The Stonehenge People*. London: Dent.

Burl, H.A.W. 1988 'Without sharp north . . .': Alexander Thom and the great stone circles of Cumbria. In: C.L.N. Ruggles (ed.) *Records in Stone: Papers in Memory of Alexander Thom*, 175–205. Cambridge: Cambridge University Press.

Burl, H.A.W. 1990 Coves: structural enigmas of the Neolithic. *Wiltshire Archaeological Magazine* 82, 1–18.

Burton, J. 1984 Quarrying in a tribal society. *World Archaeology* 16, 234–47.

Busby, C. 1997 Permeable and partible persons: a comparative analysis of gender and body in south India and Melanesia. *Journal of the Royal Anthropological Institute* 3, 261–78.

Butler, J. 1993 *Bodies that Matter*. London: Routledge.

Buxton, J. 1968 Animal identity and human peril: some Mandari images. *Man* 3, 35–49.

Calkin, J. 1947 Neolithic pit at Southbourne. *Proceedings of the Dorset Natural History and Archaeological Society* 69, 29–32.

Care, V. 1982 The collection and distribution of lithic raw materials during the Mesolithic and Neolithic periods in southern England. *Oxford Journal of Archaeology* 1, 351–65.

Carruthers, W. 1990 Carbonised plant remains. In: J. Richards (ed.) *The Stonehenge Environs Project*, 250–2. London: English Heritage.

Case, H.J. 1956 The Neolithic causewayed camp at Abingdon. *Antiquaries Journal* 36, 11–30.

Case, H.J. 1963 Notes on finds and on ring ditches in the Oxford region. *Oxoniensia* 28, 19–52.

Case, H.J. 1969a Neolithic explanations. *Antiquity* 43, 176–86.

Case, H.J. 1969b Settlement patterns in the north Irish Neolithic. *Ulster Journal of Archaeology* 32, 3–27.

Case, H.J. 1973 Illusion and meaning. In: C. Renfrew (ed.) *The Explanation of Culture Change: Models in Prehistory*, 35–46. London: Duckworth.

Case, H.J. 1977 The Beaker Culture in Britain and Ireland. In: R. Mercer (ed.) *Beakers in Britain and Europe*, 71–101. Oxford: British Archaeological Reports S26.

Case, H.J. 1982a The linear ditches and southern enclosure, North Stoke. In: H. Case and A. Whittle (eds) *Settlement Patterns in the Oxford Region*, 60–76. London: Council for British Archaeology.

Case, H.J. 1982b Cassington, 1950–52: late Neolithic pits and the big enclosure. In: H. Case and A. Whittle (eds) *Settlement Patterns in the Oxford Region*, 118–51. London: Council for British Archaeology.

Case, H.J. 1982c The Vicarage Field, Stanton Harcourt. In: H. Case and A. Whittle (eds) *Settlement Patterns in the Oxford Region*, 103–18. London: Council for British Archaeology.

Case, H.J. 1986 The Mesolithic and Neolithic in the Oxford region. In: G. Briggs, J. Cook and T. Rowley (eds) *The Archaeology of the Oxford Region*, 18–37. Oxford: Oxford University Department of External Studies.

Case, H.J. 1993 Beakers: deconstruction and after. *Proceedings of the Prehistoric Society* 59, 241–68.

Case, H.J. 1995a Irish Beakers in their European context. In: J. Waddell and E. Shee Twohig (eds) *Ireland in the Bronze Age*, 14–29. Dublin: The Stationery Office.

Case, H.J. 1995b Beakers: loosening a stereotype. In: I.A. Kinnes and G. Varndell (eds) *'Unbaked Urns of Rudely Shape'*, 55–67. Oxford: Oxbow.

Case, H.J. 1995c Some Wiltshire Beakers and their contexts. *Wiltshire Archaeological Magazine* 88, 1–17.

Case, H.J. and Whittle, A.W.R. (eds) 1982 *Settlement Patterns in the Oxford Region*. London: Council for British Archaeology.

Castleden, R. 1987 *The Stonehenge People*. London: Routledge.

Catt, J.A. 1978 The contribution of loess to soils in lowland Britain. In: S. Limbrey and J.G. Evans (eds) *The Effect of Man on the Landscape – the Lowland Zone*, 12–20. London: Council for British Archaeology.

Caulfield, S. 1978 Neolithic fields – the Irish evidence. In: H.C. Bowen and P.J. Fowler (eds) *Early Land Allotment*, 137–43. Oxford: British Archaeological Reports 48.

Chadburn, A. and Gardiner, J. 1885 A Grooved Ware pit and prehistoric spade marks on Hengistbury Head (Site 6), Dorset, 1984. *Proceedings of the Prehistoric Society* 51, 315–18.

Chapman, R. 1981 The emergence of formal disposal areas and the 'problem' of megalithic tombs in prehistoric Europe. In: R. Chapman, I.A. Kinnes and K. Randsborg (eds) *The Archaeology of Death*, 71–81. Cambridge: Cambridge University Press.

Chapman, R.C. and Randsborg, K. 1981 Approaches to the archaeology of death. In: R.C. Chapman, I.A. Kinnes and K. Randsborg (eds) *The Archaeology of Death*, 1–24. Cambridge: Cambridge University Press.

Cherry, J. 1978 Generalisation and the archaeology of the state. In: D. Green, C. Haselgrove and M. Spriggs (eds) *Social Organisation and Settlement*, 411–37. Oxford: British Archaeological Reports S47.

Chesterman, J.T. 1977 Burial rites in Cotswold long barrow. *Man* 12, 22–32.

Childe, V.G. 1925 *The Dawn of European Civilisation*. London: Kegan Paul.

Childe, V.G. 1930 *The Bronze Age*. Cambridge: Cambridge University Press.

Childe, V.G. 1931 The continental affinities of British neolithic pottery. *Archaeological Journal* 88, 37–66.

Childe, V.G. 1936 *Man Makes Himself*. London: Watts.

Childe, V.G. 1940 *Prehistoric Communities of the British Isles*. London: Chambers.

Childe, V.G. 1950 *Prehistoric Migrations in Europe*. Oslo: Aschehaug.

Childe, V.G. 1951 *Social Evolution*. New York: Schumann.

Childe, V.G. and Smith, I.F. 1954 The excavation of a Neolithic barrow on Whiteleaf Hill, Bucks. *Proceedings of the Prehistoric Society* 20, 212–30.

Christie, P. 1963 The Stonehenge Cursus. *Wiltshire Archaeological Magazine* 58, 370–82.

Clare, T. 1987 Towards a reappraisal of henge monuments: origins, evolution and hierarchies. *Proceedings of the Prehistoric Society* 53, 457–78.

Clark, J.G.D. 1966 The invasion hypothesis in British archaeology. *Antiquity* 40, 172–89.

Clark, J.G.D. 1977 *World Prehistory*. Cambridge: Cambridge University Press.

Clark, J.G.D., Higgs, E.S. and Longworth, I. 1960 Excavations at the Neolithic site of Hurst Fen, Mildenhall, Suffolk, 1954, 1957 and 1958. *Proceedings of the Prehistoric Society* 26, 202–45.

Clarke, D.L. 1968 *Analytical Archaeology*. London: Methuen.

Clarke, D.L. 1970 *Beaker Pottery of Great Britain and Ireland*. Cambridge: Cambridge University Press.

Clarke, D. L. 1976 The Beaker network: social and economic models. In: J.N. Lanting and J.D. van der Waals (eds) *Glockenbechersymposion Oberried 1974*, 459–77. Haarlem and Bussem: Fibula/Van Dishoek.

Clarke, D.V. 1983 Rinyo and the Orcadian Neolithic. In: A. O'Connor and D.V. Clarke (eds) *From the Stone Age to the 'Forty-Five*, 45–56. Edinburgh: John Donald.

Clarke, D.V. and Sharples, N. 1985 Settlements and subsistence in the third millennium B.C. In: A.C. Renfrew (ed.) *The Prehistory of Orkney*, 54–82. Edinburgh: Edinburgh University Press.

Clarke, D.V., Cowie, T. and Foxon, A. 1985 *Symbols of Power at the Time of Stonehenge*. Edinburgh: HMSO.

Cleal, R.M.J. 1984 The later Neolithic in the east of England. In: R.J. Bradley and J. Gardiner (eds) *Neolithic Studies*, 135–58. Oxford: British Archaeological Reports 133.

Cleal, R.M.J. 1986 The Later Neolithic in Eastern England, PhD thesis, University of Reading.

Cleal, R.M.J. 1988 The occurrence of drilled holes in later Neolithic pottery. *Oxford Journal of Archaeology* 7, 139–45.

Cleal, R.M.J. 1991 Cranborne Chase: the earlier prehistoric pottery. In: J.C. Barrett, R.J. Bradley and M. Hall (eds) *Papers on the Prehistoric Archaeology of Cranborne Chase*, 134–200. Oxford: Oxbow.

Cleal, R.M.J. 1992 Significant form: ceramic styles in the earlier Neolithic of southern England. In: N. Sharples and A. Sheridan (eds) *Vessels for the Ancestors*, 286–306. Edinburgh: Edinburgh University Press.

Cleal, R.M.J. 1995 Pottery fabrics in Wessex in the fourth to second millennia BC. In: I.A. Kinnes and G. Varndell (eds) *'Unbaked Urns of Rudely Shape'*, 185–94. Oxford: Oxbow.

Cleal, R.M.J. and Allen, M.J. 1994 Investigation of tree-damaged barrows on King Barrow Ridge and Luxenborough Plantation, Amesbury. *Wiltshire Archaeological Magazine* 87, 54–88.

Cleal, R.M.J., Cooper, J. and Williams, D. 1994 Shells and sherds: identification of inclusions in Grooved Ware, with associated radiocarbon dates, from Amesbury, Wiltshire. *Proceedings of the Prehistoric Society* 60, 445–8.

Cleal, R.M.J., Walker, K.E. and Montague, R. 1995 *Stonehenge in its Landscape: Twentieth-Century Excavations*. London: English Heritage.

Clifford, E.M. 1936 Notgrove long barrow, Gloucestershire. *Archaeologia* 86, 119–62.

Clifford, E.M. 1937 The Beaker folk in the Cotswolds. *Proceedings of the Prehistoric Society* 3, 159–63.

Clifford, E.M. 1938 The excavation of Nympsfield long barrow. *Proceedings of the Prehistoric Society* 4, 188–213.

Clifford, E.M. and Daniel, G. 1940 The Rodmarton and Avening portholes. *Proceedings of the Prehistoric Society* 6, 133–65.

Clough, T. and Green, B. 1972 Petrological identification of stone implements from East Anglia. *Proceedings of the Prehistoric Society* 38, 108–35.

Cohen, G.A. 1978 *Karl Marx's Theory of History: A Defence*. Oxford: Oxford University Press.

Cole, S. 1965 *The Neolithic Revolution*. London: British Museum (Natural History).

Coles, J. and Orme, B. 1976 The Sweet track: Railway site. *Somerset Levels Papers* 2, 34–65.

Coles, J. and Orme, B. 1979 The Sweet track: Drove site. *Somerset Levels Papers* 5, 43–64.

Conkey, M.W. 1978 Style and information in cultural evolution: toward a predictive model for the Palaeolithic. In: C. Redman *et al.* (eds) *Social Archaeology: Beyond Subsistence and Dating*, 61–85. London: Academic.

Conkey, M.W. 1982 Boundedness in art and society. In: I.R. Hodder (ed.) *Symbolic and Structural Archaeology*, 115–28. Cambridge: Cambridge University Press.

Connah, G. 1965 Excavations at Knap Hill, Alton Priors, 1961. *Wiltshire Archaeological Magazine* 60, 1–23.

Connerton, P. 1989 *How Societies Remember*. Cambridge: Cambridge University Press.

Cooney, G. 1997 Images of settlement and landscape in the Neolithic. In: P. Topping (ed.) *Neolithic Landscapes*, 23–31. Oxford: Oxbow.

Coppet, D. de 1994 'Are'are. In: C. Barraud, D. de Coppet, A. Iteanu and R. Jamous (eds) *Of Relations and the Dead: Four Societies Viewed from the Angle of their Exchanges*. Oxford: Berg.

Corcoran, J.W.X.P. 1960 The Carlingford culture. *Proceedings of the Prehistoric Society* 26, 98–148.

Corcoran, J.W.X.P. 1970 The Giant's Cave, Luckington (WIL2). *Wiltshire Archaeological Magazine* 65, 39–63.

Corcoran, J.W.X.P. 1972 Multi-period construction and the origins of the chambered long cairn in western Britain and Ireland. In: F. Lynch and C. Burgess (eds) *Prehistoric Man in Wales and the West*, 31–63. Bath: Adams and Dart.

Cornwall, I.W. and Hodges, H.W.M. 1964 Thin sections of British Neolithic pottery: Windmill Hill – a test site. *Bulletin of the Institute of Archaeology, London* 4, 29–33.

Cosgrove, D.E. 1984 *Social Formation and Symbolic Landscape*. London: Croom Helm.

Coudart, A. 1991 Social structure and relationships in prehistoric small-scale societies: the Bandkeramik groups in Neolithic Europe. In: S.A. Gregg (ed.) *Between Bands and States*, 295–420. Carbondale: Southern Illinois University Press.

Cowie, T. 1993 A survey of the Neolithic pottery of eastern and central Scotland. *Proceedings of the Society of Antiquaries of Scotland* 123, 13–41.

Crawford, O.G.S. 1925 *The Long Barrows of the Cotswolds*. Gloucester: John Bellows.

Cunnington, M.E. 1909 Notes on barrows on King's Play Down, Heddington. *Wiltshire Archaeological Magazine* 36, 311–17.

Cunnington, M.E. 1914 List of the long barrows of Wiltshire. *Wiltshire Archaeological Magazine* 38, 379–414.

Cunnington, M.E. 1927 Shepherd's Shore. *Wiltshire Archaeological Magazine* 43, 397–8.

Cunnington, M.E. 1929 *Woodhenge*. Devizes: Simpson.

Cunnington, M.E. 1931 The 'Sanctuary' on Overton Hill, near Avebury. *Wiltshire Archaeological Magazine* 45, 300–35.

Cunnington, W. 1872 Notes on a long barrow at Oldbury Hill. *Wiltshire Archaeological Magazine* 13, 103–4.

Curwen, E.C. 1929 Excavations at the Trundle, Goodwood, 1928. *Sussex Archaeological Collections* 70, 33–85.

Curwen, E.C. 1930 Neolithic camps. *Antiquity* 4, 22–54.

Curwen, E.C. 1934a Excavations at Whitehawk Camp, Brighton, 1932–1933. *Antiquaries Journal* 56, 11–23.

Curwen, E.C. 1934b A late Bronze Age farm and a Neolithic pit-dwelling on New Barn Down, Clapham, nr. Worthing. *Sussex Archaeological Collections* 75, 141–70.

Curwen, E.C. 1936 Excavations in Whitehawk Camp, Brighton, third season, 1935. *Sussex Archaeological Collections* 77, 60–92.

Darvill, T.C. 1981 Excavations at the Peak Camp, Cowley: an interim note. *Glevensis* 15, 52–6.

Darvill, T.C. 1982 *The Megalithic Chambered Tombs of the Cotswold–Severn Region*. Highworth: Vorda.

Darvill, T.C. 1986 Beaker pottery fabrics from Cefn caer Euni. *Archaeologia Cambrensis* 135, 111–13.

Darvill, T.C. 1987 *Prehistoric Britain*. London: Batsford.

Darvill, T.C. 1996 Neolithic buildings in England, Wales and the Isle of Man. In: T.C. Darvill and J.S. Thomas (eds) *Neolithic Houses in Northwest Europe and Beyond*, 77–112. Oxford: Oxbow.

Darvill, T.C. 1997 Ever increasing circles: the sacred geographies of Stonehenge and its landscape. In: B. Cunliffe and C. Renfrew (eds) *Science and Stonehenge*, 167–202. Oxford: Oxford University Press.

Darvill, T.C., Hingley, R., Jones, M. and Timbey, J. 1986 A Neolithic and Iron Age site at the Loders, Lechlade, Gloucestershire. *Transactions of the Bristol and Gloucester Archaeological Society* 104, 24–48.

David, N., Sterner, J. and Gavua, K. 1988 Why pots are decorated. *Current Anthropology* 29, 365–89.

Davis, M. 1990 *City of Quartz: Excavating the Future in Los Angeles*. London: Verso.

DeAtley, S.P. and Findlow, F. 1984 Exploring the limits: introduction. In: S.P. DeAtley and F. Findlow (eds) *Exploring the Limits: Frontiers and Boundaries in Prehistory*, 1–3. Oxford: British Archaeological Reports S223.

DeBoer, W. 1984 The last pottery show: system and sense in ceramic studies. In: S. van der Leeuw and A.C. Pritchard (eds) *The Many Dimensions of Pottery*, 527–68. Amsterdam: University of Amsterdam Press.

de Man, P. 1978 The epistemology of metaphor. *Critical Enquiry* 5, 13–30.

Dennell, R.W. 1972 The interpretation of plant remains: Bulgaria. In: E.S. Higgs (ed.) *Papers in Economic Prehistory*, 149–60. Cambridge: Cambridge University Press.

Dennell, R.W. 1976 Prehistoric crop cultivation in southern England: a reconsideration. *Antiquaries Journal* 56, 11–23.

Dennell, R.W. 1983 *European Economic Prehistory*. London: Academic Press.

de Roever, J.P. 1979 The pottery from Swifterbant – Dutch Ertebølle? *Helenium* 19, 13–36.

Derrida, J. 1976 *Of Grammatology*. Baltimore: Johns Hopkins University Press.

Derrida, J. 1978a Structure, sign and play in the discourse of the human sciences. In: J. Derrida, *Writing and Difference*, 278–93. London: Routledge and Kegan Paul.

Derrida, J. 1978b *Spurs: Nietzsche's Styles*. Chicago: University of Chicago Press.

Derrida, J. 1982 Différance. In: J. Derrida, *Margins of Philosophy*, 1–27. Brighton: Harvester.

Devereux, P. 1991 Three-dimensional aspects of apparent relationships between selected natural and artificial features within the topography of the Avebury complex. *Antiquity* 65, 894–9.

Dews, P. 1987 *Logics of Disintegration*. London: Verso.

Dincauze, D. and Hasenstab, R. 1989 Explaining the Iroquois: tribalisation on a prehistoric periphery. In: T.C. Champion (ed.) *Centre and Periphery: Comparative Studies in Archaeology*, 67–87. London: Unwin Hyman.

Dixon, P. 1988 The Neolithic settlements on Crickley Hill. In: C. Burgess, P. Topping, C. Mordant and M. Madison (eds) *Enclosures and Defences in the Neolithic of Western Europe*, 75–88. Oxford: British Archaeological Reports S403.

Domańska, L. 1989 Elements of a food-producing economy in the late Mesolithic of the Polish lowland. In: C. Bonsall (ed.) *The Mesolithic in Europe*, 447–55. Edinburgh: John Donald.

Donaldson, P. 1977 The excavation of a multiple round barrow at Barnack, Cambridgeshire, 1974–6. *Antiquaries Journal* 57, 197–231.

Donley, L. 1982 House power: Swahili space and symbolic markers. In: I.R. Hodder (ed.) *Symbolic and Structural Archaeology*, 63–73. Cambridge: Cambridge University Press.

Donovan, H.E. 1938 Adlestrop Hill barrow, Gloucestershire. *Transactions of the Bristol and Gloucester Archaeological Society* 60, 152–64.

Douglas, M. 1957 Animals and Lele religious symbolism. *Africa* 27, 46–58.

Douglas, M. 1966 *Purity and Danger*. London: Routledge and Kegan Paul.

Drenth, E. 1990 Flat graves and barrows of the Single Grave Culture in the Netherlands in social perspective. In: M. Buchvaldek and C. Strahm (eds) *Die Kontinentaleuropäischen Gruppen der Kultur mit Schnurkeramik*, 207–14. Prague: Palaeohistorica.

Drew, C.D. and Piggott, S. 1936 The excavation of long barrow 163a on Thickthorn Down, Dorset. *Proceedings of the Prehistoric Society* 2, 77–96.

Drewett, P. 1975 The excavation of an oval burial mound of the third millennium BC at Alfriston, East Sussex. *Proceedings of the Prehistoric Society* 41, 119–52.

Drewett, P. 1977 The excavation of a Neolithic causewayed enclosure at Offham Hill, East Sussex. *Proceedings of the Prehistoric Society* 42, 201–41.

Drewett, P. 1980 Neolithic pottery in Sussex. *Sussex Archaeological Collections* 118, 23–30.

Drewett, P. 1982 Late Bronze Age downland economy and excavations at Black Patch, East Sussex. *Proceedings of the Prehistoric Society* 48, 321–400.

Drewett, P. 1986 The excavation of a Neolithic oval barrow at North Marden, West Sussex, 1982. *Proceedings of the Prehistoric Society* 52, 31–51.

Drewett, P. 1994 Dr V. Seton Williams' excavations at Combe Hill, 1962, and the role of causewayed enclosures in Sussex. *Sussex Archaeological Collections* 132, 7–24.

Drewett, P., Rudling, D. and Gardiner, M. 1988 *The South East to AD 1000*. London: Longmans.

Dronfield, J. 1995 Subjective vision and the source of Irish megalithic art. *Antiquity* 69, 539–49.

Dronfield, J. 1996 Entering alternative realities: cognition, art and architecture in Irish passage-tombs. *Cambridge Archaeological Journal* 6, 37–72.

Duncan, J. and Duncan, N. 1988 (Re)reading the landscape. *Society and Space* 6, 117–26.

Dunning, G.C. 1966 Neolithic occupation sites in east Kent. *Antiquaries Journal* 46, 1–25.

Easthope, A. 1983 *Poetry as Discourse*. London: Methuen.

Edmonds, M.R. 1987 Rocks and risk: problems with lithic procurement strategies. In: A. Brown and M.R. Edmonds (eds) *Lithic Analysis and Later British Prehistory*, 155–80. Oxford: British Archaeological Reports 162.

Edmonds, M.R. 1993 Interpreting causewayed enclosures in the past and the present. In: C. Tilley (ed.) *Interpretative Archaeology*, 99–142. London: Berg.

Edmonds, M.R. 1995 *Stone Tools and Society: Working Stone in Neolithic and Bronze Age Britain*. London: Batsford.

Edmonds, M.R. and Thomas, J.S. 1987 The Archers: an everyday story of country folk. In: A. Brown and M.R. Edmonds (eds) *Lithic Analysis and Later British Prehistory*, 187–99. Oxford: British Archaeological Reports 162.

Edwards, K. 1979 Palynological and temporal inference in the context of prehistory. *Journal of Archaeological Science* 6, 255–70.

Edwards, K. 1982 Man, space and the woodland edge – speculations on the detection and interpretation of human impact in pollen profiles. In: M. Bell and S. Limbrey (eds) *Archaeological Aspects of Woodland Ecology*, 5–22. Oxford: British Archaeological Reports S146.

Edwards, K. and Hirons, K. 1984 Cereal pollen grains in pre-elm decline deposits: implications for the earliest agriculture in Britain and Ireland. *Journal of Archaeological Science* 11, 71–80.

Ehrenburg, M. 1980 The occurrence of Bronze Age metalwork in the Thames: an investigation. *Transactions of the London and Middlesex Archaeological Society* 31, 1–15.

Ehrenreich, R.M., Crumley, C. and Levy, J. (eds) 1995 *Heterarchy and the Analysis of Complex Societies*. Washington, DC: American Anthropological Association.

Entwistle, R. 1990 Land mollusca from Amesbury 42 long barrow. In: J. Richards (ed.) *The Stonehenge Environs Project*, 105–9. London: English Heritage.

Entwistle, R. and Bowden, M. 1991 Cranborne Chase: the molluscan evidence. In: J.C. Barrett, R.J. Bradley and M. Hall (eds) *Papers in the Prehistoric Archaeology of Cranborne Chase*, 20–48. Oxford: Oxbow.

Entwistle, R. and Grant, A. 1989 The evidence for cereal cultivation and animal husbandry in the southern British Neolithic and Bronze Age. In: A. Milles, D. Williams and N. Gardner (eds) *The Beginnings of Agriculture*, 203–15. Oxford: British Archaeological Reports S496.

Eogan, G. 1986 *Knowth*. London: Thames and Hudson.

Eogan, G. and Roche, H. 1993 Neolithic ritual at Knowth? *Archaeology Ireland* 26, 16–18.

Evans, C. 1988a Monuments and analogy: the interpretation of causewayed enclosures. In: C. Burgess, P. Topping, C. Mordant and M. Maddison (eds) *Enclosures and Defences in the Neolithic of Western Europe*, 21–46. Oxford: British Archaeological Reports S403.

Evans, C. 1988b Excavations at Haddenham, Cambridgeshire: a 'planned' enclosure and its regional affinities. In: C. Burgess, P. Topping, C. Mordant and M. Maddison (eds) *Enclosures and Defences in the Neolithic of Western Europe*, 127–48. Oxford: British Archaeological Reports S403.

Evans, C. 1988c Acts of enclosure: a consideration of concentrically-organised causewayed enclosures. In: J.C. Barrett and I.A. Kinnes (eds) *The Archaeology of Context in the Neolithic and Bronze Age: Recent Trends*, 85–96. Sheffield: Department of Archaeology and Prehistory.

Evans, J.G. 1971 Habitat change on the calcareous soils of Britain: the impact of Neolithic man. In: D.D.A. Simpson (ed.) *Settlement and Economy in Neolithic and Early Bronze Age Britain and Europe*, 27–73. Leicester: Leicester University Press.

Evans, J.G. 1975 *The Environment of Early Man in the British Isles*. London: Elek.

Evans, J.G. 1983 Stonehenge – the environment in the late Neolithic and Early Bronze Age and a Beaker-Age burial. *Wiltshire Archaeological Magazine* 78, 7–30.

Evans, J.G. 1990 Notes on some Late Neolithic and Bronze Age events in long barrow ditches in southern and eastern England. *Proceedings of the Prehistoric Society* 56, 111–16.

Evans, J.G. and Simpson, D.D.A. 1991 Giant's Hills 2 long barrow, Skendleby, Lincolnshire. *Archaeologia* 109, 1–45.

Evans, J.G. and Smith, I.F. 1983 Excavations at Cherhill, north Wiltshire, 1967. *Proceedings of the Prehistoric Society* 49, 43–117.

Evans, J.G., Rouse, A.J. and Sharples, N.M. 1988 The landscape setting of causewayed camps: some recent work on the Maiden Castle enclosure. In: J.C. Barrett and I.A. Kinnes (eds) *The Archaeology of Context in the Neolithic and Bronze Age: Recent Trends*, 73–84. Sheffield: J. Collis.

Evans, J.G., Limbrey, S., Maté, I. and Mount, R. 1993 An environmental history of the upper Kennet Valley, Wiltshire, for the past 10,000 years. *Proceedings of the Prehistoric Society* 59, 139–96.

Farrington, I. n.d. An alternative view on the transition to agriculture: American and Australian collectors compared. Paper read at the conference 'Early Man in America', Mexico City, 1989.

Farrington, I. and Urry, J. 1985 Food and the early history of cultivation. *Journal of Ethnobiology* 5, 143–57.

Field, N. and Penn, J. 1981 A late Neolithic macehead from Kingston upon Thames. *Transactions of the London and Middlesex Archaeological Society* 32, 15–17.

Field, N., Matthews, C. and Smith, I.F. 1964 New Neolithic sites in Dorset and Bedfordshire, with a note on the distribution of Neolithic storage pits in Britain. *Proceedings of the Prehistoric Society* 30, 352–81.

Finlayson, B. 1996 The basis for change. In: T. Pollard and A. Morrison (eds) *The Early Prehistory of Scotland*, 269–90. Edinburgh: Edinburgh University Press.

Fischer, A. 1982 Trade in Danubian shafthole axes and introduction of Neolithic economy in Denmark. *Journal of Danish Archaeology* 1, 7–12.

Fisher, P.F. 1982 A review of lessivage and Neolithic cultivation in southern England. *Journal of Archaeological Science* 9, 299–304.

Flannery, K.V. 1968 Archaeological systems theory and early Mesoamerica. In: B. Meggers (ed.) *Anthropological Archaeology in the Americas*, 67–87. Washington: Anthropological Society of Washington.

Flannery, K.V. 1972 The cultural evolution of civilisation. *Annual Review of Ecology and Systematics* 3, 399–426.

Fleming, A. 1973 Tombs for the living. *Man* 8, 177–93.

Ford, S. 1987a Chronological and functional aspects of flint assemblages. In: A. Brown and M.R. Edmonds (eds) *Lithic Analysis and Later British Prehistory*, 67–86. Oxford: British Archaeological Reports 162.

Ford, S. 1987b Flint scatters and prehistoric settlement patterns in south Oxfordshire and east Berkshire. In: A. Brown and M.R. Edmonds (eds) *Lithic Analysis and Later British Prehistory*, 101–33. Oxford: British Archaeological Reports 162.

Forde-Johnson, J. 1964 A hoard of flint axes from Moel Arthur, Flintshire. *Transactions of the Flintshire Historical Society* 21, 99–100.

Foucault, M. 1967 Nietzsche, Freud, Marx. In: *Nietzsche*. Paris: Cahiers du Royaumont.

Foucault, M. 1970 *The Order of Things*. London: Tavistock.

Foucault, M. 1977 *Discipline and Punish*. London: Allen Lane.

Foucault, M. 1978 *The History of Sexuality, Vol. 1: An Introduction*. London: Peregine.

Foucault, M. 1984a Nietzsche, genealogy, history. In: P. Rabinow (ed.) *The Foucault Reader*, 76–100. Harmondsworth: Peregrine.

Foucault, M. 1984b Space, knowledge, and power. In: P. Rabinow (ed.) *The Foucault Reader*, 239–56. Harmondsworth: Peregrine.

Foucault, M. 1988 Technologies of the self. In: L. Martin, H. Gutman and P. Hutton (eds) *Technologies of the Self: A Seminar with Michel Foucault*, 16–49. London: Tavistock.

Fowler, P. 1981 Wildscape to landscape: 'enclosure' in prehistoric Britain. In: R.J. Mercer (ed.) *Farming Practice in British Prehistory*, 9–54. Edinburgh: Edinburgh University Press.

Frere, D.H.S. 1943 Late Neolithic Grooved Ware near Cambridge. *Antiquaries Journal* 23, 34–41.

Friedman, J. 1975 Tribes, states and transformations. In: M. Bloch (ed.) *Marxist Analyses in Social Anthropology* 161–202. London: Malaby.

Fritz, J. 1978 Palaeopsychology today: ideational systems and human adaptation in prehistory. In: C. Redman *et al.* (eds) *Social Archaeology: Beyond Subsistence and Dating*, 37–60. London: Academic Press.

Gadamer, H.G. 1975 *Truth and Method*. London: Sheed and Ward.

Gamble, C. 1981 Social control and the economy. In: A. Sheridan and G. Bailey (eds) *Economic Archaeology*, 215–30. Oxford: British Archaeological Reports S96.

Gardin, J.C. 1980 *Archaeological Constructs*. Cambridge: Cambridge University Press.

Gardiner, J.P. 1984 Lithic distributions and settlement patterns in central southern England. In: R.J. Bradley and J.P. Gardiner (eds) *Neolithic Studies*, 15–40. Oxford: British Archaeological Reports 133.

Gardiner, J.P. 1987 Tales of the unexpected: approaches to the assessment and interpretation of museum flint collections. In: A. Brown and M.R. Edmonds (eds) *Lithic Analysis and Later British Prehistory*, 49–66. Oxford: British Archaeological Reports 162.

Garwood, P. 1991. Ritual tradition and the reconstitution of society. In P. Garwood, D. Jennings, R. Skeates and J. Toms (eds) *Sacred and Profane*, 10–32. Oxford: Oxford University Committee for Archaeology Monograph No. 32.

Gebauer, A.B. 1995 Pottery production and the introduction of agriculture in southern Scandinavia. In: W.K. Barnett and J.W. Hoopes (eds) *The Emergence of Pottery: Technology and Innovation in Ancient Societies*, 99–112. Washington, DC: Smithsonian.

Geertz, C. 1983 Blurred genres: the reconfiguration of social thought. In: C. Geertz, *Local Knowledge: Further Essays in Interpretive Anthropology*, 19–35. New York: Basic Books.

Gell, A. 1995 The language of the forest: landscape and phonological iconism in Umeda. In: E. Hirsch and M. O'Hanlon (eds) *The Anthropology of Landscape*, 232–54. Oxford: Oxford University Press.

Gell, A.S.R. 1949 Grooved Ware from West Runton, Norfolk. *Antiquaries Journal* 29, 81.

Gibson, A.M. 1985 A Neolithic enclosure at Grendon, Northants. *Antiquity* 59, 213–19.

Gibson, A.M. 1992 Possible timber circles at Dorchester on Thames. *Oxford Journal of Archaeology* 11, 85–91.

Gibson, A.M. 1994 Excavations at the Sarn-y-bryn-caled cursus complex, Welshpool, Powys, and the timber circles of Great Britain and Ireland. *Proceedings of the Prehistoric Society* 60, 143–224.

Gibson, A.M. 1995 First impressions: a review of Peterborough Ware in Wales. In: I.A. Kinnes and G. Varndell (eds) *'Unbaked Urns of Rudely Shape'*, 23–39. Oxford: Oxbow.

Gibson, A.M. and Kinnes, I.A. 1997 On the urns of a dialemma: radiocarbon and the Peterborough problem. *Oxford Journal of Archaeology* 16, 65–72.

Gibson, A.M. and Woods, A. 1990 *Prehistoric Pottery for the Archaeologist*. Leicester: Leicester University Press.

Giddens, A. 1981 *A Contemporary Critique of Historical Materialism, 1: Power, Property and the State*. London: Macmillan.

Giddens, A. 1984. *The Constitution of Society: Outline of the Theory of Structuration*. Cambridge: Polity Press.

Gilbert, A.S. 1975 Modern nomads and prehistoric pastoralists: the limits of analogy. *Journal of the Ancient Near Eastern Society, Columbia University*, 1–20.

Giot, P.R. 1988 Stones in the landscape of Brittany. In: C. Ruggles (ed.) *Records in Stone: Studies in Memory of Alexander Thom*, 319–24. Cambridge: Cambridge University Press.

Godelier, M. 1977 *Perspectives in Marxist Anthropology*. Cambridge: Cambridge University Press.

Goldsmitt, W. 1979 A general model for pastoral social systems. In: *Pastoral Production and Society*, 15–27. Cambridge: Cambridge University Press.

Goodenough, W.R. 1965 Rethinking 'status' and 'role': towards a general model of the cultural organisation of social relationships. In: M. Banton (ed.) *The Relevance of Models for Social Anthropology*, 1–29. London: Tavistock.

Gosselain, O.P. 1992 Technology and style: potters and pottery among the Bafia of Cameroon. *Man* 27, 559–86.

Gottdiener, M. 1995 *Postmodern Semiotics: Material Culture and the Forms of Postmodern Life*. Oxford: Blackwell.

Gourlay, R. and Barrett, J.C. 1984 Dail na Caraidh. *Current Archaeology* 8, 347–9.

Graves, C.P. 1989 Social space in the English medieval parish church. *Economy and Society* 18, 297–322.

Gray, H. St G. 1935 The Avebury excavations, 1902–1922. *Archaeologia* 84, 99–162.

Green, C. and Rollo-Smith, S. 1984 The excavation of eighteen round barrows near Shrewton, Wiltshire. *Proceedings of the Prehistoric Society* 50, 255–318.

Green, C.P. 1997 The provenance of rocks used in the construction of Stonehenge. In: B. Cunliffe and C. Renfrew (eds) *Science and Stonehenge*, 257–70. Oxford: Oxford University Press.

Green, F.J. 1981 Iron Age, Roman and Saxon crops: the archaeological evidence from Wessex. In: G. Dimbleby and M. Jones (eds) *The Environment of Man*, 129–53. Oxford: British Archaeological Reports 87.

Greenfield, E. 1960 Neolithic pit and other finds from Wingham. *Archaeologia Cantiana* 74, 58–72.

Greenwell, W. 1877 *British Barrows*. Oxford: Clarendon Press.

Grigson, C. 1982a Sexing Neolithic domestic cattle from skulls and horncores. In: B. Wilson, C. Grigson and S. Payne (eds) *Ageing and Sexing Animal Bones from Archaeological Sites*, 25–35. Oxford: British Archaeological Reports 109.

Grigson, C. 1982b Porridge and pannage: pig husbandry in Neolithic England. In: M. Bell and S. Limbrey (eds) *Archaeological Aspects of Woodland Ecology*, 297–314. Oxford: British Archaeological Reports S146.

Grimes, W.F. 1939 The excavation of the Ty Isaf long cairn, Breconshire. *Proceedings of the Prehistoric Society* 5, 119–42.

Grimes, W.F. 1944 Excavations at Stanton Harcourt, Oxon., 1940. *Oxoniensia* 8/9, 19–63.

Grimes, W.F. 1960 *Excavations on Defence sites, Vol. 1: Neolithic–Bronze Age*. London: HMSO.

Grimes, W.F. 1964 Excavations in the Lake group of barrows, Wilsford, Wiltshire in 1959. *Bulletin of the Institute of Archaeology, London* 4, 89–121.

Grinsell, L.V. 1957 Archaeological Gazetteer. In: *The Victoria County History of Wiltshire*, Vol. 1(1), 21–279. London: HMSO.

Grinsell, L.V. 1985 Carrying flint cores to Mendip. *Lithics* 6, 15–17.

Haggarty, A. 1991 Machrie Moor, Arran: recent excavations at two stone circles. *Proceedings of the Society of Antiquaries of Scotland* 121, 51–94.

Halpin, C. 1984 Blewbury. *Oxford Archaeological Unit Newsletter* 11, 1–2.

Halpin, C. 1987 Irthlingborough barrow excavations 1986. MS.

Halstead, P. 1996 The development of agriculture and pastoralism in Greece: when, how, who and what? In: D. Harris (ed.) *The Origins and Spread of Agriculture and Pastoralism in Eurasia*, 296–309. London: University College London Press.

Hansen, H.O. 1969 *Reports from Experiment in Lejre 1968: 1*. Lejre: Historic-Archaeological Centre.

Hansen, J. 1980 The Palaeoethnobotany of Franchthi Cave, PhD thesis, University of Minnesota.

Hardin, M. 1984 Models of decoration. In: S. van der Leeuw and A.C. Pritchard (eds) *The Many Dimensions of Pottery*, 573–614. Amsterdam: University of Amsterdam Press.

Harding, A. 1981 Excavations in the prehistoric ritual complex near Milfield, Northumberland. *Proceedings of the Prehistoric Society* 47, 87–135.

Harding, J. 1997 Interpreting the Neolithic: the monuments of North Yorkshire. *Oxford Journal of Archaeology* 16, 279–95.

Harding, P. 1988 The chalk plaque pit, Amesbury. *Proceedings of the Prehistoric Society* 54, 320–6.

Harding, P. and Gingell, C. 1986 The excavation of two long barrows by F. de M. and H.F.W.L. Vatcher. *Wiltshire Archaeological Magazine* 80, 7–22.

Harland, R. 1987 *Superstructuralism: The Philosophy of Structuralism and Post-Structuralism*. London: Methuen.

Harris, E. 1989 *Principles of Archaeological Stratigraphy*. London: Academic Press.

Harris, O. 1982 The dead and the devils among the Bolivian Laymi. In: M. Bloch and J. Parry (eds) *Death and the Regeneration of Life*, 45–73. Cambridge: Cambridge University Press.

Harrison, R.J. 1980 *The Beaker Folk*. London: Thames and Hudson.

Hastorf, C. and Johannessen, S. 1994 Becoming corn-eaters in prehistoric America. In: S. Johannessen and C. Hastorf (eds) *Corn and Culture in the Prehistoric New World*, 427–43. Boulder, CO: Westview.

Hawkes, C.F.C. 1931 Hillforts. *Antiquity* 5, 60–97.

Hawkes, C.F.C. 1940 *The Prehistoric Foundations of Europe*. London: Methuen.

Hawkes, C.F.C. 1954 Archaeological theory and method: some suggestions from the Old World. *American Anthropologist* 56, 155–68.

Hawkes, J. 1935 The place of origin of the Windmill Hill Culture. *Proceedings of the Prehistoric Society* 1, 127–9.

Hawkes, J. and Hawkes, C.F.C. 1948 *Prehistoric Britain*. London: Chatto and Windus.

Hawkes, T. 1972 *Metaphor*. London: Methuen.

Hayden, B. 1995 The emergence of prestige technologies and pottery. In: W.K. Barnett and J.W. Hoopes (eds) *The Emergence of Pottery: Technology and Innovation in Ancient Societies*, 257–65. Washington, DC: Smithsonian.

Healy, F.M. 1984 Farming and field monuments: the Neolithic of Norfolk. In C. Barringer (ed.) *Aspects of East Anglian Prehistory*, 77–140. Norwich: Geo.

Healy, F.M. 1987 Prediction or prejudice? The relationship between field survey and excavation. In: A. Brown and M.R. Edmonds (eds) *Lithic Analysis and Later Prehistory*, 9–18. Oxford: British Archaeological Reports 162.

Healy, F.M. 1988 Spong Hill part VI: 7th to 2nd millennia BC. *East Anglian Archaeology* 39.

Healy, F.M. 1995 Pits, pots and peat: ceramics and settlement in East Anglia. In: I.A. Kinnes and G. Varndell (eds) *'Unbaked Urns of Rudely Shape'*, 173–84. Oxford: Oxbow.

Healy, F., Cleal, R.M.J. and Kinnes, I.A. 1993 Excavations at Redgate Hill, Hunstanton, 1970 and 1971. *East Anglian Archaeology* 57, 1–80.

Hedges, J. and Buckley, D. 1981 *Springfield and the Cursus Problem*. Essex County Council.

Hedges, J.W. 1984 *Tomb of the Eagles*. London: John Murray.

Heidegger, M. 1962 *Being and Time*, translated by J. Macquarrie and E. Robinson. Oxford: Blackwell.

Heidegger, M. 1993 Letter on humanism. In: D.F. Krell (ed.) *Martin Heidegger: Basic Writings*, 2nd edition, 213–65. London: Routledge.

Helbaek, H. 1952 Early crops in southern England. *Proceedings of the Prehistoric Society* 18, 194–233.

Helms, M. 1979 *Ancient Panama: Chiefs in Search of Power*. Austin: University of Texas Press.

Hemp, W. 1930 The chambered cairn of Bryn Celli Ddu. *Archaeologia* 80, 179–214.

Herne, A. 1988 A time and a place for the Grimston bowl. In: J.C. Barrett and I.A. Kinnes (eds) *The Archaeology of Context in the Neolithic and Bronze Age: Recent Trends*, 2–29. Sheffield: Department of Archaeology and Prehistory.

Hertz, R. 1960 *Death and the Right Hand*. Aberdeen: Cohen and West.

Hey, G. 1997 Neolithic settlement at Yarnton, Oxfordshire. In: P. Topping (ed.) *Neolithic Landscapes*, 99–112. Oxford: Oxbow.

Higgs, E.S. and Jarman, M.R. 1975 Palaeoeconomy. In: E.S. Higgs (ed.) *Palaeoeconomy*, 1–8. Cambridge: Cambridge University Press.

Hill, J.D. 1995 *Ritual and Rubbish in the Iron Age of Wessex*. Oxford: British Archaeological Reports 242.

Hillier, W. and Hanson, J. 1984 *The Social Logic of Space*. Cambridge: Cambridge University Press.

Hillman, G. 1981a Reconstructing crop husbandry practices from charred remains of crops. In: R. Mercer (ed.) *Farming Practice in British Prehistory*, 123–62. Edinburgh: Edinburgh University Press.

Hillman, G. 1981b Crop husbandry: evidence from macroscopic remains. In: I. Simmons and M. Tooley (eds) *The Environment in British Prehistory*, 183–91. London: Duckworth.

Hirst, P.Q. 1985 Constructed space and the subject. In: R. Fardon (ed.) *Power and Knowledge*, 171–92. Edinburgh: Scottish Academic Press.

Hirth, K.G. 1978 Interregional trade and the formation of gateway communities. *American Antiquity* 43, 35–45.

Hoare, R.C. 1812 *The Ancient History of Wiltshire*. London: Miller.

Hoare, R.C. 1821 An account of a stone barrow in the parish of Wellow at Stoney Littleton. *Archaeologia* 19, 43–8.

Hodder, I.R. 1978 Social organisation and human interaction: the development of some tentative hypotheses in terms of material culture. In: I.R. Hodder (ed.) *The Spatial Organisation of Culture*, 199–269. London: Duckworth.

Hodder, I.R. 1979 Economic and social stress and material culture patterning. *American Antiquity* 44, 446–55.

Hodder, I.R. 1982a *Symbols in Action*. Cambridge: Cambridge University Press.

Hodder, I.R. 1982b Theoretical archaeology: a reactionary view. In: I. Hodder (ed.) *Symbolic and Structural Archaeology*, 1–16. Cambridge: Cambridge University Press.

Hodder, I.R. 1983 Pottery, production and use: a theoretical discussion. In: H. Howard and E. Morris (eds) *Production and Distribution: A Ceramic Viewpoint*, 215–20. Oxford: British Archaeological Reports S120.

Hodder, I.R. 1984 Burials, houses, women and men in the European Neolithic. In: D. Miller and C. Tilley (eds) *Ideology, Power and Prehistory*, 51–68. Cambridge: Cambridge University Press.

Hodder, I.R. 1986 *Reading the Past: Current Approaches to Interpretation in Archaeology*. Cambridge: Cambridge University Press.

Hodder, I.R. 1987 Contextual archaeology: an interpretation of Çatal Hüyük and a discussion of the origins of agriculture. *Bulletin of the Institute of Archaeology, London* 24, 43–56.

Hodder, I.R. 1988 Material culture texts and social change: a theoretical discussion and some archaeological examples. *Proceedings of the Prehistoric Society* 54, 67–76.

Hodder, I.R. 1990 *The Domestication of Europe*. Oxford: Blackwell.

Hodder, I.R. 1991 Interpretive archaeology and its role. *American Antiquity* 56, 7–18.

Hodder, I.R. 1992 Symbolism, meaning and context. In: I.R. Hodder, *Theory and Practice in Archaeology*, 11–23. London: Routledge.

Hodder, I.R. 1994 Architecture and meaning: the example of Neolithic houses and tombs. In: M. Parker Pearson and C.C. Richards (eds) *Architecture and Order*, 73–86. Oxford: Blackwell.

Hodder, I.R. and Lane, P. 1982 A contextual examination of Neolithic axe distribution in Britain. In: J. Ericson and T. Earle (eds) *Contexts for Prehistoric Exchange*, 213–35. London: Academic Press.

Hodder, I.R. and Shand, P. 1988 The Haddenham long barrow: an interim statement. *Antiquity* 62, 394–453.

Hodges, H. 1962 Thin sections of prehistoric pottery: an empirical study. *Bulletin of the University of London Institute of Archaeology* 3, 58–68.

Hodges, R. 1982 *Dark Age Economics*. London: Duckworth.

Hoernes, M. 1925 *Urgeschichte der bildenden Kunst in Europa von den Anfängen bis zum 500 vor Christus*, 3rd edn, revised by O. Menghin. Vienna: A. Schroll.

Holgate, R. 1984 Neolithic settlement in the Upper Thames Valley. *Current Archaeology* 8, 374–5.

Holgate, R. 1988a *Neolithic Settlement of the Thames Basin*. Oxford: British Archaeological Reports 194.

Holgate, R. 1988b A review of Neolithic domestic activity in southern Britain. In: J.C. Barrett and I.A. Kinnes (eds) *The Archaeology of Context in the Neolithic and Bronze Age: Recent Trends*, 104–12. Sheffield: Department of Archaeology and Prehistory.

Hoopes, W.K. and Barnett, J.W. 1995 The shape of early pottery studies. In: W.K. Barnett and J.W. Hoopes (eds) *The Emergence of Pottery: Technology and Innovation in Ancient Societies*, 1–7. Washington, DC: Smithsonian.

Houlder, C. 1968 The henge monuments at Llandegai. *Antiquity* 42, 216–31.

Houlder, C. 1976 Stone axes and henge-monuments. In: G.C. Boon and J.M. Lewis (eds) *Welsh Antiquity*, 55–62. Cardiff: National Museum of Wales.

Howard, H. 1981 In the wake of distribution: towards an integrated approach to ceramic studies in prehistoric Britain. In: H. Howard and E. Morris (eds) *Production and Distribution: A Ceramic Viewpoint*, 1–30. Oxford: British Archaeological Reports S120.

Howell, J. 1982 Neolithic settlement and economy in northern France. *Oxford Journal of Archaeology* 1, 115–18.

Howell, J. 1983a *Settlement and Economy in Neolithic Northern France*. Oxford: British Archaeological Reports S157.

Howell, J. 1983b The late Neolithic in the Paris Basin. In: C. Scarre (ed.) *Ancient France*, 62–90. Edinburgh: Edinburgh University Press.

Hugh-Jones, C. 1978 Food for thought: patterns of production and consumption in Pira-Pirana society. In: J.S. LaFontaine (ed.) *Age and Sex as Principles of Social Differentiation*, 41–66. London: Academic Press.

Humphreys, S.C. 1981 Death and time. In: S.C. Humphries and H. King (eds) *Mortality and Immortality: The Anthropology and Archaeology of Death*, 261–83. London: Academic Press.

Hunter, J. and MacSween, A. 1991 A sequence for the Orcadian Neolithic? *Antiquity* 65, 911–14.

Huntingdon, R. and Metcalf, P. 1979 *Celebrations of Death*. Cambridge: Cambridge University Press.

Ilett, M., Constantin, C., Coudart, A. and Demoule, J.P. 1982 The late Bandkeramik of the Aisne valley: environmental and spatial organisation. *Analecta Praehistorica Leidensia* 15, 45–61.

Ingold, T. 1980 *Hunters, Pastoralists and Ranchers*. Cambridge: Cambridge University Press.

Ingold, T. 1981 The hunter and his spear: notes on the ecological mediation of social and ecological systems.

In: A. Sheridan and G. Bailey (eds) *Economic Archaeology*, 119–30. Oxford: British Archaeological Reports S96.

Ingold, T. 1983 The significance of storage in hunting societies. *Man* 18, 553–71.

Ingold, T. 1990 Society, nature and the concept of technology. *Archaeological Review from Cambridge* 9 (1), 5–17.

Iversen, J. 1956 Forest clearance in the Stone Age. *Scientific American* 195, 36–41.

Jackson, D.A. 1976 The excavation of Neolithic and Bronze Age sites at Aldwincle, Northants, 1967–71. *Northamptonshire Archaeology* 11, 12–70.

Jackson, H.E. 1991 The trade fair in hunter-gatherer interaction: the role of intersocietal trade in the evolution of Poverty Point culture. In: S. Gregg (ed.) *Between Bands and States*, 265–86. Carbondale: Southern Illinois University.

Jackson, J.W. 1956 Letter to H. Case. Buxton Museum.

Jameson, F. 1981 *The Political Unconscious: Narrative as a Socially Symbolic Act.* London: Methuen.

Jarman, M., Bailey, G. and Jarman, H. (eds) 1982 *Early European Agriculture.* Cambridge: Cambridge University Press.

Jazdzewski, K. 1973 The relations between Kujavian barrows in Poland and Megalithic tombs in N. Germany, Denmark and West European countries. In: G. Daniel and P. Kjaerum (eds) *Megalithic Graves and Ritual*, 63–74. Copenhagen: Jutland Archaeological Society.

Jenkins, D. 1986 Petrographic analysis. In: C.A. Smith and F.M. Lynch *Trefignath and Din Dryfol*, 60–73. Cardiff: Cambrian Archaeological Association.

Johnson, G.A. 1978 Information sources and the development of decision-making organisations. In: C. Redman, M.J. Berman, E.V. Curtin, W.T. Langhorne, N.M. Versaggi and J.C. Wanser (eds) *Social Archaeology: Beyond Subsistence and Dating*, 87–112. London: Academic Press.

Johnson, H. and Olsen, B. 1992 Hermeneutics and archaeology: on the philosophy of contextual archaeology. *American Antiquity* 57 (3), 419–36.

Johnston, D. 1980 The excavation of a bell barrow at Sutton Veny, Wilts. *Wiltshire Archaeological Magazine* 72/3, 29–50.

Jones, A. 1996 Food for thought: material culture and the transformation in food use from the Mesolithic to Neolithic. In: T. Pollard and A. Morrison (eds) *The Early Prehistory of Scotland*, 291–300. Edinburgh: Edinburgh University Press.

Jones, M. 1980 Carbonised cereals from Grooved Ware contexts. *Proceedings of the Prehistoric Society* 46, 61–3.

Jones, M.U. 1976 Neolithic pottery found at Lechlade, Glos. *Oxoniensia* 41, 1–5.

Jones, S. 1997 *The Archaeology of Ethnicity.* London: Routledge.

Keeley, L.H. 1992 The introduction of agriculture to the western north European plain. In: A.B. Gebauer and T.D. Price (eds) *Transitions to Agriculture in Prehistory*, 81–95. Madison, WI: Prehistory Press.

Keeley, L.H. and Cahen, D. 1989 Early Neolithic forts and villages in N.E. Belgium: a preliminary report. *Journal of Field Archaeology* 16, 157–76.

Keiller, A. and Piggott, S. 1938 Excavation of an untouched chamber in the Lanhill long barrow. *Proceedings of the Prehistoric Society* 4, 122–50.

Kendrick, T.D. 1925 *The Axe Age.* London: Methuen.

Kenward, R. 1982 A Neolithic burial enclosure at New Wintles Farm, Eynsham. In: H.J. Case and A.W.R. Whittle (eds) *Settlement Patterns in the Oxford Region*, 51–4. London: Council for British Archaeology.

Kesby, J.D. 1979 The Rangi classification of animals and plants. In: R. Ellen and D. Reason (eds) *Classifications in their Social Context*, 33–56. London: Academic Press.

Kinnes, I.A. 1975 Monumental function in British Neolithic burial practices. *World Archaeology* 7, 16–28.

Kinnes, I.A. 1978 Neolithic pottery. In: J. Hedges and D. Buckley, Excavations at a Neolithic causewayed enclosure, Orsett, Essex, 1975. *Proceedings of the Prehistoric Society* 44, 219–308.

Kinnes, I.A. 1979 *Round Barrows and Ring Ditches in the British Neolithic.* London: British Museum.

Kinnes, I.A. 1981 Dialogues with death. In: R. Chapman, I. Kinnes and K. Randsborg (eds) *The Archaeology of Death*, 83–91. Cambridge: Cambridge University Press.

Kinnes, I.A. 1982 Les Fouillages and megalithic origins. *Antiquity* 56, 24–30.

Kinnes, I.A. 1985 Circumstance not context: the Neolithic of Scotland as seen from outside. *Proceedings of the Society of Antiquaries of Scotland* 115, 115–57.

Kinnes, I.A. 1992 *Non-Megalithic Long Barrows and Allied Structures in the British Neolithic.* London: British Museum.

Kinnes, I.A., Schadla-Hall, T., Chadwick, P. and Dean, P. 1983 Duggleby Howe reconsidered. *Archaeological Journal* 140, 83–108.

Kinnes, I.A., Gibson, A.M., Ambers, J., Bowman, S., Leese, M. and Boast, R. 1991 Radiocarbon dating and British Beakers: the British Museum programme. *Scottish Archaeological Review* 8, 35–68.

Kopytoff, I. 1986 The cultural biography of things: commodification as process. In: A. Appadurai (ed.) *The Social Life of Things*, 64–91. Cambridge: Cambridge University Press.

Kossinna, G. 1911 *Die Herkunft der Germanen: Zur Methode Siedlungsarchäologie*. Würzburg: Kabitzsch.

Kristiansen, K. 1984 Ideology and material culture: an archaeological perspective. In: M. Spriggs (ed.) *Marxist Perspectives in Archaeology*, 72–100. Cambridge: Cambridge University Press.

Kruk, J. 1980 *The Earlier Neolithic Settlement of Southern Poland*. Oxford: British Archaeological Reports S93.

Küchler, S. 1987 Malangan: art and memory in a Melanesian society. *Man* 22, 238–55.

Kus, S. 1983 The social representation of space: dimensioning the cosmological and the quotidian. In: J.A. Moore and A.S. Keene (eds) *Archaeological Hammers and Theories*, 277–98. London: Academic Press.

Laidler, D. and Young, W.E.V. 1938 A surface flint assemblage from a site near Stonehenge. *Wiltshire Archaeological Magazine* 33, 150–60.

Lambrick, G. 1988 *The Rollright Stones: Megaliths, Monuments, and the Prehistoric Landscape*. London: English Heritage.

Lane, P. 1986 Past practices in the ritual present: examples from the Welsh Bronze Age. *Archaeological Review from Cambridge* 5, 181–92.

Lanting, J.N. and van der Waals, J.D. 1972 British Beakers as seen from the continent. *Helenium* 12, 20–46.

Lanting, J.N. and van der Waals, J.D. 1976 Beaker Culture relations in the lower Rhine basin. In: *Glockenbecher Symposion Oberried 1974*, 1–80. Haarlem: Fibula-Van Dishoek.

Larrick, R. 1986 Age grading and ethnicity in Loikop (Samburu) spears. *Journal of Anthropological Archaeology* 4, 269–83.

Last, J. 1996 Neolithic houses – a central European perspective. In: T.C. Darvill and J.S. Thomas (eds) *Neolithic Houses in Northwest Europe and Beyond*, 27–40. Oxford: Oxbow.

Lawson, H. 1985 *Reflexivity: The Post-Modern Predicament*. London: Hutchinson.

Leach, E. 1976 *Culture and Communication: The Logic by which Symbols are Connected*. Cambridge: Cambridge University Press.

Leeds, E.T. 1923 A Saxon village near Sutton Courtenay, Berkshire. *Archaeologia* 73, 147–92.

Leeds, E.T. 1927 A Neolithic site at Abingdon, Berks. *Antiquaries Journal* 7, 438–63.

Leeds, E.T. 1928 A Neolithic site at Abingdon, Berks. *Antiquaries Journal* 8, 461–77.

Leeds, E.T. 1934 Recent Bronze Age discoveries in Berkshire and Oxfordshire. *Antiquaries Journal* 14, 264–76.

Leeds, E.T. 1940 New discoveries of Neolithic pottery in Oxfordshire. *Oxoniensia* 5, 1–12.

Legge, A.J. 1981 Aspects of cattle husbandry. In: R.J. Mercer (ed.) *Farming Practice in British Prehistory*, 169–81. Edinburgh: Edinburgh University Press.

Legge, A.J. 1989 Milking the evidence: a reply to Entwistle and Grant. In: A. Milles, D. Williams and N. Gardner (eds) *The Beginnings of Agriculture*, 217–42. Oxford: British Archaeological Reports S496.

Legge, A.J. 1991 The animal remains from six sites at Down Farm, Woodcutts. In: J.C. Barrett, R.J. Bradley and M. Hall (eds) *Papers in the Prehistoric Archaeology of Cranborne Chase*, 54–100. Oxford: Oxbow.

Lentricchia, F. 1980 *After the New Criticism*. London: Methuen.

Lévi-Strauss, C. 1966 *The Savage Mind*. Harmondsworth: Penguin.

Lévi-Strauss, C. 1969a *Totemism*. Harmondsworth: Penguin.

Lévi-Strauss, C. 1969b *The Raw and the Cooked*. London: Jonathan Cape.

Levitan, B., Audsley, A., Hawkes, C.J., Moody, A., Moody, P., Smart, P.L. and Thomas, J.S. 1988 Charterhouse Warren Farm Swallett, Mendip, Somerset. Exploration, Geomorphology, Taphonomy and Archaeology. *Proceedings of the University of Bristol Spelaeological Society* 18, 171–339.

Lidén, K. 1995 Megaliths, agriculture, and social complexity: a diet study of two Swedish megalith populations. *Journal of Anthropological Archaeology* 14, 404–17.

Llamazares, A.M. 1989 A semiotic approach in rock-art analysis. In: I. Hodder (ed.) *The Meanings of Things*, 242–8. London: Unwin Hyman.

Longworth, I. 1961 The origins and development of the primary series in the collared urn tradition in England and Wales. *Proceedings of the Prehistoric Society* 27, 263–306.

Longworth, I. 1984 *Collared Urns of the Bronze Age in Great Britain and Ireland*. Cambridge: Cambridge University Press.

Loveday, R. 1989 The Barford ritual complex: further excavations (1972) and a regional perspective. In: A. Gibson (ed.) *Midlands Prehistory*, 51–84. Oxford: British Archaeological Reports 204.

Lowenthal, D. 1994 European and English landscapes as national symbols. In: D. Hooson (ed.) *Geography and National Identity*, 15–38. Oxford: Blackwell.

Lubbock, J. 1865 *Pre-Historic Times*. London: Williams and Norgate.

Lucas, G. 1995 Genealogies: Classification, Narrative and Time: An Archaeological Study of Eastern Yorkshire, 3700–1300 BC, Unpublished PhD thesis, University of Cambridge.

Lukis, W. 1867 Tumuli of north Wiltshire. *Proceedings of the Society of Antiquaries of London* 2s 3, 213–16.

Lüning, J. 1982 Research into the Bandkeramik settlement of the Aldenhover Platte in the Rhineland. *Analecta Praehistorica Leidensia* 15, 1–30.

Lynch, K. 1972 *What Time is this Place?* Cambridge, MA: Massachusetts Institute of Technology.

Macdonnell, D. 1986 *Theories of Discourse*. Oxford: Blackwell.

McInnes, I.J. 1969 A Scottish Neolithic pottery sequence. *Scottish Archaeological Forum* 1, 19–30.

MacKie, E. 1977 *Science and Society in Prehistoric Britain*. London: Elek.

McMillan, A.D. 1988 *Native Peoples and Cultures of Canada*. Vancouver: Douglas and McIntyre.

MacSween, A. 1992 Orcadian Grooved Ware. In: N. Sharples and A. Sheridan (eds) *Vessels for the Ancestors: Essays on the Neolithic of Britain and Ireland*, 259–71. Edinburgh: Edinburgh University Press.

MacSween, A. 1995 Grooved Ware in Scotland: aspects of decoration. In: I.A. Kinnes and G. Varndell (eds) *'Unbaked Urns of Rudely Shape'*, 41–8. Oxford: Oxbow.

Madsen, T. 1979 Earthen long barrows and timber structures: aspects of the early Neolithic mortuary practice in Denmark. *Proceedings of the Prehistoric Society* 45, 301–20.

Madsen, T. and Jensen, H.J. 1982 Settlement and land use in early Neolithic Denmark. *Analecta Praehistorica Leidensia* 15, 63–86.

Maltby, J.M. 1979 *Faunal Studies on Urban Sites: The Animal Bones from Exeter 1971–1975*. Sheffield: Department of Prehistory and Archaeology.

Manby, T.G. 1956 Neolithic 'B' pottery from East Yorkshire. *Yorkshire Archaeological Journal* 39, 1–8.

Manby, T.G. 1963 The excavation of the Willerby Wold long barrow. *Proceedings of the Prehistoric Society* 29, 173–205.

Manby, T.G. 1967 Neolithic Cultures of the North of England, M.Phil. thesis, University of Liverpool.

Manby, T.G. 1970 Long barrows of northern England: structural and dating evidence. *Scottish Archaeological Forum* 2, 1–27.

Manby, T.G. 1974 *Grooved Ware Sites in Yorkshire and the North of England*. Oxford: British Archaeological Reports 9.

Manby, T.G. 1975 Neolithic occupation sites on the Yorkshire Wolds. *Yorkshire Archaeological Journal* 47, 23–59.

Manby, T.G. 1976 The excavation of Kilham long barrow, East Riding of Yorkshire. *Proceedings of the Prehistoric Society* 42, 111–60.

Manson, J.L. 1995 Starčevo pottery and Neolithic development in the central Balkans. In: W.K. Barnett and J.W. Hoopes (eds) *The Emergence of Pottery: Technology and Innovation in Ancient Societies*, 65–77. Washington, DC: Smithsonian.

Mark, V. 1994 Objects and their maker: bricolage of the self. In: S. Riggins (ed.) 1994 *The Socialness of Things*, 63–100. The Hague: Mouton/de Gruyter.

Marshall, D.N. 1977 Carved stone balls. *Proceedings of the Society of Antiquaries of Scotland* 108, 40–72.

Marshall, Y.M.M. and Maas, A. 1997 Dashing dishes. *World Archaeology* 28, 275–90.

Marx, K. and Engels, F. 1970 *The German Ideology*. London: Lawrence and Wishart.

Massingham, H.J. 1926 *Downland Man*. London: Jonathan Cape.

Massingham, H.J. 1936 *English Downland*. London: Batsford.

Masters, L. 1973 The Lochill long cairn. *Antiquity* 47, 96–100.

Masters, L. 1983 Chambered tombs and non-megalithic barrows in Britain. In: C. Renfrew (ed.) *The Megalithic Monuments of Western Europe*, 97–112. London: Thames and Hudson.

Maxwell, G. 1983 Recent aerial survey in Scotland. In: G. Maxwell (ed.) *The Impact of Aerial Reconnaissance in Archaeology*, 27–40. London: Council for British Archaeology.

Meadow, R. 1975 Mammal remains from Hajji Firuz: a study in methodology. In: A.T. Classon (ed.) *Archaeozoological Studies*, 265–83. Oxford: North Holland.

Megaw, J.V.S. and Simpson, D.D.A. 1979 *An Introduction to British Prehistory*. Leicester: Leicester University Press.

Meillassoux, C. 1972 From reproduction to production. *Economy and Society* 1, 93–105.

Mellars, P.A. 1976 Fire ecology, animal populations and man: a study of some ecological relationships in prehistory. *Proceedings of the Prehistoric Society* 42, 15–45.

Mercer, R.J. 1980 *Hambledon Hill: A Neolithic Landscape*. Edinburgh: Edinburgh University Press.

Mercer, R.J. 1981a Introduction. In: R.J. Mercer (ed.) *Farming Practice in British Prehistory*, ix–xxvi. Edinburgh: Edinburgh University Press.

Mercer, R.J. 1981b The excavation of a late Neolithic henge-type enclosure at Balfarg, Fife, Scotland. *Proceedings of the Society of Antiquaries of Scotland* 111, 63–171.

Mercer, R.J. 1982 Hambledon Hill, 1982: Interim Report. Manuscript.

Mercer, R.J. 1988 Hambledon Hill, Dorset, England. In: C. Burgess, P. Topping, C. Mordant and M. Madison (eds) *Enclosures and Defences in the Neolithic of Western Europe*, 89–106. Oxford: British Archaeological Reports S403.

Metcalf, P. 1981 Meaning and materialism: the ritual economy of death. *Man* 16, 563–78.

Midgley, M.S. 1985 *The Origin and Function of the Earthen Long Barrows of Northern Europe*. Oxford: British Archaeological Reports S259.

Miket, R. 1976 The evidence for Neolithic activity in the Millfield Basin, Northumberland. In: C. Burgess and R. Miket (eds) *Settlement and Economy in the Second and Third Millennia BC*, 113–42. Oxford: British Archaeological Reports 33.

Miket, R. 1981 Pit alignments in the Milfield Basin, and the excavation of Ewart 1. *Proceedings of the Prehistoric Society* 47, 137–46.

Miller, D. 1982 Structures and strategies: an aspect of the relationship between social hierarchy and cultural change. In: I. Hodder (ed.) *Symbolic and Structural Archaeology*, 89–98. Cambridge: Cambridge University Press.

Miller, D. 1985 *Artefacts as Categories: A Study of Ceramic Variability in Central India*. Cambridge: Cambridge University Press.

Miller, D. 1987 *Material Culture and Mass Consumption*. Oxford: Blackwell.

Mitchell, G.F. 1986 *Reading the Irish Landscape*. Dublin: Country House.

Mizoguchi, K. 1993 Time in the reproduction of mortuary practices. *World Archaeology* 25, 223–35.

Mizoguchi, K. 1995 The 'materiality' of Wessex Beakers. *Scottish Archaeological Review* 9, 175–86.

Modderman, P.J.R. 1988 The Linear Pottery Culture: diversity in uniformity. *Berichten Van de Rijksdienst voor het Oudheidkundig Bodermonderzoek* 38, 63–139.

Moffett, L., Robinson, M.A. and Straker, V. 1989 Cereals, fruit and nuts: charred plant remains from Neolithic sites in England and Wales and the Neolithic economy. In: A. Milles, D. Williams and N. Gardner (eds) *The Beginnings of Agriculture*, 243–61. Oxford: British Archaeological Reports S496.

Moir, G. 1981 Some archaeological and astronomical objections to scientific astronomy in British prehistory. In: C. Ruggles and A. Whittle (eds) *Astronomy and Society in Britain during the Period 4000–1000 B.C.*, 221–41. Oxford: British Archaeological Reports.

Moore, H.L. 1981 Bone refuse – possibilities for the future. In: A. Sheridan and G. Bailey (eds) *Economic Archaeology*, 87–94. Oxford: British Archaeological Reports 96.

Moore, H.L. 1982 The interpretation of spatial patterning in settlement residues. In: I. Hodder (ed.) *Symbolic and Structural Archaeology*, 74–9. Cambridge: Cambridge University Press.

Moore, H.L. 1986 *Space, Text and Gender*. Cambridge: Cambridge University Press.

Moore, H.L. 1990 Paul Ricoeur: action, meaning and text. In: C. Tilley (ed.) *Reading Material Culture*, 85–120. Oxford: Blackwell.

Moore, J. 1997 The infernal cycle of fire ecology. In: P. Topping (ed.) *Neolithic Landscapes*, 33–40. Oxford: Oxbow.

Moorey, P.R.S. 1982 A Neolithic ring ditch and Iron Age enclosure at Newnham Murren, near Wallingford. In: H.J. Case and A.W.R. Whittle (eds) *Settlement Patterns in the Oxford Region*, 55–9. London: Council for British Archaeology.

Morgan, F. de M. 1959 The excavation of a long barrow at Nutbane, Hants. *Proceedings of the Prehistoric Society* 25, 15–51.

Morphy, H. 1995 Landscape and the reproduction of the ancestral past. In: E. Hirsch and M. O'Hanlon (eds) *The Anthropology of Landscape*, 184–209. Oxford: Oxford University Press.

Morris, M. 1974 Megalithic exegesis: megalithic monuments as sources of socio-cultural meanings. *Irish Archaeological Research Forum* 1, 10–28.

Mortimer, J.R. 1905 *Forty Years' Researches in British and Saxon Burial Mounds of East Yorkshire*. London: A. Brown and Sons.

Munn, N. 1986 *The Fame of Gawa*. Cambridge: Cambridge University Press.

Murphy, P. 1990 *The Stumble, Essex (Blackwater Site 28): Carbonised Neolithic Plant Remains*. London: Ancient Monuments Laboratory Report 126/90.

Needham, S. 1988 Selective deposition in the British Early Bronze Age. *World Archaeology* 20, 229–48.

Newbiggin, N. 1937 The Neolithic pottery of Yorkshire. *Proceedings of the Prehistoric Society* 3, 189–216.

Nielsen, P.O. 1986 The beginning of the Neolithic – assimilation or complex change? *Journal of Danish Archaeology* 5, 240–3.

Nietzsche, F. 1969 *On the Genealogy of Morals* and *Ecce Homo*. New York: Vintage.

Norris, C. 1982 *Deconstruction: Theory and Practice*. London: Methuen.

Norris, C. 1987 *Derrida*. London: Fontana.

O'Kelly, C. 1969 Bryn Celli Ddu, Anglesey: a reinterpretation. *Archaeologia Cambrensis* 118, 17–48.

O'Kelly, M. and Shell, C. 1979 Stone objects and a bronze axe from Newgrange, Co. Meath. In: M. Ryan (ed.) *The Origins of Metallurgy in Atlantic Europe*, 127–44. Dublin: The Stationery Office.

Olsen, B. 1990 Roland Barthes: from sign to text. In: C. Tilley (ed.) *Reading Material Culture*, 163–205. Oxford: Blackwell.

O'Neil, H.E. 1966 Sale's Lot long barrow, Withington, Glos. *Transactions of the Bristol and Gloucester Archaeological Society* 85, 5–35.

Oswald, A. 1969 Excavations at Barford, Warwickshire. *Transactions of the Birmingham and Warwickshire Archaeological Society* 83, 3–54.

Pader, E.J. 1982 *Symbolism, Social Relations, and the Interpretation of Mortuary Remains*. Oxford: British Archaeological Reports, British series 130.

Palmer, R. 1976 Interrupted ditch enclosures in Britain. *Proceedings of the Prehistoric Society* 42, 161–86.

Panoff, S. 1970 Food and faeces: a Melanesian rite. *Man* 5, 237–52.

Parker Pearson, M. 1982 Mortuary practices, society and ideology: an ethnoarchaeological study. In: I.R. Hodder (ed.) *Symbolic and Structural Archaeology*, 99–113. Cambridge: Cambridge University Press.

Parker Pearson, M. 1990 The production and distribution of Bronze Age pottery in south-west Britain. *Cornish Archaeology* 29, 5–32.

Parker Pearson, M. 1993 *Bronze Age Britain*. London: Batsford.

Parker Pearson, M. 1995 Southwestern Bronze Age pottery. In: I.A. Kinnes and G. Varndell (eds) *'Unbaked Urns of Rudely Shape'*, 89–100. Oxford: Oxbow.

Parker Pearson, M. and Ramilsonina 1998 Stonehenge for the ancestors: the stones pass on the message. *Antiquity* 72, 308–26.

Parrington, M. 1978 *The Excavation of an Iron Age Settlement, Bronze Age Ring-Ditches and Roman Features at Ashville Trading Estate, Abingdon*. London: Council for British Archaeology.

Passmore, A.D 1923 Chambered long barrow in West Woods. *Wiltshire Archaeological Magazine* 42, 366–7.

Passmore, A.D. 1938 Gatcombe Lodge. *Proceedings of the Prehistoric Society* 4, 124.

Passmore, A.D. n.d. *Field Diary and Scrapbook*. Devizes Museum.

Patrik, L. 1985 Is there an archaeological record? In: M.B. Schiffer (ed.) *Advances in Archaeological Method and Theory*, Vol. 3, 27–62. London: Academic Press.

Pauketat, T.R. 1992 The reign and ruin of the lords of Cahokia: a dialectic of dominance. In: A.W. Barker and T.R. Pauketat (eds) *Lords of the Southeast: Social Inequality and the Native Elites of Southeastern North America*, 31–52. Washington, DC: Archaeological Papers of the American Anthropological Association 3.

Payne, S. 1975 Faunal changes at Franchthi Cave from 20,000 to 3,000 BC. In: A.T. Clason (ed.) *Archaeozoological Studies*, 120–31. Amsterdam: North Holland.

Peacock, D.P.S. 1969 Neolithic pottery production in Cornwall. *Antiquity* 43, 145–9.

Peers, C.R. and Smith, R.A. 1921 Wayland's Smithy, Berkshire. *Antiquaries Journal* 1, 183–98.

Pennington, W. 1974 *The History of British Vegetation*. London: Hodder and Stoughton.

Penny, A. and Wood, J. 1973 The Dorset Cursus complex – a Neolithic astronomical observatory? *Archaeological Journal* 130, 44–76.

Phillips, C.W. 1935 The excavation of Giant's Hill long barrow, Skendleby. *Archaeologia* 85, 37–106.

Piggott, S. 1929 Neolithic pottery and other remains from Pangbourne, Berks. and Caversham, Oxon. *Proceedings of the Prehistoric Society of East Anglia* 6, 30–9.

Piggott, S. 1931 The Neolithic pottery of the British Isles. *Archaeological Journal* 88, 67–158.

Piggott, S. 1936 Handley Hill, Dorset – a Neolithic bowl and the date of the entrenchment. *Proceedings of the Prehistoric Society* 2, 229–30.

Piggott, S. 1937 The excavation of a long barrow in Holdenhurst parish, near Christchurch, Hants. *Proceedings of the Prehistoric Society* 3, 1–14.

Piggott, S. 1938. The Early Bronze Age in Wessex. *Proceedings of the Prehistoric Society* 4, 52–106.

Piggott, S. 1940 Timber circles: a re-examination. *Archaeological Journal* 96, 193–222.

Piggott, S. 1948 The excavations at Cairnpapple Hill, West Lothian, 1947–8. *Proceedings of the Society of Antiquaries of Scotland* 10, 68–123.

Piggott, S. 1952 The Neolithic camp on Whitesheet Hill, Kilmington Parish. *Wiltshire Archaeological Magazine* 54, 404–9.

Piggott, S. 1954 *The Neolithic Cultures of the British Isles.* Cambridge: Cambridge University Press.

Piggott, S. 1958 Native economies and the Roman occupation of North Britain. In: I. Richmond (ed.) *Roman and Native in North Britain*, 1–27. London: Nelson.

Piggott, S. 1962 *The West Kennet Long Barrow.* London: HMSO.

Piggott, S. 1963 Abercromby and after: the Beaker cultures of Britain re-examined. In: I. Foster and L. Alcock (eds) *Culture and Environment*, 53–91. London: Routledge and Kegan Paul.

Piggott, S. 1966 'Unchambered' long barrows in Neolithic Britain. *Palaeohistoria* 12, 381–93.

Piggott, S. 1973 The Dalladies long barrow, N.E. Scotland. *Antiquity* 47, 32–6.

Piggott, S. and Piggott, C.M. 1944 The excavation of barrows on Crichel and Launceston Downs. *Archaeologia* 90, 47–80.

Piggott, S. and Simpson, D.D.A. 1971 Excavation of a stone circle at Croft Moraig, Perthshire, Scotland. *Proceedings of the Prehistoric Society* 37, 1–15.

Pitt Rivers, A.L.F. 1898 *Excavations in Cranborne Chase near Rushmore, on the Borders of Dorset and Wilts.*, Vol. IV. Privately printed.

Pitts, M. 1982 On the road to Stonehenge: report on the investigations beside the A344. *Proceedings of the Prehistoric Society* 48, 75–132.

Pitts, M. 1996 The stone axe in Neolithic Britain. *Proceedings of the Prehistoric Society* 62, 311–72.

Pitts, M. and Jacobi, R. 1979 Some aspects of change in flaked stone industries of the Mesolithic and Neolithic in Southern Britain. *Journal of Archaeological Science* 6, 163–77.

Pitts, M. and Whittle, A.W.R. 1992 The development and date of Avebury. *Proceedings of the Prehistoric Society* 58, 203–12.

Pollard, J. 1992 The Sanctuary, Overton Hill, Wiltshire: a reassessment. *Proceedings of the Prehistoric Society* 58, 213–26.

Pollard, J. 1995 Inscribing space: formal deposition at the later Neolithic monument of Woodhenge, Wiltshire. *Proceedings of the Prehistoric Society* 61, 137–56.

Powell, T.G.E. 1973 Excavation of the chambered cairn at Dyffryn Ardudwy, Merioneth, Wales. *Archaeologia* 54, 44–6.

Powell, T.G.E., Corcoran, J.W.X.P., Lynch, F. and Scott, J. 1969 *Megalithic Enquiries in the West of Britain.* Liverpool: Liverpool University Press.

Pred, A. 1977 The choreography of existence: comments on Hagerstrand's Time-Geography and its usefulness. *Economic Geography* 53, 207–21.

Price, T.D. 1996 The first farmers of southern Scandinavia. In: D. Harris (ed.) *The Origins and Spread of Agriculture and Pastoralism in Eurasia*, 346–62. London: University College London Press.

Proudfoot, E. 1965 Bishop's Cannings: Roughridge Hill. *Wiltshire Archaeological Magazine* 60, 132–3.

Pryor, F. 1978 *Excavation at Fengate, Peterborough, England: The Second Report.* Toronto: Royal Ontario Museum.

Pryor, F. 1988 Etton, near Maxey, Cambridgeshire: a causewayed enclosure on the fen-edge. In: C. Burgess, P. Topping, C. Mordant and M. Maddison (eds) *Enclosures and Defences in the Neolithic of Western Europe*, 107–26. Oxford: British Archaeological Reports S403.

Pryor, F., French, C. and Taylor, M. 1985 An interim report on excavations at Etton, Maxey, Cambridgeshire. *Antiquaries Journal* 65, 275–311.

Radley, J. 1967 The York hoard of flint tools. *Yorkshire Archaeological Journal* 42, 131–2.

Randsborg, K. 1980 *The Viking Age in Denmark.* London: Duckworth.

Ray, K.W. 1987 Material metaphor, social interaction and historical interactions: exploring patterns of association and symbolism in the Igbo Ukwu corpus. In: I. Hodder (ed.) *The Archaeology of Contextual Meanings*, 66–77. Cambridge: Cambridge University Press.

Ray, K.W. 1988 Context, Meaning and Metaphor in an Historical Archaeology: Igbo Ukwu, Eastern Nigeria, PhD thesis, University of Cambridge.

Redman, C. 1977 Man, domestication and culture in south-west Asia. In C.A. Reed (ed.) *Origins of Agriculture*, 523–41. The Hague: Mouton.

Rees, S. 1979 *Agricultural Implements in Prehistoric and Roman Britain.* Oxford: British Archaeological Reports 69.

Relph, E. 1976 *Place and Placelessness.* London: Pion.

Renfrew, A.C. 1972 *The Emergence of Civilisation: The Cyclades and the Aegean in the Third Millennium B.C.* London: Methuen.

Renfrew, A.C. 1973a Monuments, mobilisation and social organisation in Neolithic Wessex. In: A.C. Renfrew (ed.) *The Explanation of Culture Change*, 539–58. London: Duckworth.

Renfrew, A.C. 1973b *Before Civilization: The Radiocarbon Revolution and Prehistoric Europe*. Harmondsworth: Penguin.

Renfrew, A.C. 1976 Megaliths, territories and populations. In: S. de Laet (ed.) *Acculturation and Continuity in Atlantic Europe*, 98–220. Bruges: de Tempel.

Renfrew, A.C. 1979 *Investigations in Orkney*. London: Society of Antiquaries.

Reugg, M. 1979 Metaphor and metonymy: the logic of structuralist rhetoric. *Glyph* 6, 141–57.

Reynolds, P. 1974 Experimental Iron Age pits: an interim report. *Proceedings of the Prehistoric Society* 40, 118–31.

Reynolds, P. 1979 *Iron Age Farm*. London: British Museum.

Reynolds, P. 1981 Deadstock and livestock. In: R.J. Mercer (ed.) *Farming Practice in British Prehistory*, 97–124. Edinburgh: Edinburgh University Press.

Rice, P. 1987 *Pottery Analysis: A Sourcebook*. Chicago: Chicago University Press.

Richards, C.C. 1988 Altered images: a re-examination of Neolithic mortuary practices in Orkney. In: J.C. Barrett and I.A. Kinnes (eds) *The Archaeology of Context in the Neolithic and Bronze Age: Recent Trends*, 42–56. Sheffield: Department of Archaeology and Prehistory.

Richards, C.C. 1992 Doorways into another world: The Orkney–Cromarty chambered tombs. In A. Sheridan and N. Sharples (eds) *Vessels for the Ancestors: Essays on the Neolithic of Britain and Ireland*, 62–76. Edinburgh: Edinburgh University Press.

Richards, C.C. 1996a Life is not that simple: architecture and cosmology in the Balinese house. In: T.C. Darvill and J.S. Thomas (eds) *Neolithic Houses in Northwest Europe and Beyond*, 171–84. Oxford: Oxbow.

Richards, C.C. 1996b Henges and water: towards an elemental understanding of monumentality and landscape in late Neolithic Britain. *Journal of Material Culture* 1, 313–36.

Richards, C.C. and Thomas, J.S. 1984 Ritual activity and structured deposition in later Neolithic Wessex. In: R. Bradley and J. Gardiner (eds) *Neolithic Studies*, 189–218. Oxford: British Archaeological Reports 133.

Richards, J. 1982 The Stonehenge environs project: the story so far. *Scottish Archaeological Review* 1, 98–104.

Richards, J. 1984 The development of the Neolithic landscape in the environs of Stonehenge. In: R.J. Bradley and J. Gardiner (eds) *Neolithic Studies*, 177–88. Oxford: British Archaeological Reports 133.

Richards, J. 1985 Scouring the surface: approaches to the ploughzone in the Stonehenge environs. *Archaeological Review from Cambridge* 4, 27–42.

Richards, J. 1990 *The Stonehenge Environs Project*. London: English Heritage.

Richards, J. and Whitby, M. 1997 The engineering of Stonehenge. In: B. Cunliffe and C. Renfrew (eds) *Science and Stonehenge*, 231–56. Oxford: Oxford University Press.

Richards, M. 1996 'First farmers' with no taste for grain. *British Archaeology* 12, 6.

Richmond, A. 1996 *Preferred Economies: An Interdisciplinary Study Focusing on the Nature of the Subsistence Base Throughout Mainland Britain During Prehistory*, PhD thesis, University of Reading.

Ricoeur, P. 1978 Metaphor. *Critical Enquiry* 5, 1–12.

Ricoeur, P. 1981 *Hermeneutics and the Human Sciences*. Cambridge: Cambridge University Press.

Ricoeur, P. 1984 *The Reality of the Historical Past*. Milwaukee: Marquette University Press.

Riggins, S. (ed.) 1994 *The Socialness of Things*. The Hague: Mouton de Gruyter.

Ritchie, A. 1983 Excavation of a Neolithic farmstead at Knap of Howar, Papa Westray, Orkney. *Proceedings of the Society of Antiquaries of Scotland* 113, 40–121.

Robertson-Mackay, M.E. 1980 A 'head and hoofs' burial beneath a round barrow. *Proceedings of the Prehistoric Society* 46, 123–76.

Robertson-Mackay, R. 1962 The excavation of the causewayed camp at Staines, *Middlesex Archaeological Newsletter* 7, 131–4.

Robertson-Mackay, R. 1987 The Neolithic causewayed enclosure at Staines, Surrey; excavations 1961–63. *Proceedings of the Prehistoric Society* 53, 23–128.

Robinson, M. and Wilson, R. 1987 A survey of environmental archaeology in the south Midlands. In: H. Keeley (ed.) *Environmental Archaeology: A Regional Review*, Vol. 2, 16–100. London: HBMC.

Rogerson, A. 1995 A late Neolithic, Saxon and Medieval site at Middle Harling, Norfolk. *East Anglian Archaeology* 74.

Rolleston, G. 1876 On the people of the long barrow period. *Journal of the Anthropological Institute* 5, 120–75.

Rorty, R. 1989 *Contingency, Irony and Solidarity*. Cambridge: Cambridge University Press.

Roth, M. 1988 Narrative explanations: the case of history. *History and Theory* 27, 1–13.

Rowlands, M.J. 1976 *The Production and Distribution of Metalwork in the Middle Bronze Age in Southern Britain*. Oxford: British Archaeological Reports 32.

Rowlett, R.M. and Robbins, M.C. 1982 Estimating original assemblage content to adjust for post-depositional vertical artefact movement. *World Archaeology* 14, 73–83.

Rowley-Conwy, P. 1981 Slash and burn in the temperate European Neolithic. In: R.J.Mercer (ed.) *Farming Practice in British Prehistory*, 85–96. Edinburgh: Edinburgh University Press.

Rowley-Conwy, P. 1982 Forest grazing and clearance in temperate Europe with special reference to Denmark: an archaeological view. In: M. Bell and S. Limbrey (eds) *Archaeological Aspects of Woodland Ecology*, 199–215. Oxford: British Archaeological Reports S146.

Rowley-Conwy, P. 1983 Sedentary hunters: the Ertebølle example. In: G. Bailey (ed.) *Hunter-Gatherer Economy in Prehistory*, 111–26. Cambridge: Cambridge University Press.

Ruggles, C. 1997 Astronomy and Stonehenge. In: B. Cunliffe and C. Renfrew (eds) *Science and Stonehenge*, 203–29. Oxford: Oxford University Press.

Russel, A.D. 1990 Two Beaker burials from Chilbolton, Hampshire. *Proceedings of the Prehistoric Society* 56, 153–72.

Sackett, J.R. 1973 Style, function and artefact variability in palaeolithic assemblages. In: A.C. Renfrew (ed.) *The Explanation of Culture Change*, 317–25. London: Duckworth.

Sackett, J.R. 1986 Isochrestism and style: a clarification. *Journal of Anthropological Archaeology* 5, 266–77.

Sahlins, M. 1974 *Stone Age Economics*. London: Tavistock.

St Joseph, J.K. 1976 Air reconnaissance, recent results 40. *Antiquity* 50, 55–7.

Saville, A. 1982 Carrying cores to Gloucestershire. *Lithics* 3, 25–8.

Saville, A. 1983 Excavations at Condicote henge monument, Gloucestershire, 1977. *Transactions of the Bristol and Gloucester Archaeological Society* 101, 21–47.

Saville, A. 1984 Preliminary report on the excavation of a Cotswold–Severn tomb at Hazleton, Gloucestershire. *Antiquaries Journal* 64, 10–24.

Saville, A. 1990 *Hazleton North: The Excavation of a Neolithic Long Cairn of the Cotswold–Severn Group*. London: English Heritage.

Saville, A., Gowlett, J. and Hedges, R.E.M. 1987 Radiocarbon dates for the tomb at Hazleton (Glos.): a chronology for Neolithic collective burial. *Antiquity* 64, 10–24.

Savory, H.N. 1956 The excavation of Pipton long cairn, Brecknockshire. *Archaeologia Cambrensis* 105, 7–48.

Saxe, A.A. 1970 Social Dimensions of Mortuary Practice, Unpublished PhD thesis, University of Michigan. Ann Arbor: University Microfilms.

Scaife, R.G. 1987 A review of later Quaternary microfossil and macrofossil research in southern England; with special reference to environmental archaeology. In: H. Keeley (ed.) *Environmental Archaeology: A Regional Review*, 125–203. London: HBMC.

Schiffer, M.B. 1972 Archaeological context and systemic context. *American Antiquity* 37, 156–65.

Schiffer, M.B. 1976 *Behavioral Archaeology*. London: Academic Press.

Schiffer, M.B. 1987 *Formation Processes of the Archaeological Record*. Albuquerque: University of New Mexico Press.

Schuchhardt, C. 1919 *Alteuropa*. Berlin.

Scourse, J.D. 1997 Transport of the Stonehenge Bluestones: testing the glacial hypothesis. In: B. Cunliffe and C. Renfrew (eds) *Science and Stonehenge*, 271–314. Oxford: Oxford University Press.

Serjeantson, D. 1995 Animal bones. In: R.M.J. Cleal, K.E. Walker and R. Montague, *Stonehenge in its Landscape: Twentieth-Century Excavations*, 437–51. London: English Heritage.

Serjeantson, D. 1996 The animal bones. In: S. Needham and T. Spence (eds) *Refuse and Disposal at Area 16 East, Runnymede*, 194–223. London: British Museum.

Servet, J.M. 1982 Primitive order and archaic trade, part II. *Economy and Society* 11, 22–59.

Shanks, M. and Tilley, C.Y. 1982 Ideology, symbolic power and ritual communication: a reinterpretation of Neolithic mortuary practices. In: I. Hodder (ed.) *Symbolic and Structural Archaeology*, 129–54. Cambridge: Cambridge University Press.

Shanks, M. and Tilley, C.Y. 1987a *Social Theory and Archaeology*. London: Polity.

Shanks, M. and Tilley, C.Y. 1987b *Re-Constructing Archaeology*. Cambridge: Cambridge University Press.

Sharples, N. 1991 *Maiden Castle: Excavations and Field Survey 1985–6*. London, Batsford/English Heritage.

Shee Twohig, E. 1981 *The Megalithic Art of Western Europe*. Oxford: Clarendon Press.

Shennan, S.J. 1976 The appearance of the Bell Beaker culture assemblage in central Europe. In: R.J. Mercer (ed.) *Beakers in Britain and Europe*, 51–70. Oxford: British Archaeological Reports S26.

Shennan, S.J. 1977 Bell Beakers and their Context in Central Europe: A New Approach, PhD thesis, Cambridge University.

Shennan, S.J. 1981 Settlement history in east Hampshire. In: S.J. Shennan and R.T. Schadla-Hall (eds) *The Archaeology of Hampshire*, 106–21. Winchester: Hampshire Field Club and Archaeological Society.

Shennan, S.J. 1982 Ideology, change and the European Early Bronze Age. In: I. Hodder (ed.) *Symbolic and Structural Archaeology*, 155–61. Cambridge: Cambridge University Press.

Shennan, S.J. 1983 Monuments: an example of archaeologists' approach to the massively material. *Royal Anthropological Institute Newsletter* 59, 9–11.

Shennan, S.J. 1985 *Experiments in the Collection and Analysis of Archaeological Survey Data: The East Hampshire Survey*. Sheffield: Department of Archaeology and Prehistory.

Shennan, S.J. 1986 Interaction and change in third millennium BC western and central Europe. In: C. Renfrew and J.F. Cherry (eds) *Peer Polity Interaraction and Sociopolitical Change*, 137–48. Cambridge: Cambridge University Press.

Shennan, S.J. Healy, F.M. and Smith, I.F. 1985 The excavation of a ring-ditch at Tye Field, Lawford, Essex. *Archaeological Journal* 142, 150–215.

Shepherd, I.A.G. 1986 *Powerful Pots: Beakers in North-East Prehistory*. Aberdeen: Anthropological Museum.

Sheridan, A. 1986 Megaliths and megalomania: an account, and interpretation, of the development of passage graves in Ireland. *Journal of Irish Archaeology* 3, 17–30.

Sheridan, A. 1995 Irish Neolithic pottery: the story in 1995. In: I.A. Kinnes and G. Varndell (eds) '*Unbaked Urns of Rudely Shape*', 3–21. Oxford: Oxbow.

Sherratt, A.G. 1980 Water, soil and seasonality in early cereal cultivation. *World Archaeology* 11, 313–30.

Sherratt, A.G. 1981 Plough and pastoralism: aspects of the secondary products revolution. In: I. Hodder, N. Hammond and G. Isaac (eds) *Pattern of the Past*, 261–306. Cambridge: Cambridge University Press.

Sherratt, A.G. 1989 V. Gordon Childe: archaeology and intellectual history. *Past and Present* 125, 151–85.

Sherratt, A.G. 1990 The genesis of megaliths: monumentality, ethnicity and social complexity in Neolithic north-west Europe. *World Archaeology* 22 (2): 147–67.

Shields, R. 1994 The logic of the mall. In: S. Riggins (ed.) *The Socialness of Things*, 203–30. The Hague: Mouton de Gruyter.

Shotton, F.W. 1978 Archaeological inferences from the study of alluvium in the lower Severn-Avon valleys. In: S. Limbrey and J.G. Evans (eds) *The Effect of Man on the Landscape – the Lowland Zone*, 27–31. London: Council for British Archaeology.

Siiriänen, A. 1977 Pieces in vertical movement: a model for rock-shelter archaeology. *Proceedings of the Prehistoric Society* 43, 349–54.

Simpson, D.D.A. 1996a The Ballygalley houses, Co. Antrim, Ireland. In: T.C. Darvill and J.S. Thomas (eds) *Neolithic Houses in Northwest Europe and Beyond*, 123–32. Oxford: Oxbow.

Simpson, D.D.A. 1996b 'Crown' antler maceheads and the later Neolithic. *Proceedings of the Prehistoric Society* 62, 293–309.

Simpson, W.G., Gurney, D.A., Neve, J. and Pryor, F.M.M. 1993 The Fenland Project number 7: excavations in Peterborough and the Lower Welland Valley 1960–1969. *East Anglian Archaeology* 61.

Slichter von Bath, B.H. 1963 *The Agrarian History of Western Europe*. London: Edward Arnold.

Smith, A.G., Grigson, C., Hillman, G. and Tooley, M. 1981 The Neolithic. In: I. Simmons and M. Tooley (eds) *The Environment in British prehistory*, 125–209. London: Duckworth.

Smith, G.E. 1929 *The Migrations of Early Culture*. Manchester: Manchester University Press.

Smith, I.F. 1956 The Decorative Art of Neolithic Ceramics in S.E. England and its Relations, PhD thesis, University of London.

Smith, I.F. 1965a *Windmill Hill and Avebury*. Oxford: Clarendon Press.

Smith, I.F. 1965b Excavation of a bell barrow, Avebury G.55. *Wiltshire Archaeological Magazine* 60, 24–46.

Smith, I.F. 1966 Windmill Hill and its implications. *Palaeohistoria* 12, 469–83.

Smith, I.F. 1968 Report on late Neolithic pits at Cam, Glos. *Transactions of the Bristol and Gloucester Archaeological Society* 87, 14–28.

Smith, I.F. 1971 Causewayed enclosures. In: D.D.A. Simpson (ed.) *Economy and Settlement in Neolithic and Early Bronze Age Britain and Europe*, 89–112. Leicester: Leicester University Press.

Smith, I.F. 1974 The Neolithic. In: A.C. Renfrew (ed.) *British Prehistory: A New Outline*, 100–36. London: Duckworth.

Smith, I.F. 1991 Round barrows Wilsford cum Lake G51–G54: excavations by Ernest Greenfield in 1958. *Wiltshire Archaeological Magazine* 84, 11–39.

Smith, I.F. and Simpson, D.D.A. 1964 Excavation of three Roman tombs and a prehistoric pit on Overton Down. *Wiltshire Archaeological Magazine* 59, 68–85.

Smith, I.F. and Simpson, D.D.A. 1966 Excavation of a round barrow on Overton Hill, north Wiltshire, England. *Proceedings of the Prehistoric Society* 32, 122–55.

Smith, R., Healy, F., Allen, M., Morris, E., Barnes, I. and Woodward, P.J. 1997 *Excavations along the Route of the Dorchester By-Pass, Dorset, 1986–8*. Salisbury: Wessex Archaeology.

Smith, R.A. 1910 The development of Neolithic pottery. *Archaeologia* 73, 340–52.

Smith, R.A. 1924 Neolithic bowls from the Thames at Mongewell. *Antiquaries Journal* 4, 127.

Smith, R.W. 1984 The ecology of Neolithic farming systems as exemplified by the Avebury region of Wiltshire. *Proceedings of the Prehistoric Society* 50, 99–120.

Smith, W.G. 1915 Maiden Bower, Bedfordshire. *Proceedings of the Society of Antiquaries of London* 27, 143–161.

Sofranoff, S. 1976 A Petrological Study of a Portion of the Ceramics of the So-Called 'Windmill Hill' and 'Peterborough' Traditions of the Wessex Area of Southern England, M.Phil. thesis, University of Southampton.

Starling, N.J. 1983 Neolithic settlement patterns in central Germany. *Oxford Journal of Archaeology* 2, 1–11.

Starling, N.J. 1985a Colonisation and succession: the earlier Neolithic of central Europe. *Proceedings of the Prehistoric Society* 51, 41–58.

Starling, N.J. 1985b Social change in the later Neolithic of central Europe. *Antiquity* 59, 30–8.

Steponaitis, V.P. 1984 Technological studies of prehistoric pottery from Alabama: physical properties and vessel function. In: S.E. van der Leeuw and A.C. Pritchard (eds) *The Many Dimensions of Pottery*, 81–127. Amsterdam: Amsterdam University Press.

Stewart, M. 1985 The excavation of a henge, stone circles and metal working area at Moncreiffe, Perthshire. *Proceedings of the Society of Antiquaries of Scotland* 115, 125–50.

Stone, J.F.S. 1935 Some discoveries at Ratfyn, Amesbury and their bearing on the date of Woodhenge. *Wiltshire Archaeological Magazine* 47, 55–67.

Stone, J.F.S. 1938 An Early Bronze Age grave in Fargo Plantation near Stonehenge. *Wiltshire Archaeological Magazine* 48, 357–70.

Stone, J.F.S. 1947 The Stonehenge cursus and its affinities. *Archaeological Journal* 104, 7–19.

Stone, J.F.S. 1949 Some Grooved Ware pottery from the Woodhenge area. *Proceedings of the Prehistoric Society* 15, 122–7.

Stone, J.F.S. 1958 *Wessex*. London: Thames and Hudson.

Stone, J.F.S. and Young, W.E.V. 1948 Two pits of Grooved Ware date near Woodhenge. *Wiltshire Archaeological Magazine* 52, 287–304.

Stone, J.F.S., Piggott, S. and Booth, A. St. J. 1954 Durrington Walls, Wiltshire: recent excavations at a ceremonial site of the early second millennium BC. *Antiquaries Journal* 34, 155–77.

Strathern, A. 1982 Witchcraft, greed, cannibalism and death. In: M. Bloch and J. Parry (eds) *Death and the Regeneration of Life*, 111–33. Cambridge: Cambridge University Press.

Strathern, M. 1988 *The Gender of the Gift*. Berkeley: University of California Press.

Stukeley, W. 1740 *Stonehenge: A Temple Restor'd to the British Druids*. London: Innys and Manby.

Symmonds, J. and Simpson, D.D.A. 1975 Introduction. In: R. Colt Hoare, *The Ancient History of Wiltshire*, 1–16. Wakefield: EP publications.

Tainter, J. 1978 Mortuary practices and the study of prehistoric social systems. In: M.B. Schiffer (ed.) *Advances in Archaeological Method and Theory*, Vol. 1, 105–41. New York: Academic Press.

Tambiah, S.J. 1969 Animals are good to think with and good to prohibit. *Ethnology* 8, 423–59.

Tarlow, S. 1992 Each slow dawn a drawing down of blinds. *Archaeological Review from Cambridge* 11, 125–40.

Tarlow, S. 1994 Scraping the bottom of the barrow: an agricultural metaphor in Neolithic/Bronze-Age European burial practice. *Journal of Theoretical Archaeology* 3/4, 123–44.

Taverner, N. 1987 Bannockburn: the pit and post alignments excavated in 1984 and 1985. *Scottish Development Department Central Excavation Unit and Ancient Monuments Laboratory Annual Report* 1987, 71–6.

Ten Hove, H.A. 1968 The Ulmus fall and the transition Antlanticum/Sub-Boreal in pollen diagrams. *Palaeogeography, Palaeoclimatology, Palaeoecology* 5, 359–69.

Thomas, J.S. 1984 A tale of two polities. In: R.J. Bradley and J.C. Gardiner (eds) *Neolithic Studies*, 161–76. Oxford: British Archaeological Reports 133.

Thomas, J.S. 1987 Relations of production and social change in the Neolithic of north-west Europe. *Man* 22, 405–30.

Thomas, J.S. 1988a Neolithic explanations revisited: the Mesolithic–Neolithic transition in Britain and south Scandinavia. *Proceedings of the Prehistoric Society* 54, 59–66.

Thomas, J.S. 1988b The social significance of Cotswold–Severn burial rites. *Man* 23, 540–59.

Thomas, J.S. 1990 Monuments from the inside: the case of the Irish megalithic tombs. *World Archaeology* 22, 168–78.

Thomas, J.S. 1993a Discourse, totalisation and 'the Neolithic'. In: C. Tilley (ed.) *Interpretative Archaeology*, 357–94. London: Berg.

Thomas, J.S. 1993b The politics of vision and the archaeologies of landscape. In: B. Bender (ed.) *Landscape: Politics and Perspectives*, 19–48. London: Berg.

Thomas, J.S. 1996a *Time, Culture and Identity: An Interpretive Archaeology*. London: Routledge.

Thomas, J.S. 1996b Neolithic houses in mainland Britain and Ireland – a sceptical view. In: T.C. Darvill and J.S. Thomas (eds) *Neolithic Houses in Northwest Europe and Beyond*, 1–12. Oxford: Oxbow.

Thomas, J.S. 1996c The cultural context of the first use of domesticates in continental central and north-west Europe. In: D. Harris (ed.) *The Origins and Spread of Agriculture and Pastoralism in Eurasia*, 310–22. London: University College London Press.

Thomas, J.S. 1997 The materiality of the Mesolithic–Neolithic transition in Britain. *Analecta Praehistorica Leidensia* 29, 57–64.

Thomas, J.S. 1998 Some problems with the notion of external symbolic storage, and the case of Neolithic material culture in Britain. In: C. Renfrew and C. Scarre (eds) *Cognition and Culture: The Archaeology of External Symbolic Storage*. Cambridge: MacDonald Institute.

Thomas, J.S. 1999 An economy of substances in earlier Neolithic Britain. In: J. Robb (ed.) *Material Symbols: Culture and Economy in Prehistory*. Carbondale: Southern Illinois University Press.

Thomas, J.S. forthcoming *Prehistoric Monuments in South-West Scotland: Excavations at the Pict's Knowe, Holywood and Holm*. Oxford: Oxbow.

Thomas, J.S. and Tilley, C.Y. 1993 The axe and the torso: symbolic structures in Neolithic Brittany. In: C. Tilley (ed.) *Interpretative Archaeology*, 225–326. London: Berg.

Thomas, J.S. and Whittle, A.W.R. 1986 Anatomy of a tomb: West Kennet revisited. *Oxford Journal of Archaeology* 5, 129–56.

Thomas, K. 1982 Neolithic enclosures and woodland habitats on the south Downs in Sussex, England. In: M. Bell and S. Limbrey (eds) *Archaeological Aspects of Woodland Ecology*, 147–70. Oxford: British Archaeological Reports S146.

Thomas, N. 1955 Excavations at Vicarage Field, Stanton Harcourt, 1951. *Oxoniensia* 20, 1–28.

Thomas, N. 1956 A Neolithic pit on Waden Hill. *Wiltshire Archaeological Magazine* 56, 167–71.

Thomas, N. 1964 The Neolithic causewayed camp at Robin Hood's Ball, Shrewton. *Wiltshire Archaeological Magazine* 59, 1–25.

Thomas, R. and Wallis, J. 1982 Recent work on Neolithic and Early Bronze Age sites in the Abingdon area. *Council for British Archaeology Group 9 Newsletter* 12, 184–91.

Thorley, A. 1981 Pollen analytical evidence relating to the vegetational history of the chalk. *Journal of Biogeography* 8, 93–108.

Thorpe, I.J. 1983 Prehistoric British astronomy – towards a social context. *Archaeological Review from Cambridge* 2, 2–10.

Thorpe, I.J. 1984 Ritual, power and ideology: a reconsideration of earlier Neolithic rituals in Wessex. In: R.J. Bradley and J. Gardiner (eds) *Neolithic Studies*, 41–60. Oxford: British Archaeological Reports 133.

Thorpe, I.J. and Richards, C.C. 1984 The decline of ritual authority and the introduction of Beakers into Britain. In: R.J. Bradley and J. Gardiner (eds) *Neolithic Studies*, 67–84. Oxford: British Archaeological Reports 133.

Thorpe, R.S., Williams-Thorpe, O., Jenkins, D.J. and Watson, J.S. 1991 The geological sources and transport of the Bluestones of Stonehenge, Wiltshire, UK. *Proceedings of the Prehistoric Society* 57 (2), 103–57.

Thrift, N. 1991 For a new regional geography 2. *Progress in Human Geography* 15, 456–65.

Thurnam, J. 1857 On a cromlech-tumulus called Lugbury, near Littleton Drew. *Wiltshire Archaeological Magazine* 6, 164–73.

Thurnam, J. 1860 Barrows of the north Wiltshire downs. *Wiltshire Archaeological Magazine* 6, 317–36.

Thurnam, J. 1869 On ancient British barrows, especially those of Wiltshire and the adjoining counties (part I, long barrows). *Archaeologia* 42, 161–244.

Tilley, C.Y. 1984 Ideology and the legitimation of power in the Middle Neolithic of southern Sweden. In: D. Miller and C. Tilley (eds) *Ideology, Power and Prehistory*, 111–46. Cambridge: Cambridge University Press.

Tilley, C.Y. 1989 Interpreting material culture. In: I. Hodder (ed.) *The Meanings of Things*, 185–94. London: Unwin Hyman.

Tilley, C.Y. 1993 Introduction: Interpretation and a poetics of the past. In: C.Y. Tilley (ed.) *Interpretative Archaeology*, 1–27. London: Berg.

Tilley, C.Y. 1994 *A Phenomenology of Landscape: Places, Paths and Monuments*. London: Berg.

Tinsley, H. and Grigson, C. 1981 The Bronze Age. In: I. Simmons and M. Tooley (eds) *The Environment in British Prehistory*, 210–49. London: Duckworth.

Tipping, R. 1994 The form and fate of Scotland's woodlands. *Proceedings of the Society of Antiquaries of Scotland* 124, 1–54.

Topping, P. 1982 Excavation at the cursus at Scorton, north Yorkshire 1978. *Yorkshire Archaeological Journal* 54, 7–21.

Trigger, B.G. 1980 *Gordon Childe: Revolutions in Archaeology*. London: Thames and Hudson.

Trigger, B.G. 1989 *A History of Archaeological Thought*. Cambridge: Cambridge University Press.

Tuan, Yi-Fu 1974 Space and place: humanistic perspective. *Progress in Geography* 6, 211–52.

Tuan, Yi-Fu 1978 Space, time, place: a humanistic frame. In: T. Carlstein, D. Parkes and N. Thrift (eds) *Making Sense of Time: Timing Space and Spacing Time*, Vol. 1, 7–16. London: Edward Arnold.

Tuckwell, A. 1975 Patterns of burial orientation in the round barrows of East Yorkshire. *Bulletin of the Institute of Archaeology, University of London* 12, 95–123.

Turner, V. 1967 *The Forest of Symbols*. Ithaca, NY: Cornell University Press.

Turner, V. 1969 *The Ritual Process*. Harmondsworth: Penguin.

Tyler, J.M. 1921 *The New Stone Age in Northern Europe*. London: Bell and Sons.

Ucko, P., Hunter, M., Clark, A.J. and David, A. 1991 *Avebury Reconsidered: From the 1660s to the 1990s*. London: Unwin Hyman.

van der Leeuw, S.E. 1976 Neolithic Beakers from the Netherlands: the potter's point of view. In: J.N. Lanting and J.D. van der Waals (eds) *Glockenbecher Symposion Oberreid 1974*, 81–139. Bossum/Haarlem: Fibula-Van Dishoek.

Van Gennep, A. 1960 *The Rites of Passage*. London: Routledge and Kegan Paul.

Vatcher, F. de M. 1961 The excavation of the long mortuary enclosure on Normanton Down, Wilts. *Proceedings of the Prehistoric Society* 27, 160–73.

Vatcher, F. de M. 1969 Two incised chalk plaques from Stonehenge bottom. *Antiquity* 43, 310–11.

Veldman, M. 1994 *Fantasy, the Bomb, and the Greening of Britain: Romantic Protest, 1945–80*. Cambridge: Cambridge University Press.

Vitelli, K.D. 1995 Pots, potters and the shaping of Greek Neolithic society. In: W.K. Barnett and J.W. Hoopes (eds) *The Emergence of Pottery: Technology and Innovation in Ancient Societies*, 55–63. Washington, DC: Smithsonian.

Vulliamy, C.E. 1921 The excavation of a megalithic tomb in Breconshire. *Archaeologia Cambrensis* 76, 300–5.

Vyner, B. 1984 The excavation of a Neolithic cairn at Street House, Loftus, Cleveland. *Proceedings of the Prehistoric Society* 50, 151–96.

Wainwright, G.J. 1969 A review of henge monuments in the light of recent research. *Proceedings of the Prehistoric Society* 35, 112–33.

Wainwright, G.J. 1973 The excavation of prehistoric and Romano-British settlements at Eaton Heath, Norwich. *Archaeological Journal* 53, 1–43.

Wainwright, G.J. 1979a *Mount Pleasant, Dorset: excavations 1970–71*. London: Society of Antiquaries.

Wainwright, G.J. 1979b *Gussage All Saints – An Iron Age Settlement in Dorset*. London: HMSO.

Wainwright, G.J. and Longworth, I. 1971 *Durrington Walls: Excavations 1966–1968*. London: Society of Antiquaries.

Wainwright, G.J., Donaldson, P., Longworth, I. and Swan, V. 1971 The excavation of Prehistoric and Romano-British settlements near Durrington Walls, Wiltshire, 1970. *Wiltshire Archaeological Magazine* 66, 76–128.

Wallerstein, I. 1974 *The Modern World-System*, Vol. 1. London: Academic Press.

Wansleben, M. and Verhart, L.B.M. 1990 Meuse valley project: the transition from the Mesolithic to the Neolithic in the Dutch Meuse valley. In: P.M. Vermeersch and P. van Peer (eds) *Contributions to the Mesolithic in Europe*, 389–42. Leuven: Leuven University Press.

Warren, S.H., Piggott, S., Clarke, J.G.D., Burkitt, M.C., Godwin, H. and Godwin, M.E. 1936 Archaeology of the submerged land-surface of the Essex coast. *Proceedings of the Prehistoric Society* 2, 178–210.

Waton, P.V. 1982 Man's impact on the chalklands: some new pollen evidence. In: M. Bell and S. Limbrey (eds) *Archaeological Aspects of Woodland Ecology*, 75–91. Oxford: British Archaeological Reports S146.

Watson, P.J., Redman, C. and LeBlanc, S. 1971 *Explanation in Archaeology: An Explicitly Scientific Approach*. New York: Columbia University Press.

Watson, S.L. 1982 Of flesh and bones: the management of death pollution in Cantonese society. In: M. Bloch and J. Parry (eds) *Death and the Regeneration of Life*, 155–86. Cambridge: Cambridge University Press.

Welbourn, D.A. 1984 Endo ceramics and power strategies. In: D. Miller and C. Tilley (eds) *Ideology, Power and Prehistory*, 17–24. Cambridge: Cambridge University Press.

Welbourn, D.A. 1985 Craft specialization and complex societies: a critique. In: T.C. Champion and J.V.S. Megaw (eds) *Settlement and Society*, 123–32. Leicester: Leicester University Press.

West, S.E. 1990 West Stow: the prehistoric and Romano-British occupations. *East Anglian Archaeology* 48.

Wheatley, D. 1995 Cumulative viewshed analysis: a GIS-based method for investigating intervisibility, and its archaeological application. In: G. Lock and Z. Stancic (eds) *Archaeology and Geographical Information Systems*, 171–87. London: Taylor and Francis.

Wheeler, R.E.M. 1943 *Maiden Castle, Dorset*. London: Society of Antiquaries.

Whimster, R. 1981 *Burial Practices in Iron Age Britain*. Oxford: British Archaeological Reports 90.

Whittle, A.W.R. 1977 *The Earlier Neolithic of Southern England and its Continental Background*. Oxford: British Archaeological Reports S35.

Whittle, A.W.R. 1978 Resources and population in the British Neolithic. *Antiquity* 52, 34–41.

Whittle, A.W.R. 1980a Two Neolithics? Part one. *Current Archaeology* 70, 329–34.

Whittle, A.W.R. 1980b Two Neolithics? Part two. *Current Archaeology* 71, 371–3.

Whittle, A.W.R. 1988a *Problems in Neolithic Archaeology*. Cambridge: Cambridge University Press.

Whittle, A.W.R. 1988b Windmill Hill 1988: Preliminary Report on Excavations of the Neolithic Causewayed Enclosure, MS.

Whittle, A.W.R. 1990a A model for the Mesolithic–Neolithic transition in the upper Kennet Valley, north Wiltshire. *Proceedings of the Prehistoric Society* 56, 101–10.

Whittle, A.W.R. 1990b A pre-enclosure burial at Windmill Hill, Wiltshire. *Oxford Journal of Archaeology* 9, 25–8.

Whittle, A.W.R. 1991 Wayland's Smithy, Oxfordshire: excavations at the Neolithic tomb in 1962–3 by R.J.C. Atkinson and S. Piggott. *Proceedings of the Prehistoric Society* 57 (2), 61–102.

Whittle, A.W.R. 1993 The Neolithic of the Avebury area: sequence, environment, settlement and monuments. *Oxford Journal of Archaeology* 12, 29–53.

Whittle, A.W.R. 1994 Excavations at Millbarrow chambered tomb, Winterborne Monkton, north Wiltshire. *Wiltshire Archaeological Magazine* 87, 1–53.

Whittle, A.W.R. 1996 *Europe in the Neolithic: The Creation of New Worlds*. Cambridge: Cambridge University Press.

Whittle, A.W.R. 1997a *Sacred Mound, Holy Rings: Silbury Hill and the West Kennet Palisade Enclosures*. Oxford: Oxbow.

Whittle, A.W.R. 1997b Remembered and imagined belongings: Stonehenge in its traditions and structures of meaning. In: B. Cunliffe and C. Renfrew (eds) *Science and Stonehenge*, 145–66. Oxford: Oxford University Press.

Whittle, A.W.R. 1997c Moving on and moving around: Neolithic settlement mobility. In: P. Topping (ed.) *Neolithic Landscapes*, 14–22. Oxford: Oxbow.

Whittle, A.W.R. and Pollard, J. 1998 Windmill Hill causewayed enclosure: the harmony of symbols. In: M. Edmonds and C. Richards (eds) *Understanding the Neolithic in Northwestern Europe*, 231–47. Glasgow: Cruithne Press.

Whittle, A.W.R. and Smith, R. 1990 West Kennet. *Current Archaeology* 10, 363–5.

Whittle, A.W.R. and Wysocki, M. 1998 Parc le Breos Cwm chambered tomb. *Proceedings of the Prehistoric Society* 64, 139–82.

Whittle, A.W.R., Keith-Lucas, M., Milles, A., Noddle, B., Rees, S. and Romans, J.C. 1986 *Scord of Brouster*. Oxford: Oxford University Committee for Archaeology.

Whittle, A.W.R., Atkinson, R.J.C., Chambers, R. and Thomas, N. 1992 Excavations in the Neolithic and Bronze Age complex at Dorchester-on-Thames, Oxfordshire, 1947–1952 and 1981. *Proceedings of the Prehistoric Society* 58, 143–201.

Whittle, A.W.R., Rouse, A.J. and Evans, J.G. 1993 A Neolithic downland monument in its environment: excavations at the Easton Down long barrow, Bishop's Cannings, north Wiltshire. *Proceedings of the Prehistoric Society* 59, 197–239.

Wiessner, P. 1983 Style and social information in Kalahari San projectile points. *American Antiquity* 48, 253–76.

Wiessner, P. 1984 Reconsidering the behavioral basis for style: a case study among the Kalahari San. *Journal of Anthropological Archaeology* 3, 190–234.

Williams, A. 1940 A megalithic tomb at Nicholaston, Gower, Glamorgan. *Proceedings of the Prehistoric Society* 6, 181.

Williams, E. 1989 Dating the introduction of food production into Britain and Ireland. *Antiquity* 63, 510–21.

Wilson, D. 1975 'Causewayed camps' and 'interrupted ditch systems'. *Antiquity* 49, 178–86.

Windell, D. 1989 A late Neolithic 'ritual focus' at West Cotton, Northamptonshire. In: A.M. Gibson (ed.) *Midlands Prehistory* 85–94. Oxford: British Archaeological Reports 204.

Witts, G.B. 1881 Description of the long barrow called West Tump in the parish of Brimpsfield, Gloucestershire. *Transactions of the Bristol and Gloucester Archaeological Society* 5, 201–11.

Witts, G.B. 1883 Randwick long barrow. *Proceedings of the Cotteswold Naturalists' Field Club* 8, 156–60.

Wobst, H.M. 1977 Stylistic behavior and information exchange. In: C.E. Cleland (ed.) *For the Director: Research Essays in Honor of James B. Griffin*, 317–42. Ann Arbor: Research Papers of the University of Michigan 61.

Woodburn, J. 1982 Social dimensions of death in four African hunting and gathering societies. In: M. Bloch and J. Parry (eds) *Death and the Regeneration of Life*, 187–210. Cambridge: Cambridge University Press.

Woodward, A.B. and Woodward, P.J. 1996 The topography of some barrow cemeteries in Bronze Age Wessex. *Proceedings of the Prehistoric Society* 62, 275–91.

Woodward, P.J. 1988 Pictures from the Neolithic: discoveries from the Flagstones House excavations, Dorchester, Dorset. *Antiquity* 62, 266–74.

Woodward, P.J. 1991 *The South Dorset Ridgeway: Survey and Excavations 1977–84*. Dorchester: Dorset Natural History and Archaeological Society.

Wylie, A. 1982 Epistemological problems raised by a structuralist archaeology. In: I. Hodder (ed.) *Symbolic and Structural Archaeology*. Cambridge: Cambridge University Press.

Yates, T. 1990 Archaeology through the looking-glass. In: I. Bapty and T. Yates (eds) *Archaeology after Structuralism*, 154–202. London: Routledge.

Young, W.E.V. 1950 Beaker burial at Beckhampton Grange. *Wiltshire Archaeological Magazine* 53, 311.

Zienkiewicz, L.C. 1996 Early Neolithic Pottery from Windmill Hill Causewayed Enclosure and the Avebury Area: Style, Sequence, Context and Deposition, PhD Thesis, University College of Cardiff.

Zvelebil, M. 1989 On the transition to farming in Europe, or what was spreading with the Neolithic: a reply to Ammerman (1989). *Antiquity* 63, 379–83.

Zvelebil, M. 1994 Plant use in the Mesolithic and its role in the transition to farming. *Proceedings of the Prehistoric Society* 60, 35–74.

Zvelebil, M. 1996 The agricultural frontier and the transition to farming in the circum-Baltic region. In: D. Harris (ed.) *The Origins and Spread of Agriculture and Pastoralism in Eurasia*, 323–45. London: University College London Press.

Zvelebil, M. and Rowley-Conwy, P. 1984 Transition to farming in northern Europe: a hunter-gatherer perspective. *Norwegian Archaeological Review* 17, 104–27.

Zvelebil, M. and Rowley-Conwy, P. 1986 Foragers and farmers in Atlantic Europe. In: M. Zvelebil (ed.) *Hunters in Transition*, 67–93. Cambridge: Cambridge University Press.

Index

Abingdon 40, 43, 75, 77, 87, 103, 170, 184–8, 198, 206
Abingdon Common 192
Abingdon-style pottery 91, 99–100
Abingdon Ware 106, 188, 194
Adam's Grave 208
Adlestrop Hill 149
agriculture 7–33
Aldwincle 131
Alfriston 78, 140, 152
Ali Kosh 14
alignments 48, 50, 53, 171, 194
Allen, G. 194
Allen, M. 165, 167
Allen, N. 26
Ambohimanga 36
Amesbury: Amesbury 4 179; Amesbury 14 170–1; Amesbury 42 27–8, 139–40, 166, 171–2; Amesbury 51 179; Amesbury G71 24, 166
animal bone 66–8
antiquarians 126
Arbor Low 56
archery equipment 157
ard 24
ard marks 200
ardmarks 167
Arminghall 54
Armit, I. 101
Arreton 86
Ascott-under-Wychwood 70, 144, 148, 151
Ashbee, P. 131, 137
assumption 1
Aston Bampton 185
Astrop 68, 188
Atkinson, R. 7–8, 51, 192, 195–6, 199
Aubrey, J. 34
Avebury 26, 55, 118, 140, 165, 199–220, 210, 212–16, 218–20, 223, 228, 229; Avebury G55 201, 209–10; Avebury School 212; Cove 216; Longstones Cove 219; Obelisk 215, 217
Avening 148

Avery, M. 187
Avon: county 6, 143; River 57, 167, 169, 171–2, 178, 181; Valley 118, 199

Baker Platform 24
Balbridie 25
Balfarg 54, 60, 65, 72; Balfarg Riding School 54, 114, 117–19
Balkans 121
Ballateare 153
Ballygalley 25
Balneaves Cottage 77
Baltic 90
Baltic cord-impressed pottery 90
bank barrows 139–40
Bannockburn 77
Barclay, G. 55–6
Barford 153
Bargates 118
Barholm 109, 118
Barholm Pit 4 68
Barker, G. 38, 42,
Barnack 160–1
Barnhouse 117
Barrett, J. 40, J. 52, 96, 104, 122–3, 141, 155–7, 181
Barrow Hills 78, 119–20, 142, 153, 161, 187–8, 190, 192, 194–5, 197–8; Radley 140, 184, 187, 190, 212
barrow diggers 165
Barth, F. 164
Barton Court 184; Barton Court Farm 190, 192
Beacharra Ware 101
Beaker: associations 159–62; burials 156–62, 165, 179, 182, 192, 195, 197–8, 218–20, 227–8; folk 2, 69, 151; package 122–3; period 28, 47, 158, 179, 181, 205, 213; pottery 30, 43–5, 69, 74, 80, 86, 92, 106, 109, 120–5, 157, 166, 167, 175, 179–80, 190, 196, 200, 202, 204–6, 209–10, 213–14, 218–20, 226, 228
Beakers: AOC 120, 214; AOO 121; Bell 121; BW 219; E 120; early style 120; European Bell

157; Iberian 121; late style 120; N/NR 122; Protruding Foot 121; S 113; W/MR 120, 218

Beckhampton 28

Beckhampton Avenue 219

Beckhampton Road 28, 139, 200, 203, 207–8, 217

Begleitkeramik 122

Bender, B. 169, 171

Berkshire 6, 139, 185; Downs 211

binary structures 93

Binford, L. 126–7

Bishop's Cannings Downs 199–200

Black Patch 68

Blackdown barrow T5 161

Blewbury 66, 192

Bluestones 177–82

Boast, R. 92, 123

Bone Hole 161

bone pins 66

Borrowstone 159

Boscombe Down 166

Bourdieu, P. 45

Bowl's Barrow 27

Boyne Valley 38, 216

Brackmont Mill 110

Bradley, R. 9, 21, 29, 34, 40, 51, 53, 92, 118–19, 139, 164, 170, 172, 187, 189, 193

Bratton 140

Briar Hill 74, 77, 103

bricolage 80, 96

Britnell, W. 150

Brittany 38, 122, 216, 220, 223

Broadmayne 140

Bronze Age 17, 18, 26, 34, 46–7, 60–1, 85–6, 89–90, 106, 109, 111, 120–1, 131, 151, 153, 155–6, 165–7, 179, 194–5, 200, 209, 223, 224–5; pottery 91, 210

Broome Heath 99

Brown, A. 31

Bryn Celli Ddu 50

Brynderwen 108

buildings 45

Burgess, C. 86, 121

burial orientation 160–1

burials 224

Burl, A. 9, 48, 50, 55, 220

Burn Ground 149–50

Buscott Lock 31, 184

c-transformations 62

Cahokia 23

Cairnpapple 54–5, 72

Cannon Hill 70

Care, V. 41

carinated bowls 98, 200

Carnaby Temple: Site 7 65; Site 15 65

Carnac 210

carved stone balls 119

Case, H. 8, 34, 63, 120, 159, 205

Cassington 188, 190, 192, 198; Mill 192

Castellic pottery 99

cattle 26–7, 223; skulls 28

causewayed enclosure ditches 74–7

causewayed enclosures 38–45, 102–3

caves 161

Céide Fields 10

cenotaph barrows 140

cereals 23–4

Cerny 131

Chalk Plaque Pit 66, 118, 176

Chalkpit Field 110

chambered tombs 103, 203–8, 223, 226

Chapman, R. 37

Charterhouse Warren Farm Swallett 161

Chasséen culture 99–102

Cherhill 102, 199–200, 202–3

Cherry, J. 34

Chesham 122

Chilbolton 158

Childe, V.G. 12, 90, 102

China 136

Christie, P. 171

chronology 221

City Farm 190

Clacton style 109, 114, 116–17, 119–20, 192

Clare, T. 52

Clark, J.G.D. 64

Clarke, D.L. 113, 120, 122, 125, 160

classification 63

Clatford 212

Cleal, R. 70, 82, 102, 109, 113, 114, 117, 119, 167, 169–70, 175

Cleaven Dyke 52, 140

Clyde cairns 137

Cold Kitchen Hill 131

Collared Urns 69, 74, 106, 109, 121, 194–5

Collingwood, R. 3

Combe Hill 41, 43

Condicote 190

Coneybury 72, 118, 153, 167, 176, 181–2; 'Anomaly' 166, 70, 99, 169; Henge 116, 166; Hill 42, 56, 167, 176, 178–9

Connerton, P. 98

Conquer Barrow 216

conspicuous consumption 42, 99, 218

contextual archaeology 94–5

Coombe Hill 106

Corcoran, J. 144

Corded Ware 121–2

core areas 223

Corporation Farm 188, 190

Corton 27

Cosgrove, D. 36–7

cosmology 36–7, 45–6, 208

Cotswolds 140, 185, 187–8, 207, 211; Hills 161;

Cotswold–Severn 48, 50–1, 58, 143–51, 155, 162, 203, 208
court tombs 137
Cow Common Long 144, 148
Cowan, J. 86
Cowie, T. 110
Cranborne Chase 40, 119, 139–40, 188–9
Crawford, O. 148
cremation 227
crematoria 131, 137
Crickley Hill 41, 43, 52, 58, 77, 139, 187
Croft Moraig 47
Crofton 201
cultivation 166
cultural traits 164
culture history 11, 91, 97, 121, 126, 151, 156, 163
Cumancaya 98
Cunnington, M. 181, 199, 213
Cunnington, W. 165
cursus monuments 9, 185

dairy products 28
Daisy Banks 184
Dalladies 133
Daniel, G. 34
Danubian 90
Darvill, T. 64, 144, 150, 172
Davis, M. 36
death (the dead) 226–7
DeAtley, S. 164
DeBoer, W. 98
Decorated style pottery 225
decoration 96–8
Denmark 131, 135
depositional practice 62–88, 224–6
Derbyshire 152
Derrida, J. 4, 5, 96
design hierarchy 116
Deverel-Rimbury 70, 74
Devil's Quoits 190, 196, 198; Henge 161
Diamond 167, 174
difference 121
diffusion 90
discourse 48
dissonance 221
ditch recuts 74–5
diversification 223
Donneruplund 24
Donovan, H. 149
Dorchester 188, 190; Big Rings 190, 196; Cursus 185, 189, 196
Dorchester on Thames 47–8, 52, 77, 153–5, 184 186–8, 192–5; Cursus 68; Dorchester Site 3 52
Dorset 6, 139, 216; Cursus 26–7, 32, 34, 52–3, 73, 83, 110, 171,
Down Ampney 185

Drayton 184, 194; Cursus 185; Drayton/Sutton Courtenay Cursus 186
Drewett, P. 40, 78
Dronfeld, J. 118
Duggleby Howe 47, 152–3, 155
Durrington 24, 171, 165, 175; Married Quarters 181; Walls 27, 47, 52, 54–5, 57, 80–1, 83, 85, 114, 116–17, 166–7, 169, 171, 176–9, 181–2, 196, 210, 213; Walls style 114, 116–7, 119–20, 192
Dyffryn Ardudwy 70

Earl's Down Farm 166
earthen long barrows 103, 162, 185, 131–43, 203–8, 227
East Anglia 106, 114, 190, 227
Eastleach 185
Easton Down 199–200, 203, 207–8
Eaton Heath 72, 99
Ebbsfleet 116; Ebbsfleet Ware 91, 106–7, 110–11, 194, 209
economic system 221–2
economy 64
Edmonds, M. 21, 41
Edwards, K. 31
Elf Howe 111
elm decline 30–1
Engels, F. 12
entoptic phenomena 118
Entwhistle, R. 24
Eogan, G. 119
episodic cultivation 222
Ertebølle 15
Etton 42, 52, 54, 74, 87, 103
Europe 90; central 122; eastern 122; north-west 74
Evans, J. 24, 42, 210
event of deposition 157
exchange 42–3, 224, 228–9
extra revetment 150
Eyford 148–9, 161
Eynsham 185, 198

Fargo 177; Plantation 179; Ridge 171
Fayum 64
feasting 42, 202, 207, 218, 224
Fengate 10; Fengate Ware 91, 106–11, 113–14, 188, 194, 209; Ware 213
Fens 118
Figheldean 31 170–1
Findlow, F. 164
Finland 89
Finlayson, W. 15, 101
fire 77
Firtree Field 73–4, 109, 119; Down Farm 68
Flagstones enclosure 173
Flagstones House 72, 99, 108
Flanders Moss 31

Flannery, K. 126
Fleming, A. 139, 142
flint extraction 41, 211
folk movements 89
Food Vessels 69, 89, 109–10, 121, 160
food: processing 225; production 96
Ford 110
Ford, S. 185
forest: clearance 30–1, 42, 144, 166, 199, 222;
     regeneration 32, 200, 222
Fornham All Saints 52
Foucault, M. 4, 5, 36, 128–9
Fourknocks style 119
Fowler, P. 10
France 15
Franchthi Cave 14
Freud, S. 4
Fussell's Lodge 27, 78, 99, 131, 134, 136–7, 142

gabbroic pottery 40, 102
Garwood, P. 158–9, 195
Gatcombe Lodge 146
Gatehampton Farm 185
Gebauer, A. 102
Gee, T. 195
Geertz, C. 37
gender 97
genealogy 5, 63, 124–5, 162, 221, 226–7
Giant's Hill 2 133–4, 137
Gibson, A. 109–10, 195
Giddens, A. 36
Glenluce 110
Gloucestershire 6, 143, 184
Golden Ball Hill 200
Goodenough, W. 127
Goodland 63
Gosselain, O. 98
Grant, A. 24
Gravelly Guy 109, 184, 190
Gray, H. 83
Great Langdale 43
Greece 14
Greenland Farm 166
Grendon 194
Grey Croft 47
Grey, H. 212
Grigson, C. 27–8
Grimes, W. 144, 150
Grimston style pottery 70, 72, 99
Grimston Ware 90
Grooved Ware 11, 26, 45, 66, 69, 73–4, 86–7,
     90, 109, 113–25, 153, 165–6, 174–9, 181–2,
     190, 192, 194–5, 198, 204–6, 209–11,
     212–13, 217–18, 225, 228
Gussage All Saints 64
Gussage Cow Down 53
Gwernvale 70, 144, 146, 150

Hackpen Hill 211
Haddenham 75, 77, 131, 133–5, 137, 187
Halpin, C. 192
Hambledon Hill 27–8, 32, 40–4, 68, 74–5, 77,
     139–40, 142, 170, 187
Hampshire 139, 199
Handley Hill 40, 68, 111, 139, 155
Hanging Grimston 134
Hardin, M. 117
Hatfield Barrow 216
Hayden, B. 98
Hazleton 148–50; Hazleton North 70, 144, 146,
     147
Healy, F. 64, 72, 100, 106, 120, 190
Heathrow 72, 111
Hebridean bowls 101
Hedges, J. 118
Heelstone 177
Helmdorf 131
Hembury 40, 99; Hembury style pottery 99
Hemp Knoll 28, 157, 160, 200–1, 218
Hendriksmose 24
henges 54–60, 80–5, 196
hermeneutics 36, 95
Herne, A. 70, 98–9
Hetty Pegler's Tump 148
hierarchical theocracy 218
Higgs, E. 8
High Peak 40
Hill, J. 64
Hillend 117
Hirst, P. 36
historical materialism 12
hoards 47, 85–6
Hoare, R 165, 126, 139
Hodder, I. 3, 14, 37, 63, 92, 94–5
Holdenhurst 142
Holgate, R. 18, 21, 73, 185, 188, 199
Holland 122
Hopewell 23
Horslip 78, 142 199–200, 203, 207–8
horticulture 17, 24–5
Horton 108
houses 9–10, 14, 17, 25, 64, 222
human remains 68, 75
Hungary 122
Hungerford 199
Hurst Fen 64, 72, 99
Husserl, E. 3

ideological structure 222
ideology 127–8
Igbo-Ukwu 96
Inchbare 77
information exchange 92
Ireland 119, 122, 220; north-east 99
Irish passage tombs 118
Iron Age 64, 223

Irthlingborough 158, 160–1
Isbister 118

Jameson, F. 2
Jarman, M. 8, 24
Jarmo 14
Jones, A. 97

Kabyle 45
Keiller, A. 40, 51, 91, 165, 199, 202, 209, 212
Kemp Howe 53
Kendall 165
Kendrick, T. 90
Kennet: River 199; Valley 199, 202, 204, 210–11, 214, 216, 220, 228
Kilham 53, 131, 135
Kinalty 77
King Arthur's Round Table 55–6
King Barrow 140; Ridge 66, 74, 166–7, 171, 176, 179, 180–1; Wood 176
King's Play Down 207
Kingston Deverill 142; Kingston Deverill G1 78
Kinnes, I. 50, 85, 109, 120, 131, 135–6, 142, 152–3
Kirknewton 53
Kitchen Barrow 208
Knap Hill 40, 42–3, 200–1, 212, 218
Knap of Howar 63, 118
Knook 2 27
Knowth 83, 119
Kus, S. 36

ladder of inference 127
Laidler, D. 165,
Lake District 30
landscapes 37–8
Lane, P. 46
Langdean 212
Langford 185
Lanhill 147, 149, 151
Larkhill 66
Launceston Down 152
Lechlade 87, 192
Legge, A. 8, 23, 27–8, 42, 68
Lengyel 9
Leubingen 131
Levant 14
Lévi-Strauss, C. 92, 94
Liff's Low 107, 111
Limlow Hill 195
Linch Hill 160, 162, 198; Linch Hill Corner 189
Lincolnshire 131
Linearbandkeramik 9, 14, 15, 17, 24, 131
Links of Noltland 63
Lismore Fields 25
lithics 17–23, 66; lithic sources 41
Little Clanfield 185
Little Woodbury 64

Lizard 40
Llandegai 47, 72, 153, 155, 173
Lochill 131, 148
Loft's Farm 72
Long Bredy 140
long barrow ditches 77–80
longhouses 9, 17
Longworth, I. 83, 109
Los Angeles 36
Loughcrew style 119
Low Countries 121–2
Luckington 146, 148,
Lugbury 149
Luxenborough Plantation 166

Maas, A. 98
maceheads 119
Machrie Moor 47
MacSween, A. 117
Madagascar 36
Maes Howe 50
Maes Howe type 51
Maiden Bower 40
Maiden Castle 26–8, 40–1, 43–4, 52, 75, 87, 99, 114, 139–40, 187
Malthus, T. 10, 30
Manby, T. 65, 110, 117
Marden Henge 216
Marlborough: Downs 199–200; Mound 216
Marnhull 40, 43
Marshall, Y. 98
Marx, K. 12, 45
Marxism 3, 12
Masai 29
material culture 228–9
Maumbury Rings 54, 83
Mayburgh 47
meaning 72
Mediterranean, west 121
megalithic tombs 1, 185, 201–2
Megaw, J. 9
Meldon Bridge 110
memory 157–8, 162
Mendip Hills 161, 211
Menghin, O. 90
menhirs 223
Mercer, R. 10, 30, 38, 54, 139
Mere 13d 152
Merina 36
Mesakin 63
Mesolithic 10, 11, 15, 17, 18, 31, 90, 144, 167, 199, 203; Mesolithic/Neolithic transition 16, 30, 72
metalwork 125, 157
Michelsberg culture 102
Middle Harling 74
Migdale 86
migrations 13

Mildenhall-style pottery 91, 99–100; Mildenhall Ware 72, 91, 111
Milfield North 54
Milk Hill 200
Mill Road 65
Millbarrow 139, 144, 200, 203, 207, 208
Miller, D. 92, 97, 102
Milston 170
Milton Ferry 111
Mississippi Valley 23
mixed farming 222
Mizoguchi, K. 123, 158–9
mobility 223
Moffett, L. 24
Moncrieffe 47, 54, 56
Montelius, O. 90
monumentality 164, 223–4
monuments 212–18
Moody's Down 140
Moore, H. 38, 45, 63
Morbihan 220
Morris, M. 37
Mortlake 89, 116; Mortlake Ware 91, 106, 108–11, 120, 190, 209, 213
Mosegården 18
Mount Farm 188
Mount Pleasant 47, 54–5, 60, 82, 108, 196, 213; Mount Pleasant Site IV 213

n-transformations 62
Narmanton Down 182
Ndembu Isoma 96
Near East 14
Nempnett Thrubwell 149
Nene, River 111
Neolithic people 228–9
Netheravon 6 170
Netheravon Bake 139, 170
Nethercourt Farm 68
New Archaeology 126
New Barn Down 66
New Guinea 136
New Wintles 131, 187, 188
Newgrange 47, 50
Newnham Murren 188, 193
Nicholaston 144
Nielsen, P. 85
Nietzsche, F. 4, 5
Normanton 171–2, 177, 179; Down 170
North Mains of Strathallan 54–6
North Marden 78
North Stoke 52, 139, 185, 187, 194
Notgrove 144, 149–50, 161
Nutbane 134, 137, 141–2
Nympsfield 144, 146, 149–50

Offham 40–1, 43, 75
Old Ditch 140

Old Yeavering 53
Oldbourne Downs 211
Oldbury Hill 207
ordered adjacency 158
Orkney 9, 33, 63, 114, 117–20, 227; Orkney–Cromarty 52
Orsett 103
otherness 1, 2, 5
Overton Hill 213–14, 220
Ownes Valley Paiute 25
Oxford 185, 188; Oxfordshire 6, 143, 184
Oxford University Archaeological Society 165

Pangbourne 68
Parc le Breos Cwm 149–50
Parker-Pearson, M. 128
Passmore, A. 165, 211
past-as-same 3
past-as-other 5
pastoralism 29
Peak District 227
Penny, A. 53
Pentridge 139
Penywyrlod 148, 151
performance 222–4, 228–9
Peterborough 89; Peterborough Ware 43, 45, 73–4, 80, 86, 90–1, 106–13, 117–25, 144, 151, 173–8, 190, 198, 205, 207, 209, 211, 225
Pewsey 43; Vale of 199–201
phenomenology 214–16, 225
Pict's Knowe 72
pig 26–7, 218
Piggott, S. 34, 42, 64, 90–1, 99, 102, 113, 131, 134, 151, 163, 199, 204–6, 213
Pipton 144, 151
pit: alignments 77; morphology 64
pits 64–74, 103
Pitt Rivers, A. 139
Pitted Ware 90
Pitts, M. 212
plain bowls 178
plant foods 24
plough agriculture 18, 24
Pole's Wood: East 147–8; South 151
Pollard, J. 82, 153, 202, 213
Pool 117–18
population growth 223
portholes 148,
Portland chert 40
positivism 2
pottery 89–125, 225–6; *see also specific styles*
Poverty Point 23
Prescelli 177
prestige goods hierarchy 121
Price, T. 15
process of transformation 157

Radley 142, 153, 155, 161; *see also under* Barrow Hills
Randwick 150
Ratfyn 66, 68, 166, 176–7, 181
Raunds 10
Ray, K. 96
Redgate Hill 68, 74, 116
redistribution 29, 40
regional variation 227–8
regions 164
relations of production 12
Relph, E. 35
Renfrew, A. C. 3, 8–9, 30, 34, 37, 118, 164
revolutions 12
Reynolds, P. 64
Rhine Valley 121–2
Rice, P. 103
Richards, C. 51–2, 85, 116–17, 121, 123
Richards, J. 166, 169, 175
Ricoeur, P. 3, 5
Rinyo 63; Rinyo style 114, 117; Rinyo–Clacton culture 113
rites of passage 129
ritual authority system 121
ritual landscape 26
Robbins, M. 205
Robin Hood's Ball 40–1, 43, 77, 170–1, 182
Robinson, M. 31
Rodmarton 146, 148
role theory 127
Rolleston, G. 147–8
Roman imperial cult 96
Rorty, R. 94
Rössen 9, 15
Roth, M. 2
Rothesay/Achnacree Ware 101
rotunda graves 144, 149
Roughridge Hill 70, 200–1
Roundway 8 218
Rowden 70, 99
Rowlands, M. 86
Rowlett, R. 205
Rowley-Conwy, P. 9, 15, 30
rubbish 62–3
Rudston 52, 109; Rudston Ware 110
Runnymede 27
Rybury 43, 201, 212

Sale's Lot 47, 144, 151, 161
Salisbury Plain 26, 48, 118, 140, 165–84
Saltway Barn 144
Sanctuary 47, 199, 213–14, 216, 218, 220, 228; Bank Holiday Ring 213; Stone and Post Ring 213; Ten Foot Ring 213
Sangmeister 121
Sarsen circle 178
Saville, A. 144, 147, 150
Saxe, A. 127, 129

Scandinavia 15, 25, 131
Schiffer, M. 62
Schuchhardt, C. 90
Scorton 52, 140
Scotland 101, 106, 110, 114, 117; eastern 227; south-west 99, 227
Scottish Groved Ware 117
seasonal movement 228–9
seasonality 42
secondary burial 47, 136, 151
sedentism 10, 11, 222
seed impressions 121
Serjeantson, D. 27
settlement 9
shamanism 51, 118
Shanks, M. 2, 136, 148
Shennan, S. 121, 157
Shepherd's Shore 207–8
Shepherd, I. 159
Sheridan, A. 50, 99
Sherratt, A. 18, 28
Sherrington 1 27
Shetland 9, 33
Shipibo-Conibo 98, 109
Shrewton 5K 47
Sidlings Copse 184
Signet Hill 185
Siiriänen, A. 205
Silbury Hill 38, 199–200, 214, 216–17, 220
Simpson, D, 9
single graves 151–7
Siriano 25
Skara Brae 63
Skendleby 78, 80
skeuomorphs 90, 96
Slewcairn 133, 148
Smeath Ridge 218
Smith, I. 27, 40, 64, 77, 91, 100, 106, 114, 119, 202, 209, 212
Smith, R. 89
Smith, R.W. 199, 203
Snail Down 26
social relations 226–7
society 228–9
Somerset 6, 143; Levels 24
songlines 35
South Lodge 68
South Street 24, 139, 199–201, 203, 207–8, 217
South-Eastern style pottery 100
South-Western style pottery 99–100, 103
space 45–6, 48, 51, 60, 214–16; and place 35–6
Spartum Fen 184
Spong Hill 64, 72, 74, 106
Springfield Cursus 52
Stadhampton 187
Staines 27, 40, 75, 103, 188
Stanton Drew 56

Stanton Harcourt 160–2, 184, 187–8, 190, 195, 198; Vicarage Field 192, 198
Stanwick 10, 64
Stepleton 41, 75
Stock Close 211
Stock Lane 211
Stonehenge 26–8, 47, 50, 55, 57, 60, 77, 108, 153–5, 165–83, 196, 212–13, 223, 227, 229; Aubrey Holes 172, 174, 176; Avenue 180–2; Bottom 168, 171, 174, 179; car park post-holes 167; Cursus monuments 167; Down 167, 173–5; Environs Project 167, 174; Great Cursus 51–2, 171, 174, 176, 178; Lesser Cursus 166, 171, 178; Pallisade Ditch 176; Slaughter Stone 180; Station Stones 177
Stoney Littleton 50, 149
Stour Valley 40,
Streethouse 134, 135–6; Streethouse Farm 53, 131
structuralism 4, 92
Stukeley, W. 34, 51
Stumble 25
Sussex 42, 131, 139 185
Sutton Courtenay 87, 188, 192; Sutton Courtenay Pit Q 68
Sutton Veny 160
Sweden 89
Sweet track 111; drove 85; railway 85
Swifterbant 15

Tainter, J. 127, 129
Tan Hill 200
Tarlow, S. 128
Taversoe Tuick 118
Temple Bottom 207
Ten Hove, H. 30
texts 2, 37–8, 46, 92–6
Thames: basin 161; River 85, 111; Valley 18, 86, 100, 106, 114, 118–19, 152, 165, 184, 199, 211
Thickthorn Down 27, 45, 47, 78, 142, 162
Thirlings 65, 110
Thomsen, C. 108
Thorpe, I. 41, 121, 123, 137, 139–40
Thrupp 184; Thrupp Farm 188, 192
Thurnam, J. 126, 144, 165, 171, 204
Till, river 171
Tilley, C. 2, 136, 148
Tilshead 7 140, 170; Lodge 27; Old Ditch 139
timber coffins 160
Tipping, R. 31
Tolley's Pit 188
totalisation 13, 221
Totterdown Clump 181
transformation 162
TRB 91, 102, 131
Trefignath 102
Trundle 40, 43, 75, 103

Tuan, Y. 35
Turner, J. 31
Turner, V. 95
Ty Isaf 47, 144, 151

Uley 50, 146, 148
Unstan 118; Unstan Ware 97, 101, 117–18
Upper Ninepence 118
Upper Thames: basin 184; Valley 184–99, 201, 227–8

Vacher, F. 212
Vitelli, K. 97

Waden Hill 200–1, 214, 217
Wainwright, G. 83
Wales 110, 177
Wardour 43
Warminster 169
Waton, P. 31
Wayland's Smithy 50, 53, 131 133–5, 137, 139, 142, 149, 187
Webley, D. 38, 42
Wessex 18, 30, 34, 42, 60, 80, 86–7, 102, 131 134, 155, 160, 164, 170, 179, 184–5, 187–90, 207–8, 211, 213, 227; Wessex Archaeology Pit 418 176
West Cotton 10, 161
West Kennet 50, 83, 149–50, 199, 200–1, 204, 205–8, 210; Avenue 209, 213, 214–16, 218–20, 228; long barrow 214, 216–9, 228; palisade enclosure 1 217; palisade enclosure 2 217; palisade enclosure 2, structure 2 217; palisade enclosures 209, 217–8, 220, 228
West Lockridge 218
West Overton 199–200, 210; West Overton G19 200, 209; West Overton G6a 209; West Overton G6b 160, 209–10, 220
West Stow 153
West Tump 146, 148
West Woods 207
Westbury 7 151
wet places 111
Wheatley, D. 170, 207
Wheeler, R. 41
Whitby, M. 166
Whitegrounds 47
Whitehawk 40, 43, 75, 103; Whitehawk style pottery 99–100
Whiteleaf Hill 106, 141
Whitesheet Hill 28, 40, 43, 187
Whittle, A. 14, 29–30, 32, 42, 149, 178, 199, 202, 207, 212, 216
wild species 26–7, 65, 174, 222
Willerby Wold 134, 136–7, 142
Wilsford 30 170, 171–2, 177, 179; Down 169–70, 174, 182; Wilsford G52 176
Wilson, R. 31

Wiltshire 6, 26, 139, 143, 199; north 228; south 228

Windmill Hill 40, 42, 44, 72, 75, 91, 102–3, 106, 199–203, 206–8, 218; culture 163; Windmill Hill style pottery 91, 99–100; Windmill Hill Ware 90–1

Wingham 66, 70

Winterbourne Dauntsey, 9

Winterbourne Monkton 220

Winterbourne Stoke: Crossroads 155, 167; Winterbourne Stoke 1 140, 152, 155, 170–1; Winterbourne Stoke 44 181; Winterbourne Stoke 53 170

Wood, J. 53

Woodburn, J. 128

Woodhenge 58, 82–3, 117, 153, 177, 181–2, 199; Woodhenge style 114

Woodlands 65, 176; Woodlands style 114, 116–17, 119–20, 176, 192

Wor Barrow 27–8, 45–7, 139, 141, 155

Wyke Down 54, 82–3, 117–19

Wysocki, M. 149

Yarnton 184, 188, 190

Yates, T. 95

Yeavering 72,

Yorkshire 86, 131, 134, 110, 117, 152, 160, 216; east 227

Young, W. 165

Zagros 14

Zeuner 193

Zuni 109

Zvelebil, M. 9, 13, 15